A Carolinian Goes to War

A Carolinian Goes to War

THE CIVIL WAR NARRATIVE OF Arthur Middleton Manigault

BRIGADIER GENERAL, C.S.A.

edited by R. Lockwood Tower
with a Foreword by Thomas L. Connelly

AND WITH HIS MEXICAN WAR NARRATIVE
edited by Warren Ripley and Arthur M. Wilcox

Published for the
CHARLESTON LIBRARY SOCIETY
by the
UNIVERSITY OF SOUTH CAROLINA PRESS

FRONTISPIECE: Gen. Manigault in uniform. An imaginative miniature on wood painted by John Stolle, a prominent turn-of-the-century portraitist in Charleston, four years after the general's death. The face is taken from a photograph made after the war. The color of the uniform coat collar should be gray.

Copyright © University of South Carolina 1983

Published in Columbia, South Carolina by the

University of South Carolina Press

First Edition

Library of Congress Cataloging in Publication Data

Manigault, Arthur Middleton, 1824-1886.
   A Carolinian Goes to War.

   Bibliography: p. 283.
   Includes indexes.
   1. Manigault, Arthur Middleton, 1824-1886. 2. United
States—History—Civil War, 1861-1865—Personal
narratives, Confederate. 3. United States—History—
Civil War, 1861-1865—Campaigns. 4. Confederate States
of America. Army—Biography. 5. Generals—Southern
States—Biography. 6. United States—History—War
with Mexico, 1845-1848—Personal narratives, American.
I. Tower, R. Lockwood. II. Ripley, Warren. III. Wilcox,
Arthur M. IV. Manigault, Arthur Middleton, 1824-1886.
Mexican War narrative. 1983. V. Title.
E605.M27 1983   973.7'84   83-1063
ISBN 0-87249-422-5

Contents

(Asterisks indicate Manigault's Narrative)

Illustrations

Maps

Foreword

In the rich bluegrass plain of Middle Tennessee, the Civil War battlefield of Franklin lies only eighteen miles south of the house I grew up in in Nashville. Before I was sixteen years old I knew every inch of the battlefield, knew that General Manigault's career in the Army of Tennessee was ended by a bold night assault, and knew that I was going to write about the Civil War. Franklin was a beginning for me, an ending for General Arthur Middleton Manigault. Southern history is a maze of ironies.

In that dreary November of 1864, General John Bell Hood marched his weary Army of Tennessee out of Georgia and Alabama and spoke of capturing Nashville and even crossing the Ohio River. But when he arrived at Franklin, Hood saw that General John Schofield's Army of the Ohio blocked his way. The telescopes of Confederate officers along Winstead Hill could see across the bluegrass fields to the near-impregnable Federal breastworks around the village.

General Nathan Bedford Forrest, with whom my great-grandfather was serving, suggested that Hood alter his strategy, move northeastward and flank the Union troops from their trenches. The blond-bearded Hood, ailing still from the amputation of his leg at Chickamauga, disagreed. Someone else urged that Hood wait until his entire column was on the field. By the early afternoon of November 30, 1864, only the corps of Generals Benjamin Cheatham and A.P. Stewart had arrived. General Stephen D. Lee's corps was not present. Most of the army's batteries were still on the road as well. Again, Hood refused. The attack would come shortly after two o'clock in the afternoon.

So almost 18,000 infantry moved forward through a mile and one half of the bluegrass fields in the last great spectacle of the Civil War. Over 6,000 were killed, wounded or captured, including thirteen general officers. The percentage of men killed was the highest for any single action in the war on the Confederate side.

After the battle, the corpses were moved to a nearby plantation. The owner set aside a plot of ground amid some young cedar trees and buried the dead. Later, individual states would erect monuments there to the Confederate dead. The old cedars remain, as does the house nearby. Some 1,492 young men rest in the cemetery. I have gone there many times, and without fail the resting place has moved me deeply.

Darkness came early that evening as Manigault's brigade came up the Columbia Pike. General Hood ordered them forward, as well as other units from General Edward Johnson's division. It was the only night attack authorized by the Confederates during the war.

More than once, I have walked the length of Manigault's approach from Winstead Hill to the Federal breastworks. He led his troops along the fields just west of the Columbia Pike and skirted Merrill Hill. Then the brigade passed just west of the initial Federal skirmish line at Privet Knob. From there they veered slightly northeast and struck the Federal breastworks in the vicinity of the Carter house, which stands today as a museum. Manigault was severely wounded in this night assault.

Back home in Charleston not long after the fighting stopped, he put his own personal experience of the war down on paper for his sons, as if he were not sure how long he had to live. Being of an orderly and disciplined turn of mind, he apparently first wrote down his recollections of the Mexican War, which are here usefully edited for us by Warren Ripley and Arthur M. Wilcox. His spelling in the Mexican memoir (Appendix II) is noticeably wilder than in his Civil War narrative. Perhaps he was eager to have it done with and get on to the war that all Southern fathers tell their sons about, or perhaps he'd simply got some of his eccentric spellings straightened out in his mind by the time he came to the Civil War.

Fortunately for South Carolina he lived in tolerable health for many years and had a distinguished career as a public servant before his death some two decades after he was wounded.

The family name is pronounced MAN-i-GO, by the way, the first two syllables rhyming with "Danny" and the last one rhyming with "toe." The general's manuscript has been in the possession of the Manigault family for more than a hundred years, and few historians have known of its existence. Its publication now is a significant event in American historiography. Among the many personal recollections, diaries, and letters of men who took part in the Civil War that have been published in the last twenty years, none is as important as the Manigault manuscript.

It is important because it was written so soon after the war, while the events were still fresh in his mind. It is important because it was written not for publication: he said what he thought without fear of offending anyone and without arguing for or against the opinions of others. It is important because he was a general and knew things men of lower rank did not know. It is important because he was a remarkably careful observer whose career encompassed the major campaigns of the western front (it's all there: the geography, the politics of command, the weather, everything one could ask for). It is important because he was a sensitive, finely educated writer: an eighteenth-century man fighting the first modern war!

R. Lockwood Tower has brought skill, intelligence, and an abundance of information to the editing of this manuscript.

In a way I have known Manigault as a gallant soldier for a long time. His official reports and correspondence were often in my mind all through the years when I was working on *Army of the Heartland* and

Autumn of Glory, as was the field where he was wounded, the field I knew so thoroughly it seemed to be part of me.

Now, thanks to Lockwood Tower, I feel as though I have met General Manigault for the first time.

I still revisit Franklin's field on occasion. Often at night, I have driven out to Winstead Hill where the Confederate attack began. The landscape has changed some with the advent of shopping centers and other trappings of modern society.

But out on the high rise, the wind still chills on an autumn night, as it did over a century ago when the General and his brigade moved forward into the darkness.

Thomas L. Connelly
Columbia, South Carolina.

Introduction

On one of those incomparable spring days in the South Carolina Lowcountry in April 1976, with the azaleas and dogwood in bloom and the gently stirring air so soft you could almost reach out and touch it, I was at Drayton Hall on the west bank of the Ashley River not far from Charleston. For more than two centuries that outstanding example of the Georgian plantation architecture has been miraculously saved from the ravages of fire and hurricane, as it was from the depredations of the Northern troops who, burning and plundering, moved into the area from James Island in February 1865 as Sherman's march north from Savannah outflanked Charleston and compelled the evacuation of the unconquered city and its outlying defenses. The event was a fund-raising affair sponsored by the National Trust for Historic Preservation and the Historic Charleston Foundation, which joined with the State of South Carolina to preserve Drayton Hall for the use of the public.

After lunch under the spreading live oaks, I wandered to the river side of the great plantation house and there, on the steps overlooking the Ashley, was introduced to Edward Manigault. Recognizing a resemblance and with one of those strokes of good fortune that occur all too seldom, I remarked: "You must be related to General Manigault." Indeed he was — his grandson, in fact, and the holder of the General's unpublished Confederate War memoirs.

One thing led to another and through his great kindness and, I may add, somewhat blind but nonetheless gratifying faith in my ability to do justice to his grandfather's recollections, he authorized me to undertake the welcome task of editing them with a view to publication. Since then I have been General Manigault's almost daily companion.

More has been written about the Civil War than any other event in American history. By 1970, authoritative estimates placed the number of books and pamphlets on the subject at the staggering total of between 40,000 and 60,000 and the figure is still rising. Why another?

The answer is simple. First, these are no ordinary memoirs; second, authentic works by general officers of the Confederate Army are, contrary to the general impression, comparatively rare. Of the 299 such individuals who survived the war in grade, less than 20 set down their experiences in the conflict for publication.

General Manigault's recollections may well be the last unpublished memoir of a Confederate general. For this reason, if no other, they would be of interest. More significant is the fact that they stand on their own as one of the very best accounts written on the Southern side. They are of particular importance in that they deal chiefly with the relatively neglected Western Army of the Confederacy and are unique as the only first-hand narrative by a brigade commander of the Army of Tennessee.

Manigault's descriptions of the organization and training of the Southern army are outstanding. Seldom have the duties of the provost guard and the infirmary corps, for example, or the use of entrenchment tools, infantry target practice, the establishment of winter quarters or the issue of rations by the commissary been so adequately dealt with. And the same may be said of the development of trench warfare outside of Atlanta, which foreshadowed, along with Lee's employment of breast-works in the Wilderness campaign and during the siege of Petersburg in 1864, the tactics on the Western Front in World War I.

Anecdotes of the brigade band, the fraternization of opposing pickets, swimming in the Tennessee, baseball, wrestling and other sports, not to mention playing cards and a drink of whiskey if he could get hold of one, help bridge the years and serve as a reminder that the soldier of the 1860s was not much different from the GI of the 1940s.

Furthermore, these memoirs are extraordinarily accurate. This may be accounted for by two considerations: First, the character of the author, and, second, the fact that they were written immediately after the war, when the events described were fresh in the mind of the writer.

We know, for example, that by September 1866 he was near the mid-point of his narrative, for, in describing the death of his brother-in-law at Chickamauga on Sept. 20, 1863, he wrote, "he fell in the hour of victory, whilst endeavoring to restore a wavering line, almost overpowered by numbers, and had just succeeded in his effort, when a bullet through his heart struck him from his horse, and he expired almost instantly, (this day, three years ago)."

There is no direct evidence as to when Manigault completed his memoirs, but the strong presumption is that this was accomplished prior to 1868. On a cover sheet to the manuscript he wrote, "Arthur and Huger (his two elder sons) may on some occasion take the trouble to read these pages." Since there would have been no reason to omit reference to his third son, Stephen, had he been living, one may conclude that the memoirs were finished prior to his birth in 1868. This would tie in with Manigault's further statement that he was writing "with a view of keeping these events as fresh in my memory as possible."

Thus, these recollections, in all probability, were set down within three years of the close of the war, which makes them virtually unique in this respect. Why they were terminated abruptly in September 1864, just prior to Hood's invasion of Tennessee, remains a mystery.

As a man of informed and definite opinions, Manigault does not hesitate to speak his mind regarding some of the leading figures of the day with whom he came in contact.

Of Jefferson Davis he wrote, "I was much pleased with his manner and the ease and dignity of his demeanour. There was not the slightest affectation or pedantry about him, but he conversed easily and cleverly and with the air of a polished and highly educated gentleman. I was much impressed with him."

That Manigault admired Braxton Bragg, with all his shortcomings, is clear to see. "I have always regarded him as one of the best organizers of an army and disciplinarians that I ever met with. Full of energy, indefatigable in his labors, firm and impartial as an administrative officer, he was no respecter of person or rank...He was not, however, a great general...Yet, I rank him fourth in merit and ability amongst our Confederate generals."

Hood he regarded as "incompetent, and entirely unfit for the responsible position he occupied," and he expressed the opinion that had Joseph E. Johnston remained in command of the Army of Tennessee at Atlanta, his wise policy might have protracted the war for at least a year and the South might have obtained terms "which would have left us in a far better condition than that to which we have since been reduced." Of the military capacity of his sometime division commander, Patton Anderson, he had little respect, and for another, Hindman, nothing but contempt.

Accustomed to the structured and well-regulated life of the South Carolina Lowcountry, and to what he euphemistically referred to as "its admirable order system of labor," Manigault laid great stress on the drill, discipline and training of the troops entrusted to his care.

At Corinth, Miss., in the spring of 1862, he noted with pride that his regiment, the 10th South Carolina, "attracted much attention from its soldierly appearance and for the precision of its drill...While going through their daily exercises there would be hundreds of lookers-on, officers and private soldiers coming several miles to witness the performance of a regiment of whom they had heard so much."

Later, at Munfordville, during the invasion of Kentucky, as the skirmishers of the 10th were advancing in fine style and driving the enemy before them, his army commander, Braxton Bragg, turned to Manigault and said: "That's worth looking at, Colonel. Your regiment does you honor."

Not unpredictably, Manigault's *bete-noir* was the cavalry, to whose lack of discipline and free-wheeling ways he attributed "our lamentable deficiency in that branch of the service." He had it in particularly for "Fighting Joe" Wheeler's troopers, perhaps because he knew them best, going so far as to assert that "as a general rule, the reports brought me by the cavalry were for the most part unreliable and incorrect." He hastened, however, to absolve Bedford Forrest from these strictures, considering him by far the most able of the cavalry leaders, possessing "skill, courage, judgment and the power of organizing and disciplining his troops." With a touch of condescension, he added that Forrest's "defective education and social disadvantages were his great drawbacks," which in all probability kept him from being "the most conspicuous and useful general in the Army of the Confederate States."

In a letter to his wife, written from Ault's Gap, near Dalton, Ga., just before the commencement of the Atlanta campaign, he told how J.R. Pringle of Charleston had asked him to trace two of his horses stolen by the cavalry at Flat Rock, N.C. Pointing out the virtual impossibility of complying with the request, he got in another lick at the mounted arm, adding, "I am afraid that many of the cavalry are mounted in this way and are without doubt a most unscrupulous set...a greater terror to their countrymen than to their enemies."

Manigault's memoirs are not devoted solely to the military. He was a keen observer and possessed a felicitous descriptive ability. Recalling the Blue Grass region of Kentucky, he speaks of the extensive woods of beech, poplar, ash, and oak, the ponds, the enormous sycamores along the water courses. Whilst riding through the plantations there, he says he was "frequently reminded of the English parks," and he found the roads and pikes of Kentucky almost as good as those he had seen in England.

He had an eye for the beauties of nature amidst the horrors of war, writing in a letter to his wife just before the opening of the Atlanta campaign in the spring of 1864: "The country is beginning to look beautifully and all the trees and wild flowers are in blossom. It is painful to think that while nature is thus robing itself in all her beauties, that so many thousands of men are preparing with all the improvements of modern science to cut each others throats and destroy one another...and that how much blood must be spilled before the same leaves fall to the ground."

And he had his reflective moments, too, as on Missionary Ridge during the siege of Chattanooga, looking down on the two armies below. "At night just after dark, when all the camp fires were lighted, the effect was grand and imposing...Over and over again have I spent an hour or more in the quiet of the evening...admiring this grand illumination, thinking of home, family and friends or speculating as to the future."

Manigault was a man of deep emotion and totally devoted to his family. "God bless you my darling wife and son," he wrote to Mary during some of the bloodiest fighting of the Atlanta campaign amidst the incessant cannonading and the rattle of small arms, "let us pray to Him to reunite us once more in peace and health. My love to all, your affectionate husband, A.M. Manigault." And on a more domestic note: "In the last 17 days I have had but one clean shirt...Oh for the quiet and luxury of a home and one's family once more...I may truly say that I have had more than my share of war and am sick of it. I long for it to end."

His affection extended to Mary's brothers, three of whom lost their lives in the war. Of Dan, his favorite, who met a heroic death at Chickamauga, he wrote, "I do not think I ever knew a purer spirit, a better balanced mind, or one who had his temper and passions more thoroughly under control." In a poignant and moving passage, he tells of the parents' sorrow. "Seldom have a family had more cause to mourn, or parents been more grief-stricken...three sons lost in the service of their country in the brief period of a twelvemonth, one from disease caused by exposure, privation and fatigue; the third and youngest of them struck down, scarcely knowing what it was that hurt him, on the walls of that fortress *(Sumter),* the glorious defense of which has been a matter of pride to us, and a subject for history, as illustrating what courage, perseverance and skill can accomplish under the most adverse circumstances. The three brothers lie side by side in 'Magnolia' *(cemetery)* in their undisturbed rest, only to be awakened 'At the last trump' on that 'dreadful day'."

Religion was an integral part of Manigault's life, as was generally true in that era. He told Mary that he was glad to note "a strong and growing religious sentiment" prevailing in the army but decried the lack of participation of the Episcopal Church to which they belonged, concluding that its ministers either had "too much regard for their personal comfort or pastorate charges at home." He said he was considering writing to the newspapers or the bishop about it, but, in keeping with his character, shrank from the notoriety.

Arthur Middleton Manigault was born in Charleston in 1824 of distinguished stock on both sides of his family. His mother was a Drayton, and of his Manigault forbears the most celebrated was his great-grandfather Gabriel, that legendary French Huguenot who became the richest merchant in the province and went a long way toward financing the Revolution in South Carolina by advancing $200,000 from his own pocket to support the cause of independence from Britain.

Starting his business career as a merchant trading with England, France and the West Indies, Gabriel Manigault expanded his interests to include rice and indigo planting, as well as banking, which was but a short step from the counting house of his merchant activites. That he had the Midas touch is made evident from the fact that when he died in 1781 he left, for those days, a prodigious estate of $854,000, the chief asset of which was 47,352 acres of land, including the site of Columbia and three rice plantations, along with 490 slaves. On a more gentle note, it should be recorded that he was vice-president of the Charleston Library Society — an institution still flourishing two centuries later — for which he provided a spacious apartment near his counting house free of rent.

As a young man, Arthur Manigault set out to learn the export trade in Charleston. He did not go to college, but as was the custom of the day for sons of the rich and prominent, he took the "Grand Tour" of Europe and also joined a militia company.

When the Mexican War came along, he was ready for active service as first lieutenant of the Charleston Volunteers, which became Company F of the Palmetto Regiment, raised, in his words, "from among the best citizens of South Carolina, most of them young men of good family, and well-to-do in the world."

In his early twenties, this experience of military life made a deep impression and in later years, in a delightful memoir of the expedition in Mexico, he was to write, "in spite of the privations, fatigues and dangers to which I was at times exposed, these months were perhaps the happiest and most romantic period of my life."

One may speculate that the memory of those days did not suffer from his recollections of the Mexican senoritas whom the young lieutenant found "well-made, with good figures, small feet, and exceedingly graceful carriage, coquettish and always ready for a flirtation."

Under Winfield Scott, "Old Fuss and Feathers," he took part in five battles, including the storming of Chapultepec and the capture of the City of Mexico, and was wounded three times, never seriously — once in the left arm by a spent ball, again in the inner part of the thigh *(he described it as a scratch)* and, lastly, "by a fragment of masonry, splintered by a cannon ball at one of the gates of the city."

In those days, however, the greater danger was from disease, and he later estimated that not more than 400 of an original 1,040 in the Palmetto Regiment survived the war. As one of the luckier — or perhaps hardier — ones, after being mustered out of service, he reached home in July 1848, safe and sound.

On his return to civilian life, he entered the commission business in Charleston and, on April 18, 1851, married Mary Proctor Huger, quite appropriately a member of another distinguished Charleston family.

A few years later, he moved to the Georgetown area and became a rice planter on property inherited from his parents on the north bank of the North Santee. He was living there when, on Dec. 20, 1860, South Carolina adopted the Ordinance of Secession, withdrew from the Union and set herself up as a free and independent nation.

In retrospect, this action appears foolhardy. Yet, there were many in the South, including Manigault, who did not so regard it at the time. Although slavery may have been the immediate issue, what concerned the majority of Southern leaders most was the conviction that their constitutional rights were being abridged and that, as Manigault put it, the government of the United States had fallen into the hands of a party that would deny the South the rights and protection afforded it by the Constitution and eventually bring about its "complete and thorough ruin." Being a man of principle, his course of action was clear, and he threw himself wholeheartedly into the cause of the South.

South Carolina anticipated, correctly as it transpired, that it would be joined by most, if not all, of the slave-holding states. Eventually, the Confederacy would comprise eleven states — a vast area of some 770,000 square miles stretching from the Potomac to the Rio Grande with a population, in 1860, of more than 5,300,000 whites and 3,500,000 slaves. Although far outstripped by the manpower and industrial might of the North, the South was not without its advantages. If hostilities were to break out — and this was by no means regarded as inevitable — it would be fighting a defensive war on interior lines. Furthermore, the South could count on its strong military tradition and a homogeneous, predominantly rural population whose members generally regarded themselves as superior fighters, certainly to the city masses and foreign born of the Northern states, whether or not they really believed that one Southerner could whip five Yankees.

Then, too, there was "King Cotton." That would be the clincher and hit the avaricious North in its pocketbook, and, if war should come, bring in John Bull on the side of the South. This belief, so widely held below the Mason and Dixon Line, was not unreasonable and had, in fact, a basis in logic that appealed to the Southern people, who still clung to the rationalism of the seventeenth and eighteenth centuries.

With the invention of Eli Whitney's cotton gin, American cotton, proving itself cheaper and superior in quality, rapidly displaced the Indian variety in the British and Continental cotton manufacturing industries, the very backbone of the Industrial Revolution. Such was England's dependence on the South for raw materials, chiefly cotton, that by 1858 more than 78% of Great Britain's total imports came from there, and it was estimated that somewhere between 4,000,000 and 5,000,000 people out of a population of 21,000,000 in the United Kingdom owed their livelihood to the cotton industry. Add to this the fact that Southern exports, again mostly cotton, made up over two-thirds of the U.S. total, and the further consideration that Northern cotton manufacturers were virtually wholly dependent on the South for their source of raw material supply, and it is small wonder that many Southern leaders were convinced that cotton was indeed king. But such proved not to be the case. War came and England remained aloof, never recognizing the Confederate States as an independent nation.

When hostilities broke out, Manigault volunteered at once and, during the first 12 months of the conflict, played an active role in organizing the defense of the coast in the region of Georgetown and in raising and training the 10th Regiment of South Carolina Volunteers, of which he was elected colonel.

In the spring of 1862, he was ordered to Mississippi with his regiment and, for the next two years and seven months, served in the Western Army. Almost the entire time, he was in command of the brigade that bore his name, taking part in the invasion of Kentucky and leading his troops in the battles of Murfreesboro, Chickamauga and Missionary Ridge and throughout the Atlanta campaign.

He was with Hood in the latter's desperate invasion of Tennessee in October and November of 1864, a campaign which, he later wrote, "speedily brought to an end all our bright hopes of independence, peace and rest...hurrying on the final scene which left us a conquered and enslaved people, at the mercy of a heartless, unscrupulous, and tyrannical enemy."

At the Battle of Franklin on Nov. 30, he was severely wounded in the head by by a rifle ball. In a letter to his wife that he was able to write the next day, he described his wounding: "About fifteen minutes after getting under fire, I was struck by a minnie ball...which brought me to the ground. It entered in the back part of the ear & passing thro. & under the skin came out about two inches behind the ear & near the back part of the head. It fortunately was turned in its course by the high projecting bone back of the ear & making a slight groove along the bone passed out as I have described before.

"Altho. I was not able to stand without assistance for several hours, still I had the use of my legs. After lying on the field for an hour...with the assistance of Willie *(Huger)* & a soldier, I walked a mile and a half to the hospital."

Although the doctor spoke of his being fit for duty in two or three weeks, the wound proved more serious. Not only did it keep him out of action for the remainder of the war, but its lingering effects contributed to his death some 20 years later.

Of Manigault's conduct at Franklin and that of the division of which his brigade was a part, his corps commander, Lt. Gen. Stephen D. Lee wrote, "Brigadier General Manigault, commanding a brigade of Alabamians and South Carolinians, was severely wounded in the engagement while gallantly leading his troops to the fight...I have never seen greater evidence of gallantry than was displayed by this division, under command of that admirable and gallant soldier, Maj. Gen. Ed. Johnson."

After a long convalescence, Manigault was preparing to rejoin his command just before the surrender in North Carolina in the spring of 1865, when, as he was about to set out for that purpose, he was directed by telegraph not to do so, it being quite evident, in his words, that a surrender would soon take place.

With the war at an end, he resumed his life as a rice planter on the North Santee, added another son and daughter to his family and devoted his spare time to the writing of his memoirs.

In 1867, he received a full pardon from Andrew Johnson, President of the United States, for all offenses committed — that is to say, for taking part in the late rebellion — provided he took the oath prescribed and did not "acquire any property whatever in slaves, or make use of slave labor." Just how he might do the latter, with South Carolina an occupied military district and under the heel of the Northern troops, was not revealed.

After the withdrawal of the occupation forces in 1877, he supported Wade Hampton and his "Red Shirts" in their successful campaign to restore white rule in the state. In 1880, he was elected Adjutant and Inspector General for the State of South Carolina for a two-year term and was twice reelected. He was renominated a third time in 1886 but died on Aug. 16 before the election.

Arthur Middleton Manigault comes down to us through his letters and memoirs as a well-born South Carolina gentleman of moderate and realistic views, balanced, orderly and disciplined. Yet, in his relations with his wife and family, he exhibits a tenderness one might not expect in one whose emotions were always under such perfect control. That his character was molded by the structured life and the traditions of the antebellum South seems clear, and surely he was one of its finest representatives.

In 1913, Lieut. Col. C. Irvine Walker, who probably knew Manigault as well as anyone outside his own family, wrote an account of his military career for the Arthur M. Manigault Chapter No. 63 of the United Daughters of the Confederacy, from which the following appreciation of his old commander is taken:

> "He had high ideals of duty and to them was ever faithful. He was firm in his decisions, always formed after mature consideration and with the best of judgment. He was very even-tempered, never swayed by passion. He was pure in thought and had no vulgar impulses to clothe in blasphemous words. He was not only morally good, but a communicant of the church and a deeply religious man without fanaticism. His lofty character was an inspiration to his men. He was a guide in all noble things."

In the spring of 1862, after the Battle of Shiloh, Manigault and his regiment arrived in Corinth, Miss., accompanied by the 19th South Carolina, to reinforce Beauregard's army. For a day or two, his troops were under the command of Brig. Gen. Daniel S. Donelson, who had likewise been transferred from South Carolina to the West with the 8th and 16th Tennessee. In a reorganization on April 28, however, Manigault's 10th South Carolina was assigned to Trapier's Fourth Brigade of Wither's Division of Bragg's Second Corps, along with the 19th South Carolina, the 28th Alabama, Blythe's 44th Mississippi and Waters' Alabama Battery.

In mid May — Trapier having been temporarily placed in charge of the division due to Withers' illness — Manigault, as senior colonel present, assumed command of the brigade which was later to bear his name, and led it in the action at Farmington. Thus was formed an association which, with the exception of the period from Aug. 21 to Oct. 12, 1862, during the Kentucky campaign, and a few days prior to the Battle of Murfreesboro, was to last until Manigault was struck down at Franklin, Tenn. on Nov. 30, 1864, and put *hors de combat* for the remainder of the war.

In June 1862, Blythe's 44th Mississippi Regiment was replaced by the 34th Alabama, and at Tullahoma, about Nov. 15, the 24th Alabama was added. This completed the organization of Manigault's Brigade, which was to remain unchanged until the very end of the war in North Carolina. In April 1865, when a mere skeleton, it was consolidated with Sharp's Brigade.

The fighting efficiency of the brigade was attributable, in large measure, to the high state of discipline always maintained by its commander. When the occasion demanded, he could be ruthless — as at Missionary Ridge when, in a desperate effort to stem the Confederate rout, he ordered the provost guard to shoot down anyone attempting to go to the rear, unless wounded. A stern taskmaster, he nevertheless won the respect and devotion of his men.

Usually, the brigade was in the thick of whatever action was taking place. In one of the attacks at Chickamauga, for example, of 800 men who took part "nearly 300 were shot down in a space of time certainly not exceeding three minutes. It almost sickened one," Manigault wrote in reference to this action, "to reflect how many of those sturdy forms moving steadily forward, in all the vigor and strength of manhood, ere the setting sun would lie cold and stiff on that bloody field."

Manigault's personal bravery was never questioned. As one would expect, he was determined to do his duty regardless of the risks involved. This was made clear on two occasions — at Chattanooga and the Battle of the Poor House, or Lick Skillet Road, outside of Atlanta when he was prepared to carry out orders, mistaken as he knew them to be, and lead his brigade in hopeless attacks against overwhelming numbers, although fully expecting not to come back alive.

His coolness under fire was shown near Atlanta, when, refusing to take a longer but safer route, he led his troops to the relief of another portion of the line across "a high bare hill, entirely exposed to the enemy, for the space of about two hundred yards...Four Yankee batteries opened on us, and firing with the greatest rapidity; shrapnel and spherical case all bursting with admirable regularity, over, under, and around us, threatened to destroy or sweep us away...This was the severest artillery fire that I have ever been exposed to. The air seemed alive with shells, bursting, it seemed to me, within only a few feet of my head."

By his own account, Manigault led his brigade in 13 battles and 30 skirmishes. "Its strength, when most full, never exceeded 3,500 men on paper — 2,500 men was its greatest number present for duty at any one period. Its losses in killed and wounded up to 30th November, 1864 (Battle of Franklin) was a little in excess of 2,700 men...I do not think it surrendered more than 450 strong."

Although rarely mentioned, except in the *Official Records,* Manigault's Brigade was a solid, reliable, no-nonsense outfit that, with few exceptions, conducted itself with courage and gallantry. Along with similar unsung commands, it formed the fighting backbone of the Army of Tennessee.

R.L.T.

Acknowledgments

My chief debt of gratitude is to Edward Manigault for his confidence in entrusting me with his grandfather's memoirs and his unfailing courtesy, kindness and encouragement. I wish also to express my thanks to Thomas R. Waring, former editor of the Charleston, S.C., *News and Courier* and *The Evening Post,* for putting in a good word in my behalf with his former boss, Mr. Manigault; and to Warren Ripley, author and leading authority on Confederate ordnance, for his help in arranging the details of publication.

My appreciation also goes to Arthur Manigault Wilcox, editor of *The News and Courier,* for his kindness in making available most of the photographs reproduced in the illustrations, as well as a number of letters from Gen. Manigault to his wife which contain interesting sidelights and personal reflections on the course of events; to Minnie Haigh for courtesies graciously extended as assistant librarian of the Charleston Library Society, particularly in connection with access to the microfilm records of the issues of the *Charleston Courier* and *Mercury* during the war years and afterwards; and to Peter Manigault, great-grandson of the General, for helpful suggestions.

The libraries of the Virginia and South Carolina Historical Societies and the Wyles Collection of the University of California at Santa Barbara have been valuable sources of information and to the directors and librarians of these institutions I express my thanks, as I do to the Western Reserve Historical Society in Cleveland for kindly making available a letter of Gen. Manigault's which throws considerable light on the intriguing question of why his promotion to brigadier general was held up for so long by the Confederate authorities in Richmond. In addition, I wish to extend my appreciation to the librarians and staffs of the Southern Historical Collection, University of North Carolina, Chapel Hill, and Duke University Library, Durham, N.C. who were most kind and cooperative.

And, finally, I am grateful to my wife, Betsy, for encouragement and forbearance along the way and for the many hours she put in working on the index; to my son, Richard, for assistance in clearing up one or two obscure points, including the location of Proctor's Station on the Louisville & Nashville Railroad; and to my stepson, John Belmont, for proofreading the manuscript and making helpful comments thereon.

R.L.T.

xv

Editor's Note

The original manuscript, in the beautiful handwriting so typical of the days before the invention of the typewriter, has been followed essentially without change. Minor corrections have been made in the spelling of the names of individuals and places, as have occasional adjustments in punctuation and paragraphing where they contribute to the ease of reading.

For all practical purposes, however, General Manigault's narrative is presented exactly as he wrote it in the years immediately following the close of hostilities, when his memory was fresh and the emotions evoked by the South's war for independence, ending as it did in the bitterness of defeat, were still very much alive.

Introductions to the various chapters have been included in the belief that, particularly for the general reader, they will provide a background against which the memoirs themselves will not only take on added meaning but will be more enjoyable to read as well.

Parenthetical inserts have been kept to a minimum. Where included by General Manigault, they are in the same type as that of the manuscript. If inserted by the editor, contrast is accomplished by use of *(italics)*.

Notes follow each chapter and are numbered consecutively for that chapter.

R.L.T. — 1982

PROLOGUE

(The Narrative)

M y purpose is simply and in as concise a manner as possible to narrate for my own amusement and with a view of keeping these events as fresh in memory as possible, the part I took in the war between the United States and the Confederate States and the impressions made on my mind during that period.

Arthur and Huger* may on some occasion take the trouble to read these pages. If they ever do, I wish them to bear in mind that this does not profess to be a history, nor is it intended to be read outside my own family, and that owing to the loss of my memorandums and the papers pertaining to my command near the end of the war, I have been obliged to rely almost entirely on my memory and have forgotten the names of several points of interest and at times *(may)* be somewhat inaccurate as to the dates, numbers, etc. I do not think, however, that in any instance I am much out of the way.

My account also relates almost entirely to such occurrences as I personally took part in, or is based on intelligence received from others whose opinions I thought worth something. These remarks must also apply to what I have before written concerning the campaigns in Mexico. The scraps and memorandums which I had relating to that period were also destroyed at the time that my furniture and other household effects were plundered by Yankees and my own negroes, at the house on Wambaw** where they had been deposited for safe keeping, or at my residence, White Oak, on North Santee.

A.M. MANIGAULT

Gen. Manigault's children — Arthur Middleton Manigault II and Daniel Elliott Huger Manigault. — Editor.

**A tributary of the South Santee, across the rivers and a few miles upstream from White Oak. — Editor.*

1

SOUTH CAROLINA

and

TRANSFER TO THE WEST

(Editor's Preface)

On Feb. 27, 1861, A.M. Manigault wrote to the Secretary of War of the fledgling nation of South Carolina:

> *"I beg leave to report to you the formation of a cavalry Corps, raised in this neighborhood, for its protection or for such service as you may see fit to require of us. Said Corps has been inspected and numbers fifty (50) men, a muster roll of which as been furnished the Adjutant General by Major Price, inspecting officer, detailed for that purpose. The company is armed with sabers, and arrangements have been made for the purchase of rifled carbines to complete our equipment."*
> (Signed)   A.M. MANIGAULT
> Capt. North Santee Mounted Rifles.

A few days later, Manigault received official confirmation of his election as captain of this volunteer outfit in the form of a commission signed by F.W. Pickens, governor and commander-in-chief, "reposing special trust and confidence in your courage and good conduct *(and)* in your fidelity to the STATE OF SOUTH CAROLINA." Said company, "You are to Lead, Train, Muster and Exercise according to Military Discipline." This document was rather pointedly dated in the "Eighty-fifth year of the Sovereignty and Independence of the State of South Carolina," declaring in unmistakable terms that South Carolina had been independent all along anyway, that is to say, since 1776.

Some weeks thereafter, Manigault made a trip to Montgomery, Ala. — the then seat of the Confederate government — bearing with him a letter of introduction from Gov. Pickens to President Jefferson Davis. Recommending the bearer for an officer's commission, Pickens wrote: "He is a gentleman of the highest standing" and in the Mexican War "was considered a thoroughly informed and brave officer." Indeed, Pickens continued, he had intended to appoint him a Captain of Infantry of South Carolina troops but understood at the time, he rather quaintly explained, that Manigault was sick in the country with rheumatism.

Returning to Charleston, Manigault found that events were moving swiftly.

At half past four o'clock on the morning of Friday, April 12, 1861, a burst of flame flashed from the muzzle of one of the mortars at Fort Johnson on James Island, and the pre-dawn stillness of Charleston Harbor was shattered by a deep-throated roar. Its spluttering fuse marking its course, a 10-inch shell rose slowly in a graceful arc, hesitated, started downward with ever increasing velocity and exploded directly over Fort Sumter. In the ringing prose of the day, "a white smoke floated after it, parted from its upmost course and melted in the higher air of heaven, like a departing angel of peace, as the missile sped on its errand of ruin and affright."

The questions dividing the North and the South had at last been committed to the sword, and the strife that would tear the nation apart and bring with it immeasurable suffering, destruction and death had begun. As Lincoln so aptly put it in his Second Inaugural, "Both parties deprecated war, but one of them would make war rather than let the nation survive, and the other would accept war rather than let it perish. And the war came."

Appointed the first brigadier general of the Provisional Army of the Confederate States, Pierre Gustave Toutant Beauregard commanded the troops in Charleston and the forts ringing the bay. Among his aides was a Captain Manigault of whom Beauregard wrote: "I cannot close my report without reference to...A.M. Manigault, of my staff...who did effective and gallant service on Morris Island during the fight."

On May 1, Manigault was appointed a special aide-de-camp on Gov. Pickens' staff, with the rank of lieutenant colonel, and ordered to report 'to Gen. Beauregard for whom he served for several weeks as a volunteer assistant inspector general. In recognition of his services, Beauregard, when he was called away to take command of the Confederate troops massing in northern Virginia, wrote Manigault a cordial letter expressing gratitude for his "very valuable assistance" and assuring him of his "high esteem and respect."

In the months following the heady and virtually bloodless triumph of Fort Sumter — two privates on the Southern side were slightly wounded — South Carolina's energies were directed to fortifying her coast and raising troops for her defense. In this, Manigault played an active part in the Georgetown region and was held in high esteem by the Governor who referred to him as "an officer of experience" and "a thorough military man...of the highest standing."

Late in December 1860, the legislature had divided South Carolina into 10 districts in each of which a regiment was to be formed for state defense. In the northern district along the coast, embracing the districts of Horry, Marion, Georgetown, Williamsburg and part of the Charleston District, the 10th South Carolina Volunteers was organized on May 31 and Arthur M. Manigault elected its colonel. The recruits, whose only military qualifications were strong physiques, courage and ardent patriotism, assembled at Camp Marion near Georgetown on July 19 and the long and trying process of training in the school of the soldier was begun.

Capt. C. Irvine Walker, the first adjutant of the regiment and later to command it as a lieutenant colonel, wrote in his *Historical Sketch of the Tenth Regiment South Carolina Volunteers:*

> *"Col. Manigault was a disciplinarian by nature and devoted himself earnestly to making trained soldiers out of the raw recruits who had come to him. So marked was his success, that his Regiment went into active service one of the best drilled and disciplined commands which South Carolina offered to the Southern Confederacy."*

Later, at the front, this period of the regiment's history would seem almost idyllic. "Dear old Camp Marion," Walker remembered, "and those dress parades...wives, daughters, sweethearts and friends looking admiring on to make each one of us do his best, and our negro band marching down the line to the tune of 'Walk in the Light'...and the colonel's two setters...and then the chat with our friends in the cool twilight after parade."

Company A of the Tenth was the former Georgetown Rifle Guards and its historian told how they "drilled in Hardee's light infantry tactics and Scott's heavy infantry tactics. Later, an expert teacher in the Zouave drill was employed to instruct the company. A drum and fife corps led by George Douglas, a worthy and respected colored barber, furnished music for the company. His favorite air was 'Walk in the Light', so often played that a very staid member of the company, Joseph Tuttle, dryly remarked that if he were in hell and heard that tune he would know the Rifle Guards were coming."

The proficiency in drill and excellence in discipline of the regiment were materially contributed to by a number of the cadets of the South Carolina Military Academy, who did their bit for the cause by forsaking their summer vacation and devoting their tactical knowledge to the training of the recruits. The result was a splendidly drilled and disciplined regiment which, when it joined the Western Army in Mississippi in the spring of 1862, was to receive the praise of that strict taskmaster, Braxton Bragg.

On one occasion two companies, along with the Georgetown Artillery, were called out to oppose a reported enemy landing on one of the

Waccamaw beaches. While this proved a false alarm, it gave rise to a long-remembered event for those fortunate enough to be involved. In his *Historical Sketch of the Georgetown Rifle Guards*, S. Emanuel, a member of the company, describes the scene:

> *Capt. Weston...invited the detachment of more than 150 men to dine with him at his plantation, Hagely...Col. Manigault accepted the pressing invitation. Capt. Weston was entirely unprepared, yet from the resources of his palatial home he served a course dinner for the entire party. He seated all in his house, had table capacity, silver, crockery, servants, provisions for the impromptu affair...Think of the stupendous undertaking and the lavish hospitality of dining more than 150 men and giving them a really fine dinner without a moment's warning! ...I may add that the wines furnished were of the rarest, and were plentiful."*

Capt. Plowden C.J. Weston, who had joined the Georgetown Rifle Guards as a private, typified those patriotic and wealthy Southern planters who willingly sacrificed everything for the cause of their state and the Southern Confederacy. From his own purse, he provided Company A of the 10th with 155 English Enfield rifles, accoutrements and knapsacks, and material for both summer and winter uniforms. As a crowning touch, he "had uniformed and attached to his company a pioneer corps composed of four of his able-bodied and most trusted servants, by name: Flanders, Caesar, Cooper and Cudjoe, who, armed with picks, axes and spade, moved in advance of the company when on the march to clear its path of obstructions."

His generosity, as Emanuel points out, did not stop there. He also "assisted companies elsewhere in procuring their equipment and in the incipiency of the war he sent a check for $5,000 to the State Ordnance Department, a part of which was invested in perhaps the first rifle gun made in the South, manufactured by Cameron & Co. of Charleston. The name of Capt. Weston was placed on the gun as a compliment to that noble patriot."

When Robert E. Lee was placed in command of the Department of South Carolina, Georgia and East Florida in the fall of 1861, at the time of the seizure of Port Royal Sound by the Federals, he assigned the First, or Eastern, District — extending from Little River Inlet to the South Santee River — to Manigault, with headquarters at Georgetown. In this capacity Manigault corresponded with Lee regarding the construction and armament of the fortifications near the mouth of the North Santee and Winyah Bay and on Cat and South Islands, as well as the equipment and training of the troops.

On Nov. 15 he wrote, "I will do the best I can, should the enemy appear." Yet, no attacks of any consequence occurred. Nonetheless, there were other problems of camp and garrison duty of which the health of the troops was perhaps the most pressing. On Christmas Day, writing from Coosawhatchie, Capt. Walter H. Taylor, Lee's assistant adjutant general, informed Manigault that Lee was "sorry to hear that the Tenth Regiment is suffering from measles, but hopes the cases continue trifling and that the number of sick is on the decrease."

When the spring campaigns of 1862 opened, the necessity of concentrating as many men as possible at the points of greatest danger in the overall conduct of the war became evident. As a result, the 10th South Carolina, which had entered Confederate service in August of the previous year and now reenlisted for three years or the war, was transferred from the region about Georgetown to Charleston and thence to the West to reinforce Gen. Beauregard's army at Corinth, Miss. The latter, his forces severely reduced in numbers by the combined losses of some 25,000 men at Fort Donelson, Island No. 10 and Shiloh, not to mention a severe outbreak of illness among his troops, was calling for reinforcements.

Lee had telegraphed Pemberton, now in command of the department of which South Carolina was a part, on April 10: "Beauregard is pressed for troops. If Mississippi Valley is lost, Atlantic states will be ruined." To, meet the emergency, two Tennessee regiments and two from South Carolina, the 10th and the 19th, were dispatched by rail to Corinth.

When, on the evening of April 11, the men of the 10th Regiment boarded the cars at the South Carolina Rail Road depot in Charleston for the two weeks' roundabout journey to Mississippi over the rickety railroads of the Confederacy, most of them, as Manigault points out, were leaving home forever. But that was all in the future, and now their spirits were high and they were on their way to join in the real fighting. "Every where along the route," wrote Irvine Walker, "the wildest enthusiasm prevailed, and we went to the front encouraged by the smiles and blessings of the women."

They found Corinth a depressing place — hot, at times wet and muddy, at others dry and dusty. The army there, made up largely of raw recruits, was riddled with disease and in a state of considerable disarray.

The Tenth's baptism of fire occurred a few days later, when, on picket duty, they came in contact with the vanguard of the Northern army under Halleck moving cautiously southward on Corinth. Describing the conduct of Company A, the old Georgetown Rifle Guards, the war correspondent of the *Charleston Daily Courier* wrote: "Capt. Plowden Weston himself was on the field and acted with the coolness of a veteran soldier; balls tore up the earth around his feet and cut the limbs above his head, yet his most intimate friends would have discovered no difference between the calm, imperturbable soldier on the field of strife and the dignified gentleman whose society they had enjoyed at his princely home on the Waccamaw."

Opposed by Halleck's overwhelming numbers and his own army seriously reduced by illness, Beauregard evacuated Corinth on the 29th of May, withdrawing to Tupelo and subsequently Saltillo, Miss., whence, on July 30, Manigault and his brigade were transferred by rail to Chattanooga.

R.L.T.

PREPARING FOR BATTLE

(The Narrative)

T he election of Abraham Lincoln as President of the United States by the Republican party of the North, in October 1860,[1] satisfied the people of the Southern States that the time long since foreseen by our wiser statesmen, had at last arrived when the South must withdraw from the Union.

It was now evident that the party into whose hands the direction of the government had fallen would to a greater extent pervert the Constitution to the advancement of their own ends, and denying us through the majority which they possessed in Congress, the rights and protection which it secured us, eventually bring about our complete and thorough ruin. To save themselves from the threatened danger, most of the Southern slaveholding States, with remarkable unanimity, one after another, called conventions of the people and passed Ordinances of Secession, beginning with South Carolina, on the 20th of December, 1860, and expressing a desire peaceably to withdraw from the Union, adopted a Constitution of their own, and formed a Government known as the Confederate States of America. The remaining States of the old Union, denying the sovereignty of these States and their right to secede, began to make war-like preparations, with the intention of coercing the South back into the Union, or forcibly to subjugate her. The government of the Confederate States determined at all hazards to maintain their independence and separate nationality.[2]

All efforts at conciliation having failed, in April, 1861, the first conflict occurred, and that war, so familiar and fresh in the minds of many, was commenced, which after lasting four years, resulted, as we have bitter cause to remember, in our complete overthrow and subjugation.

Towards the latter part of 1860, many volunteer organizations were formed in the State with a view to future military service. In December, the residents of North Santee formed themselves into a corps, known as the North Santee Mounted Rifles and I was elected the Captain. During the winter and spring of 1861, my time was much occupied in superintending the construction of several batteries for the defence of Winyah Bay and North Santee River, and in the drill and instruction of the Company. Early in April, I made a visit to Montgomery, then the seat of government. On my return through Charleston, it being very generally believed that an attack on Fort Sumter in that harbor would soon take place, I offered my services to General Beauregard, then in command, which he accepted, and assigned me to duty on his staff as a volunteer Aide-de-Camp.[3]

On the 11th of April, Major Anderson,[4] Commander at Fort Sumter, having refused to give up that fortress to the Confederate States, it was determined to attack the place before reinforcements, both military and naval, which were known to be on the way with a considerable amount of supplies, could arrive. Preparations with a view to its bombardment and capture had been pushed forward with great activity, and were by this time tolerably complete. These works carried on under the eye of the Commandant of the Fort, he had allowed to proceed without molestation on his part.

General James Simons, South Carolina Militia, was placed in command of Morris Island on the 11th, most of the troops there belonging to his Brigade, and by order and at the request of General Beauregard, I was temporarily assigned to duty with him, as was also Major Whiting, of the Engineers, (afterwards a Major-General, C.S.A., and killed near the end of the war at Fort Fisher, N.C.).[5] With General Simons, I reached the Island on the same day, and at about three o'clock[6] on the morning of the 12th, our mortar batteries opened fire on the Fort. The bombardment lasted day and night until the following morning, and was replied to with great spirit by the enemy. At about eleven o'clock on the 13th, the barracks of the Fort took fire, and were destroyed, and eventually caused the surrender of the Fort that afternoon.

The battle, as it is called, is remarkable only as being the first contest of the war, and as one in which no person was killed.[7] General Simons remained about ten days longer on the Island, and was then relieved.[8] I found on my return to the city that General Beauregard had obtained for me from the Governor of the State (Pickens) the commission of Lieutenant Colonel, and that I had been assigned the duty on his staff of Assistant Inspector General for his Military department. Shortly after I made a short tour on duties connected with my position, and found on my return that General Beauregard had received orders to proceed to Virginia to take some command there.[9] He was kind enough to offer to carry me with him, promising an appointment as soon as he could obtain one. His offer I however declined, as I had every reason to believe that in a short time I would receive a position which in every respect would suit me better.

On the 31st of May, I was elected without opposition colonel of the 10th S.C.V., a regiment made up of companies from the districts of Marion, Horry, Williamsburg, and Georgetown.[10] The honor conferred on me by this regiment was peculiarly agreeable to me, from the fact that previous to my election, I did not know, personally, ten men in it. My connection with it ceased only with the war, it having been under my command either as Colonel or Brigadier General, during the whole of that period, and we shared together all its hardships and privations, and there were but three engagements in all the bloody fields through which they passed, that I was not present with them, a severe wound preventing.[11]

My connection with it from first to last was of a most satisfactory character, and the respect and confidence with which they treated me, I never can forget, and I look back now with sentiments of regard and affection to my old companions in arms, both the living and the dead, — of the former, how few are left!

The 10th South Carolina assembled at Camp Marion, two and a half miles from Georgetown, S.C., on the 16th of July, 1861. Shortly after they were mustered into the Confederate States Service, and two companies were added, making twelve in all, and numbering eleven hundred and seventy-five men (1,175).[12]

For several months the Regiment remained at this place, busily engaged, drilling, and receiving the more necessary instructions for the more active duties of the field.[13]

General Ripley,[14] commanding the troops in South Carolina, and charged with its defence, shortly after the organization of my Regiment, divided the coast and country adjacent into three Military Districts, appointing me to the command of the first, which extended from the South Santee River to the North Carolina line. During the latter part of the summer, much apprehension existed as to a descent upon some part of our coast, as it was known that the Yankees were preparing an expedition for some such purpose. Its destination was, of course, unknown, yet it had been pretty well ascertained that the attack would be made on some point in this State. The military force of the first district was in consequence largely increased, and consisted of the following named commands and the strength of each:

10th S.C.	Col. A.M.M.	—	12	Compy	—	1,175	
21st S.C.	Col. Graham		10	"	—	750	
Smith's Battalion	Lt. Col. Smith		7	"	—	500	
						2,425	Inf.
Wilson's "	Maj. Wilson		4	"	—	200	
Tucker's Troop	Capt. Tucker		1	"	—	80	
N. Santee Mounted Rifles	Capt. Cordes		1	"	—	40	
						320	Cav.
Ward's Battery	Capt. Ward		1	"	—	90	
						90	Art.
Troops continually on duty in 1st Military District						2,835	Total

To the above must be added several other Companies not in Confederate States Service, but liable to be called out at any time, and were on several occasions in the field for a week or two, giving an additional force, should there be occasion, of about 180 Men — 3,015.

This Command was necessarily much scattered, and, although a very respectable force when brought together, it would have been a very difficult matter to do so under three days, owing to the nature of the country, intersected as it was by rivers, creeks, and inlets. Three steamers, however, were furnished by the Government, and they were all important to us.

The great bulk of these troops were retained in the neighbourhood of Winyah Bay, at Georgetown, South Island and Cat Island. Smith's Battalion, Ward's Battery, and the greater part of the Cavalry, were stationed at various points of that part of the coast known as Waccamaw Neck. Henning's Battery, a company of Militia belonging to Georgetown, though not in camp, was held in readiness for any service that might be required of it.

The principal works constructed were on Winyah Bay and at the mouth of North Santee River. For the defence of the first, quite a respectable battery, mounting ten guns, was thrown up at Cat Island, and another, mounting five, on South Island. At the southwest point of the last island was a third battery as a protection to the North Santee.

The guns, however, were deficient in calibre, the largest 32 pounders, and only two of these. The others consisted of 24, 18, and 12 pounders, several of the latter being rifled.

On Waccamaw Neck, at *(Murrell's)* Inlet, there was a small battery for three guns, and near the mouth of Little River was another for four guns. The intervening inlets were comparatively insignificant, the water on the bars being very shallow, and no attraction for an enemy in the neighbourhood.

These batteries were manned by Infantry detailed for the purpose, and drilled as Artillerists. Their practice in a short time was very creditable. As a general thing, a good deal of anxiety was expressed by the Command to try their hands with the enemy, and the Companies serving as Artillery were very confident of their ability to sink the finest frigate in the United States Navy, or a fleet of gunboats. It is a matter of congratulation to me that such an opportunity never offered itself, for our experience during later periods of the war leaves no doubt in my mind but that our popguns not only would have done them little damage, but would soon have been dismounted or the gunners driven from them.

It was a matter of great importance that this region of country should have been preserved, for a very large portion of the rice crop of the South was grown on the two Santees, and on the rivers emptying into Winyah Bay, — the Pee Dee, Waccamaw, Sampit, and Black Rivers. The additional means it furnished of subsistence to our armies, was a matter of great consequence, and so valuable and productive a district should have been preserved even at a considerable cost. General Lee, who superceeded Ripley in November,[15] fully understood its value, and I do not think that had he continued in the department, he would have consented to abandon it, and leave it in the defenceless state that his successor[16] afterwards did.[17]

The organizing, inspection, and disposition of the troops, the general supervision of the defences and obstructions, together with the special attention which I liked to give to my own Regiment kept me continually busy, and scarcely left me a spare moment.[18] On several occasions, my anxiety was very great, but needlessly so, as it turned out. No serious demonstration was ever made against any part of the coast for which I was responsible, during my stay there and with the exception of a repulse of a boat party by the 10th S.C.[19] and a like skirmish in which a number of cavalry was engaged, we never came in collision with the enemy. Their blockaders were constantly in sight, and could at high water have crossed the bar at pleasure. With them on two occasions were several transports, with troops on board, but no attempt to enter or land troops was ever made.

In March, General Lee was ordered to Virginia, and General Pemberton succeeded him in the command of the department in which South Carolina was included.[20] Shortly after, he opened a correspondence with me on matters relating to my district, and in the latter part of March, 1862, I received orders to dismantle the batteries, send all the guns, ordnance stores, etc., by rail to Charleston, and, after having done so, to report with my Regiment to General Ripley, commanding there, also stating that it was his intention to abandon that district, likewise to remove all the infantry, and a portion of the cavalry, leaving only a few companies of the latter and Ward's Battery as a guard or police force. There was nothing to do but to obey. On the 28th, his instructions were carried out, and on the following morning, the 10th Regiment began their march to Charleston.[21]

So far as General Pemberton's orders applied to myself and Regiment, I did not regret the change, for we were all anxious for one, and for service of a more active character, with one of the largest armies in the fields but knowing his intention as to an abandonment of this most productive grain-growing country, believing that its loss would be very seriously felt by the Confederacy in one way or another, and knowing that the destruction of the batteries and removal of the troops would prove an invitation to the enemy too strong and too important to be resisted, the whole country lying at the mercy of a single gunboat, I took leave of my old district rather low in spirits, and with a strong presentiment of coming evil. My forebodings were soon verified. A few weeks after we left, two U. S. gunboats entered the bay, and proceeded to Georgetown and up the neighbouring rivers, and carried off many Negroes, destroyed much property, and created great alarm. These visits were repeated several times, and on the Santees like raids were undertaken by the enemy. Those of the planters who were able to do so removed their Negroes and such property as could conveniently be transported into the interior or out of reach of the enemy, their plantations abandoned, and the growing crops left to perish in the fields. An effort was afterwards made to repair the error of General Pemberton. Batteries were constructed higher up Winyah (but below the mouths of the rivers emptying into it), under the cover of night, and during the temporary absences of the enemy's vessels. When completed, they were unmasked, and although they attacked them *(on)* one occasion, no effort of a determined character was ever made to pass them, and they afterwards confined themselves to the lower Bay.

A certain amount of protection was thus again secured to the planters, but the mistake, excepting to a very limited extent, could not be corrected. Those of them who had removed their Negroes were unwilling to return, having lost much confidence in the wisdom of the military authorities, and not knowing how soon again they might have to flee. Such gangs as had not been removed were much demoralized. The admirable order system of labor which had hitherto existed in the cultivation of these valuable plantations could not be restored. They ceased to become productive, barely making a sufficiency for the labourers themselves. In this way, a very considerable portion of our labouring population, instead of producing as they might have done, a large amount of subsistence for our soldiers in the field, besides supplying themselves, had to be provided for from other portions of the State, at a time when the country could ill afford to spare anything in the shape of food. This instance is only one of the many where mismanagement on the part of the Government or its officials, by sacrificing their resources and multiplying their incumbrances, contributed to our final failure.

After a march of four days, the Regiment reached Mount Pleasant, near Charleston, and went into camp at that place. Reporting to General Ripley, he directed me to remain where I was, but to be in readiness to move to Cole's Island, at the mouth of the Stono, in the course of a week. I was also permitted to furlough a good many of my men, who had re-enlisted in advance of the expiration of their term of service.[22]

On the morning of the 11th of April, at nine o'clock, A. M., I received a message from General Ripley, directing me to report to him. On doing so, he ordered me to proceed without delay by rail to Corinth, Mississippi, there to join the army under General Beauregard. At nine P. M., the Regiment, with its baggage, horses of officers, and supplies for the journey, were in the trains prepared for them, at the depot of the S.C. R.Rd. A short time after, we started, and bid farewell to Charleston and South Carolina. To most of them, it was forever.[23]

On reaching Atlanta, we were informed that a telegram had just been received there, giving the information that a Federal column had captured Huntsville, Alabama.[24] Consequently, the railroad being in their possession, we were obliged to change our route, and proceeding to Montgomery, we there took a steamer down the Alabama River to Mobile. Here we were detained several days, but finally got off in two detachments by the Mobile and Ohio R.Rd., and on the 25th and 26th, the right and left wings, respectively, reached Corinth. Owing to the tapping of the road before mentioned and various other causes, we were much delayed on the road, the journey having occupied fifteen instead of five days.[25]

On our arrival in Corinth, we were temporarily placed under the command of Brig. Gen. Donelson, together with the 19th S.C., and two

Tennessee Regiments, the four regiments having arrived there very nearly together, and had been drawn from the forces in South Carolina.[26] A few days later, an entire reorganization of the army was made, and we were placed in Wither's[27] Division, Trapier's[28] Brigade, consisting of the 10th and 19th South Carolina, 28th Alabama, and Blythe's *(44th)* Mississippi, with Water's Battery attached.

The Division consisted of four Brigades, the troops from the states of South Carolina, Alabama, and Mississippi. The two South Carolina regiments were the only ones from that state in the Western Army for very nearly eighteen months. The Division and Brigade, with some occasional exceptions, and frequent change of Commanders, remained as at first organized throughout the remainder of the War.

The Battle of Shiloh had been fought about twenty days previous to my arrival. It was claimed by both sides as a victory. I was not at it, and it is not my purpose to say anything about it here. We found our Army, I thought, in rather a bad condition. It had suffered a good deal in the late fight, and the men had not been long enough in the Service at that time to recuperate rapidly. After a great battle, there is always a laxness of discipline and a slovenly manner about the men in discharging their duties. To a certain extent, this state of things is unavoidable, but it was in excess here. It must be said, however, in justice to General Beauregard, that the bulk of his troops were newly-raised regiments and raw recruits, both officers and men sadly wanting in experience.

I have never before or since seen so little order, discipline, or such complete absence of martial appearance amongst the troops as was here exhibited. Our own Division, however, may be regarded as an exception, as the greater part of them had been in Service for more than a year, and many of the regiments had been at Pensacola, under the command of General Braxton Bragg, the best disciplinarian and organizer of an army that I ever served under. He was second in command here, and commanded a Corps of the Army. At Shiloh he had greatly distinguished himself, and I think it cause for regret that after the fall of General Albert Sidney Johnston on the first day that he did not succeed to the command, instead of another officer. As far as he was able, he laboured hard to correct the bad state of things existing, and to a great extent succeeded in doing so.[29]

Early in May, the Federal Army, under the command of General Halleck, began its forward movement against us, approaching slowly and with great caution. Their number must have been fully one hundred thousand men. To resist them, General Beauregard was believed to have seventy-five thousand. I doubt if his force exceeded sixty thousand. He certainly never had that number for duty at any one time, and his strength was daily diminishing from sickness and other causes.[30] Corinth had been encircled with breastworks and redoubts for artillery, located wherever the ground was favorable for it, and it appeared that General Beauregard had determined to await the enemy, and receive his attack, if he made one, behind his defences. The ground upon which the Army lay was too contracted, and had been camped on for months. But little attention had been paid to the policing of the camps, and as the weather became hot, the atmosphere was offensive and unwholesome in the extreme. The supplies were of bad quality, and not the full allowance. Towards the latter part of our stay, or from the 10th of May to the 30th, owing to excessive heat and want of rain, the water in the pools or wet weather branches became stagnant or altogether disappeared, and much suffering was caused from this deficiency. Most of the men were unaccustomed to the exposure attendant upon their new mode of life, and suffering from diseases generally attendant upon camps and large bodies of men brought together for the first time. The consequence of all this was that the army lost daily a large number of men, and I have been told that on many occasions as many as fifteen hundred were sent to the rear in the course of one day.[31]

Our first tour of duty occurred in the beginning of May, and the Brigade was ordered on outpost duty to relieve another from our Division, stationed on one of the principal roads leading to Corinth, at a point known as "The White House," distant from our lines about seven miles. General Withers having gone to the rear sick, the senior Brigadier, Trapier, was at the time commanding the Division. As senior Colonel, the command of the Brigade fell to me. Leaving our camp at daylight, we reached "The White House" about 8 A. M., and began at once to relieve Colonel Smith,* commanding Chalmer's Brigade.[32] He informed me that his Cavalry scouts had reported to him a short time previous to my arrival, the advance of the enemy in heavy force, and that their Cavalry was at that time within a mile or two of him.

The prospect before me was not pleasant, particularly so as my orders were "to resist any attack, to fight obstinately, and on no account to retire unless forced to do so." The means at my command with which to make a fight consisted of about 2,300 Infantry, 300 Cavalry, and four pieces of light Artillery, six pounder guns and twelve pounder howitzers. There could be little doubt but that the enemy were approaching in large numbers, and it proved afterwards to be Pope's Corps, some 20,000 strong. Our skirmish line extended over a space of about one mile, connecting with a like line of Cavalry. In front of this were my own videttes. To the right and left of the line of battle selected, there was no considerable body of troops within two miles, the nearest of these at the small village of Farmington, in strength corresponding very nearly with my own. Shortly after Col. Smith left me, the enemy Cavalry made its appearance, and our Videttes were driven in. Some slight skirmishing occurred at intervals during the day, but the enemy, cavalry alone, did not seem disposed to attack us.

As soon as it became dark, we could see distinctly the reflected light from the fires of the Infantry, apparently not more than four miles off. On the following day, their Cavalry, still in our front, but only occasionally showing themselves, were evidently employed for the purpose of covering the movement of their column.

*Afterwards killed at Munfordville, Ky. — A.M.M.

16

It being important that information of their movements should be obtained, about 150 of our Cavalry, supported by a small force of Infantry, were sent out to skirmish with and drive back theirs, so that an opportunity might be had of noting the movements of the main body. The result was, after a slight skirmish, that it was evident that the enemy were moving towards Farmington, on a road parallel with our front, and distant about one and a half miles. The force was clearly a large one, but it could not be seen, and was estimated at not less than 10,000 men. Several of our scouts during the afternoon managed to get within 200 or 300 yards of their line of march, and after remaining in view of them for some time, safely returned with the information they had obtained.

At about five o'clock P.M., sharp firing, increasing in rapidity, both of Artillery and small arms, was heard in the direction of Farmington. It continued for about ten or twelve minutes, when it became evident that the Yankees were gaining ground, and we soon after heard their cheers, as they successfully charged and drove our men from the field. It could not well have been otherwise considering the great disparity of the opposing forces.

Anxious as we had been for the past few days we were more so now, and fully expected that, if not before dark, certainly at daylight, our turn would come, if not sooner removed. During the evening and before dark, I had discovered that the troops at Farmington on my right had been attacked and driven from that place, and had lost severely. The line of skirmishers beyond me in that direction had disappeared. On the left also, no one connected with me, and a regiment of Cavalry two miles from me had disappeared, no one knew where to. The Colonel commanding it had sent me word not an hour before that he would not leave his position until I did mine, and that if I required any assistance he would readily give it. My position was a very awkward one. My orders forbade my retiring, both flanks were exposed, several very good country roads on each side led to my rear, the enemy were gathering in our front in irresistible force, and if their commander had any knowledge of the country, or a guide, with a little management on his part, it would not have been difficult for him to have captured the whole Command.

Capt. D.E. Huger,[33] the Inspector General of the Brigade, was dispatched with information of our position to General Bragg, a little after dark, he, being familiar with the condition of affairs, and, as he always was, thoroughly posted, could explain everything to the General. He was to return without loss of time with whatever instructions he might receive. I waited anxiously for him all night, but there was no appearance of him.

The Cavalry portion of the detachment was in the saddle all night, and several times came in contact with that of the enemy. At daylight the men were all under arms. I had determined not to lose my command by allowing the enemy to get in the rear, and felt pretty secure thus far. Soon after daylight, Capt. Huger made his appearance and told me that General Bragg's orders were to retire without a moment's delay. He had only learned a short time before that the other outposts had retired without orders, and he expressed a good deal of uneasiness about my safety. The Captain had, during the night, (it being very dark) taken the wrong road, and finally lost himself in the woods. Daylight only enabled him with the two couriers to rejoin us. Anticipating such an order, we were ready in a few minutes to move. The line having been withdrawn within the outer edge of a thick wood, we moved off without attracting attention. Before the enemy discovered our retreat, we had gained an hour's start of them. They followed our Cavalry for a short distance, and then halted. After retiring to a new line that had been selected, about four miles from the White House, we were relieved by another Brigade.

On the evening of the 8th, the enemy made a reconnaissance in force, driving our pickets, etc., to within a half-mile of our breastworks on the Farmington and Monterey road. Several Brigades were ordered out to repel them. Ours, with a regiment of Cavalry, was sent out for this purpose on the last named road. They had obtained, however, some information, and retired before our advance. There was some skirmishing between them and one or two regiments.

After having re-established our outposts, etc., we were recalled and reached our camp about 10 o'clock P.M.

At four on the following morning, May 9th, we were under arms again, and, taking the direction of Farmington, moved through the breastworks. The Federal General, Pope,[34] with his Command, had taken up a position around and in the neighborhood of Farmington, about six or seven miles from Corinth. It was believed that he was beyond the support of the main body of the Yankee Army, and the Commanding General determined to make an effort to destroy or capture him. Generals Price and Van Dorn,[35] with one Corps and a large body of Cavalry, under cover of night, were to make a considerable circuit to our right and around Pope's left flank, get in his rear and attack him. At the same time, Bragg's corps was to leave the lines, advance as near as possible towards their front, remaining unperceived if possible, and so soon as the firing in the rear or to our right began, they also were to move rapidly over the intervening ground and fall upon him. For several hours after the expected time, we remained anxiously awaiting the commencement of the actions, but unfortunately too much time had been lost — unavoidably, I believe — and the enemy discovered the trap set for him just in time to save himself. It was soon discovered that he was withdrawing as rapidly as he could, and although nothing could be seen or heard of Van Dorn and Price, General Bragg determined to attack alone. The troops were immediately pushed forward, and became engaged. The Yankees did not stand at all, but gave way almost instantly. From the first gun to the last fired, I do not think that more than a half-hour elapsed. The hasty retreat made by them was no doubt owing to their being aware of the movement taking place to their rear. The battle was not quite over when the head of Price's column became visible to many of us. He and Van Dorn were just an hour too late. The loss amongst the troops on either side was comparatively small.

A large quantity of stores was captured, and much personal baggage of officers. It appeared to me that the Yankee soldiers must, to a man, have left either their knapsacks or their blankets behind them. There was no pursuit on our part, and by sunset we were all again within our lines at Corinth. On two other occasions, General Beauregard offered battle, leaving the intrenchments and advancing towards the enemy. On one of them, a large portion of our Army endeavored to reach the enemy's rear by a flank movement,[36] but owing to their position, and the protection afforded them by bad roads and impassable swamps, so much time was lost that a surprise, which it was hoped would be effected, proved a failure. The enemy had become very cautious since the Farmington affair, advancing very slowly and always intrenching. Although ready always to receive an attack, everything being in their favor so to fight, they would not accept our offer of battle but on their own terms, and these efforts of ours to bring about one resulted in nothing more than desultory and, at times severe, skirmishing.

Slowly but surely, Halleck with his numerous Army drew his lines around us, gaining ground foot by foot, and the skirmishing was incessant with heavy losses on both sides. In one of these, Captain Weston,[37] with his company of the 10th S.C., gained much applause and reputation for himself and command. He was in charge of two other companies besides his own, but the brunt of the fighting fell on Co. A. An effort was made to break through the picket line at the point where he was stationed, but he repulsed every attack made upon him. Finally, the enemy having tried the experiment at another point at some distance to his left, and succeeding, he was forced to submit to being captured. On another occasion, Major Porcher[38] of the 10th, (he having succeeded Major Shaw[39] in that position) commanding the detachment on outpost duty from the Brigade, was much praised for his conduct, bravery, and skill.

By the 28th of May, the enemy's lines were within 800 or 900 yards of our works, and his skirmish line within 500, and his batteries at several points began to open on us. On the 29th and 30th, they were still nearer. Our Army was now much reduced by sickness. The invalids who had been going to the rear during the whole of the month by trains, did not return from the hospitals. My own Regiment, which, on its arrival at Corinth had numbered over 900 men (many had been furloughed before leaving Charleston), could not now muster for duty but 500, and many of these were far from being robust. Theirs was a fair criterion of the rest of the Army. I was told that during the 29th, 30th, and 31st, that 17,000 sick had been sent to the rear. My authority, I think, knew what he was talking about, and from my own observation, I do not think that he could have been far wrong.[40]

On the morning of the 30th, it began to be rumored that an evacuation was about to take place. During the day, I became satisfied that the rumor was correct. On the 30th, the Commanders of Brigades received their instructions as to the manner in which it was to be conducted, and by nine o'clock in the evening the movement was commenced. By midnight all troops were out of Corinth, excepting the rear guard of Cavalry, and by sunrise the entire army had placed the Tuscumbia River in their rear,

Corinth distant from it six and one-half or seven miles. The enemy did not follow with their whole army, only a portion of it pursued us. Some slight engagements took place with our rear guard, but they did not amount to much. The most serious was at Blackland, in which a portion of our division took part. Twice the Commanding General halted, and formed a line of battle on favorable ground, but the Yankees would not advance. At Clear Creek, we remained several days, and, it being evident that all pursuit had ceased, the line of march was resumed. On the Mobile and Ohio R.R., we encamped with every reason to believe that for some time at least we might expect to be undisturbed.

Many reasons rendered it necessary that Corinth should be abandoned, although by doing so, the Confederacy lost heavily. The chief one was that the army had been so diminished by sickness that it was no longer able to cope with the enemy in the open field. Of Infantry and Artillery, I do not believe that we abandoned the place with more than 35,000 men.[41] What our strength in Cavalry was I had no means of learning with any accuracy. I doubt if it exceeded 3,000. To have remained in our works and withstood a siege would have been to insure our final capture, for though we might have repulsed the enemy in any attack made on our lines, yet eventually, our communications being cut off, and our supplies failing, we must have been starved out and forced to surrender. It was well that we extricated ourselves when we did, for there was no time to lose.

I have already endeavored to account in some measure for the miserable state of health of the Army, to which I will add that the preparations made by the medical officers were lamentably deficient, a great deficiency existing of the most ordinary means of protecting the sick, or of the commonest medicines with which to work a cure. I never witnessed a more reckless waste of human life than during this short period, owing to a great degree to the inefficiency or ignorance shown in the management of the Quarter Masters, Subsistence, and Medical Departments. Over and over again it has happened that the sick destined for hospitals in the rear, after being transported by wagons to the R.R., would be left in and around the depot without food or shelter for 24 hours, often for a longer period, awaiting some train which was to carry them off. The consequences of such treatment may easily be imagined.

The evacuation and retreat from Corinth was conducted in the most orderly and skillful manner. There was no confusion or interruption whatever, no column clashing one with another. No mistake could be made about roads, and so silently was it conducted, that the enemy, whose pickets, were in many instances within 400 or 500 yards of our lines, were not aware that we had abandoned our position until shortly before sunrise on the following morning.

The most stringent and positive orders had been issued by General Bragg to prevent straggling, firing of arms, and other breaches of discipline, all violations of which he firmly and promptly punished. The wholesome and necessary lessons which he taught his command on this occasion, had a most excellent effect, and were perceptible throughout its after career.

It was generally believed that to General Bragg had been intrusted all the arrangements and details for the evacuation. It was one of his happiest exhibitions of generalship, and the reputation that he derived from it was well deserved.

Shortly after reaching Tupelo, General Beauregard retired from the command of the Army of the Mississippi, owing to some differences between himself and President Davis, and General Bragg was appointed his successor.[42] This latter officer laboured indefatigably during the six weeks that the army remained in the neighbourhood of Tupelo. A thorough and complete reorganization took place, many abuses were corrected, discipline and the strictest obedience to orders was rigidly enforced by the Commander and in turn by those under him. The country was favorable for our purposes, camps were carefully selected, well laid out, excellent water was obtained by sinking wells to a depth of from 15 to 20 feet.

In the neighbourhood of our camps were extensive, open fields, well adapted to drill and evolutions of the line. Our supplies were abundant and of good quality, and the health and spirits of our men improved rapidly, and they performed their duties cheerfully and with spirit. Our invalids now began to return in large numbers, and the regiments were approximating their old numbers. Towards the end of that period, it would have been difficult to recognize this one as the same army that a few weeks ago had marched out of Corinth, dejected and crestfallen, now performing their duties and exercises with a martial air that made them at last begin to look like soldiers.

The 10th S.C. had at Corinth attracted much attention from its soldierly appearance and for the precision of its drill. Here a better opportunity was afforded for exhibiting their proficiency.

Whilst going through their daily exercises there would be hundreds of lookers-on, officers and private soldiers coming several miles to witness the performances of a regiment of whom they had heard so much. The commander-in-chief, as well as many general officers, were frequent spectators. Much praise and many compliments were lavished upon them, and I am afraid that there was a good deal of envy mixed up with it. So much notoriety was very gratifying to the pride of the 10th, and I believe that they at last forgave me for what they had previously regarded as an unnecessary amount of labor and annoyance which they thought I had imposed upon them.

Brigadier General Trapier's health failing immediately after reaching this place, he was at his own request relieved from duty with the army, and returned to S.C.[43] As senior Colonel, the Brigade remained under my command. I afterwards learned that towards the end of July, my name had been forwarded to Richmond with an earnest recommendation for promotion to the rank of Brigadier General.[44]

Blythe's Mississippi, during our stay here, was removed from the Brigade, and the 34th Alabama, a fine regiment, but newly raised, substituted in its place. The exchange was very favorable for us, as for 250 men we got nearly 800. The material of this Regiment was most excellent, and one of the finest-looking bodies of men that I ever saw, but unfortunately it never had a field officer that could be called a soldier, until the latter part of the war. The 19th S.C. very nearly equaled them, but they also were unfortunate in the same way.

Between the 1st and 3rd of July, General Withers was sent on an expedition, with two of his Brigades.[45] The two remaining ones were placed under my command, there being no officer above the rank of Colonel present. On the 6th, I received orders to advance with this command to a place called Saltillo, about fourteen miles north of Tupelo, and on the line of the Mobile & Ohio R.R. Early on the morning of the 7th, we started, and after a hot, dusty, and tiresome march reached Saltillo about 1 P.M. We were afterwards joined by General Withers, who, with his Division, continued to discharge this outpost duty until our departure for a new line of operations. I think the distance from Corinth to Saltillo is about 45 miles. The enemy never disturbed us whilst there. An occasional reconnoitring party made its appearance, but never attacked or got within our Cavalry Videttes.

The enemy had retired to Corinth, and the campaign in Mississippi seemed to be ended. I do not see how one could well have been carried on, for the country was completely parched up, the streams were all dry, the greatest scarcity of water existing, and the troops, and even the stock, dependent almost entirely on the wells that we were obliged to dig in order to supply ourselves.

NOTES TO CHAPTER 1

[1] Nov. 6, 1860.

[2] South Carolina was followed out of the Union by Mississippi on Jan. 9, 1861; by Florida on the 10th; Alabama the 11th; Georgia the 19th; Louisiana the 26th; and by Texas Feb. 1. These seven so-called "Cotton States" established on Feb. 4, 1861, in Montgomery, Ala., the Provisional Government of the Confederate States of America. Several months passed by, during which Fort Sumter was fired on and Lincoln issued a call for 75,000 troops to put down the rebellion, before the northern tier of slave-holding states joined their sisters to the south. On May 6, Arkansas seceded and on the 20th North Carolina. On May 23, the voters of Virginia ratified an ordinance of secession and, finally, Tennessee took similar action June 8.

[3] The appointment was made April 10, 1861. *War of the Rebellion: A Compilation of the Official Records of the Union and Confederate Armies,* 128 vols., (Washington, 1880-1901), Series I, Vol. LIII, 141-142. Hereafter cited as *O.R.* All citations will be Series I unless otherwise indicated.

[4] Major Robert Anderson, First Artillery, United States Army. A native of Kentucky, married to a Georgian and until recently the owner of a few slaves, the mild-mannered and deeply religious Anderson had impeccable Southern connections, numbering among his warm friends Jefferson Davis and P.G.T. Beauregard. And yet, withall, he was a dedicated Regular Army man, opposed to secesion and devoted to the flag of the Union. This combination of characteristics appeared to make him an ideal choice to take over the delicate responsibility of command in Charleston harbor. W.A. Swanberg, *First Blood: The Story of Fort Sumter,* (New York, 1957), 33-36.

[5] Fort Fisher, at the mouth of the Cape Fear River, protected Wilmington, N.C., one of the major Southern ports to which the blockade runners brought arms and supplies for the Confederacy. During the bombardment, two days before the fort was captured by Northern forces on Jan. 15, 1865, Gen. W.H.C. Whiting, the district commander, accompanied only by his staff, arrived and volunteered his services to its commander, Col. William Lamb, remarking: "Lamb, my boy, I have come to share your fate. You and your garrison are to be sacrificed!" Whiting was referring to the failure of Braxton Bragg to lead his troops in the vicinity to the defense of Fort Fisher now under attack. In the final Northern assault, Whiting, although a major general, fought with conspicuous gallantry under Col. Lamb, was twice severely wounded, captured and removed to Fort Columbus in New York Harbor. There, he died from his wounds on May 10, 1865, after the war was over. Robert Underwood Johnson and Clarence Clough Buell (eds.), *Battles and Leaders of the Civil War,* 4 vols., (New York, 1887), Vol. IV, 642-654. Hereafter cited as *Battles and Leaders. Southern Historical Society Papers,* 52 vols., (Richmond, Va., 1876-1953), Vol. XXI, 277, 289. Hereafter cited as *S.H.S.P.*

[6] The signal gun for the attack on Fort Sumter was fired at 4:30 A.M. *O.R.* I, 31.

[7] Ironically, the only loss of life occurred when one member of the garrison was killed and another mortally wounded by a premature explosion during a 50-gun salute fired as the fort was being evacuated April 14th. *O.R.* I, 66; E. Milby Burton, *The Siege of Charleston, 1861-1865,* (Columbia, S.C., 1970), 56-57.

[8] Brig. Gen. James Simons was relieved on April 29 from the command of Morris Island to which he had been appointed on April 11 (*O.R.,* I, 33, 305; LIII, 158). A high-spirited gentleman, Speaker of the S.C. House of Representatives and a militia officer for almost 28 years, Simons for months carried on an ill-disguised vendetta with Gov. Pickens, claiming his honor had been impungned and that he had not been given command and authority commensurate with his rank. He resigned his commission in a huff on July 10, 1861, and took no further active part in the war. See: James Simons, *Address to the Officers of the Fourth Brigade, Giving the Grounds of his Resignation.* (Charleston, 1861).

[9] Beauregard was relieved from duty in South Carolina on May 27 and left on the 29th to take command of the troops massing in northern Virginia to oppose the anticipated Federal advance on Richmond, *O.R.* VI, 1; LI, pt. 2, pp. 19-20.

[10] On Dec. 17, 1860, three days before the passage of the Ordinance of Secession by the State Convention, the legislature of South Carolina passed an act providing for an armed military force, which resulted, at the call of the governor, in the raising and organizing of 10 regiments of volunteers for 12 months service, Manigault's being designated the Tenth. It is of interest to note that the convention adopting the Ordinance of Secession also provided for a regiment of six months volunteers, in addition to which the legislature, on Jan. 28, 1861, further authorized the governor to raise a battalion of artillery and a regiment of infantry to serve as regulars and form the basis of a Regular Army of South Carolina. Thus it came about that there were three "First South Carolina Regiments" — the regulars, commanded by Col. Richard H. Anderson, later known as "Fighting Dick" and destined to rise to the rank of lieutenant general in the Army of Northern Virginia; the 12 months volunteers under Col. Johnson Hagood; and Col. Maxcy Gregg's six months volunteers. To confuse matters even further, Orr's First South Carolina Rifles were subsequently organized. Such were the complications of starting from scratch and arming a newly independent nation! Clement A. Evans, *Confederate Military History,* 12 vols., (Atlanta, 1899), Vol. V, 12-13. Hereafter cited as *C.M.H.*; Johnson Hagood, *Memoirs of the War of Secession,* (Columbia, S.C., 1910), 27-29.

[11] Manigault refers here to the battles of Nashville, Tenn., in December 1864, and Kinston and Bentonville, N.C., in the spring of 1865.

[12] Although on March 6, 1861, States Rights Gist, Adjutant and Inspector General of South Carolina, informed Maj. Gen. Bonham, commanding the volunteer forces of the state, that 10 regiments of volunteers under the act of Dec. 17, 1860, had been organized and received (*O.R.,* I, 265), it is evident that the Tenth was not ready for active service at that time. On June 27th, Gov. Pickens wrote President Davis that he had recently ordered two new regiments to the seacoast for exclusive state service, both of which "will require arms." (*O.R.,* Series IV, I, 404). That one of these regiments was the Tenth is confirmed by the fact that the governor informed the Confederate Secretary of War three days later that he had ordered into encampment on the Georgetown coast a regiment "under Colonel Manigault, who is an officer of experience." (*Ibid.,* 413-414). Prior to that time, an infantry company of regulars, training as artillery, had garrisoned the forts or redoubts on North and South Islands at the entrance of Georgetown Harbor. *Ibid.,* 186, 413.

[13] Of the 10 regiments of 12 months volunteers raised under the legislative act of Dec. 17, 1860, all but two were sent to Virginia in the spring and summer of 1861. The First (Hagood) declined to enter Confederate service at the time, and the Tenth (Manigault) remained in state service at Georgetown defending the coast. Accompanying the eight regiments dispatched to the North were Orr's First South Carolina Rifles, Gregg's six months volunteers and the Hampton Legion consisting of "six companies of infantry or voltigeurs, four of cavalry, and one of flying artillery." *O.R.*, Series IV, I, 296, 303-305, 413-415, 487.

[14] A native of Ohio, graduate of West Point and twice brevetted for gallantry in the Mexican War, Brig. Gen. Roswell S. Ripley married into the Middleton family of Charleston in 1852 and was engaged in business there when the war broke out. On Aug. 21, 1861, Ripley was assigned to the command of the Department of South Carolina. *O.R.*, VI, 267; Ezra J. Warner, *Generals in Gray*, (Baton Rouge, 1959), 257. Hereafter cited as *Generals in Gray*.

[15] By Special Orders No. 206 from the Adjutant and Inspector General's office in Richmond, dated Nov. 5, 1861, the coasts of South Carolina, Georgia and East Florida were constituted a military department and Gen. Robert E. Lee assigned to its command. *O.R.*, VI, 309.

[16] Maj. Gen. John C. Pemberton, who succeeded Lee (*O.R.*, VI, 402), had a remarkable subsequent career. Born in Philadelphia, he was vilified by many Southerners because of his Northern birth, and his loyalty to the Confederate cause was unjustifiably questioned. Promoted lieutenant general, he was in command at Vicksburg when that vital fortress controlling the Mississippi River was surrendered to U.S. Grant July 4, 1863. He was later exchanged, resigned his commission as lieutenant general in 1864 and was appointed by his friend and supporter, Jefferson Davis, a lieutenant colonel of artillery. In that capacity he served at the siege of Petersburg. Douglas Southall Freeman told the editor in 1940 that Pemberton was one of the first officers to make use of indirect control of artillery fire. It is likely that his decision to resign from the U.S. Army in 1861 and offer his services to the Confederacy was influenced by the fact that his wife was a native of Norfolk, Va. *Generals in Gray*, 232-233.

[17] In December, Manigault instructed his officers, in the event of a threatened or actual occupation of any portion of the coast by the enemy, to direct "the rice planters to destroy all the rice and provision crops on their plantations; and, in the event of their failing to do so, to cause it to be destroyed themselves as a military necessity; the negroes to be removed also by force if necessary." He further wrote to the department adjutant general, "over two-thirds of the rice crop of the state is made in this neighborhood and...it would be disastrous...should our enemies ever succeed in possessing themselves of so large an amount of provisions...So satisfied am I that our true policy is to destroy all that we cannot remove or hold, that unless otherwise directed, I shall carry out the instructions I have previously mentioned having given. I do not, however, intend that they shall take possession quietly or without a struggle while I have the means of opposing them." (*O.R.*, VI, 337). Three weeks later, Manigault reported that, due to transfers, termination of terms of enlistment and the breaking out of measles and mumps in the 10th South Carolina, his effective force in the First Military District had been reduced to 925 men. This figure apparently did not include the 21st South Carolina, commanded by Col. R.F. Graham. *O.R.*, VI, 360.

[18] An interesting sidelight on the problems involved in supplying equipment for the troops is provided by Gov. Pickens, who wrote to the Confederate Secretary of War at this time, "I can order a large supply of the best tents made here of heavy drill at $12 each, with poles and all complete. I can have them made by a Frenchman, in the best style." *O.R.*, Series IV, I, 490.

[19] This doubtless refers to the occasion Dec. 24, 1861, when the schooner *Prince of Wales* from Nassau, loaded with salt, oranges and other cargo, ran into North Inlet, went aground and was fired on by the blockading squadron. Boats from the enemy vessel twice attempted to seize her and tow her out but were driven off by the Confederate troops. The captain of the *Prince of Wales,* fearful of capture, fired his vessel. She burned to the water line and with her cargo was a total loss. She was owned, Manigault believed, by the house of John Fraser & Co. of Charleston. *O.R.,* VI, 352; *Official Records of the Union and Confederate Navies in the War of the Rebellion,* 24 vols. (Washington, 1899-1922), Series I, Vol. 12, 428-430.

[20] It was at this time that Lee was called to Richmond to become Davis' military advisor. Pemberton was assigned to the command of the Department of South Carolina and Georgia with headquarters at Pocotaligo Station. *O.R.,* VI, 402, 407.

[21] In his order of March 25th, Pemberton gave no explanation for his decision, nor did he leave Manigault any discretion, stating, "Having maturely considered the subject, I have determined to withdraw the forces from Georgetown, and therefore abandon the position...You will proceed with all the infantry force under your command...to this city, Charleston, and report to Brigadier-General Ripley." *Ibid.,* 417-418.

[22] On his arrival April 3rd in Charleston, Manigault reported the 10th Regiment's aggregate strength at 1,103, consisting of 903 present for duty, 123 sick and convalescent and 77 on furlough. *Ibid,* 426.

[23] It was originally intended that the reinforcements being sent to Beauregard be dispatched on a temporary basis only, and that they be returned to South Carolina as soon as their services could be dispensed with. As events transpired, however, the latter contingency never occurred and Manigault was to remain with the Western Army for the balance of his active militry career. *Ibid,* 433-434.

[24] Huntsville had been captured April 11 by a force of some 7,000 men under Gen. Ormsby M. Mitchel, who had been placed in command of an expedition against the Memphis and Charleston Railroad. He reported seizing 15 locomotives and a large amount of rolling stock, boasting that he had "at length succeeded in cutting the great artery of rebel communications between the Southern States." *O.R.,* X, pt. 2, 104.

[25] The direct and far shorter route would have been by the South Carolina Railroad to Augusta, the Georgia R.R. to Atlanta, the Western & Atlantic to Chattanooga and thence by the Memphis & Charleston to Corinth. See: Robert C. Black III, *The Railroads of the Confederacy,* (Chapel Hill, N.C., 1952).

[26] A nephew of Andrew Jackson and a man of considerable distinction in his own right, Daniel S. Donelson graduated from West Point in the class of 1825. Active in public affairs, he was Speaker of the Tennessee House of Representatives when the war broke out. After service in Western Virginia, he was ordered to South Carolina, where he commanded the Fifth Military District and a brigade consisting of the Eighth and Sixteenth Regiments of Tennessee Volunteers. With these troops, he was transferred to Corinth, Miss., to reinforce Beauregard at the same time Manigault was sent there with the 10th and 19th South Carolina. At Murfreesboro, Donelson commanded a brigade in Cheatham's division. He died April 17, 1863, in his 62nd year. His brother, Andrew Jackson Donelson, adhered to the Union cause — yet another example of brother against brother in the war. *Generals In Gray,* 74-75; *O.R.,* VI, 433.

[27] Jones M. Withers was a graduate of the U.S. Military Academy in the class of 1835 and a veteran of the Mexican War. Leaving the army, he played an active role in the business and political life of Alabama, serving in the state legislature and as mayor of Mobile. At the outbreak of the war, he entered Confederate service as colonel of the 3rd Alabama Infantry and rose to the rank of major general early in 1862. *Generals In Gray,* 342-343.

[28] A planter of the Georgetown area, Brig. Gen. James Heyward Trapier never lived up to the seemingly bright promise of a distinguished career in the Confederate Army. After graduating third in his class (1838) at West Point, he served in the elite Corps of Engineers until 1848 when he resigned from the army and returned to his plantation. Called on to assist with the fortifications in Charleston Harbor, he was praised for his work by both Beauregard and Ripley and was considered by Gov. Pickens as "by far the most accomplished and scientific engineer we have." In October 1861, he offered his services to the Confederacy and was made a brigadier general by President Davis and given command of the Department of Eastern and Middle Florida, with instructions to organize the defense of that state. There, he struggled manfully with the well-nigh insoluble problems of inadequate manpower, equipment and supplies, not to mention the jurisdictional quarrels between the state and Confederate governments.

Early the next year, incensed and outraged by a critical resolution introduced into the Florida State Convention, in a bitter letter to Davis he asked to be relieved of his command. Transferred to the Western Army, he led a brigade and, briefly, a division, but being found wanting by Braxton Bragg, the army commander, he was shipped back to South Carolina. Shunted from one command to another, often protesting, he spent most of the remainder of the war commanding the Fourth Military District, which embraced the territory east and north of the Santee and South Santee Rivers. At the end, in Hardee's army in the Carolinas opposing Sherman's march northward, he led a skeleton brigade that in the return of Jan. 31, 1865, could muster only 14 officers and 170 men, including those serving the four remaining guns of the German and Waccamaw Light Artillery.

Although limited in ability and touchy where his honor was concerned, Trapier never flagged in his loyalty and devotion to the Southern cause. He died Dec. 21, 1865. *O.R.,* I, 34, 42; VI, 292-293, 412-413; X, pt. 2, 419, 461, 642; XIV, 669-670, 818, 937, 966; XVII, pt. 2, 673; XXXVIII, pt. 2, 143; XLVII, 1069; LIII, 174, 217; *Generals in Gray,* 309-310.

[29] On April 12, 1862, Braxton Bragg was appointed and confirmed as the sixth and last full general of permanent rank in the regular army of the Confederate States.

Thus he joined that select group composed, in order of rank, of Samuel Cooper, Adjutant and Inspector General, Albert S. Johnston, Robert E. Lee, Joseph E. Johnston and P.G.T. Beauregard. Bragg was a controversial figure throughout the war. His partisans, of whom Manigault was one, regarded him as an outstanding strategist, organizer and disciplinarian; while his detractors looked on him as a scheming favorite of Jefferson Davis, lacking in daring and decisiveness on the battlefield. Unpopular with many subordinates, his curt manner and shortness of temper may have been due, at least in some measure, to the migraine, dyspepsia and other assorted ills from which he suffered. Despite his shortcomings, his wholehearted devotion to the cause of the South was never questioned. Ironically, Bragg is perhaps best rememberd for a trivial incident that occurred when he was serving as a young artillery officer at the Battle of Buena Vista in the Mexican War. At a critical juncture, Gen. Zachary Taylor, future president and father-in-law of Jefferson Davis, is reputed to have called out: "A little more grape, Captain Bragg!" Whether apocryphal or true, the expression stuck and made Bragg's name a household word. Bragg maintained that what Taylor actually said was, "Captain, give them hell!" *Battles and Leaders,* III, 605; Horn, *The Army of Tennessee,* 112; Marcus J. Wright, *General Officers of the Confederate Army,* (New York, 1911), 9-11.

[30] The April 30, 1862, return for the Union army under Halleck showed 95,076 present for duty and 124,172 aggregate present. (*O.R.,* X, pt. 2, 146-154), while the comparable figures for Beauregard's Army of the Mississippi were 45,440 and 66,903 respectively. (*O.R.,* X, pt. 2, 475). To the latter figures should be added the reinforcements received from the Trans-Mississippi, Van Dorn's Army of the West, so that Beauregard's total effective strength may be estimated at between 50,000 and 60,000 men.

[31] "Corinth became one vast ward, with 18,000 soldiers on the sick list. The sinister yellow flag of the hospital corps fluttered over hotels, public buildings, homes, schools and churches — wherever a wounded man could be laid full length on the floor." Horn, *The Army of Tennessee,* 146.

[32] Col. Robert A. Smith of the Tenth Misssissippi regiment of Brig. Gen. James R. Chalmers' brigade. (*O.R.,* X, pt. 1, 788). A Virginian, Chalmers led his brigade at Shiloh, during the invasion of Kentucky and at Murfreesboro. Thereafter, he was transferred to the cavalry, where he had a distinguished career under Gen. Forrest. *Generals in Gray,* 46.

[33] Daniel Elliott Huger, Manigault's brother-in-law, for whom he named his second son and to whom he was totally devoted. Bravest of the brave, Capt. Huger met a hero's death at Chickamauga. *O.R.,* X, pt. 1, 535; XX, pt. 1, 578; XXX, pt. 2, 343, 353.

[34] Maj. Gen. John Pope, who shortly thereafter was transferred to the East to take command of the Army of Virginia and was soundly thrashed by Lee and Jackson at Second Manassas. Denied by Pope and never proved, a story got around that he wrote his orders from "Headquarters in the Saddle," which made him the butt of an obvious joke. His instructions to his troops regarding the treatment of non-combatants led Lee to refer to him as the "miscreant Pope" and to write that he must be "suppressed" — which was about as far as Robert E. Lee ever went in denouncing an adversary, even one whom he held in contempt as he did the boastful and bombastic Pope. Gen. S.D. Sturgis of the Federal army

sized the latter up in more vivid language: "I don't care for John Pope one pinch of owl dung." After his crushing defeat at Second Manassas, Pope was shipped off to fight Indians in Minnesota and there his active career came to an end. Douglas Southall Freeman, *R.E. Lee*, 4 vols., (New York, 1934), II, 264; *Civil War Times Illustrated*, Vol. XIX, No. 1, April 1980, 4-9, 43-47.

[35] Sterling Price was born in Virginia but as a young man moved west to Missouri where he had a distinguished public career, serving in the state legislature, as a member of Congress and as governor of the state from 1853 to 1857. Although not a secessionist, he cast his lot with the South, accepted a commission as major general in the Confederate army and fought in Mississippi, Arkansas and Missouri. Known familiarly to his men as "Old Pap," he went to Mexico when the war ended. After the collapse of Maximilian's empire, he died there in 1867. (*Generals In Gray*, 246-247).

A West Pointer and Mexican War veteran, Earl Van Dorn had risen to the rank of major in the 2nd United States Cavalry when the war broke out. He was in good company. Albert Sydney Johnston was colonel of the regiment, Robert E. Lee was lieutenant colonel and George H. Thomas the other major. Most of Van Dorn's Confederate service was in the West. His best known exploit was the capture and destruction of Grant's supply depot at Holly Springs, Miss., in December 1862, which compelled the latter to temporarily abandon his campaign against Vicksburg. He was assassinated in May 1863 by a Dr. Peters who claimed Van Dorn had "violated the sanctity of his home." *Generals in Gray*, 314-315.

[36] During one of these abortive flank movements, Gen. Price seized the enemy's telegraph office and impudently wired his compliments to President Lincoln in Washington. Horn, *The Army of Tennessee*, 146-148.

[37] This was the same Capt. Weston who had entertained the Georgetown Rifle Guards so royally at his plantation on the Waccamaw in the early days of the war. At the end of the invasion of Kentucky, Capt. Weston, worn down by the exposure and fatigues of the campaign, left the 10th Regiment never to return. "His age, pursuits, and responsibilities," wrote the war correspondent of the *Charleston Courier*, "might fairly have excused him from service in the field and his wealth would easily have purchased immunity from hardship and danger. To prevent his return to the army, his admiring friends in the Legislature..." elected him lieutenant governor "...which made it his duty to remain in the state; and before the war ended, he succumbed to his disease, and yielded up his life, as much a victim of the war as those who fell by shot and shell..." When the state "...shall make up the roll of her tried and true sons, few names will be inscribed higher than that of Plowden Weston!" C.I. Walker, *Rolls and Historical Sketch of the Tenth Regiment, So. Ca. Volunteers in the Confederate Army*, (Charleston, S.C., 1881), 12-13, 85-86; S. Emanuel, *A Historical Sketch of the Georgetown Rifle Guards*, (n. p., 1909), 11-13.

[38] Julius Porcher, later promoted lieutenant colonel of the regiment and killed at Missionary Ridge. Walker *Tenth Regiment*, 9.

[39] Maj. A.J. Shaw, who was not reelected in the reorganization of the regiment in 1862. Walker, *Ibid.*

[40] The *Official Records* confirm the accuracy of Manigault's information. In the field return of the Confederate forces prior to the evacuation of Corinth on May

30th, 17,418 men of a total present of 70,124 were carried on the sick rolls. *O.R., X,* pt. 1, 791.

[41] If Manigault is referring here to the Army of the Mississippi, he is essentially correct. If Van Dorn's Army of the West is included, however, the total effective strength of the Confederate infantry and artillery on the evacuation of Corinth was 48,606. The cavalry of both armies amounted to 4,100 effectives. *Ibid.*

[42] Bragg was given command of the Army of the Mississippi on May 6 and, on June 20, of the Western Department, replacing Beauregard. On June 27, he issued an address to his troops calling for "a resolute resistance to the wicked invasion of our country" and assuring them that "discipline at all times and obedience to the orders of your officers on all points, as a sacred duty, an act of patriotism, is of absolute necessity." These sentiments were fully shared by Manigault and basic to his admiration of Bragg as a commanding officer. *O.R., XVII,* pt. 2, 626.

[43] More than Trapier's health was involved, for Bragg wrote to the Confederate Secretary of War on Aug. 8, 1862, "In reference to the want of qualifications in some general officers, I alluded in particular to ...Brigadiers Carrol, Trapier and Hawes as, in my judgment, unsuited for their responsible positions, and, as far as I can learn, not recommended from here." On Oct. 17, Trapier reported for duty to Beauregard, commanding at Charleston, S.C. *O.R., XVII,* pt. 2, 673; LIII, 262.

[44] On June 29, 1862, Bragg wrote to the Adjutant and Inspector General in Richmond, stressing the need for qualified division and brigade commanders in the army, to the command of which he had recently been appointed, and enclosed recommendations for promotions. Manigault's name may well have been included in the list which, unfortunately, is not to be found with the Confederate correspondence bearing on the matter in the *Official Records.* Cooper replied on July 22nd pointing out that Bragg already had on the rolls nine major generals and 34 brigadiers to command seven divisions and 29 brigades, thus making a surplus of two major generals and seven brigadier generals. Although some of these officers were absent for various causes, President Davis, ever the bureaucrat hewing to the letter of the law, maintained he had no power to remove them and appoint successors. By inference, this also applied to general officers Bragg considered unfit for command. Thus for the first, but not the last, time Manigault's hopes for promotion died on the vine. *O.R., XVII,* pt. 2, 628, 654-655.

[45] The purpose of this move was to harass the enemy and strike at the Memphis & Charleston Railroad, then in enemy hands. *Ibid,* 629, 638-639.

2

THE INVASION OF KENTUCKY

(Editor's Preface)

Having occupied Corinth with his huge army, estimated at close to 125,000 men, Halleck contemplated his next move. Remaining there seemed impractical due to the difficulty of supplying so many troops so far from their base of supply, as well as the unhealthy conditions in that barren area, especially in the heat of summer. These two factors likewise persuaded the unenterprising Northern commander that further offensive operations were out of the question. The upshot of it all was that the Federal army was broken up. Pope was transferred to Virginia. Buell was assigned to eastern Tennessee and Grant was left to hold the line of the Memphis and Charleston Railroad in northern Mississippi.

With Buell's army threatening Chattanooga, Gen. Kirby Smith, commanding a Confederate force of some 18,000 men in East Tennessee, telegraphed Bragg on July 20 urging him to come to his support. Following this with another communication a few days later, Smith told Bragg there was yet time for a brilliant summer campaign, with every prospect of regaining possession of Middle Tennessee and possibly Kentucky. He assured Bragg not only of his cooperation but of his cheerful willingness to serve under him. Such additional urging, however, was superfluous, for Bragg on July 21 had ordered the transfer of his Army of the Mississippi to Chattanooga, and the troops began arriving on the 27th.

Bragg and Smith agreed on a plan whereby the latter would advance from Knoxville against Cumberland Gap and, if successful, proceed into Middle Tennessee, where he would be joined by Bragg advancing from Chattanooga "with the fairest prospect of cutting off General Buell."

As the days passed, Bragg's horizons widened and on Aug. 10, referring to a proposed simultaneous advance of Van Dorn and Price into West Tennessee, he ventured, "I trust we may all unite in Ohio." In fact, his spirits were so high at the prospect before him that he wrote Gen. Breckinridge Aug. 8: "My army has promised to make me 'Military Governor' of Ohio in 'ninety days' — Seward's time for crushing the rebellion. We only await our trains and the capture of the forces at Cumberland Gap...Our prospects were never more encouraging." Aware of Breckinridge's great popularity in his native Kentucky, Bragg went on to assure him that his presence during the invasion would be worth an extra division of troops. As events transpired, Breckinridge, occupied with the relief of the Vicksburg garrison and the reoccupation of Baton Rouge, arrived too late to take an active part in the Kentucky campaign.

Kirby Smith left Knoxville Aug. 14, outflanked the Federal forces at Cumberland Gap, and, by the 29th had entered the lush Blue Grass region of Kentucky. There he annihilated, at Richmond, a Union army of more than 6,000 men and swept on to Lexington, his cavalry raiding as far as the outskirts of Louisville and Covington, across the Ohio from Cincinnati, and occupying Frankfort the state capital.

Having reorganized his army of close to 28,000 effectives at Chattanooga into two wings under Polk and Hardee, Bragg crossed the Tennessee River on Aug. 28, proceeded north up the Sequatchie Valley to Pikeville, and thence, via Sparta, to Carthage and Gainsboro, where he crossed the Cumberland. Encouraged by Kirby Smith's victory at Richmond, he entered Kentucky and reached Glasgow, about 30 miles east of Bowling Green, on the 13th of September.

Meanwhile, Buell had retreated through Murfreesboro and Nashville, which he fortified against attack. Shortly thereafter, in response to Bragg's advance, he set out for Louisville, his leading units reaching Bowling Green on the 14th. His intention was to join Col. Wilder and his force of some 4,000 at Munfordville on the Green River about 40 miles to the northeast, but, delayed by Wheeler's cavalry, he was too late. The town and the fort protecting it, along with the entire garrison, its artillery, stores and 5,000 stand of small arms, fell to the advancing Southerners.

Having conducted a successful offensive campaign into Kentucky, flushed with victory and buoyed by news of Kirby Smith's progress, Bragg had now placed his army squarely across the enemy's direct escape route to Louisville. This presented him with a dilemma — and an opportunity. Should he turn on Buell and force a showdown battle then and there? In a congratulatory order to his troops he issued a ringing call to action. "A powerful foe is assembling in our front and we must prepare to strike him a sudden and decisive blow." On the other hand, was it the part of wisdom to continue north, keeping between Buell and his base of supply at Louisville, and wait for Kirby Smith to join him? Then, together they could fight the decisive battle at maximum strength.

Either course of action posed tempting prospects of success. Testifying at the Court of Inquiry into Buell's conduct of the Kentucky campaign a few months later, Maj. Gen. George H. Thomas of the Union army was asked the following questions by the Judge-Advocate: "Had the enemy made a stand at Munfordville what would have been the effect on our army? Could we have passed that place without a battle, and if defeated what would have been the result?" Thomas' reply was unequivocal: "If the enemy had made a stand at Munfordville it would have been necessary for us to have fought him, and if defeated it would have been disastrous, as it was a difficult position for us to get out of." In reference to the alternative, Kirby Smith was later to write: "Had Bragg called my command to his support, holding Buell's line of communications and retreat upon Louisville, the latter's destruction was inevitable."

The potential results of a Confederate victory, coming at a time when Lee had crushed Pope at Second Manassas and invaded Maryland, would have been incalculable. Doubtless, Louisville and Nashville would have fallen. Would Cincinnati have been next, to be followed by an invasion of Ohio? And then, perhaps, foreign recognition? Who can tell?

But in this, his first great test as an independent army commander, Braxton Bragg's resolution faltered at the decisive moment, and thus was established a pattern with dire portents for the future of the Army of Tennessee. Lamely pleading a shortage of supplies, although he had previously written Polk, "we shall be in a plentiful country at Glasgow and beyond," he called a council, of his generals on the night of the 17th, at which a proposal was made to double back and capture Nashville. Bragg appeared to favor this but on the 19th announced his intention to turn aside and march on Bardstown to the northeast. This left the way open to Louisville, and Buell, taking advantage of this unexpected turn of events, marched there, his right flank exposed but unthreatened by a hesitant and vacillating Bragg. The moment for victory had come and gone.

On Oct. 1, his army merged with the untrained recruits of the Louisville garrison, Buell moved out to confront Bragg at Bardstown, feinting in the direction of Frankfort, held by Kirby Smith, where Bragg had repaired to witness the inauguration of a Confederate governor of the state.

This maneuver succeeded in confusing Bragg as to the main thrust of the Union army, so that when battle was joined at Perryville his troops were dangerously divided, despite prior warnings from Smith and Hardee. Nevertheless, Polk, now commanding the Southern forces at Perryville, attacked and routed the Federal left wing, driving it back a mile or more in a savage and bloody struggle, which, in his official report, Bragg characterized as "for the time engaged...the severest and most desperately contested engagement within my knowledge."

Rather than follow up this success, Bragg broke off contact and withdrew to Harrodsburg, where at long last, he was joined by Kirby Smith's troops. Now the Confederate forces were at their maximum strength, and hopes ran high once more that a decisive battle would be joined. "For God's sake, General, let us fight Buell here," Kirby Smith is reported to have said. To which Bragg replied, "I will do it, sir." But once more, when the decisive moment was at hand, Bragg shrank from the reponsibility.

Later, Gen. Basil Duke was to write: "It would have been the only great field of the war — east or west — on which the Confederate forces were numerically the stronger, and every other conceivable factor was in their favor. Never was the morale of an army better than that of General Bragg's on the eve of the anticipated conflict. The men seemed to realize what was at stake and to fear nothing but retreat, which should carry back war and invasion to their homes and people...General Bragg should have fought then and there and must have won. But the gloomy and hostile destiny which seemed to pursue the Confederacy, and became manifest when victory was about to visit her banners...smote our commander at Harrodsburg with a consternation which no man in his ardent and undaunted ranks shared then or can understand now."

There is little more to say regarding the Kentucky invasion of 1862. On Oct. 13, Bragg began his withdrawal, weakly complaining in a letter to his wife that it would have been unpardonable for him to have kept his "noble little army to be ice-bound in a Northern clime, without tents or shoes, and obliged to forage daily for bread, etc." Unwittingly, perhaps, Bragg was revealing his true character.

Its rear protected by the gallant troopers of Wheeler's cavalry, the long column wended its weary way across the mountains, through Cumberland Gap, and back to Knoxville, whence Kirby Smith had departed two months before, with hopes so high and prospects so bright. It was a dismal end to a campaign that might have changed the course of the war.

R.L.T.

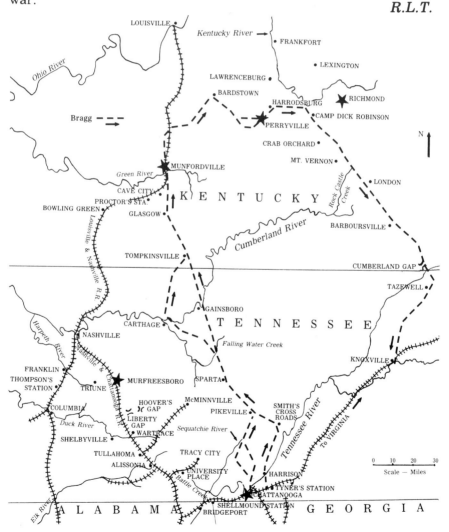

Operations in Kentucky and Tennessee 1862-1863.

INVADING KENTUCKY

(The Narrative)

At as early a period as the 15th of July, it became known to the men, who find out everything by some means or another, that active operations were about to recommence, and that some design of a novel character was about to be inaugurated. It had been discovered that large numbers of wagons and mules had been purchased and impressed all over the country, and that orders had been issued which indicated clearly that the army would not long remain in their present position, but it was not until the 25th or 26th of the month that we as a general thing became aware that Tennessee and perhaps Kentucky would be invaded, from some point east of us and from the Tennessee River. The greater part of Tennessee had slipped through our fingers, and it was high time that some effort should be made to relieve the state of its enemies, and it was well worth the effort to offer Kentucky an opportunity of joining the Southern Confederacy, as it was well known that we had many friends there, and it was hoped by far the greater portion of its population would prove favorable to us. The only way in which they could be induced to throw off the yoke would be by marching a Southern army within the limits of the state, insuring to the inhabitants the support and assistance of a powerful force.

During the last few days of July all was life, bustle, and activity within our lines. Trains of wagons, horses, mules, and artillery, escorted by Cavalry, took the route across the country in the direction of Chattanooga. A few Regiments of Infantry were carried across in wagons, only as a guard, however, and the remainder of the army destined for this new scene of action were transported by rail, first to Mobile, thence by the Alabama River or R.R. to Montgomery, Atlanta, and Chattanooga. About 30,000 men (Infantry) were drawn from the force in Mississippi for this purpose. That portion of the old Army of Mississippi which remained was placed under the command of Major-General Van Dorn, having under him Generals Price, Lovell, and others, and was deemed sufficient at that period for the further protection of that state.[1]

On the 30th of July, 1862, our Brigade took the trains for Mobile, and on the 7th day after leaving Saltillo arrived at a small village situated near the Chickamauga Creek, about ten miles from Chattanooga. On the 2nd day after our arrival here, we moved across, about three miles, to the Knoxville road, and went into rather a pleasant camp, with an abundance of fine spring water, near a station known as Tyner's. Here we were to await the arrival of our trains, Artillery, etc., coming across the country, whose movements were necessarily slower.

On the 28th of August, we moved from Tyner's Station to Harrison's Ferry on the Tennessee River, a distance of about 8 miles, and crossed it the same evening, joining the other Brigades of the Division, which had preceded us. Cheatham's Division of Tennesseans also crossed at this point, the two Divisions forming one Corps under the command of Lieut. Gen. (Bishop) Leonidas Polk.

On the 24th, Brig. Gen. Duncan, having some days previously joined the Army, had been assigned to the command of our Brigade, joined us, and on the 26th relieved me of the command, I returning to my regiment. This Gen. Duncan was the officer who commanded the forts near the mouth of the Mississippi, and after a gallant and long defence was forced to surrender in the preceding April to the U. S. Naval force. He proved himself to be a good and efficient officer, by far the most capable one in the entire Division. My association with him was of the pleasantest character until death ended his career.[2]

Shortly after crossing the river, our wagons joined us, also the Artillery, but our large trains of provisions, ordnance, and other stores, detained us until the 30th inst.

The force with which General Bragg opened this campaign consisted, I believe, of about 30,000 Infantry and Artillery,* and perhaps 3,000 Cavalry. It had been arranged that a corresponding movement from *(Knoxville)* was to be made by General E. Kirby Smith, and that the two forces should move forward towards a common point in Kentucky, and there joining would afterwards manouvre together as one army. The strength of General Smith's army I estimated at about 15,000 men, exclusive of Cavalry.[3]

At an early hour on the morning of the 30th of August our Division commenced the march, the right wing to which we were attached moving in the direction of Sparta, Pikeville, and Gainsboro; the left wing, commanded by Lieut. Gen. Hardee, crossing at Chattanooga, following a road parallel to our own, and distant from 10 to 15 miles, I should judge.

Our first day's march ended, we bivouacked at a large spring, which excited much surprise on the part of our men for its immense size, they never before having seen anything like it, but very common in some parts of Tennessee, Kentucky, and North Alabama. I must not neglect to mention that the strength of the 10th Regiment about this time was 600 men for duty.

On the 3rd day we reached the Cumberland Mountains, and were detained at a camp known as Smith's Crossroads one day, in consequence of the delay occasioned in getting our trains up the steep ascent. I think that after reaching the highest point we travelled on the mountain a distance of 20 miles, before beginning to descend. The road was by no means a bad one and less hilly than is usually found in the valley.

On the 5th of September, we reached a small dilapidated village, known as Bunker Hill, on the Falling Water Creek. Here we remained on the 6th,

*About 75 or 80 pieces of Artillery. — A.M.M.

that the two columns might close well up, and partially to rest our men and the wagon teams.

A few miles north of Gainsboro, an ancient and most un-American-looking village with the most picturesque surroundings, we reached the Cumberland River, and crossed it by a good and shallow ford, the river being very low. On the morning of the 10th, we passed the Kentucky line, and later in the day reached Tompkinsville, where we halted for the night. It was evident that we had no friends there.

Our marches had been very fatiguing, for although we had on no occasion exceeded 20 miles a day, yet the long delays which our trains caused us, for they were obliged to be well up so as to be protected by the columns, made it frequently nine and ten o'clock at night before we could reach our destined camping grounds, and the route had been commenced before sunrise.

The portion of Tennessee through which we passed is generally regarded as poor and unproductive, yet the lands planted, being of course a selection of the best quality, appeared to be producing good crops of corn, the yield from which must have averaged fully 25 bushels to the acre. The lands in the *(Sequatchie)* valley, a long strip of land perhaps 100 by from 3½ to 5 miles wide, is exceedingly fertile and productive in grain crops, but the climate is unsuited to cotton. Indeed throughout the whole of this part of Tennessee, I did not see 1,000 acres of land that had apparently been planted in cotton. The scenery at times was quite imposing, but there was no indication of wealth or any high degree of civilization or comfort.

From Tompkinsville we moved in the direction of Glasgow, a very considerable and apparently flourishing town. Our Brigade, however, only remained here a few hours, although the greater part of the army converged to this point, and remained in its vicinity several days. We were sent on detached duty a little before day closed to Proctor's Station, distant about 12 miles, for the purpose of interrupting the passage of trains on the Louisville & Nashville R.R., and if possible to capture some of them. We arrived at the station during the night and made all arrangements for our prey, but they proved to be too wary for us, and although one ran up within a mile of our men who were in ambush, timely warning must have been given by some citizen hostile to us, and their escape, thereby secured.[4]

Proctor's Station was distant only for a few miles from the "Great Mammoth Cave." However anxious we may have been to visit it, we had not time just then to do so.

The difficulties of obtaining information as to our own and the enemy's movements, on the part of the soldiers and officers of lower grade, is at times very great. Those entrusted with information of future plans are very reticent, necessarily and properly so. So that at this time, as it frequently happened afterwards, we were almost entirely ignorant of the position and movement of the enemy, and it was a matter of much speculation with us as to where they were, and how it happened that up to the present time we had seen no hostile forces, and no attempts had been made to check us. But on the evening of the day of our arrival here, we learned that they were not many miles distant in our front, at the Railroad Bridge crossing Green River, near Munfordville, where a considerable force was awaiting us, and also that General Buell, to whom had been entrusted the task of driving General Bragg out of Kentucky, was fast approaching with his army by the L. & N. R.R. from Nashville.[5]

During the day of the 14th, we learned that General Chalmers[6] who, with his Brigade, belonging to our Division, had been sent out to reconnoitre the position of the enemy at Green River, deceiving himself as to their strength, both in numbers and position, and no doubt encouraged by stratagems of the enemy, had most unadvisedly and rashly made an attack upon their works, and had been easily repulsed with heavy loss, losing several most excellent and promising officers.[7] At about four o'clock (Gen. Duncan) received orders to join him at *(Cave City)*, to which place he had retired. Early on the morning of the 15th, Gen. Duncan, commanding his own and Chalmer's Brigades in obedience to the instructions of the Commanding General, moved forward to the enemy's position (eight miles), and at about eight o'clock began to skirmish with them. It was known that heavy reinforcements would soon be up to assist us. Being temporarily in command of the Brigade, I had just ordered forward the 10th S. C. as skirmishers, they had deployed and were just advancing to engage and drive the enemy's light troops into their defences — the ground they had to pass over was an open, low, and tolerable level meadow — I was sitting on horseback on rather a high hill overlooking the movement, when General Bragg with his staff, just arrived upon the ground, rode up to, and addressed me. The movement in progress immediately caught his eye. He remained watching it, apparently with intense interest, and occasional exclamations of satisfaction would escape him, as the bold fellows steadily and skillfully pushed forward in an unbroken line of skirmishes, followed by their supports, regardless of shot and shell which the enemy dealt them. The time occupied did not exceed five or six minutes. When completed, he turned to me, and said as he rode off, "That's worth looking at, Colonel. Your Regiment does you honor."

General Bragg's combinations for the reduction of the Federal positions were well planned, and skillfully executed. The selection of ground chosen by them to impede our further advance into Kentucky was most judicious. A very considerable chain of earthworks, consisting of three enclosed redoubts or batteries, connected by strong Infantry breastworks protected by ditches, palisades, and abattis, had been thrown up on the south side of Green River, near the little town of Munfordville. The growth of trees had been cut away for a very considerable distance, and all obstacles to a wide field of fire had been removed. The banks of the river were much higher than the country immediately around it, and the position could not be approached or attacked but with the certainty of considerable loss to the attacking party. Their engineer had shown a good deal of skill in the arrangement of the batteries, and in the general configuration of the works. The garrison consisted of about 4,500 Infantry.

It was well for us that we had reached this place before Buell, who was fast hurrying to it also. With his army in line of battle on ground as favorable to them as this neighborhood offered, there can be but little doubt but that our further advance would have been effectually checked.

General Polk with his command had been sent round to the enemy's left to cross the river some 15 miles above, and if possible to reach their rear on the evening of the 15th. During the night of that day, he got possession of the north bank of the river, and crowning its height with Artillery, which from its greater altitude commanded and controlled the works of the Yankees from their rear, was ready by daybreak on the morning of the 16th to take his share in the combat. During the 15th we skirmished with the enemy, hemming him in, and forcing them into their works. Our batteries were planted in the best positions to be had for them, and on the morning of the 16th, 25,000 men, assisted by 75 pieces of Artillery, were ready and awaiting the signal for attack.

The Yankee commander, seeing that there was no possibility of making a successful resistance against such odds and advantages, very prudently and wisely yielded to a demand for surrender, and did so unconditionally.[8]

It was well for us that the place had fallen so quickly, for in twelve hours after General Buell was within 12 miles of us, with a very considerable force, but too late to save his comrades. For two days we expected him to move on us, and now desired it, for we now had the advantage of position, but he declined doing so, and his army drew no nearer, but moving to our right (as we faced to the rear) crossed the Green River lower down and moved rapidly north towards Louisville. General Bragg, however, was ahead, and on the most direct road to the same place, having also started in the same direction as soon as he found out his adversaries' intentions.

It was now fully expected that a battle would take place. Any hour one might have been brought on by General Bragg. The two armies were about equal in strength, they were marching on parallel roads. We were ahead, and could consequently select the position. If we offered battle it could not be declined. The Federal commander, owing to his forced marches to be before us, had been obliged to leave his baggage and provision trains behind. His troops had scarcely anything served out to them, were footsore and tired. They had lost almost all that they had gained in Tennessee, and were much dejected and demoralized. Many thought, and I could not help but agreeing with them, that a more favorable opportunity to fight could scarcely offer itself, and were most anxious to do so. I think the sequel proved that they were right. General Bragg, however, thought otherwise. Perhaps his reasons were good. His opportunities of gaining information were of course as thorough as they could be, and his plans to effect a junction with General Kirby Smith may have influenced him in his decision, as well as the reason which I afterwards heard that he gave to the effect that owing to this and other delays, his provisions which he had brought were exhausted. The country immediately adjacent offered him no means of supply. Even if he succeeded in gaining a victory, starvation would threaten him, and a failure or defeat would be fatal to the army, as well as the plans of the Government at Richmond. The difficulty as to subsistence, I think, might have been overcome, and this reason given I have never regarded as a good one. I have ever thought, and have seen but little reason since to change my mind, that a fatal mistake was made when the Federal General, Buell, with his army was allowed to reach Louisville without being forced to fight a battle.[9]

For 20 miles the two armies marched on parallel roads. At that distance from Munfordville, General Bragg turned to the right, and apparently abandoning his intention against Louisville, marched towards Bardstown reaching and camping in the vicinity that night, after one of our longest day's marches. We were delayed a considerable time on the road, being apprehensive of an attack, our advanced guard having been engaged with a body of cavalry, and our trains threatened by a force reported to be on our flank. We did not reach our place of bivouac until 11 o'clock at night, I think on the 23rd of September. On the afternoon of the following day, we marched through Bardstown, quite a large and flourishing inland town, and were received with much enthusiasm by the inhabitants. Not only in the town itself, but in the country around it, the people, both men and women, appeared to be decidedly on our side and of our way of thinking. We met with much hospitality and kindness. Here we at last found ourselves in a comparatively wealthy portion of the state. There were much evidences of wealth, comfort, and profusion.

Passing through Bardstown, our Brigade proceeded on the Louisville Pike to Turkey Creek, a distance of seven miles, and there went into camp, being in advance of the army and on outpost duty. From Louisville we were about 30 miles.

Remained here about five days, and were then relieved by another Brigade. Returning through the town, we rejoined our Division encamped about three miles off on the Springfield Pike.

PERRYVILLE TO KNOXVILLE

(The Narrative)

On the 4th of October, our Division moved towards Springfield, and passing through that place, also through Perryville, reached Harrodsburg on the 6th, the entire army moving in the same direction. Bardstown was abandoned, and the enemy pressing towards it in heavy force. Buell, who had received heavy reinforcements, had also refreshed his weary men, now took the initiative, and was eager for battle. Our Army, weakened to a considerable extent by sickness caused by overfatigue and exhaustion, was now far inferior to the enemy in number, theirs having been probably doubled by the reinforcements drawn from the Northern

States.[10] It became absolutely necessary that the junction with Kirby Smith should be effected without delay, and at Harrodsburg it was accomplished.

General Bragg here made a division of the forces under him. With the greater part of his own army, he advanced from Harrodsburg to Perryville.[11] And General Smith with his own command and Withers's Division, moved against Lawrenceburg, hoping to capture or destroy a column of the enemy passing through that place on their way to join Buell's main body.[12] With his immediate command, he succeeded in cutting them off, and to General Withers was entrusted the duty of closing in their rear, the only opening by which they could extricate themselves. Withers's force, it is true, was rather small for this purpose. Still, had he displayed a little more energy or forced an engagement, he could have held the enemy in check sufficiently long to have enabled General Smith to come up, and the result of such a combination must have been a complete and overwhelming success; but the enemy, whilst showing a bold front and apparently remaining stationary, were really hurrying away with all speed, and what was supposed by General Withers to be the enemy in force was only a skirmish line, making up in noise and bluster for what they lacked in numbers. The mistake was discovered too late. The enemy escaped, and Smith found, on reaching the ground where he expected to fight, not the enemy, who had slipped away, but the Division which had been placed there to prevent his doing so. The whole arrangement resulted in nothing more than a skirmish with their rear guard, the loss of several hundred prisoners, a few wagons, and some hours uneasiness to the Yankees, whose General must have prided himself not a little, in the skillful strategy which he had exhibited, in extracting himself from a very perilous position.

At Perryville, on the *(8th of October)*, General Bragg was forced to give battle, which he did successfully against a greatly superior army and with only a portion of his own. On the following day he fell back to Harrodsburg, the entire army concentrating there. A line of battle west and south of Harrodsburg was selected, and on the 10th the troops were ready for the enemy.

This arrangement did not suit the Federal commander. His purpose was evidently so to place himself as first to cut off our line of retreat, and then probably to fight at his own convenience.

On the morning of the 11th, his plan was developed, for, declining our offer of battle, he was moving rapidly to our left. General Bragg's position was now a critical one. The enemy once securely in his rear, and we were gone. It would have been an easy matter to secure the mountain passes, only a few of which were practicable for a large army with its Artillery and trains, and almost the only one still in our possession was through the Cumberland Mountains. The Kentuckians had failed to respond to the offer made them, although showing no decided hostility to us, and in many instances expressing a hearty desire for the success of our cause, but they refused to take up arms, except in small numbers here and there, perhaps to the extent of 200, and of these the greater part deserted so soon as it became apparent to them that the army was retreating. Our failure to strike a decided blow and cripple the military strength of the United States in that state, had also a bad effect. They required to be assured of our earnestness and ability to protect them before they would venture anything.[13]

By 10 o'clock on the morning of the 11th of October, the army was in full retreat through Harrodsburg, and in the afternoon, crossing Dick's River, encamped that night on its right bank, and in the neighbourhood of Camp Dick Robinson. Here they remained on the 12th, and on the following day the retreat commenced in good earnest. General Withers was, on the 12th, for some purpose or other, sent in advance of the army to Tennessee. I never could learn the object. General Duncan succeeded to the Division, and I again took charge of the Brigade.[14]

The route by which we retreated was as follows: Crab Orchard, Mt. Vernon, London, Barboursville, Cumberland Gap, and Tazewell to Knoxville. The greater part of the country through which we passed was wild and picturesque in the extreme. It is perhaps the poorest part of either state, Kentucky or Tennessee.

Buell followed closely for some days, and daily engagements occurred between our Cavalry, who covered our retreat, and that of the enemy. It seemed to me that there were many positions where we might have turned and fought to great advantage against almost any odds, but no time could be lost. The country offered us no support, and of breadstuffs, we were almost without any supply. On the 17th, I received orders whilst on the march from Little Rock Castle Creek to return there and assist the Cavalry under General Wheeler, in holding the enemy in check, he having applied for an Infantry force to assist him, as they were pressing him hard, and his men were much exhausted and were unable longer to sustain the continued conflict without some assistance.

The Brigade immediately retraced its steps, and soon reached its destination. Here I found him awaiting my arrival, and a skirmish going on. The position was a strong one, almost a mountain pass, and scarcely possible to be turned. The troops, three regiments of Infantry and a battery of Artillery, were soon placed in position, the most favorable that presented itself, and the fourth regiment, (28th Alabama, a fighting regiment that never failed to give a good account of itself) was deployed as skirmishers to the front. All my dispositions being made, the Cavalry was withdrawn in rear of our line, and we awaited the advance of our adversaries, who seeing that their opponents were retiring, came on with much confidence and exulting in their supposed success. To their astonishment they were received with a deadly and well-directed fire from the rifles of the 28th and Water's Battery, which sent them back in confusion and surprise. I fully expected that after a short time our skirmishers would be forced to retire, and that our main body would have an opportunity of punishing them severely, but the brave 28th would not yield an inch, and successfully held their entire force in check throughout the day. Our purpose having been accomplished, on the following morning we started to rejoin our command, now a day's march in advance, and overtook them at Barboursville.[15]

At Barboursville, General Duncan was forced to leave us on account of illness, he suffering from an attack of typhoid fever, brought on by exposure, anxiety, and hard-living — poor fellow, he never recovered, but died at Marietta, Georgia, about a month after. Had he lived, there can be no doubt but that in a short time he would have been a Major General, and in all probablity would have retained the command of our Division.

On the 24th of October, the army reached the neighborhood of Knoxville, Tennessee, and there rested from their fatigues. The pursuit by the enemy had long since ended. Indeed they ceased to annoy us to any extent after the Rock Castle Creek affair, and disappeared altogether at the Cumberland River.

A considerable detachment from our army, perhaps 3,000 men, was left at the Cumberland Gap,[16] an ample garrison for its security, and the army after a march of 518 miles, being the distance we traveled from Harrison's Ferry on the Tennessee River to the close of our "Kentucky Campaign" at Knoxville, went into quarters for a brief period, and enjoyed much their rest after their exciting and arduous labors.

NOTES TO CHAPTER 2

[1] In the reorganization following the dispersal of the Army of the Mississippi, Bragg moved to Chattanooga with a force of about 35,000, leaving Van Dorn at Vicksburg with some 16,000 men and Price at Tupelo with about the same number. (*O.R.*, XVII, pt. 2, 656).

West Point graduate and Mexican War veteran, Mansfield Lovell was deputy street commissioner of New York City at the outbreak of the war. Resigning his position, he went South, was appointed a major general in the Confederate army and commanded at New Orleans prior to its capitulation in the spring of 1862. Subseqently, he commanded a division and later a small corps in Van Dorn's Confederate Army of West Tennessee and conducted himself with credit at the Battle of Corinth, Oct. 3 and 4, 1862. He was relieved Dec. 7, 1862, and instructed to await further orders from the War Department. They never came and, despite the fact that he was eventually relieved of responsibility for the loss of New Orleans by a court of inquiry, he held no further active command during the war. *O.R.*, XVII, pt. 1, 374-375, 503, 507; *Ibid.*, pt. 2, 697, 711, 787; *Generals in Gray*, 194-195; Archer Jones, *Confederate Strategy from Shiloh to Vicksburg*, (Baton Rouge, 1961), 70-88.

[2] It will be recalled that Manigault had been commanding the brigade as senior colonel. Brig. Gen. Johnson K. Duncan, a Pennsylvanian by birth and graduate of West Point, moved to New Orleans in 1855 and served there as chief engineer of the Board of Public Works of Louisiana. When the war came, he cast his lot with the South. In command of Forts Jackson and St. Philip on the lower Mississippi guarding New Orleans, he was forced to capitulate to Farragut's fleet in April 1862, was taken prisoner, exchanged and served in Bragg's army during the invasion of Kentucky in command of Manigault's brigade and, for a brief period, Wither's division. At the close of the campaign, Bragg appointed him chief of staff to the commanding general. Shortly thereafter, on Dec. 18, 1862, he succumbed to a painful and protracted illness. In announcing his death in General Orders, Bragg was generous in praise. "The army and the country will lament the loss of this distinguished soldier...By his zeal, efficiency and gallantry, he had so won the confidence of his Government and the admiration of his associates in arms as to attain a position second only in importance to that of commander-in-chief of an army...Dead to his family and friends, he will still live in the hearts of his countrymen as among the brightest and bravest spirits of the many who have given their lives to the holy cause of freedom." *O.R.*, XVI, pt. 2, 768, 938; XX, pt. 2, 411, 457; *Generals in Gray*, 77-78.

[3] On Aug. 27, 1862, Bragg had available in Chattanooga for the invasion of Kentucky 27,816 men present for duty in the Army of the Mississippi. This force consisted almost entirely of infantry and artillery, since the cavalry was already operating in Middle Tennessee and Kentucky under Forrest and Wheeler. Kirby Smith estimated his strength in the Department of East Tennessee at approximately 20,000, plus 1,300 cavalry under John Morgan in Kentucky. In his advance on Lexington, Ky., however, he wrote Bragg he would have with him "about 12,000 effective men." *O.R.*, XVI, pt. 2, 727, 784; *Battles and Leaders*, III, 2-3; Arthur Howard Noll, *General Kirby Smith*, (Sewanee, Tenn., 1907), 204-208.

[4] Although ordered to capture all trains, Gen. Duncan, commanding the Fourth Brigade of Withers' Division at Proctor's Station, and Gen. Chalmers, the Second at Cave City, were instructed that no unnecessary damage be done to the road or rolling stock, since both might become of importance to Bragg's army. *O.R.,* XVI, pt. 2, 816-818.

[5] Buell's army, after leaving Nashville, had been retreating on a line parallel to and west of Bragg's line of march, with the purpose of concentrating at Bowling Green, Ky. *Ibid.,* 811, 815.

[6] James R. Chalmers later commanded a division under Forrest. After the war he played an active role in politics and served three terms as a representative from Mississippi in the U. S. Congress. *Generals in Gray,* 46.

[7] Bragg characterized the attack as "unauthorized and injudicious." *O.R.,* XVI, pt. 1, 980.

[8] The Federal losses were reported as 4,148 of whom 4,076 were unwounded prisoners. (*Ibid.,* 967). In his official report, however, Bragg stated that his army "secured 4,267 prisoners, 10 pieces of artillery, 5,000 small arms, and a proportional quantity of ammunition, horses, mules and military stores." *Ibid.,* 290.

[9] Defending himself against criticism, Bragg maintained that efforts were made to induce Buell to attack but that "I failed to accomplish this object." (*Ibid.,* 1090). Be that as it may, it is generally agreed that he missed a major opportunity to crush his adversary by opposing, with his victorious army, Buell's passage of the Green River. Certainly Manigault shared this opinion, as did Colonel, later Brigadier General, Adam R. Johnson of the Partisan Rangers of the 10th Kentucky Cavalry. Years later he wrote: "I feel confident to this day that if Bragg had fought Buell at Green River, as he intended, or as he declared he intended, he could have crushed the Federal army, and with the aid of many thousand assured recruits could have held the State; here was the turning point of the war in the West." Adam R. Johnson, *The Partisan Rangers of the Confederate States Army,* (Louisville, Ky, 1904), 125.

[10] Buell stated that the effective force under his command in the advance on Perryville amounted to about 58,000, of whom approximately 22,000 were raw recruits with very little instruction or none at all. The latter represented the reinforcements received by Buell from the hastily augmented Louisville garrison. Buell put the Confederate invasion force at 55,000 to 60,000. *O.R.,* XVI, pt. 1, 1028.

[11] Preoccupied with the inauguration of a Confederate governor of Kentucky at the state capitol in Frankfort, Bragg ordered Kirby Smith to concentrate there. Also, in the erroneous belief that Buell's main thrust was toward Frankfort, he ordered Withers' division, which included Manigault's brigade, to support Smith. In actuality, Buell's entire force, with the exception of Sill's division that had been pushed out toward Frankfort as a feint, was closing on Perryville where it collided with Hardee's corps and Cheatham's division of Polk's corps under overall command of the latter. There the Battle of Perryville was fought, with less than half of Bragg's troops, including Smith's, present. Manigault gives the impression that the junction with Kirby Smith took place before Perryville, whereas, in fact, it occurred two days later. Horn, *The Army of Tennessee,* 176-187.

[12] This was Sill's division of McCook's corps sent out toward Frankfort as a feint by Buell.

[13] Manigault makes no reference to Bragg's opportunity, after the tactical victory at Perryville, of linking up with Kirby Smith and turning on Buell in a show-down battle for the control of Kentucky. Had Bragg done so, it would have been one of the very few, if not the only, instances during the war when, in a major battle, the Confederates would have had a numerical superiority of effective troops. With McCook's corps of Buell's army knocked out of action by the crushing Southern attack on the Federal left wing at Perryville, Buell had only two corps of about 36,000 men in fighting trim. Gen. C.C. Gilbert, commanding one of these, wrote later: "In not returning to Perryville and resuming the battle, he *(Bragg)* lost for the Confederacy perhaps the only opportunity it ever had of fighting a great battle with a decisive preponderance in numbers and the character of its troops." (*The Southern Bivouac*, Vol. I, 551). Noll, in *General Kirby Smith*, 220, put it this way: "For the first time in the history of the Confederacy, an army of veterans retreated before an inferior force largely made up of new levies."

[14] On Oct. 12, Withers was relieved from command and ordered to the rear for the purpose of procuring supplies of clothing, shoes, tents, etc. to be held at Knoxville and Chattanooga subject to Bragg's further orders. *O.R.*, XVI, pt. 2, 938.

[15] This is probably the most complete account of the affair at Little Rock Castle Creek (or River). It would appear, however, that the action occurred on Oct. 19, rather than on the 17th as stated by Manigault. In his official report of the Kentucky campaign, Col. Joseph Wheeler, who was shortly to be promoted brigadier general, makes this terse comment: "On the evening of the 19th I took a small portion of Fraser's infantry regiment *(the 28th Alabama)*, which was sent to assist me, to feel the enemy." As a cavalryman, Wheeler was not inclined to give much credit to the infantry on the only occasion on which it was called to assist him in his brilliant defense of Bragg's rear during the retreat. Involving no less than 26 separate engagements in five days, Wheeler's feat undoubtedly saved Bragg's immense train of some 4,000 wagons and firmly established the cavalry leader's reputation. His subsequent career as "Fighting Joe" entitled him to rank with Jeb Stuart, Bedford Forrest and Wade Hampton as one of the oustanding commanders of the mounted arm produced by the Confederacy. One observer, a colonel of artillery, called Bragg's retreat "most disgraceful" and said that many of the wagons were "loaded with dry goods, shoes, trimmings and trumpery of all kinds." *O.R.*, XVI, pt. 1, 899; John W. DuBose, *General Joseph Wheeler and the Army of Tennessee*, (New York, 1912), 102-111. (hereafter cited as *DuBose*); W.C. Dodson (ed.), *Campaigns of Wheeler and his Cavalry, 1862-1865*, (Atlanta, Ga., 1909), 26-30. (hereafter cited as *Wheeler and his Cavalry*); Horn, *The Army of Tennessee*, 189; William R. Boggs, *Military Reminiscences*, (Durham, N.C., 1913), 48.

[16] An example of Manigault's habitual accuracy. Bragg directed Kirby Smith to leave precisely that number of infantry at Cumberland Gap. *O.R.*, XVI, pt. 2, 975.

3

KNOXVILLE TO MURFREESBORO

(Editor's Preface)

In his official report written in the spring of 1863, Bragg was at pains to point out to the authorities in Richmond his accomplishments during the invasion of Kentucky. On paper, they indeed seemed impressive. "We had redeemed," he wrote, "North Alabama and Middle Tennessee and recovered possession of Cumberland Gap, the gateway to the heart of the Confederacy. We had killed, wounded, and captured no less than 25,000 of the enemy; taken over 30 pieces of artillery, 17,000 small arms, some 2,000,000 cartridges for the same; destroyed some hundreds of wagons and brought off several hundreds more with their teams and harness complete; replaced our jaded horses by a fine mount; lived two months upon the supplies wrested from the enemy's possession; secured material to clothe the army, and finally secured subsistence from the redeemed country to support not only the army but also a large force of the Confederacy to the present time."

Despite all this, there were those in the high command, not to mention many of the rank and file, who both at the time and in later years, did not hesitate to brand the campaign a failure and to lay the responsibility at the door of the commanding general. With considerable justification, they pointed out the lost opportunities after Munfordville and Perryville and the failure to come to grips with Buell's army. In point of fact, they were probing the weakness of character that was to plague Bragg during his entire career as an army commander — the lack of moral courage, when fortune called, to close with the enemy, to risk all at the critical moment, and, for better or for worse, force a decision. Perhaps Bragg himself revealed this most clearly when he told Col. Urquhart of his staff during the invasion, "This campaign must be won by marching, not fighting."

In any case, after the return to Knoxville, Bragg was summoned to the Confederate capital for consultation and to report to President Davis. He lost no time in attempting to lay the blame for the shortcomings of his Kentucky campaign on General Polk, with the result that the latter, who happened also to be a favorite of the president, was duly called to Richmond, where he told Davis that Bragg was "wanting in the higher elements of generalship," and suggested he be replaced by Joseph E. Johnston, now recovered from his wound at Seven Pines. This did not sit well with the president, who had little use for Johnston, and the upshot of it all was that Davis, in trying to please every one, ended up pleasing no one. Bragg was left in direct command of the army but under the overall supervision of Johnston, who was made department commander. Polk, along with Hardee and Kirby Smith, the latter soon to be shipped off to the Trans-Mississippi, was promoted lieutenant general and returned to the command of his corps.

From Knoxville, Bragg moved, via Chattanooga and Tullahoma, to Murfreesboro to occupy the rich farming area of central Tennessee and threaten Nashville 30 miles to the northward. There, he assembled a force of some 40,000 troops, henceforth to be known as the Army of Tennessee, a name made famous by its exploits.

President Davis, on an inspection trip to the West in December, visited the army and was favorably impressed by its condition and appearance, but he dealt it a serious blow by insisting, over the protests of Bragg and Johnston, on the transfer to reinforce Pemberton in Mississippi, where Vicksburg was threatened, of Stevenson's division of close to 10,000 men — troops that would be sorely needed when, later in the month, Rosecrans advanced on Murfreesboro from Nashville. The latter had replaced Buell, who had been roundly criticised for his conduct of the Kentucky campaign, much as Bragg had.

With the Army of Tennessee thus weakened, and Forrest and Morgan away on cavalry raids in west Tennessee and Kentucky, Rosecrans moved south from Nashville on Dec. 26. Bragg decided to oppose his advance at Murfreesboro and thus was joined, particularly for the numbers involved, one of the severest conflicts of the entire war, the Battle of Murfreesboro, as it was known in the South, or Stone's River in the North. Bragg had approximately 37,000 men present for duty, Rosecrans some 10,000 more — a disparity accounted for by the departure of Stevenson's division.

From south to north the battlefield was divided by the meandering course of Stone's River, generally fordable and intersected by the Nashville Turnpike and the Nashville and Chattanooga Railway, both of which, in close proximity, crossed the stream in a northwest-southeast direction a short distance to the northwest of the town.

In preparing to make his stand against Rosecrans' advancing troops, Bragg placed the left wing of his army, consisting of Polk's corps, of which Manigault's brigade was a part, on the west side of the river and his right, under Hardee, on the east.

Curiously enough, both commanders determined to take the offensive on the same day in the same way — that is to say, by assaulting the enemy's right and driving it in a clockwise direction in a right wheel, the pivot based on Stone's River. Thus, the prospect arose of a sort of revolving door action. However, this did not occur because Bragg beat Rosecrans to the punch and attacked first.

In order to confuse his Southern opponent and mislead him as to the true point of intended attack, Rosecrans demonstrated, by heavy skirmishing, against Bragg's left. This maneuver had the desired effect but an unanticipated result. Bragg, mistaking the feint for the main attack, transferred Cleburne's division of Hardee's corps, as well as his reserve division, McCown's, to the extreme left of his line, thus concentrating the bulk of his troops against Rosecrans' right and overlapping it. This left only Breckinridge's division on the right or east side of the river, where, it will be recalled, Rosecrans intended to make his main thrust.

Orders were issued for the Northern attack to be delivered at 7 A.M., Dec. 31, but it never took place as Bragg had anticipated his opponent and seized the initiative by directing his heavily reinforced left wing to assault Rosecrans' right "as early as it is light enough to see." This was done with a vengeance. The Southern troops, attacking in succession from left to right in one of the most brilliant charges of the war, crushed Rosecrans' right and drove it back some four or five miles against the Nashville Pike, as one half-closes a knife blade, so that the Federal line ended up at right angles to its original position.

In the formation of the Southern forces preparatory to the attack, Bragg had placed Withers' division in the front line with its right resting on Stone's River, thus forming the pivot or fulcrum on which the sweeping right wheel of the army would be based. From the river westerly, from right to left, Withers' four brigades were formed in the following order — Chalmers, Anderson, Manigault, Loomis (Deas). Since the Confederate attack was commenced on the extreme left and was taken up in succession by units to the right, Manigault's was one of the last of the Confederate brigades to go into action and, as he explains, under difficult circumstances in that a salient, or protruding angle, had been formed when his right was pushed forward to connect with Anderson's left. This meant that when Manigault attacked, his right was in advance of his left and thus exposed to an enfilading fire of artillery and small arms, with devastating results.

Twice beaten back in desperate fighting, Manigault's brigade, now supported by Maney's, assaulted the enemy once more, this time with success as it joined in the victorious attack on the Federal right wing, sweeping it back against the Nashville Turnpike. There, heavily reinforced from his left wing, which had been withdrawn from its originally intended attack on Bragg's right, Rosecrans made a successful stand.

The next day, New Year's day, the exhausted combatants reformed their lines and rested on their arms, the Southerners remaining in possession of the field. On the 2nd, under the mistaken impression that Rosecrans was withdrawing, Bragg ordered Breckinridge, despite the latter's vehement protests, to attack the Federal left on the east side of the river. As Breckinridge had foreseen, his division was torn to pieces by the Northern artillery, posted in a commanding position on the west bank, and hurled back with a loss of 1,500 men. The Kentucky or Orphan Brigade alone suffered more than 400 casualties, causing Breckinridge to cry out in anguish, "My poor Orphans! My poor Orphans!" He never forgave Braxton Bragg.

Discouraged and urged by his generals to retreat, the Southern commander accepted their advice and the Confederate withdrawal began the night of Jan. 3. It had been the story of Perryville all over again. Bragg's men had met the enemy and given him a good thrashing, but there had been no follow-through and now they were retreating once more. Where would it all end?

That Manigault had led his troops with bravery and distinction is attested to by the tributes paid him by his division commander, Withers, and Lt. Gen. Polk in command of the corps of which his brigade was a part. The former wrote in his official report: "His command had been subjected to a most trying ordeal and had suffered heavily. The calm determination and persistent energy and gallantry which rendered Colonel Manigault proof against discouragements had a marked influence on and was admirably responded to by his command." To which Polk added: "The gallant South Carolinian returned to the charge a second and a third time, and the enemy gave way and joined his comrades of the right in their precipitate retreat."

Manigault's brigade had, indeed, distinguished itself in this its first major action and against troops commanded by Phil Sheridan, who went on to fame and bore the reputation of being one of the hardest fighters in the Union army.

R.L.T.

KNOXVILLE TO MURFREESBORO

(The Narrative)

W e were much in need of rest and refreshment. During the retreat our sufferings were not light. The clothing of the men was in rags, their shoes completely worn out, and many had marched out of the country without any. Our provisions gave out — I mean bread, or its substitute — we had to subsist on meat alone and parched corn.[1] The army, when it started on the expedition, was not as fully equipped and provided as it should have been. Many suits of clothing and pairs of shoes were wanted. There was an insufficient supply of ambulances and wagons for the sick and footsore, by which means we lost many men. Our supply train contained not more than twenty days' provisions. Its early failure and the difficulty of obtaining subsistence prevented a battle being fought at the only time when it might have been done to great advantage, and when the result, if successful, would have had, I believe, a very decided effect on the Kentuckians, and may have made the campaign a successful one in many ways, apart from the beneficial influence it would have produced to our cause generally. Unfortunately our resources were too limited, and we had not time to make as thorough preparation as we should have done, but I have always thought the plan of the campaign a good one, and the motives for carrying it into operation wise. Our commanding general had many difficulties to contend against. He could not supply himself with everything, and the different departments in Richmond gave him no assistance. Although the army criticized him severely for not fighting on one or two occasions,[2] they could not do otherwise than give him credit for a good deal of skill and judgment displayed at all other times, and it would be unfair to condemn him before hearing his defence on the points at issue.[3]

I was much pleased with what I saw of Kentucky. As a farming and stock-raising country, I can not conceive that it can easily be surpassed. The appearance of abundance and comfort that you see everywhere can not fail to strike one, and makes a most favorable impression, but I must confess that I thought I saw a want of neatness and refinement, even amongst the better-off, which somewhat surprised me, and was not in keeping with my preconceived notions of Kentucky civilization.

Their roads and pikes, in many instances, were nearly if not quite as good as those I saw in England. One drawback to the country was the water, which is generally bad, and as their branches or creeks almost invariably go dry in summer, their stock, of which there is an immense quantity, would suffer much, but for the ponds, which retain water, though stagnant throughout the dry seasons. One of the ponds or pools can be seen on every farm of any size, always situated in a basin surrounded by hills, the rain water falling on which finds its level in the basin at their feet, and is there retained, unable to find a vent. For centuries past, animals would gather at such places to quench their thirst, and the constant trampling of the earth exactly suited to the purpose, in the course of years reduced it to a consistency and crust which prevented the earth from absorbing the moisture to such a degree as to seriously diminish the contents of the basin. Evaporation alone caused any diminution of the quantity. They vary in size, and I have seen them covering an area of from a half to four or five acres, and on one or two occasions where I had an opportunity of measuring the depth, they proved to be from 12 to 15 feet deep, and these were rather small specimens.

There are no forests in Kentucky, I mean in the richer and more fertile counties, but extensive woods of from 20 to 300 acres, the timber of which is of the largest size and most carefully preserved, the growth consisting of beech, poplar, ash, and oak, but the two former are much the most common. The sycamore tree grows to an enormous size, and is found in large numbers near the water courses. There is little or no underbrush, and I was frequently reminded of the English parks, whilst riding by, or through one of these plantations.

There was very little of interest to us about Knoxville, and indeed we had very little inclination to rove just then. I remember that whilst here we had an exceedingly cold spell of weather, even at that latitude at that season of the year. On the 26th of October, it snowed all day, and it was four or five days before it thawed, the snow being several inches deep.

The army began to move by rail from Knoxville to Chattanooga during the last day or two of the month of October. Our Brigade took the cars, I think, on the 31st. On the morning of the 1st of November, reached Bridgeport on the Tennessee River, only remaining long enough in Chattanooga to change cars. On the same evening we crossed the river in a steamer, the R.R. bridge having been burned more than a year previously,[4] and went into camp on the north bank of the river, where we remained for three days. From there we marched to Tullahoma, where we rested a week, and then proceeded to Murfreesboro, where the entire army was soon assembled, and went into winter quarters for as long a period as the Yankees would permit us to do so. This latter place is distant from Bridgeport about 110 miles, and from Chattanooga about 138 miles. We reached it about the (22nd) of November, and our location was a most comfortable one on Stone River (130 yards wide) with plenty of wood around us, and a large open field nearby, admirably suited for drill and such purposes, Murfreesboro distant about 2¼ miles.[5]

At this place the command recruited rapidly and recovered from its fatigues and losses. Our supplies were abundant and of good quality.[6] The country around us was rich and productive, and supplies, by sending out foragers a few miles, could be easily and reasonably obtained. Blankets, clothing, and shoes were issued to the men, their spirits were excellent, everybody was cheerful, the ordinary duties of the soldier were performed with spirit, and when not occupied in such manner, various games and athletic amusements were encouraged and indulged in freely.

Our time here passed away pleasantly and rapidly.

About the middle of December, Mr. Davis, President of the Confederacy, paid the army a visit, and remained a guest of General Bragg for several days.[7] Whilst there, the army was reviewed by him, and acquitted itself very creditably. Our Division, I think, distinguished itself more on the occasion than any other.[8] After the review, I was invited by the Commanding General, as well as many other officers, to visit him (the President) at his quarters, where I had a short conversation with him, having seen him on one occasion only previous to this day. He was quite agreeable and gentlemanly in manner, and on the whole I was rather favorably impressed by him.

Whilst there, unfortunately for the country, he issued an order directing that a very considerable body of men, amounting in number to 10,000, should be detached and sent immediately to Vicksburg, Mississippi, or that neighborhood. This was done, I have always understood, against the earnest protestations of General Bragg and his Lieutenant Generals, who endeavored to dissuade him from his determination, stating that by doing so he would be reducing the army of one-fourth of its effective force, thereby seriously interfering with its ability to cope with the enemy, who, it was well-known, were at that moment gathering in large numbers at Nashville, distant 33 miles, whose numbers already considerably exceeded our own, and an advance upon us was looked for from week to week. No arguments could avail, however, and he persistently adhered to his resolution.[9]

Towards the latter part of the month, all the information that we could gather confirmed us in the impression that but a short time would now elapse before the Yankees would be down upon us, and a desperate struggle take place. We had long been prepared to receive them, and the condition of the troops was excellent, though they were not as numerous as could be desired.

I should have mentioned in the proper place that General Withers had rejoined us at Tullahoma, and had resumed the command of the Division.[10] I was not a little mortified on the 24th of December to learn that a General Patton Anderson had been assigned to the command of our Brigade, he making his appearance the same day, and assuming the duties of its commander. I was told that General Bragg, backed by General Polk and Withers, had been making repeated applications for my promotion, but without success, and they had been led to believe that some influence had been working against me in Richmond. This, I afterwards learned, was really the case. The individual who interfered and for a considerable time prevented my promotion, was actuated in his conduct, not from any knowledge of me or my merits, for he was not even personally acquainted with me, but from a mean, petty spite he bore a relative and near connection of mine for some old difference that had taken place between them, and the opportunity of revenging himself on him through me was too tempting to be lost.[11]

Several false rumors of the advance of the enemy had occurred, and we were all on the alert, but on the 26th, at about 3 o'clock P. M., heavy Artillery firing at a great distance off on the Nashville Pike gave notice that a serious affair was then going on. At dark we learned that the enemy were advancing, our Cavalry was being driven back, and in a day or two at farthest, we would have to meet our old adversaries face to face.

On the 27th we were occupied cutting roads, preparing crossings over the Stone River, and many other matters of importance. Our Generals of higher rank were busily engaged in viewing the ground, and selecting positions most favorable for receiving the attack. During the evening of this day, General Withers came to my quarters, and informed me that he had assigned General Anderson to Walthall's Brigade, of his Division, the latter General having been sent to the rear sick, about a week before, and that I would assume the command of the Brigade and fight it, and if he could possibly prevent it, I should not again be interfered with.

He also directed me to meet him at daylight on the following morning, with the other Brigade Commanders, to join and ride with General Polk over the ground on which we intended to fight.

Shortly after daylight on the morning of the 28th, as agreed upon the evening before, General Withers and his Brigade Commanders met at the place indicated about 2½ miles from Murfreesboro, on the Nashville Pike. It was a cold, raw, foggy morning. Icicles were hanging from the branches of the trees, the roads frozen and slippery, and the water in the ditches and pools thickly coated with ice. General Polk had not made his appearance, and we had to await his arrival.[12] The scene before and around us was very impressive. An occasional gun could be heard even at that early hour, reverberating in the distance, and giving notice that our foes had begun to move. A little in the rear of where we sat on our horses, long lines of troops were moving in different directions, as they filed towards their respective positions. Groups of Cavalry constantly passed us, and as they approached on the Pike, at first scarcely to be distinguished through the mist, consisted of sick, or, as a bloody garment or handkerchief indicated, wounded troopers, also parties of detailed men, with led horses, many of them showing that they too had been in the fray. Several such parties would pass us, and then would come a train of heavily loaded wagons, looming up through the fog to twice their real size. Interspersed amongst them here and there or perhaps toiling along, with some interval between them, would appear the larger and more cumbrous machine of some unfortunate farmer, his household goods piled to an immense height, far beyond what one would suppose to be the capacity of the vehicle, women and children occupying every available position, apparently at great risk to their necks. Horses, cows, sheep, hogs, and pigs, formed an attendant drove, in charge of the lads or Negroes belonging to the family, the proprietor himself assisting in some way or superintending everything, leaving behind him his once happy home, possibly even then a heap of ashes, and seeking shelter and protection in the rear of our lines, unwilling to place himself and family in the power of an enemy in whose honor or humanity, he could place no reliance. I was much interested in all I saw during this half-hour, and could not help thinking what a subject it would be for a picture. The variety of the expressions of the different groups of men, women, animals, and all the other features of the scene, well handled by a skillful artist, would indicate beyond the possibility of doubt, "A Battle Imminent".

General Polk arriving, we accompanied him over a good portion of the ground, and had our respective positions pointed out. My Brigade soon after joined me, and was placed in the line at the point assigned it.[13]

Commanders, whatsoever their rank or importance of their commands, are almost always dissatisfied with the positions assigned them in the line of battle, regarding that point entrusted to them as the weakest in the whole line, and I may be no exception to the rule. Certainly on this occasion I was far from being satisfied, for my right formed one of the points of an obtuse angle, only a little more than a right angle, which formed a salient towards the enemy, and necessarily was a very weak point. It is true that my neighbour was no better off than myself, in case we were attacked, but it happened otherwise. We were the attackers, and it will appear afterwards why our position was an unfortunate one for us. I do not believe that either Generals Bragg, Polk, or Withers, knows to this day[14] how excessively sharp an angle existed in the line of battle at this point, which line throughout the remainder of it was comparatively straight. In other respects our ground was not unfavorable. The entire line of the Brigade was slightly retired in a wood of cedar, but sufficiently near its edge to allow an almost uninterrupted view of an open cotton field which lay in our front, the ground gradually arising towards us. This field was about 400 yards, wide, and at its other extremity the ground rose abruptly for 100 yards, forming the crest of a long regular hill, at least twenty feet higher than where we were located. One-half of this hill in our front was heavily timbered, and much broken up by large boulders of rock. On the extreme right of our line the woods ran out to a point, and the right of ours, and left of the Brigade next on our right (Anderson's) was completely hidden from the enemy by the trees and foliage.

The enemy advanced very slowly and did not begin to make his appearance until the afternoon of the 29th. About four o'clock our Cavalry on the Nolensville Pike, just to our right, retired within our lines. Company A, 10th South Carolina, commanded by Lieutenant C.C. White, one of my best officers, who lived through the war and distinguished himself on many occasions, being on picket duty near this road, was attacked by a large body of Cavalry, a Philadelphia Battalion, numbering by their own account 300 men, being deployed as skirmishers. Co. A was at first thrown into some little confusion, owing also to the fact that the skirmish line of Anderson's Brigade on our right had been retired without notice having been given, and a portion of the Cavalry getting in their rear. Lieutenant White, however, succeeded in rallying his men, first by fours, afterwards in platoons, and finally by company. He at last succeeded in getting a position where he was somewhat protected by a rail fence. Secure of their prey, as they thought, the enemy now charged them, but were repulsed with heavy loss, leaving 17 N.C. *(non-commis-*

sioned officers) and privates dead on the field, as well as (2) two Majors also killed, and a number of wounded. They were forced to retire, and the company re-established their line, having met with the loss of only one killed, one wounded, and two captured. Lieutenant White was himself for a minute or so in the hands of the enemy, but succeeded in extricating himself after a sharp hand-to-hand conflict with an officer and two men. We were not disturbed again during the evening.[15]

On the following morning the enemy's columns began to deploy, and gradually during the day to form their lines in our front but out of view. Skirmishing began in our front at nine o'clock, and continued unceasingly throughout the day. An exciting and obstinate contest for the wood on our right was carried on for several hours, resulting eventually in favor of the enemy. Late in the afternoon, our Battery, assisted by a section of rifle guns, sent from Stewart's Brigade, was engaged with two Yankee Batteries, one of them distant 500 yards, which was silenced and forced to retire. With the other it was a drawn battle. The Lieutenant commanding the rifle section was unfortunately killed as he was returning to his command, I, having just relieved him, a rifle cannon shell cutting him in two.[16]

At four o'clock on the morning of the 31st of December, 1862, I received the order for battle.[17] At seven o'clock the firing commenced on the extreme left of our line, and was taken up to the right by each Brigade in succession. The first Divisions engaged taking the enemy by surprise, met with great success, and drove the Federal troops rapidly before them. But by the time our turn came, they were somewhat prepared for us. Our instructions were to attack the troops in our front, defeat and drive them back, endeavoring to swing ourselves round, so as to form a line continuous with the one to the right of our Brigade,[18] having accomplished which, the remainder of the troops beyond and to the right of the angle would in like manner advance and attack.

Deas's Brigade to our left, temporarily commanded by its senior Colonel Loomis,[19] soon became engaged, and our own immediately afterwards, the 34th Alabama, Col. Mitchell, advancing first in line, the others following by an echelon movement, a distance of about 50 yards between them, in the following order: 28th Alabama, Col. Reid; 24th Alabama, Col. Buck;* 19th South Carolina, Col. Lythgoe; 10th South Carolina, Lieut. Col. Pressley.[20] Their advance was met by a heavy fire in front, and as they cleared the woods and got well into the cotton field which lay between the lines, the Yankee troops and two Batteries *(to the right)* who, themselves not being attacked, could devote their attention to us, the formation of their lines corresponding to our own, enabled them to pour into our flank a heavy fire in addition to that from the lines against which our movement was directed. Their first lines were broken by each regiment in succession, but their second line, owing to the disadvantages operating against us, was too much for us.[21] We were

This regiment was added to our Brigade at Tullahoma, about the 15th of November, 1862. — A.M.M.

forced to retire, our supports, Maney's Brigade of Tennesseans,[22] of Cheatham's Division, not coming to our support. Hastily reforming the Brigade, and sending an officer to General Maney informing him of our failure of complete success, and that I was preparing for a second effort, urging him to support me promptly, I received his answer that he would do so. Again we advanced, carrying everything before us in the first line of the enemy, suffering and losing many men from the fire to our right which we could not return, and which no other troops drew from us, the time not having arrived for them to advance[23] and our reserves, still tardy in their movements, not appearing, reluctantly we were compelled again to withdraw. Scarce had we done so, when our supports made their appearance. By this time, Loomis's command[24] had also been forced to retire. Seeing that the enemy were much shaken and gave evidence of uneasiness, their right wing having been driven back, and exposing the right of the troops opposed to us, in concert with General Maney, he moving a portion of his command still further to the left than my Brigade front, a third advance was made, before which the enemy gave way, making but feeble resistance.

These two Brigades now swung round and prolonged the line, making a straight one.[25] The enemy in our front were awaiting our attack. Their right wing was in full retreat, and unfortunately, the troops who had defeated them, instead of immediately rejoining their comrades and taking a part against that portion of the Yankee army still holding their ground, followed for a considerable distance in pursuit.

Scarcely was our new line formed when I received orders to carry a battery in my front with a part of the troops under my command. This battery was near the Nolensville Pike, somewhat in advance of their line, but supported by a Brigade. The 10th and 19th were ordered to carry and capture it if possible, the 10th in advance. A partial support was given on the right by an Alabama regiment, temporarily attached to Anderson's Mississippi Brigade, but this regiment soon gave way.[26] The South Carolina regiments drove the gunners and supports from the battery, shot down the horses as they were endeavoring to retire the guns, and had succeeded in their undertaking, when the Yankee reserve in turn advanced and drove them back.[27] These regiments had barely time to reform when our entire line moved forward, and the battle, excepting on our extreme right (Breckinridge's Division), became general.

In our front the enemy gave way almost without a struggle. The battery before alluded to again fell into our hands, and we gained a full mile from our last position. Here, however, we at last met with a serious check. General Rosecrans, finding his right defeated, made a desperate stand with his left wing. His position was a very strong one, his left protected by Stone River, the bank of which was high and precipitous, and a commanding hill nearby, on which he had massed a large number of guns that swept all the approaches to it;[28] his Infantry protected by the embankments of the railroad. The troops, already worn out with hard fighting and much reduced in number, found it impossible to dislodge him. By the time the army had concentrated, and those who had been pursuing the enemy had returned and been reformed, he, Rosecrans, was thoroughly prepared to receive us with as many as 30,000 men who had not as yet been seriously engaged.

Had Stevenson's Division of 10,000 men still been with us, instead of at Vicksburg, or rather on its way there, to have been thrown against the enemy before they had time to recover from the confusion and alarm attendant on the defeat of their right and center, Rosecrans's army would in all probability have been destroyed. His loss in killed, wounded, and prisoners could not have fallen short of 25,000 men, and thirty-five (35) pieces of Artillery.

Our strength did not quite reach 30,000 Infantry and Artillery, and about 6,000 Cavalry.[29] The enemy's force by General Rosecrans's own admission exceeded 60,000 men of all arms.[30] It would not surprise me if he had that number in Infantry and Artillery alone. The army of Tennessee lost in killed and wounded 9,000 men and about 1,000 prisoners.[31]

In our Brigade we suffered heavily, losing in men and officers, killed and wounded, 530 men, with not more than five or six missing.[32] We inflicted heavy loss upon the enemy, capturing also four pieces Artillery.

Col. Lythgoe of the 19th S.C. was killed, Major Crowder, same regiment, mortally wounded, Col. Buck, 24th Alabama, wounded, also the acting Major of the 28th, and a number of officers of lower rank. In the 10th S.C., five out of seven Captains were either killed or wounded. Captain Nettles, an excellent and reliable officer, was thrice wounded and eventually died in consequence.

During the following three days, we were constantly in line of battle, and within 400 or 500 yards of the enemy. Several severe but partial engagements took place, but with the exception of much sharp skirmishing and a continual cannonade to which we were subjected, we were not again seriously involved in any affair. On the night of the 3rd of January, 1863, General Bragg retired unmolested from Murfreesboro. His reason for doing so will be found in his published report of the battle, attached. It is, I think, a very fair, and as far as I can judge, accurate, report of the engagement. The censure that he bestows in one or two instances is generally believed to have been deserved.[33]

Although we were ultimately obliged to retire from Murfreesboro, and a council of war thought it advisable to do so, yet there can be no question of its having been a victory for us, and although Rosecrans did finally get possession of the town, his army was so much crippled that for more than five months he was not able to move forward again, but had to remain stationary to repair damages.[34]

The total effective of the Brigade at the Battle of Murfreesboro was about 2,200.

The sketch of the battle which is attached is the copy of a rough one made by me a week after and sent home to Mary in a letter.* My purpose was only to give some idea of the position, etc., of my own command. It is

*The Manuscript includes a copy (see page 59) of the sketch Manigault sent to his wife. — Editor.

58

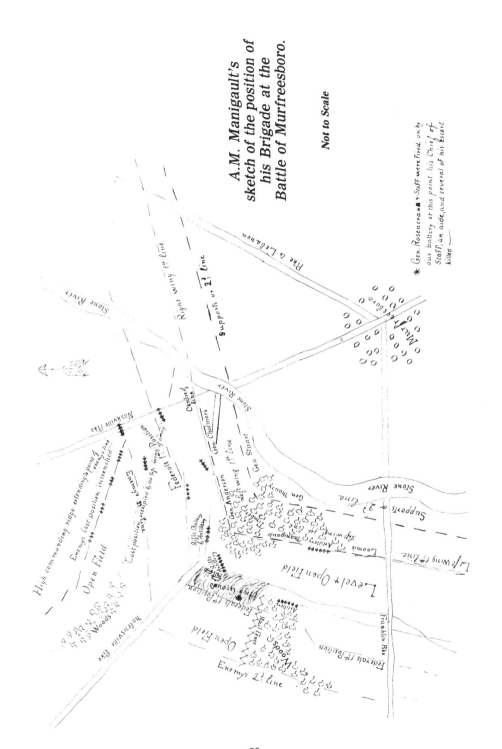

A.M. Manigault's sketch of the position of his Brigade at the Battle of Murfreesboro.

Not to Scale

* Gen. Rosencrans & Staff were fired on by our battery at this point, his Chief of Staff, an aide, and several of his Escort killed

not drawn by a scale, makes no pretensions to great accuracy. The foregoing account also is in reference almost entirely to the part taken in the battle by our Brigade. General Polk's and Withers's reports I had, but have unfortunately lost them. They refer more particularly to their more immediate commands, and would be more interesting here than that of General Bragg.[35]

In a Northern paper I found the following piece of information, professing to be from the reports of General Rosecrans: 2,000,000 rifle & musket cartridges expended at Stone River; 20,000 rounds of Artillery ammunition expended at Stone River; 2,650,000 rifle and musket ammunition expended at Chickamauga; 7,325 rounds of Artillery ammunition expended at Chickamauga.[36]

Col. I.C. Reid and Captain Turpin, 28th Alabama; Captains Welch and Carter, 34th Alabama; Lieutenants Hall and Parham, 24th Alabama, afterwards Captains; Col. Lythgoe and Major Crowder, 19th S.C.; Lieut. Col. Pressley, Major Porcher, Captain Nettles, and Lieut. White (shortly after made a Captain for his gallantry), all were conspicuous for their courage and coolness.

The three Brigade staff officers — Captain C.I. Walker, Acting Assistant Adjutant General of the 10th S.C., Captain D.E. Huger, Inspector General, and Dr. Joe Cain, Acting Volunteer Aide-de-Camp — did good service and behaved with great spirit.

Captain D.E. Huger led the 24th Alabama in the second charge, their Colonel having been wounded, the Major seriously injured by a fall, and the Lieutenant Colonel having disappeared rather mysteriously (a few weeks after he also found it advisable to resign), and made much reputation by his conduct on that occasion.

NOTES TO CHAPTER 3

[1] In a letter of May 20, 1863, to Adjutant General Cooper in Richmond, Bragg stated that after Perryville the army's rations of breadstuffs had been reduced to a four days' supply, and, although there was plenty of grain available, many of the larger mills had been destroyed by the enemy and accumulation from small country mills was impractical. *O.R.*, XVI, pt. 2, 1093.

[2] That is to say, after the capture of the Federal garrison at Munfordville and following the Battle of Perryville, when Bragg's and Kirby Smith's armies were finally united.

[3] Here Manigault discloses his partiality for Bragg for whom he had great respect.

[4] Under Bragg's direction, this bridge was subsequently rebuilt.

[5] Withers' division, of which Manigault's brigade was a part, was ordered to move from Tullahoma to Murfreesboro at sunrise Nov. 22. *O.R.*, XX, pt. 2, 416.

[6] On Nov. 24, Bragg wrote President Davis: "We are securing a rich harvest of supplies. Subsistence is abundant, not only for us, but a surplus may be had." *Ibid.*, 422.

[7] The President arrived at Murfreesboro Dec. 10, accompanied by his aide, George Washington Custis Lee, eldest son of Robert E. Lee.

[8] Gen. Polk, Manigault's corps commander, described the scene in a letter to his wife: "We have had a royal visit, from a royal visitor. The President himself has been with us...The review was a great affair; everything went off admirably, and he was highly gratified with the result...said they were the best appearing troops he had seen, well appointed and well clad. The sight was imposing, and, as it was my corps, very gratifying to me." William M. Polk, *Leonidas Polk: Bishop and General,* 2 vols., (New York, 1893), II, 169. Hereafter cited as *Polk.*

[9] Manigault here refers to the transfer of Stevenson's division on Dec. 18 to reinforce Pemberton in Mississippi. The move was carried out at Davis' insistence over the protests of Joseph E. Johnston and Bragg, who wrote after the Battle of Murfreesboro, "The unfortunate withdrawal of my troops *(Stevenson's division)...*has saved Rosecrans from destruction." Don C. Seitz, *Braxton Bragg: General of the Confederacy,* (Columbia, S.C., 1924), 255. Hereafter cited as *Seitz.*

[10] Nov. 10, 1862. *O.R.*, XX, pt. 2, 418.

[11] Nov. 22 Bragg forwarded to the Adjutant General in Richmond a recommendation, dated the previous day, from Gen. Withers for the promotion to brigadier general of Cols. E.C. Walthall of the 29th Mississippi, Z.C. Deas of the 22nd

Alabama, and A.M. Manigault of the 10th South Carolina. "These officers," he wrote, "have been connected with this command for many months, and creditably represent their respective states. Bold, energetic, and capable, they have served the country well and proved themselves worthy. In the camp, on the march, and before the enemy they have been tried and not 'found wanting.' I but discharge a duty in presenting their names for the favorable consideration of the Government." When Bragg listed these names, along with three others, for promotion, he ranked them in what he considered their order of merit, as follows: R.W. Hanson, E.C. Walthall, Z.C. Deas, A.M. Manigault, Thomas H. Hunt and Lucius E. Polk. When the promotions came through on Dec. 14, Manigault's name was not among them, nor was that of Hunt, who never did become a brigadier general, resigning from the army April 22, 1863, and turning down a commission subsequently offered him.

A word of explanation is in order here as to the method of creating general officers in the Confederate army. Normally, if the Senate were in session, the President, on the recommendation of the Secretary of War, would nominate to that body an officer to one of the four grades of general. The Senate, in turn, would refer the nomination to the Committee on Military Affairs, and, on receipt of its recommendation, either "advise and consent" to the nomination or, occasionally, reject it. If the Senate were not in session, as was the case in the present instance, the appointments were made first and the nominations sent over at the next session. Thus, Hanson, Deas and Polk were confirmed on April 22, 1863, and Walthall on the 23rd, all to rank from Dec. 13, 1862.

Since no evidence has been uncovered as to the identity of the individual Manigault says held up his promotion, one can only speculate. It seems reasonable to suppose, however, that it was someone in a position to influence President Davis or the War Department, possibly a member of the Confederate Congress from South Carolina.

There is more to the matter than this, however, for Manigault had recently written a letter critical of the Davis administration, which, contrary to his intention, had been made public. In reference thereto he wrote Bragg Nov. 30, 1862, "I deeply regret the publicity that has unfortunately been given to a private letter mailed from a point of supposed safety. I have nothing to say in extenuation. I admit having written the letter & must abide the consequences...It is a matter of as great surprise to me as to yourself, its publication in any newspaper...I need scarcely say, that after the communication received this evening (were it possible for the opportunity to offer for my doing so) I would of course decline any elevation obtained thro the joint interest of yourself & Genl. Withers, which recommendation you would under existing circumstances, very properly withdraw."

In any case, Davis, on the recommendation of the Secretary of War, finally nominated Manigault for the rank of brigadier general April 30, 1863, and he was confirmed by the Senate on the same day. *O.R.*, XX, pt. 2, 417-418, 499, 508-509; *Generals in Gray*, xv; *Journal of the Congress of the Confederate States of America, 1861-1865*, 7 vols., (Washington, 1904-5), Vol. III, 330, 334, 400; Ed Porter Thompson, *History of the Orphan Brigade*, (Louisville, Ky., 1898), 375-379, 429-433.; Letter from Manigault to Bragg, dated Nov. 30, 1862, in the Palmer Collection of Bragg papers in the Western Reserve Historical Society, Cleveland, Ohio; Grady McWhiney, *Braxton Bragg and Confederate Defeat, Vol. 1, Field Command*, (New York, 1969), 344.

[12] At 9:45 p.m. on the 27th, Polk had ordered Withers, along with his other division commander, Cheatham, to meet him punctually at 7:30 a.m. on the 28th at the crossing of the Nashville Turnpike and Stone's River for the purpose of

reconnoitering the ground on which his corps was to be posted. The troops were to be in position by 9 a.m. Withers directed his brigade commanders to accompany him to this meeting. *O.R.*, XX, pt. 2, 464-465.

[13] When it took position on Dec. 28, Polk's corps, its right resting on Stone's River, constituted the left of the army. Withers' division was in the front line, his four brigades stretching westward and southwestward from the river, from right to left in the following order: Chalmers, Anderson, Manigault, Deas. Due to the configuration of the ground, Anderson's left and Manigault's right were pushed forward, forming the protruding angle, or salient, to which Manigault refers. Withers described this angle as "near 60" degrees, while Manigault puts it as close to 90. *O.R.*, XX, pt. 1, 754.

[14] The evidence indicates that Manigault wrote this in 1866. By then, of course, Polk was in his grave, killed at Pine Mountain June 14, 1864, during the Atlanta campaign.

[15] For outstanding gallantry, Lt. C.C. White, commanding Company A (formerly the Georgetown Rifle Guards) of the 10th South Carolina, was, at Gen. Bragg's direction, promoted captain on the field. As Manigault relates, Lt. White, along with eight of his men, was temporarily captured and left in the charge of a Northern lieutenant. C.I. Walker, in his sketch of the 10th South Carolina, described the scene that ensued: "Seeing the Lieutenant tremulous, Capt. White in his stentorian voice commanded, 'Company A, rally on the right.' Rallying, they hesitated to shoot for fear of wounding their friends. 'Never mind us, fire!' came from Capt. White, and grappling their captors, the prisoners secured them, regained their arms and rejoined their Company." The Federal cavalry was the 15th Pennsylvania (Anderson Troop), which reported its loss as seven killed and five desperately wounded, including a major in each category, although a Northern participant later wrote: "Our loss...was exceedingly heavy in proportion to the number participating." Southern accounts placed the Federal dead at 13 or more in addition to many wounded and some prisoners. Referring to this action, Gen. Withers wrote: "There was a dash made by a portion of the enemy's cavalry on Manigault's skirmishers, which was creditably punished by Companies A and C of the Tenth South Carolina Regiment." *O.R.*, XX, pt. 1, 617, 754; Walker, *Tenth Regiment*, 89-90; Emanuel, *Georgetown Rifle Guards*, 15-16.

[16] Brig. Gen. A.P. Stewart was critical of the use made of the section of long-ranged rifled guns loaned to Manigault at the latter's request, stating that they were not properly supported and accomplished no useful purpose. The officer killed was Lt. A.A. Hardin, whom Stewart characterized as "a most estimable and gallant young officer." Stewart went on to become a lieutenant general and commanded a corps in the Army of Tennessee under Johnston and Hood. *O.R.*, XX, pt. 1, 724.

[17] Bragg instructed Withers, in an order dated Dec. 30, 1862, — 1:50 p.m., to make a vigorous assault on the enemy "tomorrow morning as early as it is light enough to see." Withers' right, on Stone's River, was to be the pivot on which the movement was to be executed, his left swinging around in a right wheel, corresponding to the advance of Gen. McCown's division on his left. *O.R.*, XX, pt. 2, 469.

[18] Thus substantially eliminating the angle formed with Anderson's brigade referred to above.

[19] With Loomis reporting himself disabled, command of the brigade was assumed by Col. J.G. Coltart of the 26th Alabama. *O.R., XX*, pt. 1, 754-755.

[20] These five regiments were to constitute Manigault's Brigade for the remainder of the war. The 34th Alabama, Col. Julius C.B. Mitchell, was organized at Loachapoka, Ala., in April 1862; the 28th, Col. J.C. Reid, at Shelby Springs in March of that year; and the 24th, Col. William A. Buck, at Mobile in August 1861. *C.M.H.,* VII, 131-132, 146-147, 164-165.

[21] "Manigault's brigade moved promptly at the proper moment, and his left swinging around, drove the enemy from the wooded ridge back on his second line. In the wheel through the open field, and before his command had completed the angle necessary to bring it on a line with Anderson's *(on his right)*, a heavy fire from two batteries and a column of infantry was opened on him from his right, which, enfilading his line, checked and finally forced him back to his former position." (Withers' Report, *O.R., XX*, pt. 1, 755). The two batteries were Battery C of the 1st Illinois, Capt. Charles Houghtaling, and Battery G of the 1st Missouri, Capt. Henry Hescock, attached respectively to the Third and Second Brigades of Sheridan's Third Division. In addition, the 4th Indiana Battery, Capt. Asahel K. Bush, attached to the First Brigade, was pouring in a destructive fire immediately in Manigault's front. *O.R.,* XX, pt. 1, 177; Alexander F. Stevenson, *The Battle of Stone's River,* (Boston, 1884), 53-73.

[22] George F. Maney, a Nashville lawyer and Mexican War veteran, was elected colonel of the First Tennessee Regiment in the spring of 1861 and served in western Virginia under Robert E. Lee and Stonewall Jackson before joining the Army of Tennessee. Promoted brigadier general for gallantry at Shiloh, he fought at Perryville, Murfreesboro, Chickamauga, Chattanooga and in the Atlanta campaign. In the Battle of Jonesboro, just before the fall of Atlanta, he was in temporary command of Cheatham's division but apparently was relieved on the night of Aug. 31 for failure to carry out an attack ordered by his corps commander. Regarding Maney's subsequent military career, the *Official Records* are silent. Certain it is that he held no further command of importance, as the division he led at Jonesboro was assigned to brigadier generals John C. Carter and States Rights Gist, both killed at Franklin, and Maj. Gen. John C. Brown, severely wounded in that battle. A Federal officer reported seeing Maney at Dalton, Ga., when Hood moved north for his invasion of Tennessee, and it may be that he served out the war in a staff capacity. His old brigade remained under other commanders. Maney was paroled at Greensboro, N.C., May 1, 1865, after Johnston's surrender to Sherman. *O.R.,* XXXVIII, pt. 3, 709-712; XXXIX, pt. 1, 723; XLV, pt. 1, 682, 733; *Generals in Gray,* 210, 384; Howell and Elizabeth Purdue, *Pat Cleburne: Confederate General,* (Hillsboro, Texas, 1973), 376; Marcus J. Wright, *General Officers of the Confederate Army,* (New York, 1911), 80.

[23] That is to say, Anderson's brigade on Manigault's right.

[24] Deas' brigade, on Manigault's left. A South Carolinian, Deas was related to Brig. Gen. James Chesnut Jr., former U.S. senator and husband of Mary Boykin Chesnut, author of the celebrated *Diary From Dixie.* His family moved from Charleston to Mobile, Ala., when he was 16 and he entered the army from that state in 1861. Deas was badly wounded at Shiloh, but recovered and subsequently led a brigade throughout the remainder of the conflict. He moved to New York following the war and became a successful cotton broker and member of the stock exchange. *Dictionary of American Biography,* V, 178.

[25] Thus eliminating at last the fatal angle with Anderson's brigade on Manigault's right.

[26] This was the 45th Alabama, Col. James G. Gilchrist, which suffered severely, losing 13 killed, 71 wounded and 7 missing. *O.R.*, XX, pt. 1, 659, 677.

[27] The battery attacked by Manigault's South Carolinans was Houghtaling's Battery C of the First Illinois Light Artillery mentioned above. Houghtaling, who was wounded in the action, reported a loss of 95 horses. The Union troops engaged in the bitter fighting that took place on Manigault's front were commanded by Brig. Gen. Philip H. Sheridan, the doughty Irishman who went on to fame in the Shenadoah Valley campaign of 1864 and as commander of Grant's cavalry in the closing operations in Virginia that culminated in Lee's surrender at Appomattox Court House in the spring of 1865. *O.R.*, XX, pt. 1, 352-354; *Battles and Leaders*, III, 620.

[28] This heavily defended point was known as the Round Forest or "Hell's Half Acre." Since it formed the pivot, or anchor, on which Rosecrans' line on the west side of the river was based, its loss probably would have led to the destruction of a large portion of his army. Horn, *The Army of Tennessee*, 203.

[29] Present for duty in Bragg's army the morning of Dec. 31, 1862, were 37,312 officers and men of whom 4,237 were cavalry. *O.R.*, XX, pt. 1, 674.

[30] Bragg made this assertion, but Rosecrans himself, in his official report, stated that he moved on the enemy with 46,940 troops and fought the battle with 43,400. Total losses in the Northern army were 13,429, of whom 1,730 were killed in action, 7,802 wounded and 3,717 captured or missing, or a total of more than 30% of those Rosecrans said were engaged. *Ibid.*, 196, 215, 663.

[31] Bragg reported an aggregate loss at the Battle of Murfreesboro of 10,266 of whom the killed and wounded amounted to 9,239 and the missing 1,027. *Ibid.*, 674.

[32] Bragg's report lists the losses in Manigault's brigade as 501 killed and wounded and 16 missing or a total of 517. *Ibid.*, 678.

[33] The criticisms levelled by Bragg were essentially these: Against Gen. McCown for failing to carry out an order to rectify his line of battle, thereby causing a slight delay in the assault on Rosecrans' right; against Gen. Cheatham for lack of promptness in the attack; and, finally, at Gen. Breckinridge, posted on the right or east bank of Stone's River, for faulty reconnaissance which resulted in three of his brigades being unnecessarily withheld, according to Bragg, from supporting the main attack. *Ibid.*, 663-672, 685-694, 702-703, 783.

[34] Bragg's decision to withdraw from Murfreesboro on Jan. 4, 1863, and abandon the field was the cause of much controversy. While it was approved in varying degrees by his chief subordinates, a number of them, including Hardee, Breckinridge and Cleburne, told Bragg bluntly that, in their opinion, he had lost the confidence of the army and should be replaced. Polk was of like mind. On Johnston's recommendation, however, Davis retained Bragg in command. *Ibid.*, 682-684, 698-701.

[35] These reports will be found in Vol. XX, part 1, of the *Official Records*. Manigault's report, although listed in the index, is missing.

[36] These figures are taken from Gen. Rosecrans' official reports of the battles of Stone's River and Chickamauga. *O.R.*, XX, pt. 1, 197; XXX, pt. 1, 62.

4

THE MIDDLE TENNESSEE

Or

TULLAHOMA CAMPAIGN

(Editor's Preface)

As the 3rd of January, 1863, drew to a close, the Army of Tennessee, in the rain, the cold and the pelting sleet, silently withdrew from its lines, turned southward and abandoned the field of Murfreesboro. Bloodied but far from beaten, it had inflicted on its more numerous opponent losses of between 13,000 and 14,000 men at a cost to itself of some 10,000 casualties, killed, wounded and missing.

Like two stags who had fought each other to exhaustion, each army, for the time being, was satisfied to leave the other alone. When Rosecrans awoke on the morning of the 4th, he was as surprised as he was delighted to find the Confederate army gone. Pursuit was out of the question, and the Southern columns, unopposed, wearily slogged their way south to the valley of the Duck River, where Polk's corps occupied Shelbyville on the left and Hardee's Wartrace on the right.

Bragg established his headquarters at Tullahoma below the river on the line of the Nashville & Chattanooga Railroad, the Confederate lifeline for supplies and reinforcements. Cavalry patrols were thrown westward to Columbia and eastward to McMinnville, a distance of some 70 miles. Here the army licked its wounds and began to reform and refit, a process at which Bragg was at his best.

All might have gone smoothly had he been willing to let well enough alone, but his conscience gnawed at him over the responsibility of ordering the retreat from Murfreesboro, and he was stung by the bitter criticisms levelled at him from all sides. A hardier soul would have brushed them aside, but not Braxton Bragg, who once again exhibited that weakness of character that limited his accomplishments. Showing a tragic lack of self-confidence, he made the mistake of addressing a communication on Jan. 11 to his corps commanders, Polk and Hardee, and two of his chief division commanders, Breckinridge and Cleburne, asking them, in order to save his fair name and hopefully stop the deluge of abuse that threatened to destroy his usefulness and demoralize the army, to consult their subordinates and attest in writing that they had been unanimous in verbally advising a withdrawal and thus get him off the hook. Had he dropped the matter there, he would have been on fairly safe ground. But he went on to say that Kirby Smith had "been called to Richmond, it is supposed, with a view to supercede me. I shall retire without a regret if I find I have lost the good opinion of my generals, upon whom I have ever relied as upon a foundation of rock."

If Bragg had any thoughts that the replies of his generals would set the matter at rest, he was in for a rude awakening. Far from quieting things down, his implied request for a vote of confidence opened a pandora's box. In varying degrees, they all indicated they had approved or acquiesced in the decision to retreat, but when it came to Bragg's capacity to lead the army, that was quite a different matter. Their statements were devastating.

Hardee, a soldier's soldier of even temperament and wide experience, wrote, "I feel that frankness compels me to say that the general officers, whose judgment you have invoked, are unanimous in their opinion that a change in the command of the army is necessary. In this opinion, I concur." And then, to soften the blow, he assured Bragg of his continued respect and consideration for the purity of his motives, his energy and personal character. And this from Cleburne: "I consulted with all my brigade commanders...and they unite with me in personal regard for yourself, in a high appreciation of your patriotism and gallantry, and in a conviction of your great capacity for organization, but at the same time they see, with regret, and it has also met my observation, that you do not possess the confidence of the army in other respects in that degree necessary to secure success."

Breckinridge, still smarting from the sacrifice of his division in the abortive attack on the Federal left Jan. 2, with a loss of 1,700 men and nothing to show for it, an attack Breckinridge himself had bitterly opposed, laid it on the line. "Acting with the candor you invoke (my brigade commanders) request me to say that, while they entertain the highest respect for your patriotism, it is their opinion that you do not possess the confidence of the army to an extent that will enable you to be useful as its commander. In this opinion I feel bound to state that I concur."

Polk, who was absent on leave at the time, was spared the embarassment of joining in this chorus of denunciation of his commander, although it was well known that, after the Kentucky campaign, he had urged the removal of Bragg and his replacement by Joseph E. Johnston. In any case, after returning from leave, he wrote Bragg asking for a clarification of the latter's letter of Jan. 11, and Bragg replied that he had really intended only to elicit comments as to what had transpired in regard to the retreat from Murfreesboro and that "the paragraph relating to my supercedure was only an expression of the feeling with which I would receive your replies should they prove that I had been misled in my construction of your opinion and advice" regarding the retreat. Under the circumstances, Polk remained silent, although he did send copies of the correspondence to President Davis and again urged that Bragg be transferred elsewhere and replaced by Johnston.

Even though Davis maintained that his confidence in Bragg was "unshaken," he admitted that if the latter were distrusted by his officers and his troops, a disaster might result. Accordingly, he ordered Johnston to look into the whole matter and report back. This put Johnston, as the logical successor to the command of the army, on the spot. Pointing out to Davis that it would be inconsistent with his personal honor to occupy that position, he nevertheless dutifully carried out his assignment. After an investigation of three weeks, he concluded that Bragg was entitled to praise for his skill as a commander at Murfreesboro and, in view of the spirit and condition of the troops, he recommended against his removal.

Apparently this did not fully reassure Davis, for on March 9 Johnston was ordered to direct Bragg to report to the War Department in Richmond and to assume command of the army himself. When Johnston arrived at Tullahoma, however, he found Bragg devastated by the critical illness of his wife and tactfully refrained from mentioning the War Department order. By the time Mrs. Bragg was out of the woods, Johnston himself fell ill and, perhaps with a sigh of relief, was declared unfit for active service. There the matter rested.

Despite the torrent of abuse that had been heaped on him, Bragg abandoned any idea of retiring "without a regret" and continued at his post, as contentious as ever, having learned little from the experience. His relations with his subordinates remained strained, and he even attempted to initiate an investigation of Polk for alleged failure to obey orders at Perryville, but, fortunately, his generals squelched it. That the army was able to function at all under such circumstances was a tribute to the spirit of the troops and the loyalty to the Southern cause of its generals, despite their lack of confidence in Bragg's capacity to command.

For the first six months of 1863, while Lee was routing Hooker at Chancellorsville and invading the North, the two Western armies remained in position at Murfreesboro and along the line of the Duck River, enjoying the longest period of inactivity they were to experience during the war. Rosecrans devoted his efforts to fortifying Murfreesboro as a future base of supply and building up the strength and efficiency of his cavalry, and Bragg was afforded an opportunity to apply his talents for administration, organization and discipline. The results spoke for themselves.

On March 30, Polk wrote to his wife: "I have today had a review of the whole corps for the benefit of President Davis, in the person of his aide-de-camp, Col. W. Preston Johnston...The troops looked very well and I never saw them march so well. My corps was never in better condition and is now about 20,000 strong...Johnston was highly pleased and very complimentary." Even Col. Fremantle, visiting the army from Britain, admitted that the troops "drilled tolerably well, and an advance in line was remarkably good," praise indeed from an adjutant of the Coldstream Guards. He further remarked, "the discipline in this army is the strictest in the Confederacy."

Yet all was not drill, drudgery and discipline. A succession of visitors, including, in addition to Fremantle, George St. Leger Grenfell, a flamboyant British soldier of fortune, and Clement Vallandigham, the well-known "Copperhead" congressman from Ohio, enlivened the monotony of camp life. Vallandigham had been banished by President Lincoln from the United States for disloyalty, and, after a brief stay at Bragg's headquarters, was sent to Wilmington, N.C., whence he ran the blockade and reached Canada. Bishop Quintard found Vallandigham a man "of remarkably fine features, a frank, open countenance, beautiful teeth and a color indicating very high health. He wore no side-whiskers nor moustache but a beard slightly tinged with grey, on his chin. In manner he was extremely easy and polite; conversation very fluent and entertaining. He was greatly pleased with the kind reception he had met from the officers of the army and the citizens of Shelbyville, but was very desirous of avoiding all public demonstration."

A remarkable character in his own right was the Rev. Charles Todd Quintard, M.D., chaplain of the First Tennessee Infantry and, after the war, second bishop of Tennessee. A mere wisp of a man, but of boundless energy and unshakable faith, he epitomized the part religion played in the lives of many of the soldiers and leaders of the Confederacy. Of Huguenot descent, he was born at Stamford, Conn., in 1824, took his master's degree at Columbia and graduated Doctor of Medicine at the University of the City of New York in 1847. After some years devoted to the practice of medicine, he became a candidate for Holy Orders, studied theology under the direction of Bishop Otey of Tennessee and was advanced to the priesthood. When the war broke out, he was rector of the Church of the Advent in Nashville. Ever loyal to the Confederacy and the righteousness of its cause, after his retirement as bishop of Tennessee, he served as vice-chancellor of the University of the South at Sewanee.

While there were many visitations to the army by bishops and other clergy and much preaching, there was still plenty of time left over for social activities on the part of the officers and the usual diversions of the rank and file, including, for the more adventurous and less righteously inclined, keno, cockfighting and whiskey. Army reviews, often attended by the ladies of the neighborhood, offered diversion, especially when they were accompanied by horse racing and other sports. Bishop-General Polk, in referring to one such occasion, wrote to this wife that the whole affair was quite gay and everybody seemed much pleased. He allowed that he was planning a similar event for his own corps the following week, but lest she be upset at the prospect of a bishop of the church sponsoring a horse race, he was careful to point out that that activity was to be turned over to Gen. Cheatham, a less inhibited individual, given at times to the bottle.

Broken only by the cavalry exploits of Van Dorn at Thompson's Station south of Franklin, Tenn., and Bedford Forrest's spectacular capture of Col. Streight and his command of some 1,800 troopers (Forrest had less than 500) between Gadsden, Ala., and Rome, Ga., the period of inaction at length drew to a close as Rosecrans began a series of maneuvers that forced Bragg to abandon Middle Tennessee in a virtually bloodless campaign, regarded by many as a strategic masterpiece of its kind.

Feinting heavily at the Confederate left at Shelbyville, the Northern commander, after forcing Hoover's and Liberty Gaps in the foothills separating the two armies, executed a sweeping movement around the Confederate right flank. As a result of John Morgan's ill-fated raid into Indiana and Ohio, during which he was captured, Bragg was short of cavalry to keep him informed and was misled by the demonstration against Shelbyville. Anticipating that the enemy would advance in a frontal attack against his center, he was unaware of the direction of Rosecrans' main thrust until it was too late. Before he knew it, Northern troops were on his flank and a detachment had cut the railroad in his rear.

With his communications at least temporarily severed, his position was critical and he appealed to Polk and Hardee for advice. While the latter procrastinated, Polk was adamant that the army must withdraw.

"Then," said Bragg, "you propose that we shall retreat?"

"I do," replied Polk, "and that is my counsel."

And so it was. With Forrest guarding the rear, the withdrawal began, continued across the Elk River and southeastward to the Cumberland Mountains, which were crossed at University Place, the seat of the future University of the South at Sewanee. From there, the army wended its way down to the Tennessee River and finally crossed it to Chattanooga.

Had it not been for the torrential rains that fell during the campaign and hindered the pursuit, Bragg might well have found himself cut off. The retreat, however, was successfully accomplished and the army saved to fight another day. Yet, even Bragg himself was under no illusions. Never robust, and now suffering from an onset of boils, he told Dr. Quintard just before crossing the mountains. "Yes, I am utterly broken down."

And then, leaning over his saddle, he whispered: "This is a great disaster."

R.L.T.

THE MIDDLE TENNESSEE

Or

TULLAHOMA CAMPAIGN

(The Narrative)

O n the afternoon of the 4th of January, the Army reached Shelbyville, 25 miles from Murfreesboro, remained there on the 5th. On the 6th and 7th, they continued the march towards the Tennessee River, but were halted on the evening of the last date at a place called Allisonia, a small village made up for the most part of the cottages and dwellings of the operatives attached to a large factory, situated on the Elk River.[1] The factory and many of the houses had been destroyed by the enemy four or five months before.

Here we remained on the 8th, and on the 9th retraced our steps to Shelbyville, which we reached on the following day, and went into camp about two miles from the town. Here we commenced immediately the construction of winter quarters, which were soon completed, and made ourselves as comfortable as the circumstances would allow.

During the remainder of January, and the months of February and March, the weather was exceedingly cold, raw, and disagreeable, confining us much to our tents and cabins. Frequent snowstorms occurred, covering everything for a week or more to the depth of many inches. Ice of considerable thickness was formed in the different water courses adjacent. Much rain fell at different times, overflowing the low lands adjacent to Duck River, which stream ran along the southern side of Shelbyville, at such times completely cutting off all communication with that place. In consequence of the inclemency of the weather and the extreme cold very little drilling or instruction could be imparted to the troops. It did not however interfere with our ordinary camp duties, or picket and outpost duty necessary for the safety of the army.

The army of General Rosecrans lay also in winter quarters in and around Murfreesboro. The Infantry outposts of each were generally distant from the respective towns from six to seven miles, the Cavalry two or three miles nearer. Each camp was protected in this way by successive cordons of sentinels.

Occasionally a reconnaissance by one or the other would be made, and a sharp engagement take place, and perhaps the line would be broken through at some point for a short time, but a timely re-inforcement would again set all things to rights. There being four Brigades in our Division[2] and the Division being entrusted with the protection of the army by one of the important avenues leading to our lines, known as the Triune Pike, our turn would come every fourth week for such duty. While so occupied, of course the work was comparatively hard, a third of the men being daily on duty, but upon the whole, I think it was of service to the Command — relieving the monotony of camp life, furnishing useful and valuable instruction to the men, keeping them on the alert and rubbing off the rust which otherwise would have resulted from a life of comparative inactivity. I always found that after a tour of this kind the health of the Brigade benefitted, and the spirits of the men improved. Up to this time we were exceedingly well provided by our subsistence department, and to a certain extent by the Quarter Masters also, excepting in the article of clothing, which could not be obtained in sufficient quantities, and in texture and warmth was entirely unsuited to the rough usage required of it, or to the severe cold of the climate.

Polk's Corps occuped Shelbyville, Hardee's occupied Tullahoma, the two separated from each other about 12 miles.[3]

The front of the Cavalry line of outposts covered a distance of from 60 to 65 miles. The line of the Infantry was, of course, much shorter, and they only took the precaution of guarding the roads, or such gaps as our security rendered necessary.[4]

As spring advanced, and the weather moderated, the country drying off and presenting a good surface, the regular drills, etc., were re-established, and no time was lost in perfecting ourselves in the school of the company and battalion, both as heavy and light Infantry, and in the evolutions of the line, and our progress was steady and satisfactory.[5]

Early in April, for the greater convenience of pasturage and obtaining forage, General Polk collected in an Artillery camp about five miles from Shelbyville, on the Louisburg Pike, all the light batteries of his Corps. Our Brigade was detached as a guard for their protection, and were located in a beautiful country and most delightful camp, where we enjoyed the gradual approach of a most charming spring. When fully ushered in, it was almost impossible to recognize in the fresh, green, and fertile country, the brown, bare hills and leafless forests with which we had been so long familiar.[6]

In this camp we remained about six weeks, when the Artillery was called in and we were ordered on outpost duty on the Triune and Columbia Pike, where we remained, with the exception of one interval of two weeks, until about the 20th of June. Keeping for so long a period on this duty was a great drawback in one respect to the Command. Our teams of mules, horses of the Brigade and battery, suffered much. Green food and pasturage at this season was very necessary for them, after the exposure to which they had been exposed during the past severe winter. Whilst on picket, to turn them out to graze was out of the question, as at all times it was necessary that they should be in such a position that everything could be geared up at a moment's notice. The consequence was that the stock of all the other Brigades had a great advantage over ours, and were in much better condition for the long march, with heavy loads, over the bad roads, that was soon to take place. Our wagons also were much out of order and the necessary repairs could not be done to them.

After being relieved on the 20th, we occupied a new camp on the right bank of the Duck River, and large details were made daily for fatigue duty on breastworks and batteries with which Shelbyville was being encircled. An advance of the Yankee army was now looked for daily. Rumours and indications of an early recommencement of hostilities were of daily occurrence.

On the 25th and 26th, accounts reached us of fighting taking place at Hoover's Gap, and at another important point on our lines in front of Tullahoma.[7] On the morning of the 26th, we learned that the enemy had possession of both these points, and that the entire Yankee army was moving upon Tullahoma, situated on the Chattanooga & Nashville R.R. That place was seriously threatened, and General Bragg, believing that at that point the enemy intended to strike, ordered Polk's Command to move rapidly to the assistance of Hardee.[8]

On the morning of the 27th of June, at daylight, the troops evacuated Shelbyville and moved towards Tullahoma, reaching it about dark on the same evening. The enemy at that time had not shown themselves there, although sharp skirmishing had been going on about 8 or 9 miles in advance of it.

General Wheeler, commanding the Cavalry, had been left at Shelby-ville to protect our rear, and to hold as long as possible, or until all of the public property and army stores had been removed. At about 12 M. the same day, heavy columns of Federal Cavalry showed themselves in his front, and shortly afterwards commenced an attack on him. For some time he resisted successfully, but finally a considerable body succeeded in getting around his right flank. From some carelessness also the arms of the Cavalry, having been exposed to the heavy rains of the two preceding days, and no inspections having been made of them — a piece of carelessness habitual in this branch of the service — could not be made to fire. A panic soon seized upon the men, and in a short time a complete rout was the consequence. Many were killed and captured, and General Wheeler only succeeded in saving what was left of his command by swimming the Duck River. Several pieces of horse Artillery were also captured, and the engagement was disastrous in the extreme.[9]

This command, never very remarkable for efficiency or discipline, but who had always had a certain degree of confidence in themselves, and believed themselves superior to the enemy's Cavalry, lost all their previous prestige and never afterwards recovered it, but deteriorated steadily from that day. Occasionally at subsequent periods they would conduct themselves in a bold and dashing manner, apparently giving promise of a return to their old position of superiority, but they would fall back again, losing what they had temporarily gained, and becoming, if possible, more inefficient than ever.[10]

On the 28th, the Division remained in bivouac, the purposes of the enemy apparently undeveloped. On the 29th, about sunrise, I received an order to form the Brigade and to move rapidly to the front, as the enemy was reported moving on us and within two miles. Marching quickly, in a short time we reached some hastily constructed breastworks about a mile to the north of the village. Here the other Brigades, as well as the greater part of the Corps, soon joined us, and we fell to work strengthening and improving our defenses.

Sharp firing was going on apparently about two miles in our front, and to our right, our Cavalry and that of the enemy being engaged, our own skirmish line about a half-mile in front of us unemployed, although the Infantry of the enemy was said to be steadily advancing. This state of things lasted all day, and during the earlier part of the afternoon of the 30th, after which time the firing slackened, and finally ceased entirely. We soon learned that the enemy had merely been covering their movement to our right by threatening an attack, and that several corps had then reached or were passing our right flank and moving to our rear, evidently with a view to cutting us off from our line of retreat and base of supplies at Chattanooga.[11]

Orders to move in a short time followed this information, and at sunset the route was taken up towards Allisonia, on the Elk River, a very important and strong position, which it was very desirable that we should secure. Tullahoma was evacuated and I believe a considerable amount of supplies of various kinds were there destroyed or abandoned. Marching the entire night, over the most execrable roads, a distance of 18 miles, we reached Allisonia about 7 o'clock the following morning. Other troops had arrived before us, and the position was secure. Here we remained on the 1st of July, the enemy feeling his way towards us, principally with Cavalry. Their General, finding that he could not cut us off from this point and not daring to atack us, as strongly situated as we were, still endeavored to deceive us, whilst passing still further to our right, hoping to intercept us before we could reach the Cumberland Mountains, and trusting to our not finding out his strategy. The roads leading over this high ridge of mountains are few in number and at a great distance apart. Should he succeed in gaining possession of the one for which we were making, a comparatively small force might keep us at bay, whilst the remainder of their army, making for the Tennessee River, would cross and capture Chattanooga, thereby destroying our communications with the most important portions of the Confederacy, having Georgia and N. Alabama at their mercy, besides cutting us off in a comparatively poor and already devastated country, from which we could only have extricated ourselves after much suffering and heavy losses both in men and material.[12]

On the morning of the second, General Bragg began falling back towards the mountains, reaching the foot of them that evening, and our trains immediately commenced the ascent. During the night, after much labor and anxiety, they all passed over, and before day, most of the troops had also begun to ascend. Marching all day, we reached within six miles of the Tennessee River, after a march of some 30 miles, and there went into camp.

After leaving Allisonia, our Cavalry remaining in rear to keep back the enemy, assisted by one or two brigades of Infantry, an attack was made, which resulted in a complete repulse of the Yankees, with heavy losses to them and only a trifling one to our forces engaged. The place was abandoned soon after, and although the enemy followed, they did not again make any serious attack upon our rear guard.

The army crossed the Tennessee River on the 4th of July, a pontoon bridge having been laid down for that purpose, near *(Battle)* Creek, and about six miles above Bridgeport, the last 12 miles of our march being through the *(Battle Creek)* Valley. On the same evening we reached the Nickagack Cave, and encamped a little beyond it, near to *(Shellmound)* Station, on the Nashville & Chattanooga R.R. The following day we reached Whitesides Station, and the day after, July 6th, Chattanooga. From the moment of our leaving Shelbyville, we had nothing but hard marching, and a most fatiguing time of it, in the construction of breastworks, etc. The weather was very warm, and much rain fell. The consequence was that the roads were in a wretched condition, and after the passage over them of some 2,000 wagons and over 100 guns, with their caissons, forges, etc., they became almost impossible. Many wagons broke down and had to be abandoned with their contents. In my own Brigade, we lost five, and many mules, owing partially to our being for some time previous to our leaving Shelbyville on outpost duty, where it was impossible to give them the thorough overhauling they required, and the bad condition of our mules, caused by it being necessary to keep them in constant readiness in case of attack.

General Bragg had succeeded in securing the two important roads over the Cumberland Mountains before the enemy could do so, and thus made good his retreat and the safety of Chattanooga, and on the mountains he could have bid defiance to the Yankee army, but as there still lay other roads to his right and left, between which there was no communication through the mountains, or at least such as an army could make use of, and the mountainous ridges reached almost to the river, the enemy having the advantage of a more level and practicable country on their side, could by concealing their movements and passing far to our right, get into our rear, threaten and capture Chattanooga before we could prevent it.

It was his policy, therefore, to retire to that place, and put the Tennessee River between himself and the Federal army. Having declined to fight, he could not well do otherwise than take up the position he did, the convenience and advantage of it being very great. I have never been able to learn why it was that no battle was fought during this short campaign. Certainly at Tullahoma it appeared to be the intention of our General to receive the attack of the enemy, should he make one, and after finding out that it was not their intention to do so, as it turned out he had time to place himself across the path of the Federal commander, and force him either to fight or to retire. This he did not do. Why, I do not know, but can only conjecture that he did not regard himself as sufficiently strong to resist, and that success was too doubtful under the circumstances to render a battle advisable or prudent, or that owing to the inferiority of our cavalry, or their inability or failure to furnish him information, he remained in ignorance of the enemy's movements or plans, until it was too late to check or prevent them, or to take such steps as under other circumstances and with more general information he would have done. It often appeared to me that many of our failures or misfortunes arose from our lamentable deficiency in this branch of the service.[13]

Of course my opportunities of forming an opinion on this and many other subjects, owing to my comparatively humble position in the army, were necessarily limited, but such are my impressions, and in which I was by no means singular, many others making the same observations. On many occasions, when exercising an independent and separate command, I found as a general rule that the reports brought me by the cavalry were for the most part unreliable and incorrect.

I must, however, say for General Forrest and his Command of whom at a later date we had an opportunity of seeing much, that the remarks made above ought not to apply to them. As a Cavalry leader, for such troops as were so called in our Confederate Armies, he was by far the most able and combined many qualities, such as skill, courage, judgment, and the power of organizing and disciplining troops, which would have made him conspicuous anywhere. His defective education and social disadvantages were his great drawbacks. Had he been more fortunate in these respects, he would in all probability have been the most conspicuous and useful general in the Army of the Confederate States.[14]

This campaign of General Rosecrans, lasting not more than two weeks, was, I think, the most brilliant of the war, and although no battle was fought, his skillful maneuvering of Bragg out of Tennessee (for although Chattanooga and a strip of the state along the river, as well as East Tennessee, were still in our possession, yet all the most fertile and more wealthy portion of the state was lost to us), even though he never before or afterwards did anything, ought to stamp him as an able general. His army at the time was supposed to be from 70,000 to 75,000 men. The army of General Bragg could not have exceeded 38,000 men, all told, but in fine health and training and reasonably well supplied.[15]

After reaching Chattanooga, and it appearing that the enemy had halted and did not for the present intend to push their successes any further, the Army of Tennessee went into permanent camps, and the usual duties of camp life recommenced. The climate was very pleasant, though very hot during the day. The nights were cool and refreshing. By this time there were very few tents in use amongst the men, and but few officers were allowed them. In lieu of them, the men protected themselves with brush arbors, an old blanket, oil cloth, or piece of a fly, serving as a roof to keep the rain out. The health of the army was good. The delicate and infirm had become pretty well weeded out, and only the hardiest and more robust, now thoroughly inured to all the exposure and hardships of a soldier's life in the field, filled the ranks. It was impossible to behold their physical condition and development, and their ruddy cheeks browned by exposure, without a feeling of admiration and satisfaction. As a regiment or brigade would pass on its way to or from some tour of duty; its intervals well closed; the men marching with the ease, good order, and steady, swinging stride peculiar to the "Army of

Tennessee"; in high spirits, and with the greatest good humor laughing and jesting with each other; rather rusty looking, however, with shoes and clothing much the worse for wear, the involuntary exclamation would arise, "What splendid condition! What hardihood! Nothing but bone, sinew, and muscle! Not a pound too much of flesh. How cheerful they all seem! Can those men be beaten? Will they not prove irresistible? In the just cause in which they are fighting, can anyone doubt the issue?"

And then perhaps a sad train of thought would take the place of exultation. "Alas! how many of those brave fellows are destined to a short career! Possibly in a few months or weeks their bodies may fill a bloody grave, or, denied the right of sepulture, their bones ere long lie bleaching on some hard-fought battlefield, or lingering, torn and mangled, in some wayside hospital, far from their homes, the thoughts of which come thick and fast as life slowly ebbs away, no gentle heart or kind hand to soothe their way to the "Dark Valley". "How many hearts, too, yearning in their dreary homes for the loved ones, already apprehensive of the coming tidings of woe, too soon to be fulfilled!" As I write, my memory fills with the well-remembered forms and features of many friends and comrades, passed away, gone to their last, long homes, their work on earth finished, their duty done, their lives given, a willing sacrifice for country, and by her almost already forgotten in the ill success of a "Lost Cause", but still enshrined in the hearts of bereaved parents and loving wives, who now live in the memory of the past.

On the 25th of July, Mary and my son, Arthur,[16] arrived at our camp, having come to pay me a visit for a month or two, provided the enemy did not run them away sooner. We had been separated very nearly eighteen months, and our reunion was, as may be supposed, a most happy one. They spent all of the time in camp sleeping in tents.

General Withers, at his own request, was about the same time relieved of his command, his health failing, and too delicate to undergo the privations and exposure attendant upon an army in the field. We parted from him with regret, for although during our earlier connection with him, he was not only personally unpopular, but very little confidence also was felt in his military ability, he had latterly changed and improved very much, and had on several occasions shown much skill and good judgment, and was now regarded by his command with affection and much good-will, and as an officer he was thought well of, in spite of general mistakes which at an earlier period he had committed.[17]

Major General Hindman was assigned to the command of our Division, and the change was truly an unfortunate one for us. He had been a member of Congress from the State of Arkansas, was a secessionist, and at the commencement of hostilities had raised a regiment. As a Colonel and Brigadier, he had made some reputation, and previous to his joining us, he had held some important commands. He had the reputation of being a desperate fighter, good disciplinarian, but a scheming, maneuvering, political general, with whom it was dangerous to come in contact. Morally, he stood deservedly low in the opinions of most of the officers of the Army, but he was certainly a man of talent, and the cunningest, most slippery intriguer that I ever met with.[18] Our Division, from being the first in point of numbers, drill, efficiency and discipline, in the whole Army, under his administration, which lasted about a year, sank to that of a third-rate one. His senior Brigadier, Patton Anderson, also had much to do with its deterioration.

Shortly after our arrival at Chattanooga, my long looked-for commission of Brigadier General in the Army of the Confederate States, was received, dated several months before, (26 April, 1863). I was immediately in general orders, and assigned the old Brigade.[19] Its organization was as follows:

A.M.M.	Brig. Gen'l Comdg.
C. Irvine Walker	Capt. & A.A.G., late A.A.A.G. & Adj. 10 S.C.
Dan'l E. Huger	'' & A. & Inspector Gen'l. Had held the same position since the organization of the Brigade.
Wm. E. Huger	Lieut. & A.D.C., late Actg. A.D.C. & Sergt. Maj. 10th S.C.
S.C. Muldon	Maj. & A.Q.M., late Quarter Master, 24th Ala.
Henry Hawkins	Maj. & Surgeon, of Brigade, from Arkansas.
S.E. Lucas	'' '' A.C.S., late Lieut. 10th S.C.
Jos. Johnson	Lieut. and Ordnance Officer.

34th Alabama Reg't — Col. J.C.B. Mitchell
28th   ''   ''   — Col. J.C. Reid
24th   ''   ''   — Col. J.N. Davis
10th S.C. Reg't — Col. J.F. Pressley
19th ''   ''   — Col. Thomas Shaw
Water's Battery of Artillery — Capt. D. Waters
These Regiments were consolidated:
10th and 19th — Col. Pressley
24th and 28th — Col. Reid

The effective strength of the Brigade at this time was about 2,400 men, including litter bearers and cooks, but exclusive of officers, and it was one of the strongest in the Army.

Its strength, present and absent, was about 3,200 men, which included many who were absent without leave, such as were on furlough, and detailed men, of whom there were an unusually large number. The largest number that we ever reported, Total Aggregate, was 3,800, whilst in Mississippi, but at no time did our reports ever show a "Total effective, present for duty", exceeding 2,525 men, and at that time there were about 175 men sick in camp.

The condition of the command at this period was excellent. The sick list averaged about 2 to 2½%, and the cases of indisposition were of a trifling character. Our transportation was fair, and the equipment otherwise quite satisfactory.

NOTES TO CHAPTER 4

[1] This factory was evidently Emory's, located on the north side of the river.

[2] Commanded by Brig. Gens. Z.C. Deas, E.C. Walthall, Patton Anderson and Col. A.M. Manigault. The latter's brigade, it will be recalled, consisted of two South Carolina regiments and three from Alabama. Deas' troops were from Alabama, Walthall's and Patton Anderson's from Mississippi.

[3] For some six months, Polk's corps was encamped in the vicinity of Shelbyville. Hardee's corps, constituting the right wing, was based on Wartrace. Bragg's headquarters were at Tullahoma.

[4] Ably led by "Fighting Joe" Wheeler, now a major general, Bragg's cavalry was both numerous and efficient. In the tri-monthly return of the Army of Tennessee dated April 20, 1863, Wheeler's cavalry corps showed more than 9,000 officers and men present for duty. *O.R., XXIII, pt. 2, 779.*

[5] This was Braxton Bragg at his best.

[6] May 26, Dr. Quintard visited Manigault's brigade with Bishop Elliott of Georgia. In his memoirs, he described the occasion: "On Tuesday I was very unwell but felt it my duty to drive six miles to the front and visit, with the Bishop, the Brigade of General Manigault of South Carolina. He was on outpost duty and only a few miles from the pickets of General Rosecrans' army. The service was at five o'clock. The whole brigade was in attendance, having been marched to the grove arranged for the service under arms...The Bishop preached to the assembled officers and soldiers seated on the ground in concentric circles. It was an admirable extempore discourse which fell with great effect upon the hearts of all who heard it." Arthur H. Noll (ed.), *Doctor Quintard, Chaplain C.S.A. and Second Bishop of Tennessee,* (Sewanee, Tenn., 1905), 74-75. Hereafter cited as *Quintard.*

[7] Liberty Gap. Hardee's corps had been moved to support the outposts at the gaps through which the roads from Murfreesboro ran.

[8] On the 26th, Bragg had ordered Polk to advance his corps though Guy's Gap north of Shelbyville and assail the forces pressing Hardee at Liberty Gap. Polk considered the move imprudent. It was abandoned when Bragg learned that his right was being turned in the direction of Manchester to the northeast of Tullahoma and ordered Polk and Hardee to concentrate at the latter place. *Polk,* II, 211.

[9] Manigault's disdain for the lack of discipline in the mounted branch of the service is here evident, as, indeed, it is throughout his memoirs. In this instance, Wheeler's command was scattered and he was opposing, with only some 1,000 effectives, an overwhelming enemy force of cavalry supported by infantry. His

troopers were routed in this, the Battle of Shelbyville, and driven across the Duck River, but his personal courage displayed throughout the running fight and in his escape across the river was praised by both sides. Captured by the Northern troops when Wheeler was driven from Shelbyville were 3,000 sacks of corn and corn meal, a few animals and a quantity of meat, whiskey, ammunition and small arms. In his report, Maj. Gen. Gordon Granger, who was in overall command of the Federal forces engaged, put the Confederate loss at 200 to 250 killed, wounded and drowned, 600 to 700 prisoners and three pieces of artillery, at a cost of about 50 killed and wounded. As was so often the case, Southern accounts differ radically. They put Wheeler's casualties at 380 and those of the enemy at "over 500." *Wheeler and his Cavalry,* 85-95; *O.R.,* XXIII, pt. 1, 537; John A. Wyeth, *With Sabre and Scalpel,* (New York, 1914), 219-222.

[10] As an infantryman and strict disciplinarián, Manigault may be pardoned for a somewhat overdrawn censure of Wheeler and his cavalry. Wheeler was not pursued after crossing the river and continued, with considerable success, to guard Bragg's rear during the retreat from Middle Tennessee. Nevertheless, the end of the marked superiority of the Southern horse in the Western theatre may be dated from approximately this time. Gen. Granger, in praising the bold and gallant conduct of the Northern cavalry in this engagement, said: "The efficiency of this branch of the service...has been established beyond a doubt. The enemy can no longer boast of the superiority of their cavalry and its accomplishments." And Col. McCook of the Second Indiana Cavalry called Shelbyville "the most gallant and successful cavalry affair of the war," a pardonable exaggeration. *O.R.,* XXIII, pt. 1, 535-537, 548.

[11] By a heavy demonstration in front of Shelbyville, Rosecrans had successfully misled Bragg, who had left his right flank exposed. Taking advantage of this, the Northern commander, in a masterful exhibition of strategy, turned Bragg's right, temporarily cutting the railroad in his rear near Decherd and forcing the retreat of the Army of Tennessee to Chattanooga.

[12] These considerations, virtually point by point, formed the basis of Polk's argument, when he urged Bragg on the 29th to retreat before he was cut off. *Polk,* II, 213.

[13] Bragg had, on June 29, determined to give the enemy battle at Tullahoma. Gen. Polk, however, as already indicated, thought this decision an injudicious one under the circumstances and had so informed Hardee. The two of them went to headquarters about 3 p.m. for a conference at which were present Bragg, Gen. Mackall, his chief of staff, and Col. Urquhart, his military secretary. In response to a request from Bragg for his counsel, Polk said that he expected the enemy to seize and hold the army's communications, in which event the Southern forces would be as effectually besieged as Pemberton at Vicksburg, with their sources of supply cut off. He advised retreat, and, although Hardee equivocated, Bragg accepted Polk's advice and the withdrawal of the army began the next day. (*O.R.,* XXIII, pt. 1, 621-622). On July 3, Bragg wrote Johnston that he had offered the enemy battle prior to Tullahoma and that at the latter place, "having failed to bring him to that issue, so much desired by myself and troops, I reluctantly yielded to the necessity imposed by my position and inferior strength, and put the army in motion for the Tennessee River." The plain fact of the matter was that Bragg had been outgeneraled. *O.R.,* XXIII, pt. 1, 584.

[14] Nathan Bedford Forrest, a small planter and slave trader in Tennessee before the war, was a self-made cavalry genius possessing to a high degree the very

qualities of initiative, decision and daring that Bragg so sorely lacked.

[15] The return for July 10, with the Army of Tennessee back in Chattanooga, showed an effective total present of 38,313. Manigault's estimate of the size of the Federal army closely approximates the number of troops reported present for duty in the field. *O.R.,* XXIII, pt. 1, 410-411, 585-586.

[16] Five children were born to Gen. Manigault and his wife, Mary Proctor Huger. The eldest, Carolina Huger, died in infancy, so that at the time mentioned their only child was their son, Arthur M., born in 1851. After the war, they had two additional sons and a daughter — Daniel Elliott Huger (1866), namesake of his mother's brother killed at Chickamauga, Stephen Huger (1868) and Mary Huger (1870).

[17] Although he was a West Point graduate, class of 1835, and had served in the Creek uprising and the war with Mexico, Withers had spent most of his life prior to 1861 in business and political pursuits in Mobile. Following his relief from active service with the Army of Tennessee, he was in charge of the reserve forces of Alabama until the close of the war. *Generals in Gray,* 342-343.

[18] Prior to taking command of the division of which Manigault's brigade was a part, Maj. Gen. Thomas C. Hindman had commanded the Trans-Mississippi Department until relieved by Theophilus Holmes, a deaf and rather stubborn individual whose limitations were overlooked as he was one of Jefferson Davis' favorites. In 1868, Hindman was assassinated by an unidentified assailant in his home at Helena, Ark., possibly for political reasons. *Ibid.,* 137-138.

[19] It will be recalled that Manigault had been nominated by the President for promotion to brigadier general April 30, 1863 (the date of his commission), and confirmed by the Senate on the same day. No explanation has been found why — or even how — his promotion could have been pigeonholed for the better part of three months.

5

CHICKAMAUGA

(Editor's Preface)

Outmaneuvered by Rosecrans and compelled to abandon mid and south Tennessee, Bragg withdrew his weary and dispirited troops south of the Tennessee River and posted them guarding the fords and crossings up and downstream from Chattanooga. The latter became his main base, supplied from Atlanta to the southeast by the Western and Atlantic Railroad. The men complained of mid-summer heat and the scarcity of rations, the chief item of which was parched corn. But they chiefly grumbled at their idleness and the failure of their commander to bring the enemy to battle.

Uncertain of his next move, Bragg appealed to the War Department in Richmond for instructions, but Richmond was preoccupied with the disastrous campaigns of Gettysburg in the East and Vicksburg in the West and for the time being he was largely ignored. At length, a discussion was had regarding the possibility of reinforcing him from Johnston in Mississippi and Buckner at Knoxville to enable his army to invade Tennessee once more. Bragg blew hot and blew cold, however, and in the end, his caution prevailing, resigned himself to the defensive, a position with which Davis declined to interfere on the basis that the final decision should be left to the commanding general on the spot.

An understanding of the Chickamauga campaign and the part played in it by Manigault's brigade requires a look at the map* and at least a rudimentary knowledge of the geographical and topographical features of the region.

From its headwaters above Knoxville, the Tennessee River flows in a southwesterly direction into the northeast corner of Alabama. Chattanooga, an important railroad junction, is located on its southern bank, where the river follows its meandering course a few miles north of the Georgia-Tennessee border.

To the south and east of the river, the rugged country is divided by a series of ridges or mountains, rising at their highest point to some 3,000 feet and extending southward like the fingers of a hand, separated by valleys in which the creeks flow in a generally north or northeasterly

See Page 84 — Editor.

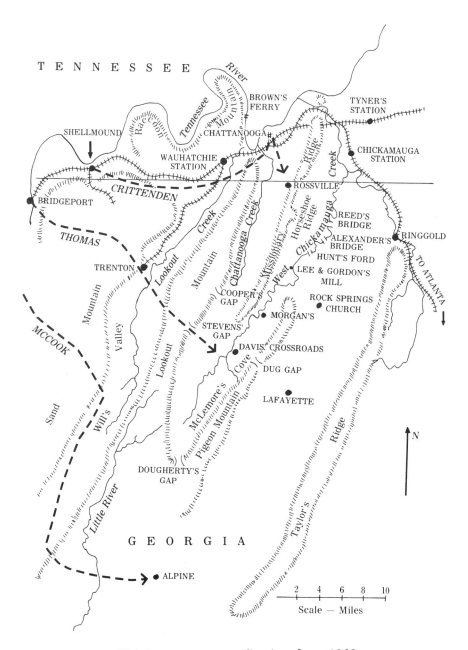

TENNESSEE

River

Tennessee

BROWN'S
FERRY

TYNER'S
STATION

SHELLMOUND

CHATTANOOGA

CHICKAMAUGA
STATION

WAUHATCHIE
STATION

Raccoon
Mountain

Mountain

CRITTENDEN

ROSSVILLE

Ridge

Chickamauga Creek

BRIDGEPORT

THOMAS

Creek

REED'S
BRIDGE

Horseshoe
Ridge

RINGGOLD

TRENTON

Lookout

Mountain

Chattanooga Creek

Missionary Ridge

West Chickamauga

ALEXANDER'S
BRIDGE

HUNT'S FORD

LEE & GORDON'S
MILL

TO ATLANTA

Mountain

COOPER'S
GAP

ROCK SPRINGS
CHURCH

MCCOOK

Valley

Lookout

STEVENS'
GAP

MORGAN'S

DAVIS' CROSSROADS

Sand

Will's

Cove

DUG GAP

McLemore's

LAFAYETTE

Little River

Pigeon Mountain

N

DOUGHERTY'S
GAP

Taylor's Ridge

GEORGIA

ALPINE

2   4   6   8   10

Scale — Miles

Chickamauga — September 1863

direction, emptying into the Tennessee. From the river itself, as it flows southwestward into northern Alabama, one encounters from west to east: Sand Mountain (and its northern spur, Raccoon); Will's Valley containing Lookout Creek; Lookout Mountain; Chattanooga Creek; Missionary Ridge; and, finally, Chickamauga Creek. The headwaters of the latter rise in McLemore's Cove, a natural cul-de-sac formed on the east by Pigeon Mountain, which juts out in a northeasterly direction from Lookout on the west. McLemore's Cove is some 45 miles south of Chattanooga.

This formidable country, penetrated only by rough and narrow roads that crossed the mountains in a series of gaps, caused Bragg to complain to Hill, "Mountains hide your foe from you, while they are full of gaps through which he can pounce on you at any time. A mountain is like the wall of a house full of rat holes. The rat lies hidden at his hole, ready to pop out when no one is watching. Who can tell what lies behind that wall?" Apparently it didn't occur to Bragg that it was up to him to find out.

By early September, the Army of Tennessee had been strengthened substantially. From Johnston's troops in Mississippi had come Breckinridge's division and W.H.T. Walker's small corps, amounting between them to some 9,000 men. Subsequently, the brigades of Gregg and McNair, totaling about 2,500, were added. Buckner, with roughly 8,000, had abandoned Knoxville and also joined Bragg from the east. In addition, two divisions of the redoubtable Army of Northern Virginia, about 6,000 men, were on the way under the command of Lee's "old war horse," Lt. Gen. James Longstreet.

All of them would be needed soon, for Rosecrans had thrown his three corps across the Tennessee near Bridgeport, Ala., and at Caperton's Ferry below Chattanooga.

Leaving Crittenden to watch the city, Rosecrans had dispatched McCook in a wide swing up Will's Valley to the south and east toward Alpine in order to threaten Bragg's communications with Atlanta. Under the misapprehension that the Confederates were in full retreat down the railroad toward Atlanta — an impression Bragg had done his best to foster through judiciously placed "deserters" — Rosecrans ordered Thomas, with his remaining corps, to cross the mountains from west to east and strike the supposedly withdrawing Army of Tennessee in the flank near Lafayette.

Thus Rosecrans had scattered his forces over a front of some 50 miles, with his three corps widely separated from one another. In the words of Gen. Turchin, one of Thomas' brigade commanders, "Seldom in the annals of warfare has such a magnificent opportunity been presented to completely defeat the opposing force in detail as that which was now offered to the rebel general Bragg."

When Thomas pushed his lead divisions, Negley's and Baird's, into McLemore's Cove, surrounded by sheer mountain walls and accessible only by widely scattered, narrow country roads, Bragg, who had concentrated his troops near Lafayette, got his first great opportunity to cripple his reckless adversary. He moved to seize it by directing Hindman's division, of which Manigault's brigade was a part, to march south up the headwaters of Chickamauga Creek and bottle up and attack Thomas's isolated divisions from the north. Hindman was to be supported by Cleburne's division, which was holding the gaps in Pigeon Mountain, which confronted Thomas's men on the east side of the Cove.

But then, as they often did when Bragg undertook to carry out his plans, things began to go wrong. Gen. Hill, Cleburne's corps commander, told Bragg that Cleburne was sick, that some of his best troops were absent, that the roads through the gaps in Pigeon Mountain were blocked by felled timber and that Bragg's orders could not be complied with. Thereupon, the latter told Buckner to follow Hindman and support him in Cleburne's stead. Despite his best efforts, however, Buckner was unable to get his men up and in position until it was too late that afternoon to accomplish anything and the day was wasted.

Early on the morrow, having cleared the roads, Cleburne was finally ready to join from the east in Hindman's attack, but now the latter hesitated, unable to comprehend Bragg's orders received during the night. A political general from Arkansas for whom Manigault had little use, Hindman, lacking experience in independent command, became confused and took the whole morning to advance less than four miles. Then, when he at last joined Cleburne and Hill, and finally Bragg himself, a misunderstanding arose as to who should attack first, with the result that neither Hindman nor Cleburne did, save for a skirmish late in the day. The upshot of all this was that Negley and Baird were given warning and ample time to escape from impending destruction or capture. In his biography of Forrest, Wyeth summed it up. "Any student of the art of war," he wrote, "desiring to learn how badly a bit of strategy may be spoiled, is referred to the official record of this affair."

As a result of inadequate information, ambiguous orders and the lack of a firm hand at the critical moment, Bragg had failed once more to answer when fortune knocked at his door. Thus, to the missed opportunity to bring Buell to battle following the capture of the garrison at Munfordville, when his army was squarely across the latter's line of communication, and his failure to follow up the first day's victory at Perryville after he had been joined by Kirby Smith's army, was added another bitter disappointment when Bragg bungled the attack in McLemore's Cove. His first great opening of the Chickamauga campaign had come and gone.

While Bragg was bombarding Hindman in McLemore's Cove with messages, he further upset that harrassed individual by telling him to finish up as quickly as possible, as Crittenden was rapidly advancing from the north. In fact, the latter, who had occupied Chattanooga Sept. 9, the day after Bragg's withdrawal to Lafayette, far from threatening attack, was proceeding deliberately after Bragg's supposedly retreating army. Two of Crittenden's divisions were near Ringgold, and the third was at Lee and Gordon's Mill on the west bank of Chickamauga Creek. Thus, not only was his corps divided, but Bragg stood squarely between him and Thomas at McLemore's Cove and in a position, with his cavalry, to cut off Crittenden's retreat if the latter should attempt to withdraw.

Instead of moving to develop this new opportunity, Bragg now started worrying about McCook, who, in reality, was completely out of the picture at Alpine some 25 air miles to the south and much farther by road. By the time Bragg realized that McCook was not such a threat after all and turned his attention to Crittenden, it was too late. The latter, taking advantage of the delay, had concentrated his corps at Lee and Gordon's Mill. Thus it transpired that when Polk, to whom Hindman had been returned, moved to attack what Bragg had told him were the two divisions of Crittenden marching from Ringgold, he found no enemy in his front.

Even with Crittenden's entire corps safely at the mill, it was still in a vulnerable spot and substantially outnumbered by the 25,000 Confederate troops concentrated nearby or within call. But Bragg started worrying about McCook again, lost his nerve and returned to Lafayette, where the army lay inactive for four days. It was the same old story all over again, — faulty information, indecision, and lack of energy and daring at the critical moment. Bragg had now failed twice when the chips were down.

Rosecrans, finally realizing that Bragg was not retreating after all, called up McCook from the south and concentrated his army on the west bank of Chickamauga Creek, with his left at Lee and Gordon's Mill and his line extending through McLemore's Cove to Steven's Gap on Lookout Mountain on his right. Bragg moved up from Lafayette and placed his left at the Cove, center at Lee and Gordon's Mill and his right at Reed's Bridge to the north. Thus, the two adversaries at last faced each other in full strength. It had been an extraordinary campaign. By good fortune and the shortcomings of his opponent, Rosecrans had escaped paying the penalty for the dispersal of his army. Now the moment of decision was at hand.

As was usually the case, Bragg's plan for the impending battle was strategically sound. It was, in broad outline, to throw his right across the Chickamauga downstream (i.e., to the north), cut off Rosecrans from his main line of retreat to Chattanooga and sweep southward up the west bank, driving the Federal army into McLemore's Cove where it could be cut to pieces or captured. Fearing just such an envelopment, Rosecrans countered by sliding his army to the left until it actually overlapped Bragg's right.

All the same, Bragg persisted and on the 19th of September heavy but indecisive fighting erupted between the Confederate right wing and the Federal Left under Thomas. As Harvey Hill was later to remark: "It was the sparring of an amateur boxer and not the crushing blows of the trained pugilist." On this day, Manigault's brigade was at Lee and Gordon's Mill, demonstrating, but not engaged in heavy hostilities.

That night, risking a change of organization in the face of the enemy, the Southern commander divided his forces into a right wing under Polk, consisting of Hill's and Walker's corps plus Cheatham's division, and a left wing commanded by Longstreet, freshly arrived that day from Virginia, made up of Buckner's and Hood's corps and Hindman's division.

It was Bragg's decision to renew the battle at daylight on the 20th, assaulting by division successively from right to left, but the failure of Polk's courier to find Hill during the night with the order to begin the attack held things up all along the line. Breckinridge of Hill's corps was on the extreme right, and the other divisions to his left were waiting for the sound of his guns before going into action. Seeking once more for a scapegoat on whom to throw the blame, Bragg, furious at the delay, angrily told Hill that he had "found Polk after sunrise sitting down reading a newspaper at Alexander's Bridge, two miles from the line of battle, when he ought to have been fighting." Stoutly denied by Polk, the charge was never proved.

Whether, in fact, this delay was of critical importance is a moot point. Hill maintained that the time was needed to make essential preparations for battle, readjust the Confederate line and get Breckinridge into position. In any case, when the attack finally was launched against Thomas at 9:30 a.m., it was delivered, in Hill's words, "with unsurpassed and unsurpassable valor," Breckinridge and Cleburne hurling their men against four divisions of the enemy protected by breastworks. Although the attack was finally repulsed with heavy loss, Thomas, alarmed for the safety of the Federal left, began crying for reinforcements and Rosecrans responded by weakening his right, a process which, in time, was to lead to his undoing.

When, in compliance with an order Rosecrans maintained was misinterpreted, Wood's division was pulled out of the line on the Union right, a hole was created in the Federal front just as Longstreet threw forward Hood's eight brigades in three lines. This impetuous assault struck the gap in Rosecrans' front at the critical moment, and Longstreet's victorious troops swept irresistibly onward. In one of the great charges of the war, the Federal front was torn wide open and Longstreet, quick to seize the opportunity, disregarded orders to bear to the left and, instead, wheeled to the right, taking the Federal right wing in reverse. There was no stopping his exultant troops. Sensing victory, they drove ahead, smashed five of McCook's brigades, as well as two of Crittenden's, and forced them into wild retreat along the Dry Valley Road to McFarland's Gap and on to Chattanooga. His headquarters captured, Rosecrans joined the fugitives in their flight.

Thomas, witnessing the collapse of the Federal right, moved to stave off complete disaster by establishing, with the remaining troops capable of resistance (shortly to be reinforced by Granger's reserve corps), a defense line along the southern side of Horseshoe Ridge. This line was virtually at right angles to that of his forces who had been defending the eastern end of that spur of Missionary Ridge against the morning attack of Breckinridge and Cleburne, later joined by Walker's corps. Thus, Thomas was now fighting on two fronts and, although eventually driven from the field, his stubborn defense saved the Union army from complete disaster and won him fame as the "Rock of Chickamauga."

Shortly after 2:30 p.m., Longstreet was summoned to Bragg's presence and was astounded to find the Confederate commander unable to comprehend the extent of Longstreet's success and the opportunity that lay before him to finish off Rosecrans' army. Longstreet suggested that the Confederate right wing go on the defensive and reinforcements from it be added to his victorious troops in order to sweep behind Thomas and cut off his line of retreat. Apparently piqued that the battle had not gone as he had planned — that is, an attack by his right wing to turn Rosecrans left and drive him into McLemore's Cove — Bragg started making excuses, turned on his heel and withdrew to his headquarters, saying to the astonished Longstreet: "General, if anything happens, communicate with me at Reed's Bridge." In the words of Stanley Horn, in his admirable work *The Army of Tennessee,* "thus was presented the strange spectacle of a major conflict fought to its decisive close, one commander having fled the field, and the other sulking in his tent." One would never see the "light of battle" in Braxton Bragg's eyes!

Left to his own devices, Longstreet renewed the assault again and again, in the face of desperate resistance. He was now joined by Polk's right wing where Breckinridge, Cleburne and Cheatham had returned to the attack after licking their wounds from the morning repulse.

The combined pressure was more than even Thomas's stubborn defenders could withstand, and at last the two wings of the Confederate army were united in triumph. Years later, Longstreet was to remember: "The Army of Tennessee knew how to enjoy its first grand victory. The dews of twilight hung heavy about the trees as if to hold down the voice of victory; but the two lines nearing as they advanced, joined their continuous shouts in increasing volume, not as the burstings from the cannon's mouth, but in a tremendous swell of heroic harmony that seemed almost to lift from their roots the great trees of the forest." Hill's recollection of the scene was no less poignant. "The cheers that went up when the two wings met were such as I have never heard before and shall never hear again." By sunset, at 6 p.m., what was left of the Federal army was in full retreat, and it did not pause until it reached Rossville on the outskirts of Chattanooga itself.

In Longstreet's assaults, Manigault was posted on the extreme left of the line. Early in the fighting, his brigade's flank was turned by Wilder's mounted infantry and his troops driven back in disorder, but they reformed and returned to the attack, distinguishing themselves in the desperate final assaults on Thomas's right at Dyer's Farm. In his report, Manigault's division commander, Hindman, says, "I never saw Confederate troops fight better...The relation of what they performed ought to immortalize them...For signal gallantry and efficiency, the army and the country are indebted to...the three brigade commanders of my division *(Anderson, Deas and Manigault)*."

The strange lethargy and impulse that led Bragg to seek the comforting protection of his headquarters behind the lines revealed once more the fatal flaw that plagued him as a commander, the inability to seize the initiative and deliver the decisive blow. Longstreet wrote D.H. Hill in 1884: "It is my opinion that Bragg thought at 3 P.M. that the battle was lost." One may well ask why?

That night, Polk sent Col. Spence of his staff to the army commander "to report the situation of the right wing, and to say that the enemy had been driven from every position in his front and now was in full retreat.'' Bragg summoned Polk to his presence and what occurred at their nocturnal meeting was described by Col. Gale, an aide-de-camp of Polk, who was present. ''About eleven or twelve at night, on the last day of the battle, I rode with General Polk from his bivouac amid the dead and dying in Thomas's intrenched line, to General Bragg's headquarters. General Bragg had gone to bed but got up to listen to his report of the day's work of his forces. General Polk urged upon him the fact that the enemy was routed and flying precipitately from the field, and that then was the opportunity to finish the work by the capture or destruction of his army by prompt pursuit, before he had time to reorganize and throw up defenses at Chattanooga. General Bragg could not be induced to look at it in that light, and refused to believe that he had won a victory.''

Whether or not pursuit that night, as urged by Polk and Buckner, was practicable (Longstreet did not think so), certainly on the morning of the 21st the way was open. Polk and Longstreet waited in vain for word from Bragg to go forward. None came.

Longstreet commented later: ''In reading Bragg's report, I was struck with his remark that the morning after the battle 'he found the ever-vigilant General Liddell feeling his way to find the enemy.' Inasmuch as every one in the army was supposed to know on the night of the battle that we had won a complete victory, it seemed to me quite ludicrous that an officer should be commended for his vigilance the next morning in looking for the enemy in his immediate presence...It did not occur to me on the night of the 20th to send Bragg word of our complete success. I thought that the loud huzzas that spread over the field just at dark were a sufficient assurance and notice to any one within five miles of us.''

But so it was, and, to his shortcomings at McLemore's Cove and his failure to crush Crittenden's isolated corps a few days later, Bragg added the crowning tragedy of allowing Rosecrans' army to escape and fortify itself in the works surrounding Chattanooga. Years later, Longstreet was to say that Chickamauga was the turning point of the war, and D.H. Hill wrote, ''It seems to me that the *élan* of the Southern soldier was never seen after Chickamauga...that brilliant dash that had distinguished him was gone forever. He was too intelligent not to know that the cutting in two of Georgia meant death to all his hopes...The failure to strike after the success *(on the 20th)* was crushing to all his longing for an independent South. He fought stoutly to the last, but, after Chickamauga, with the sullenness of despair and without the enthusiasm of hope. That 'barren victory' sealed the fate of the Southern Confederacy.''

R.L.T.

CHICKAMAUGA

(The Narrative)

About the middle of August, information found its way to us that the Yankee General, Rosecrans, was busily preparing for an advance, and preparations on our side were being made to take the field promptly, and as soon as the Yankee General's movements became known, the outlying Regiments and Brigades and the Cavalry Divisions were called in and so disposed on the left bank of the river as to resist an effort of the enemy to cross, at such points as it was thought most likely he would endeavor to do so.[1] For some time previously, large working parties had been busily engaged in constructing three enclosed works on the most commanding points around Chattanooga. Smaller ones were also being thrown up, and I believe it was intended to connect them by a line of Infantry breastworks. The three larger works were very nearly completed, when it became positively known that the enemy was on the move.

On the 20th August, our Division received marching orders, and starting about 2 o'clock P.M., crossed the Lookout Mountain, and moving several miles in a westerly direction up the Wauhatchie Valley,[2] halted and went into camp. Pickets were thrown out along the banks of the river, and strong guards at one or two points favorable for crossing, but the main body of the Division remained in the Valley, distant from the river about from 2½ to 3 miles, its position being such that it could easily reach and give assistance at any point seriously threatened. At about 11 o'clock on the 21st, frequent discharges of Artillery were heard in the direction of Chattanooga, which occasioned a good deal of surmise on our part.

We soon afterwards learned that the enemy had appeared on the opposite side of the river to Chattanooga, surprised a small guard of 20 or 30 men, killing or making prisoners of most of them, and then, unlimbering a battery of Artillery, had opened fire on the town, to the surprise and consternation of citizens, soldiers, and even the Commanding General.[3] The alarm and confusion caused by this sudden surprise was very great, and General Bragg was much censured, and deservedly so, for not having guarded against such an event. It was known that the enemy was on the move, and reasonably to be supposed that he would show himself at just this point, if not prevented, and yet no defensive work had been thrown up to protect the ferry. I could never learn that any body of Cavalry had been thrown forward on this road to give notice of the approach of the enemy, and many of our wagons had been allowed to cross the river and forage in that direction. At least 100 of the latter fell into their hands with teamsters, mules, etc. The ferry steamer was disabled by their fire, and eventually sunk. The town of Chattanooga lay directly under their guns, and they shelled it rapidly, without being replied to for some time, directing their fire principally at the railroad depots and the Quarter Master's and Commissary's store houses. All this was accomplished by a Brigade of Cavalry, accompanied by a battery or two of horse Artillery, who met with no resistance at all, and permanently secured a position of great advantage to themselves in the coming operations, from which it was almost impossible to drive them, and which seriously interfered with us in many ways. This incident was another of the very many instances of mismanagement, or culpable and careless negligence on the part of someone, that has never been cleared up or explained.[4]

Orders came at 12 M. this day for all citizens to leave the front and go to the rear. Mary and Arthur who were still with me were hastily hurried off. The enemy's movements were quicker than we had apprehended they would be, and, like myself, the wives and families of many officers were caught in a very perplexing and disagreeable dilemma.

Fortunately, however, altho they had to pass through the town, they got off safely and without accident in the afternoon.

On the 22nd (and 23rd), our Division retained the same position. Scouting parties of the enemy showed themselves at several points across the river opposite our pickets, and some little firing took place between them, but not amounting to much. After skirmishing a little, they retired. On the evening of the last day, our pickets were drawn in, and at dark we recrossed the mountain, and bivouacked some three miles from Chattanooga, leaving the 28th Alabama of our brigade to hold the pass, and a small force of cavalry to watch the river in their front.

Our Division was being retained as a reserve force, and was held constantly in readiness to march to any threatened point. Our camp was at McFarland's Springs, about five miles from Chattanooga, a delightful location at the foot of a continuation of the range known as Missionary Ridge, with a fine spring of excellent water. Here we remained until the 30th, when we marched to join General D.H. Hill,[5] who, with his corps, was guarding the river seven miles east of Chattanooga, and in the neighborhood of the mouth of the Chickamauga Creek. It was apprehended that the enemy would attempt a crossing somewhere near that point.

On joining him, we found the Federals apparently in large numbers on the opposite side of the river, the distance between our pickets on each bank being about 300 yards.

The enemy, however, were quiet, and as far as we could judge, no active preparations were going on to force a passage. General Hill, however, was very apprehensive. Here the pickets were on the most friendly terms, conversing freely with each other across the river. Not a shot was exchanged between them, the men on both sides went into bathe in large numbers, and in several instances swam out into the middle of the river to meet and talk with each other. This conduct, however, was in violation or orders, and the parties when discovered, were punished. After remaining here three days, it appearing that the enemy had no intention of making an effort to cross here, and it being discovered that they were only making a parade of a greater force than they really had,[6] on the afternoon of the 2nd of September the Division returned to McFarland's Springs, reaching the camp about nine o'clock.

September the 8th, the Division left McFarland's Springs for the last time. Marching fifteen miles, reached in the afternoon Lee and Gordon's Mill on the Chickamauga, and bivouacked on the right bank. On the 9th we remained in this neighborhood, and at about 1 A.M. on the morning of the 10th, we moved in direction S.W. from Chattanooga towards McLemore's Cove (Valley) in the neighborhood of Pigeon Mountain,[7] to find out something about the enemy, it having been reported that one of their corps had crossed at Bridgeport, and was then making its way into the Cove before mentioned. Crossing Lookout Mountain at Stevens' Gap,[8] at about ten A.M. we reached the point known as *(Morgan's)* about three miles from *(Davis')* Cross Roads, where the road by which we were moving intersected with the one leading from Stevens' Gap, and by which the enemy must pass.[9] Our scouts soon discovered the enemy's cavalry, but as it was desirable that our own presence in their vicinity should not be known, they did not show themselves during the afternoon. General Buckner, commanding a small corps, joined General Hindman, who, being the senior Major General, assumed command of all the troops. During the night, information reached us that McCook's corps was upon the mountain, and would in all probability on the following day endeavor to march forward and secure Dug Gap.[10] The enemy had now crossed the river at three points — Bridgeport, at Chattanooga (General Bragg having evacuated it), and at some other crossing higher up.[11] Thus their different army corps were widely separated. General Hindman had under his command about 11,000 men, and he received orders to attack the enemy at as early an hour on the following morning as he could find him, with instructions to cut him off from a retreat from the way he came into the Valley, whilst General Bragg himself with a portion of Hardee's corps,[12] already in the neighborhood of Dug Gap, would fall upon his right as soon as the action commenced. Our orders were to move at daylight, but much time was lost by General Buckner, whose corps was to move in advance. Our Division did not move until nine o'clock. My brigade was in the rear. Hours passed without our advancing more than two and a half miles. At about two o'clock we could hear that our skirmishers in front were becoming engaged. The enemy had marched into the cove, leaving the mountain and pass in their rear. The opportunity offered General Hindman for distinguishing himself and striking a terrible blow was favorable in the extreme, but he was not up to the work, it being far beyond his capacity as a general. So much time was lost in selecting his line and forming his troops, that the enemy discovered a trap laid for them to their peril, and whilst keeping up a show of resistance, rapidly retreated towards the mountain. By the time General Hindman had completed his arrangements, the Federal General had also completed his. Our advance commenced, but we soon found out that only a skirmish line and a brigade or two of infantry were in our front to resist us, who gave way easily, and the main body had secured its retreat, holding the pass, and their line strongly posted a short distance up the mountain side.

Several hundred prisoners were taken and perhaps as many killed and wounded. The whole affair proved a miserable failure, altho had there been a proper man to manage for us, I have little doubt but that a most brilliant success would have been achieved. It was one of several most favorable opportunities that offered themselves during my connection with the Western Army, not taken advantage of, and lost from incapacity on the part of the officer to profit by the error or folly of his opponent.[13]

General Bragg never forgave Hindman for this, and I am by no means surprised at it. As I have already stated, my brigade brought up the rear, and I was consequently not in a position to observe what was going on in the vicinity of the enemy, but I was thoroughly posted as to the plan of operations, and afterwards saw the enemy in full retreat. I know that seven hours elapsed between the time that our line was within two and a half miles of the enemy, and the time that I saw the enemy retreating towards the gap. Our Division, which was to have been thrust in between the Federals and their line of retreat, was stationary for hours, and when moved forward, they were too late to accomplish their purpose. The troops alluded to with General Bragg were in the proper position to attack with great advantage the enemy's right, and only waited the commencement of the action on Hindman's part, to take their share. The enemy were evidently unaware of the proximity of so large a hostile force. In numbers there is every reason to believe that we were nearly if not quite equal to them, and an attack from three different points at very nearly the same time, or with but a short interval between them, with the way of retreat cut off, and their corps hemmed in in a narrow valley, would most likely have resulted in the complete defeat and almost entire destruction of the enemy.[14]

Foiled in our effort, and the enemy making good in his retreat, General Bragg ordered the Division and other troops to Lafayette, a small village near the Georgia and Tennessee line, and in the former state.[15] We made a tedious and rough night march, and reached that point a little before day. There we rested until sunset of the same day, when we were ordered under arms, and making another night march, at daylight on the morning of the 12th,[16] joined General Polk, who, with Cheatham's Division and a small corps under General W.H.T. Walker, were in line of battle near what is known as Pea Vine Ridge, and within a few hundred yards of Rock Springs Church, on the road from Lafayette to Chattanooga, and about eleven miles from the former.

A considerable portion of the enemy's army, but what corps I do not remember,[17] had been discovered in their front the day before. Polk was too weak to attack alone, hence we were sent to reinforce him.[18] Altho the two forces had lain within a mile or two of each other the preceding afternoon and night, yet in the morning they had retired. A brigade or two was pushed forward to feel for them, our own amongst the number, but were almost immediately recalled. Only one of them came in contact with their rear guard for a short time.[19] It will appear that both armies were cut up into separate columns, General Rosecrans, as stated, having crossed the river in three separate detachments, and General Bragg having been obliged also to divide his army in like manner, merely, however, for the purpose of gaining information, and he having a shorter distance to travel, hoped to be able to concentrate more rapidly, and a favorable opportunity offering reasonably, expected to be able to attack and overpower some one of these detached corps of the enemy. One opportunity he had lost, as described, at McLemore's Cove, and in the present instance the enemy proved to be too wary. It was evidently their intention not to fight until their entire army was concentrated. It is as well to mention here that the enemy were unopposed at any of their crossings, whether purposely or otherwise, I could never learn.[20]

On the 13th we returned to Lafayette, and there remained until the night of the 17th, when orders again came for a night march. The enemy were reported concentrating somewhere in the neighborhood of Chickamauga Creek, but where exactly, none of us knew. On the 18th at 8 o'clock A.M., we reached the vicinity of Lee and Gordon's Mill. The greater part of our army was still in advance, or rather east of us, our position at Lafayette having been the extreme left, and we were now closing upon the main body, distant 4 or 5 miles, our entire force being on the south, the enemy on the north bank of the creek. It was well-known that no great distance separated us from our foes, still we were not a little surprised when three or four rifle shots whizzed over our heads, or struck near the road on which we were marching. Without paying much regard to them for the stream separated us, we moved on until near the mills, where we formed a line of battle and moved forward to within a half mile of the creek, and an artillery duel began between several batteries. Our skirmishers were also pushed forward, and sharp firing commenced. The Division commander had been ordered to make a feint, as tho an effort was about to be made to secure the crossing at that point. Here we had a disagreeable day of it, the bullets and cannon shot flying unpleasantly thick about us. This state of things lasted until about two o'clock on the 19th, when orders were received to move to the right, rapidly. The battle of Chickamauga had commenced, and we were wanted.[21] About the same time the enemy opposing us must have received like orders, for they also, even before us, had commenced to move to their left. Both parties knew full well that what had taken place between them was merely child's play to what was about to follow. General Bragg had issued an address to the army two days previously in which he informed them that his intention was to seek the enemy, and wherever he could find them, force a battle.[22] His army had been materially strengthened by the arrival of several divisions from Knoxville and Mississippi, and Longstreet's corps from Virginia was momentarily expected. About 7,000 of the latter joined him that evening and took part in the battle on the following day. One or two brigades were engaged as early as that evening.[23]

Our army must have amounted to 47,000 men who took part in the battle, exclusive of cavalry. The enemy numbered a little over 70,000 men. These are my estimates, and if I am not mistaken they correspond very nearly with the reports of the two generals, which I once had, but have latterly lost.[24] The equipments of both armies were thorough and complete, and their physical condition, I take it, about as good as could well be.

On the night of the 18th, two important fords of the Chickamauga were captured, the enemy driven from them, and during the morning of the 19th, our troops crossed.[25] I think the battle commenced about twelve o'clock, when we first began to hear heavy firing. We were distant about four miles. The engagement, however, was not general, but at intervals during the afternoon several divisions became seriously engaged,[26] but neither army had completed its line of battle, nor had all troops on either side come up.

Moving rapidly at the hour before mentioned from Lee and Gordon's Mills, and after a march of about three and a half miles crossing the Chickamauga at Hunt's Ford, we began to near the scene of strife. After some little delay, we were ordered forward to relieve Cheatham's Division, which was reported to be hard pressed, and likely to be driven back. As we advanced there was every evidence that a hard struggle had taken place on the ground over which we were moving. Yankees and Confederates lay within a few feet of each other, in the calm sleep of death. It was a wooded country and the trees gave visible tokens of a severe cannonade, but we had the satisfaction of knowing that our comrades had driven the enemy. The firing was still in advance, and a constant stream of ambulances, litter bearers, and wounded men were passing to the rear.

By the time we reached the troops who had been fighting, firing had greatly slackened, and soon almost entirely ceased at this point. The enemy had retired, and Cheatham, not strong enough to push forward, had halted. Our division was then placed in front and advanced about 4 or 500 yards, but with the exception of their skirmishers we found no force of any consequence. The woods and underbrush was so thick that it was impossible to see more than one hundred and fifty yards, or thereabouts. Here we also were halted, and remained until after dark, our skirmish line firing slowly. The 34th Alabama on the left of the brigade had its left wing in an open field. After dark, what was supposed to be a scouting party of the enemy, came up within fifty or sixty yards of them and fired a volley into them. The commander ordered his men to return the fire and a volley from 300 rifles was discharged. On the following evening a Yankee captain who had been made prisoner during the day, in conversation with our Provost Marshal, mentioned that on the previous evening he had been sent out about dusk with a detachment numbering about sixty men, to make a reconnaissance. When returning he lost his way in the dark, and suddenly found himself in front of a large body of men, who he rightly conjectured were Confederates. Before he could assure himself of the fact, or make arrangements to extricate himself, some of his men began to fire. It was immediately replied to by a volley, so fatal in effect that only himself and two others were left standing. There can be but little doubt the incident he related was the same that occurred to the 34th, and his was the party they fired into, tho in all probability he did not lose as many men as he supposed.[27]

About eight o'clock we retired to take our position in the line of battle, which was being formed 400 yards in our rear, as well as circumstances and the darkness would permit.

CHICKAMAUGA

September 20, 1863

(The Narrative)

Thus battle really commenced on the 19th, tho the engagement was not general, not more than a third of the Army, if so much, having been under fire that day.[28] On the 20th the action was general and decisive.

At daylight on the 20th, the troops were under arms, irregularities in the line were rectified and a few alterations made. There were at the time only three of the brigades with the Division — Deas on the right, my own on the left, and Anderson's supporting the two. To my left was a division of Buckner's corps, which I was told would advance with us. This turned out to be a mistake, and it seems that a later order kept them in reserve.[29] Consequently the position of our brigade was on the extreme left of the whole army, when we moved forward into action. By seven o'clock all was in readiness, and the men rested on the ground, awaiting the order to advance.

The order of battle was for the attack to commence at daylight, and to begin on the right. As, from the nature of the country, it was impossible to see, except at intervals, to any great distance either to the right or left, the movement could not be simultaneous, so that each brigade was ordered to move as soon as the left of that upon its right started. The enemy were known to be awaiting us in our front, but at what distance was unknown to most of us. Hour after hour passed, still there was no indication of the fight having commenced. Everything was quiet as though no human being was within miles, not even a scattering picket shot. Various were the surmises as to the cause of the delay.

Had the enemy retreated? Was the order of battle changed? Were we to await the enemy? and such like expressions.[30] But suddenly and just as we began to breathe more freely, and the intense suspense began to wear off, the report of a distant gun at the extreme right of our line sounded in our ears, followed by another and another, and then in rapid succession, the fire was taken up by half a dozen batteries on either side. This lasted several minutes, and then commenced the rattle of musketry, not easily distinguished, so great was the distance, but gradually growing larger and increasing in volume as the engagement progressed from right to left. All were now at attention, awaiting our turn, yet it was very nearly an hour, 11:20 A.M., before we began to move. It almost sickened one to reflect how many of those sturdy forms moving steadily forward, in all the vigor and strength of manhood, ere the setting sun would lie cold and stiff upon that bloody field. But there was little time for such thoughts, the attention of all the officers being necessarily engaged in preserving as nearly as possible a perfect form, and closing any gaps that the irregularities of the ground or various obstacles might cause. A line of skirmishers covering our front preceded us about 150 yards. For nearly a half-mile we advanced in this way through the woods, when we struck a piece of open ground and meadow land. Immediately beyond, some six hundred yards from us was the crest of a hill, the ascent gradual and easy, emerging from the meadow. The two right regiments, 10th and 19th S.C., again got into a thick wood, also a portion of the 24th Alabama. The 28th and 34th Alabama found themselves in a large corn field. The greater portion of the 34th (left wing) extended into a wood beyond the field.

On the crest of the hill, the enemy was posted. Their artillery opened upon us as soon as we began the ascent. The enemy's line was not parallel to our own, the right regiments being at least three hundred yards nearer to them than the regiment on the left. The 10th, 19th, and a portion of the 24th, moving through the woods were still unaware of the position of the enemy, and could not distinguish anything for more than a hundred yards in their front. Suddenly the character of the growth changed from comparatively small trees and thick underbrush, to heavy timber and no shrubs or small trees. Before reaching it, they were prepared to find the enemy, for the sharpshooters had halted and from behind the trees were firing on the enemy, but unfortunately without drawing their fire. Even their skirmish line had retired, without discharging a rifle. This portion of our line had just got well into this comparatively open place when they found themselves within 90 or 100 yards of the enemy's line of battle, the men screened and lying down behind a rough breastwork of logs. Instantly a fringe of smoke rose above their works, and a terrific fire assailed *(our men)*, crashing through their ranks, and laying low many a poor fellow. It brought them up in an instant and produced much confusion. The order to charge was given, but altho no one turned to retreat, it was impossible to make them advance. The only thing to do was to return the fire. This had the effect of reducing the fire of the Yankees, restored confidence somewhat, and they gradually advanced whilst doing so. After a few minutes, in obedience to orders, and following the examples set by several gallant officers, they rushed in and carried the works, driving the enemy, such as were not killed or wounded, before them. Still, in a few moments they were again hard pressed, the Yankee reserves coming up. During this contest on the right, the centre and left were hotly engaged. The 34th and a part of the 28th carried an advance work on the left, but the 24th, (centre) could do but little, the enemy's line having in their front a considerable concavity. They got into a cross fire, as also the right of the 28th, and suffered severely. The enemy fought with much obstinacy, and served their artillery with fatal effect. Eventually, I have no doubt but that we would have broken through the entire line opposed to us, but as far to the left as I could see, the enemy overlapped us, and there were no troops opposing or attacking him. What had become of the troops on my left, I could not imagine. A staff officer sent to discover the cause of the delay and to urge them forward, brought the information at this juncture, that they were not advancing and were kept back as a reserve force.[31] A message reached me from the left that the enemy were moving in large numbers against their flank, and a considerable body were making their way round our left and to our rear.[32] Our position was becoming critical, and knowing now that I had no support, and that if I sent for assistance it could not reach me in time to save me, I was reluctantly compelled to retire the whole line (the right) some three hundred yards, and the left double that distance, presenting a different front from that by which we had advanced. I had not a moment to lose, and even then the left regiment, a very large one, was for a short time seriously involved, lost considerably, and had forty men of the left companies captured.[33]

Sending information to General Buckner, commanding the reserve, after waiting a half-hour a brigade came to my support.[34] The remainder of our division and others to its right had by this time broken through the enemy's lines, and were in pursuit of them. The troops with which I had been engaged, as also those to my left, the extreme right of the Federal army, must also have become aware of the defeat of other portions of their army, knew that the Confederates were already in their rear, and might at any moment abandon the pursuit, turn upon them, hem in, and capture them. They abandoned their works, and retreated precipitately, whilst we moved forward almost unopposed, and after some time found and rejoined our Division, two miles in advance of the original line of battle. We now enjoyed a short breathing spell, secured and sent our prisoners to the rear, and the men were permitted to fill their canteens.[35]

The battle was still raging some distance to the right and rear. The enemy's centre, owing to its location on ground of the most favorable character for them, and fighting behind strong and well-constructed breastworks of logs of heavy timber piled one on top of the other, still remained unbroken. Their right and left had been broken, and the troops generally had fled. Still, fully 30,000 men remained on the field, their lines much contracted, and now presenting a front resembling a half circle. Rosecrans, their commanding general, had fled, regarding all as lost, but their second in command, General Thomas, held on with dogged resolution, and must have imparted much of his own resolution to those under him. They now occupied a strong and almost impregnable position,[36] amongst a range of high, abrupt, and rugged hills.

Orders came for the division to return and again take part in the fight, and to desist from the pursuit. Anderson's Brigade was detached to some other point. My own and General Deas's were directed to move to the right, retracing somewhat our steps, to form a line continuous with that of a General Bushrod Johnson, who, with two brigades, supposed himself on the right flank of the Federal line. It was hard to find out their exact position, for these hills were heavily timbered, and their men somewhat retired behind the opposite slope. At about two P.M., the connection was made, our brigade on the right, Deas on the left. Our instructions were to swing round to the right, my right being the pivot, and to endeavor to close in the enemy or to endeavor to take him in flank. Unfortunately a fresh corps of Federal troops, commanded by General Granger, came up just as we got in position, who had not been engaged that day, and only then arrived on the ground. We were not aware of this until sometime after the attack commenced. Our men at the word of command, at 3 o'clock, went boldly forward, descending a hill into the gorge and advancing up the one opposite, Dent's Battery, 6 Napoleon guns, opening behind and above us on the enemy. A steady and rapid fire assailed us as we advanced, both artillery and infantry. After an unavailing effort we were driven back, the enemy in turn charged us, and the battery for a moment or two was in great danger. But the gunners served their pieces like veterans, and their gallant captain set an example worthy of emulation. Our men who had been charged when in a state of some confusion, and it was an equal chance whether they would stand or run, rallied and drove their assailants back with heavy loss. Taking advantage of the disorder in their ranks, the brigade charged in turn, and gained some distance. Again moving forward, they were driven back a space, and the enemy repeating their first maneuver, but with less success, laid themselves open to another attack. The first ridge was carried, but on a second just as strong, the enemy again rallied and showed fight. From this one they were driven to a third, the fight resembling and being of the same character as that at the first hill. There was no more obstinately contested ground anywhere on that day than at this point. The blood of the men seemed to be up, and there was but little flinching. On several occasions the colors of two of the regiments fell into the enemy's hands, their bearers killed or wounded, but were quickly recovered. For two hours this contest lasted. Our ammunition was expended again and again in many instances, but the men supplied themselves from their dead or wounded comrades, or those of the Yankees, and when it did not suit their own weapons, threw them away and seized their arms. Towards the latter part of the fight, there was scarcely any order preserved, and no defined line. Regiments and companies were inextricably mixed up, and it resembled more a skirmish on a grand scale than the conflict of a line of battle. Officers and men never before or after behaved better, or showed more indomitable pluck. This series of attacks and counterattacks was confined to the 10th, 19th, 24th, 28th Alabama. The 34th, as well as Deas's brigade, could gain no ground, and had hard work to hold their own. Yet the enemy's line was broken where the four regiments mentioned struck them, was completely separated from their right, doubled up, forced back, and the troops opposing finally captured, but not by ourselves. They had been driven into a ravine, and whilst preparing for a final onslaught, a brigade sent to our assistance coming up from a different direction, took them almost in rear, and seeing that further resistance was useless, they surrendered to the newcomers, without their having fired a gun.[37] It was now some time after sunset, and the battle closed. I think our brigade was almost the last engaged, for I noticed that the firing had entirely ceased elsewhere, except an occasional scattering shot.[38]

Thomas, tho much reduced in numbers and driven from his first positions, still had the semblance of an army left, and showed an apparent front. His lines now resembled a horseshoe, and the distance between our extreme right and left could not have exceeded a half-mile, but neither wing nor any of the generals, knew the relative position of the two extremes of our lines. Otherwise advantage might have been taken of it, the gap closed, and General Thomas and his men would, on the following morning, have found themselves prisoners of war. Through that opening, at a late hour of the night, when our men, worn out with fatigue and labor, were resting on the ground over which they had fought so hard, the Yankee General succeeded in extricating the remains of his shattered army, and on the following day, reached his intrenched camp at Chattanooga. The courage, firmness, and skill of the Federal general is deserving of the highest praise. He saved that army, and his conduct on this occasion, and the success that met his efforts, may have had a most important bearing on the after results of the war, for had he followed the example set him by his commanders, and by many other generals of rank on that day, I believe that the victory to us would have been one of the most thorough, in the history of nations and the army completely destroyed. At an early hour on the following morning it was discovered that the enemy had escaped us. Our cavalry was despatched in pursuit, and soon overtook him, yet, tho again losing heavily, he made good his retreat, and thus ended the battle of Chickamauga.[39] No pursuit on the part of General Bragg with his infantry was attempted, a mistake much to be regretted. Yet his men were much exhausted, had suffered heavily, and there was much to be done on the battlefield. Still, these reasons should not have deterred him. It is possible that had he followed at once, and threatened Chattanooga, that the place would have fallen into his hands with many prisoners and much material. We knew from our victory of the day before that the Union Army was much demoralized, and we heard from various sources afterwards that the country was filled with stragglers, and detached and disorganized bodies of troops flying to the nearest crossing on the Tennessee River, and on reaching it, making their way over forcibly, regardless of orders to the contrary, or the means employed to prevent it.

I do not believe that the force in Chattanooga in the condition that it was in, would have awaited an assault, but would have yielded to what they regarded as an inevitable fate.

But the energy of the Yankee officers, never more conspicuous than when reverses had befallen them, and in this widely differing from our own, lost no time in making their position as secure as possible, and in restoring order and discipline amongst the rank and file. Uninterrupted in these labors by General Bragg, they succeeded but too well, as we learned afterwards to our cost.

The loss on both sides in this battle was fearful, and in proportion to the numbers engaged was nearly equal. In killed, wounded, and prisoners, I understood at the time that our loss amounted to a little over 17,000 men. This estimate I believe, was reduced afterwards, but I still think that it was very near the mark. The enemy, in killed and wounded, must have lost not less than 20,000 men, besides 7,000 prisoners, and about 50 pieces of artillery, together with many wagons, ambulances, and other materials of war.[40]

The strength of our division (three brigades) in this battle, was:

Commissioned Officers	501
N.C. and privates	5,621
	6,122

The losses were as follows:

Killed on the field	272
Wounded	1,480
Missing	98
	1,850[41]

Our brigade carried into action:

Officers	169
N.C. and privates	1,856
Total	2,025

Killed or wounded, severely, dangerously, or mortally	540
Slightly wounded, or contused, but so injured as to be unfit for duty for days	69
Prisoners captured by the enemy	47
	656

Strength of brigade after battle	1,369

The infirmary corps, or litter bearers, numbered 102 men, 2 N.C. officers, 1 commissioned officer.

There was also a wagon guard of 64 men, 2 N.C. officers, 1 commissioned officer.

Of these details, the litter bearers only were to some extent under fire. Neither of them is included in the 2,025 men.

The exemption on the part of the field officers from casualties was very remarkable. Out of the eight, not one was killed or dangerously wounded, (in obedience to orders they were all on foot) but in line officers the loss was very severe. The greatest blow to me was the death of my much-loved brother-in-law, Captain Daniel E. Huger, Brigade Inspector, a true friend, tried soldier and most promising officer. There were not many in that Army, young as he was, who equalled him for judgment, courage, and skill as an officer. I never was associated as an officer with anyone on whom I could more implicitly rely in times of danger, or when prompt and decided measures were to be adopted. In discharging the duties of the office which he held, in which he was liable to incur the ill will of many, so firm, fair, and impartial was he at all times, that officers and men alike, respected and admired him, and the regret for his early and heroic death, was, I believe, universal and sincere. He fell in the hour of victory, whilst endeavoring to restore a wavering line, almost overpowered by numbers, and had just succeeded in his effort, when a bullet through his heart struck him from his horse, and he expired almost instantly, (this day, three years ago). I do not think I ever knew a purer spirit, a better balanced mind, or one who had his temper and his passions more thoroughly under control than he had.[42]

The battle of Chickamauga was, I think, the hardest fight that I have ever been engaged in. It lasted longer, and was more obstinately contested than any other, and from the numbers engaged, it certainly was on a grander scale and more imposing. The fire we got under when first we became engaged in the morning exceeded anything I ever before or after experienced. The air seemed alive with bullets, and an officer afterwards remarked to me, "General, all you had to do was to hold out your hand, and catch them." Out of about 800 men that came into the full fury of this storm, nearly 300 were shot down in a space of time certainly not exceeding three minutes.[43]

The events in which the brigade was engaged after leaving our camp at McFarland's Springs are so well described and accurately told in the letter attached that I will substitute this account for my own:*

Lookout Mountain,
Near Chattanooga, October 7, 1863.

In connection with the Battle of Chickamauga, nothing has been written concerning one of the most gallant Brigades in the Western Army, and two of the best of South Carolina's regiments. I refer to the command of General Arthur Manigault, formerly the Colonel of the 10th South Carolina Volunteers. A portion of this letter is therefore devoted to a narrative of its achievements, during and prior to the battle.

The Brigade, as at present constituted, is composed of the 10th and 19th South Carolina Regiments, (consolidated), Col. J.F. Pressley, commanding; Lieut. Col. Julius T. Porcher, Major J.L. White, and Adjutant Ferrell; the 24th Alabama, Col. N.N. Davis; 28th Alabama, Col. J.C. Reid; 34th Alabama, Major J.N. Slaughter; and Waters' Battery of Artillery.

After leaving McFarland's Spring, at the foot of Missionary Ridge, a few miles from Chattanooga, which for some time had been

---

*Col. C. Irvine Walker, when examining Manigault's unpublished manuscript apparently some time after the turn of the century, made the following marginal notation: "Your account is better than that of Personne. C.I.W." — Editor.

the camping ground of the Brigade, the first active movements of the campaign commenced.

On the 8th of September, the Brigade moved under the command of General Hindman, who, with his own division and the corps of General Buckner, had been ordered to make a reconnaissance in force, learn the position of the enemy in McLemore's Cove, and attack them. The latter, it is supposed, under the command of General McCook, of Ohio, had, by orders of Rosecrans, crossed the Lookout Mountain through one of its passes with a view to make a left flank or rear demonstration;[44] while Crittenden with a similar corps was advancing on our right towards Ringgold and Lafayette, to make a similar movement there and burn railroad and other bridges. General Thomas, with Rosecrans and the main body of the Federal Army, remained in our front, doubtless watching an opportunity to swoop down upon Bragg and destroy his army in detail.

After a march of 15 miles, the enemy was discovered on the afternoon of the 10th inst. Our Artillery was immediately brought forward, and opened fire preparatory to a general attack; but the Federals, evidently aware that our force was superior to their own, hastily retreated to a mountainous pass, from which he could not be dislodged — one of the thousand strong positions in this Switzerland of our continent, which must be seen before their military value can be appreciated.[45]

Failing to cut the Federals off, Hindman was now ordered to Lafayette, and on the evening of the 11th, received instructions to join Gen. Polk, who, with Cheatham's Division and the corps of Gen. W.H.T. Walker, was in line of battle near Rocky Spring Church, not far from Pea Vine Ridge, and eight or ten miles directly north of Lafayette, on the Chattanooga road. A long night march ensued, and at sunrise the destination was reached.

The wary enemy, however, had changed his position, and when sought for in the morning, was not to be found. Thus he had eluded his pursuers a second time, on both occasions having been offered battle with very nearly equal forces.

(The reader will properly surmise that it was the object of Bragg, not less than that of Rosecrans, to meet and whip his adversary in detail.)

On the 13th, Hindman's Division, and probably other portions of the Confederate Army, returned to Lafayette, where they remained until the night of the 17th. Orders were then again received to advance to the Chickamauga Creek, where, on arriving, the enemy was found in strong force, posted on the opposite side in the vicinity of what is known as Lee and Gordon's Mill. Hindman's Division was there formed in line of battle. During that and the following day, skirmishing took place along our entire front, the troops on both sides being subjected to an annoying artillery fire from the contending batteries. Hindman's Division at this time constituted the extreme left of the army.

On the 19th, battle was joined by the two armies, the firing commencing on the right and rolling steadily towards the left. About two o'clock the division commander received orders to push forward to General Polk's command. Marching about four miles, he crossed the river at Hunt's Ford, and about five o'clock, got within range of the enemy's artillery, near that point. Soon after the line was formed and advanced to the front. Before getting fairly under the musketry fire, orders came to retire, which was done, and this portion of the line was then re-formed in the following order — Hood on the right, Buckner on the left, and Hindman in the centre. The brigades of Hindman's division stood in the following order — Deas on the right, Manigault on the left, and Anderson supporting the two.

(The object of the present narrative being only to show that portion of the picture in which Manigault's Brigade had a place, I have not attempted to give the general outline of the whole battle, which is reserved for another communication.)

On Sunday, Hindman's division, with Buckner's Corps, was placed under Gen. Longstreet, who commanded the left wing of the army. The battle commenced on the right, and the orders were that each brigade should move forward as the fight progressed from right to left. The tide of musketry was thus rolling on at half-past eleven o'clock; regiment after regiment and brigade after brigade having previously gone into the bloody surge with varying success. The animating yells of our men, mingling with the steady, ceaseless rattle of artillery, told that the battle was at its flood, while floating above all, and enveloping the combatants until they were almost obscured from view, was a huge shroud of dust and smoke. Such was the contest into which Manigault's brigade — all true and trusty men — now that their time had come, plunged with a battle shout.

The three right regiments advancing, found the enemy strongly posted in a dense wood, the two left regiments and Waters' Battery being exposed in an open corn field, but with a thick wood upon their left. The ground was uneven, and ascended gradually in front, partaking of the broken and irregular character of the country.

The first notice of the position occupied by the Federals was on finding them confronting our line on the right at a distance of only eighty yards, the thickness of the woods and the recumbent attitude of the men preventing the discovery at an earlier moment. Instantly a fringe of fire leaped from the muzzles of our rifles, and then the fearful whir of bullets and the falling of the dead and wounded bespoke the fray commenced.

Manigault was now fighting on the extreme left of the entire army, a post at once of honor and of danger, but nobly maintained throughout. As far as he could see — to the length of a full brigade — the Federal line overlapped him and stretched away to the left. The firing from this superior force was harassing in the extreme, as well as that from a battery posted on the summit of a hill in our front, and required the strongest nerve and the best discipline to withstand. For a moment our men flinched before its fury; the line wavered and reeled like a broken ship in the grasp of a whirlwind, but, finally recovering, pressed forward; the breastworks were carried, the artillery captured, and that portion of the field won.

General Manigault, however, finding that his left was still entirely exposed, the regiments there being overlapped by the Federal line, and suffering severely from an enfilading fire, ordered the brigade to fall back about three hundred yards for the purpose of reforming his command and awaiting his support.

Meanwhile, Deas and Anderson had likewise driven the enemy before them, and the latter, finding themselves about to be flanked on their left, also retired. There was now a brief breathing spell, during which Manigault advanced and joined the remainder of his division. After proceeding about half a mile, the enemy were again encountered — as before, admirably posted upon a ridge of commanding hills, and General Bushrod Johnson industriously engaging their attention. Manigault was at once ordered to his support. It was now about half-past two o'clock. Again the battle raged thickly in the little brigade, and again it won new titles to honor.

At half-past three o'clock, the order having been given to make a right half wheel for the purpose of enfilading the right of the Federal line, Manigault came in collision with a heavy force of fresh troops, and now ensued the most desperate struggle in which that brigade, or any other on the field during the day, were engaged.[46] The enemy outnumbered us, and held every advantage of position. Whipped elsewhere, they struggled like men who had cast their last die in the balance, and were resolved "to meet the shuddering battle shocks until their lives ran ruddy rain." But they were encountered by braver soldiers than even they — by men whose banners were stirred by old battle memories — whose hearts held royal throbbings, and beat with noble blood, and in whose eyes was already flashing the light of another victory. Such troops were not to be conquered.

Time after time they were driven back by the overwhelming forces in front, yet, rallying, each fresh attack drove the enemy further from his original position than before. Large numbers were here killed or wounded, and owing to the nature of the country, it being thickly wooded and much broken, it was almost impossible to preserve a regular line of battle. Nothing but the gallant conduct of the officers and men, individually, enabled them to sustain the heavy fire to which they were exposed. The different regiments became mixed with each other, and here and there the faint-hearted were stealing to safer positions in the rear; still, there was no thought of defeat. Men fought from behind trees and coverts, loading and firing while they dodged from point to point, but always gaining ground. In short, the character of the battle at this juncture was that of skirmishing on a grand scale. Eventually the enemy were thus driven a distance of three-fourths of a mile.

During this stubborn resistance, the colors of one of our regiments fell into the hands of the Federals. The flag of the 10th South Carolina was also captured during one of the attacks of the enemy, and its bearer, Sergeant Glysson,[47] was killed, but the regiment rallying promptly in this emergency, the Federals were in turn attacked, and the colors re-captured.

Such was the intensity of the fire that our cartridges were exhausted in the very heat of battle, but many of the brigade, unwilling to fall back, abandoned their own muskets, and seizing the rifles of the dead Yankees, and stripping the ammunition boxes from the corpses, thus supplied their wants, and with the enemy's own guns and bullets whipped them from the field.

About sunset, the Federals were driven from their last position, and a large number who had been partially surrounded by Manigault's brigade, were captured by fresh troops just entering the field. Properly they were the prize of Manigault and his men, who had fought them during the most desperate hour of the day; but it is one of the fortunes of war that the trophy was snatched from his grasp by those not entitled to it, at the very moment it seemed ready to fall into our own grasp.[48]

The battle ceased about sunset, at which time the Federals had been driven from every position on the left, a distance of two miles and a half, and that, too, not merely over an open plain, but across ravines, and from ridge to ridge, and wood to wood, where positions were almost impregnable to attack by an army less determined than our own.

General Longstreet subsequently paid a compliment to the division by saying that troops who could carry such points were capable of winning a victory on any field.

On the following morning skirmishers were thrown out to discover the position of the enemy, but Rosecrans was then many miles distant on his way to Chattanooga. The loss of the brigade was 539 killed and wounded, out of 1,850 men.[49] Among the noblest spirits who fell was Capt. D.E. Huger, the Inspector General of Manigault's brigade — one of the most promising officers in the entire army. While gallantly rallying a portion of the command about an hour before sunset, he was struck by a ball which killed him instantly.

In the language of another, "there was none whose judgment was more reliable, decision more prompt, or energy more untiring. He had won the esteem of the whole brigade, and his loss is one that can not well be replaced."

In connection with the battle, the names of Colonel Pressley, Lieut. Col. Porcher, Major White, Capt. White, Capt. Ferrell, Colonels Reid, Davis, Major Butler, of the 28th Alabama, Captain Walker,[50] the present Adjutant General, and others, are conspicuously mentioned for their splendid bearing on the field.

It is a significant fact, although it has been noticed in former *letters from other localities, that nearly all the officers who went in on horseback were either killed or wounded, while a considerable portion of those on foot were unhurt.*

General Manigault himself had a narrow escape. His horse was shot diagonally through under the saddle, the bullet coming through one of the legs of the General's pantaloons, and his sword was nearly cut in twain.[51] On dismounting, other bullets perforated portions of his clothing, but, fortunately, not one inflicted a personal injury.

In this connection I may add that officers and men attached to brigades other than his own, speak in the highest terms of Gen. Manigault, as one of the ablest, coolest, and most gallant commanders in the Western Army.

All quiet today along the line, except occasional shelling of Lookout Mountain by the enemy's batteries. We make no response. Weather cool, at night, balmy by day, and admirably suited to the work in which we are engaged. Fever and ague and dysentery prevail throughout the army, especially in Longstreet's Corps, who are unused to the water and climate, but the mortality thus far is comparatively slight. There are no evidences of an immediate change of our present attitude, though we are still in line of battle.

PERSONNE.[52]

NOTES TO CHAPTER 5

[1] Polk's corps had been quartered in and about the city, with the exception of Anderson's Brigade which was posted for observation at Bridgeport. Horn, *The Army of Tennessee*, 241; *Polk*, II, 219.

[2] Wauhatchie Valley runs between Lookout Mountain on the east and Raccoon Mountain on the west.

[3] The firing to which Manigault refers was done by Capt. Lilly's 18th Indiana Battery of Hazen's brigade of Crittenden's corps. The purpose of the demonstration was to lead Bragg to believe that the Federals intended to cross there. (Horn, *The Army of Tennessee*, 246). Polk added that it "had the more pregnant significance of an announcement that the enemy's plans were completed, and were about being put in active operation." (*Polk*, II, 220). Harvey Hill, brought from the East to command Hardee's corps, recounted years later that the shelling occurred on Fast Day, while religious services were in progress, and that the "Rev. B.M. Palmer, D.D., of New Orleans, was in the act of prayer when a shell came hissing near the church. He went on calmly with his petition to the Great Being 'who rules in the armies of heaven and among the inhabitants of the earth,' but at its close, the preacher, opening his eyes, noticed a perceptible diminution of his congregation." *Battles and Leaders*, III, 640.

[4] The Northern forces engaged in this action were three regiments of a brigade of mounted infantry commanded by Col. John T. Wilder of the 17th Indiana and Capt. Eli Lilly's battery, the latter comprised of six 3-inch rifled guns and four mountain howitzers. It may well be that Manigault was referring to the mountain howitzers when he mentioned "a battery or two of horse artillery." Col. Wilder stated that the troops and people in the town seemed in great consternation, running in all directions. In addition to shelling Chattanooga, Capt. Lilly sank the steamer *Paint Rock* and disabled another lying at the landing, as well as a number of pontoons. *O.R.*, XXX, pt. 1, 234, 445.

[5] In mid-July a major change had taken place in the high command of the Army of Tennessee. Hardee, one of Bragg's two corps commanders, was transferred to Mississippi to devote his talents to the reorganization of the troops there after the fall of Vicksburg and the surrender of its garrison. Since Bragg had been critical of Polk's alleged failure to carry out orders promptly, doubtless he would have preferred to have seen the latter shipped off to the West. Be that as it may, it was Hardee who received the appointment. Later, at Chickamauga, the steady and capable hand of "Old Reliable," as Hardee had come to be known, was to be sorely missed.

Rather than advance one of the major generals in the army to corps command to replace Hardee, Davis turned to D.H. Hill, then serving in temporary command of the Department of Richmond, promoted him to lieutenant general July 11 and gave him Hardee's old job. The strained relations existing between Bragg and his subordinate commanders doubtless played a part in Davis' decision to tap an outsider.

Harvey Hill was a member of the celebrated class of 1842 at West Point, which gave the Confederacy 13 general officers of whom four, Longstreet, Dick Anderson, A.P. Stewart and Hill, attained the rank of lieutenant general. Interestingly enough, Rosecrans also was a member of this class. Twice brevetted for gallantry in the Mexican War, Hill had resigned from the army in 1849 and, in the years between wars, had served as professor of mathematics at Washington College, later to become Washington and Lee, and at Davidson College in North Carolina. In 1861 he was superintendent of the North Carolina Military Institute. A brother-in-law of Stonewall Jackson, of whom he was an ardent admirer, Hill was a rather cantankerous individual, but no one denied that he could fight. This he had amply demonstrated during the Seven Days and at Sharpsburg, where he had held the "Bloody Lane." Of him years later, Douglas Freeman would write: "Few division commanders could get more from a given number of men."

Hill was no stranger to Bragg, having served in the old army as a lieutenant in the latter's battery, along with George H. Thomas, the ablest general officer in Rosecrans' army, who was to gain fame for his stubborn, but in the end hopeless, rear guard stand against the victorious Southerners on the second day at Chickamauga, for which he was to go down in the history books as the "Rock of Chickamauga." Hill was rather shocked at his first interview with his old commander, finding him prematurely old, despondent, nervous and non-communicative.

Relations between the two went from bad to worse and, after Chickamauga, Hill joined other senior officers in urging the President to remove Bragg from command of the Army of Tennessee, a request with which Davis declined to comply. The upshot of it all was that Hill was sent back to North Carolina, where he remained inactive and without a command until the early summer of 1864.

One may speculate on the reasons that induced Davis to cling to Bragg, even when the latter had become thoroughly discredited and had lost the confidence, not only of his chief subordinates, but of many of the men in the ranks as well. Bragg's good points were clear to see — a fine administrator, an outstanding disciplinarian and trainer of troops, a good strategist, a devoted patriot. On the other hand, his glaring shortcomings as an army commander should have been obvious to all, especially Davis, a West Point graduate, former U.S. Secretary of War and field officer in the Mexican War. Bragg often acted on insufficient information, his orders were at times ambiguous, he shrank from assuming active personal command of the fighting when the chips were down. Lacking confidence in himself, he failed to inspire it in others. He was vindictive in his repeated efforts to find a scapegoat to cover up his own failures. Beyond all this, and most important of all, he lacked the audacity and courage to risk everything at the critical moment and force a decision on the field of battle regardless of the odds — the killer instinct, if you will. Why then, one may ask, did not Davis get rid of him?

A clue may be found in the similarities of their characters. Both were gifted, honorable men, devoted to the cause of the South, ready to make any sacrifice for what they conceived to be its best interest. Essentially, however, they were not men of action. Each was given to grandiose plans, a predilection shared by Beauregard. If one planned thoroughly enough, they were inclined to believe, and foresaw all the eventualities and placed the pieces on the chessboard in just the right positions, all would be well. Davis had an obsession for creating departments, districts and administrative procedures, a game he played to the very end. Somehow this gave him comfort and confidence, just as Bragg was reassured by devoting his energies to the discipline, training and preparation of his troops. A further factor may well have played its part. Neither Davis nor Bragg was a popular man. An ill-defined feeling that they deserved better of their fellow men and an unrequited yearning for acceptance may have welded an unconscious bond that drew the two men together in a sort of mutual sympathy that recognised in each other their own strengths and weaknesses. In any case, Davis never forsook Bragg and the Confederate cause paid the price of his blind devotion.

[6] This, of course, was precisely the impression the Northern forces were doing their best to create. "Details were made nearly every night to build fires indicating large camps, and by throwing boards upon others and hammering on barrels and sawing up boards and throwing the pieces in streams that would float them into the river, we made them believe we were preparing to cross with boats. This was kept up until Chattanooga was evacuated." Col. Wilder's Report, *O.R.*, XXX, pt. 1, 446.

[7] "Forty-five miles south of Chattanooga, Lookout Mountain throws out from its eastern side a spur or range called Pigeon Mountain, crescent shaped, with the west branch of Chickamauga Creek flowing in the valley between it and Lookout. As this valley narrows to the southward, where the mountains join, it forms a natural triangular cul-de-sac called McLemore's Cove, some six miles wide. Fertile farm lands lie in the bed of McLemore's Cove, but the sheer mountain walls rise around it, passable only by widely separated, rough, narrow and circuitous roads. Dougherty's Gap is at the southernmost extremity. Pigeon Mountain is crossed by Catlett's, Dug and Bluebird Gaps. Lookout is crossed at Stevens' and Cooper's Gaps." Horn, *The Army of Tennessee,* 243.

[8] This is one of the rare instances in which Manigault's memory played him false, quite understandably considering the extremely involved topography of the area south of Chattanooga, cut up as it is by mountain ridges crossed by narrow gaps. He should have said, "Crossing Pigeon Mountain at Worthen's Gap." Lookout Mountain forms the **western** wall of McLemore's Cove, which Manigault was approaching from the northeast. See Hindman's Report, *O.R., XXX,* pt. 2, 292.

[9] Hindman stated in his official report that he ordered a halt at Morgan's "shortly after sunrise." *O.R., XXX,* pt. 2, 293.

[10] This obviously would have been impossible, since McCook's corps on the 10th was at Alpine some 20 miles to the south. Doubtless Manigault was referring to Crittenden's corps, which was reported to be advancing from the direction of Chattanooga.

[11] Part of Crittenden's Twenty-first corps crossed at Friar's Island upstream from Chattanooga. *O.R., XXX,* pt. 1, 760-761.

[12] Hardee had been transferred to Mississippi. Manigault here refers to D.H. Hill's corps, consisting of the divisions of Cleburne and Breckinridge.

[13] In fairness to Hindman, it must be recognized that Bragg's vacillating and often ambiguous orders might well have confused a more experienced and better qualified division commander (*O.R., XXX,* pt. 2, 292-302). Later, Gen. Hill wrote that the principal causes of Bragg's failure to beat Rosecrans in detail were, first, lack of knowledge of the situation; second, inadequate personal supervision of the execution of his orders. Both shortcomings were illustrated here (*Battles and Leaders,* III, 641-642). Hindman was suspended from command, whereupon he demanded a court of inquiry. This, however, was denied him by President Davis as

not deemed necessary to the honor of Gen. Hindman in view of his subsequent gallant conduct at Chickamauga, generously attested to by Bragg. *O.R.* XXX, pt. 2, 298, 309-311.

[14] The Confederate force in McLemore's Cove or within supporting distance was clearly superior in numbers to the Federal divisions that had entered the cove. It consisted of the corps of D.H. Hill, Buckner and W.H.T. Walker, as well as Hindman's division of Polk's corps.

[15] Bragg was still concerned over the possibility of an attack by McCook. Actually, the latter was isolated at Alpine and completely out of the picture. Thus, another day was given to Crittenden to concentrate his scattered troops so vulnerable to attack. Horn, *The Army of Tennessee,* 252-253.

[16] Actually the 13th. *Polk,* II, 226.

[17] It was Crittenden's Twenty-first Corps of Rosecrans' Army of the Cumberland.

[18] Before Hindman's arrival, Polk had with him only Cheatham's division.

[19] After demonstrating in the direction of Peavine Church, Crittenden's troops had been withdrawn to Lee and Gordon's Mill, west of Chickamauga Creek, where his three divisions were now concentrated. This was discovered about noon and Polk, with some 25,000 men (his own corps reinforced by Buckner's and Walker's), was ready to move upon him. Bragg, however, ordered a halt and, taking Buckner's corps with him, returned to Lafayette. Another opportunity had been lost. Once more Bragg had failed because of faulty information and a reluctance to take personal command when the chips were down. It was the same old story all over again. *Polk,* II, 226-229.

[20] Although not specifically stated in his official report of the Chickamauga campaign, it is clear that Bragg, covering a front of more than 50 miles with an army he estimated at 35,000 (not including cavalry and prior to the accession of Buckner) was in no position to oppose crossings of the Tennessee at widely scattered points. Chattanooga was voluntarily abandoned so that Bragg could keep his army concentrated and meet the Federal threat from the west against his life-line to Atlanta (*O.R.,* XXX, pt. 2, 26-37). Sept. 2 Bragg wrote to the Secretary of War: "Unable to hold so long a line without sacrificing my force in detail" (*O.R.,* XXX, pt. 4, 583-584). Sept 9 he wrote: "The loss of Chattanooga...is unavoidable." *O.R.,* XXX, pt. 2, 22.

[21] In his report of the Battle of Chickamauga dated Missionary Ridge, Tenn., Oct. 8, 1863, Manigault said that orders to move with the division to join the main body of the army were received on the afternoon of Sept. 19 and that the Brigade, moving by the right flank, crossed the Chickamauga at Hunt's Ford, wading to the west bank, and, on the morning of the 20th, took position in the front line of battle between Deas' brigade on the right and Col. Trigg's brigade of Preston's division of Buckner's corps on the left. *O.R.,* XXX, pt. 2, 340-344.

[22] In General Orders No. 180, dated "In the Field, Sept. 16, 1863," Bragg had pulled out all the stops: "Soldiers, you are largely reinforced; you must now seek the contest...Relying on your gallantry and patriotism, *(your general)* asks you to add the crowning glory to the wreath you wear...You have but to respond to assure

us a glorious triumph over an insolent foe...I know what your response will be. Trusting in God, and the justice of our cause, and nerved by the love of the dear ones at home, failure is impossible and victory must be ours." *O.R.*, XXX,pt. 2, 37-38.

[23] From Knoxville came Buckner's corps made up of Stewart's and Preston's divisions. From Mississippi, Joseph E. Johnston sent Breckinridge's division and the small corps of W.H.T. Walker. Hood's and McLaws' divisions from the First corps of the Army of Northern Virginia (Pickett's was left in Virginia) were brought west by Longstreet, but not all of Longstreet's troops arrived in time to take part in the fighting. Livermore, in his authoritative work, estimated that Longstreet had 6,390 men present for duty at Chickamauga. Thomas L. Livermore, *Numbers and Losses in the Civil War in America 1861-1865,* (Boston, 1900), 106.

[24] Manigault may have minimized somewhat the Confederate strength at Chickamauga and over-stated that of the enemy, a not uncommon practice on both sides, but the numbers he gives are reasonably close to the mark. It should be noted that the Northern figure of 70,000 includes cavalry, while the Southern total of 47,000 does not. On Aug. 20, the cavalry in Bragg's army amounted to approximately 11,000 present for duty (*O.R.*, XXX, pt. 4, 518). Estimates often vary because of terminology, i.e., present for duty, effectives, whether or not cavalry is included and, especially, whether the figures refer only to those actually engaged in combat. Balancing all the factors involved, a realistic estimate indicates that the Union forces at Chickamauga actually engaged exceeded the Confederate by about 5,000 men or roughly 10%.

[25] At Hunt's Ford, also known as Dalton's Ford. *O.R.*, XXX, pt. 2, 302.

[26] Particularly the troops led by W.H.T. Walker, Cheatham, Stewart and Hood. Although the latter had been severely wounded at Gettysburg in July and his left arm crippled, he rejoined his men as they passed through Richmond on their way to the West and on Sept. 19 commanded his own division as well as those of Kershaw and Bushrod Johnson. That evening, in the gloomy atmosphere of Bragg's headquarters, Hood later wrote in his memoirs, "I found the gallant Breckinridge, whom I had known from early youth *(they were both Kentuckians),* seated by the root of a tree, with a heavy slouch hat upon his head. When, in the course of a brief conversation, I stated that we would rout the enemy the following day, he sprang to his feet, exclaiming, 'My dear Hood, I am delighted to hear you say so. You give me renewed hope. God grant it may be so!'" The next day Hood was once more severely wounded, this time it was thought fatally, as his victorious troops were breaking the Union line in their celebrated charge. Although he lost a leg, he lived to fight another day. John B. Hood, *Advance and Retreat,* (New Orleans, 1880), 62. Hereafter cited as *Hood.*

[27] This incident is briefly discussed in Hindman's report in the following words: "After dark, in the readjustment of my line, a sharp skirmish occurred on Manigault's left, the enemy retiring." Manigault reported that the left companies of the 34th Alabama "a short time after nightfall, twice became engaged with a force of the enemy, believed to be a reconnoitering party, in which that regiment lost some 12 or 13 men killed and wounded, but in each instance inflicting a severe loss upon the enemy and driving them back." *O.R.*, XXX, pt. 2, 341.

[28] An underestimate. The true figure probably was closer to one-half. *Battles and Leaders,* III, 652. Horn, *The Army of Tennessee,* 258-259.

[29] The division on the left, to which Manigault refers, was Brig. Gen. William Preston's. The bulk of this command was held in reserve and later withdrawn on Longstreet's order to reinforce the Confederate attack farther to the right. *O.R.,* XXX, pt. 2, 288, 357-358.

[30] The delay was caused by the failure of Bragg's courier to reach D.H. Hill, on the extreme right, with the order to commence the attack at daylight.

[31] The force on his left, to which Manigault refers, was Trigg's brigade of Preston's division, which had been ordered to support Manigault and conform with his movements. In his report, Trigg stated that he followed Manigault's brigade, which he found in some confusion, and offered to support it as ordered. Just at this juncture, however, word came that an enemy force was threatening to turn the Confederate left and Trigg was dispatched to deal with it, thus leaving Manigault to his own devices. *O.R.,* XXX, pt. 2, 431.

[32] The enemy force consisted of Wilder's brigade of mounted infantry support by cavalry. James Longstreet, *From Manassas to Appomattox,* (Philadelphia, 1896), 449. Hereafter cited as *Longstreet.*

[33] Maj. Slaughter, commanding the 34th Alabama, reported a loss in falling back of two men killed, 28 wounded and 28 captured (*O.R.,* XXX, pt. 2, 352). Although Manigault, in describing this withdrawal, maintained he was "reluctantly compelled to retire the whole line," others were less charitable. Longstreet said Manigault's left "had been forced back...in disorder." Polk referred to the action as a "repulse." As seen from the Northern side, one of Wilder's men later wrote, "At a distance of less than fifty yards six solid lines of gray were coming with their hats down, their bayonets at a charge, and the old familiar rebel yell. Our first volley did not check their advance, but as volley after volley from our Spencer rifles followed, with scarce a second's intermission...they broke and fled...In a few moments those lines of gray once more emerged from the sheltering timber on the opposite side of the field, and steadily, as if on parade, they advanced to the charge till the line had reached to the point at which they broke before, when the command 'Fire' was given, and again they broke and fled in wild confusion. Three times more did those brave men advance at a charge, and each time they were hurled back." *Longstreet,* 449; *Polk,* II, 262; *Battles and Leaders,* III, 658-659.

[34] This was Trigg's brigade of Preston's division once again. *O.R.,* XXX, pt. 2, 342.

[35] In addition to "many" prisoners, Manigault's troops had captured three pieces of artillery. *Ibid.*

[36] Horseshoe Ridge.

[37] The 22nd Michigan, 89th Ohio and part of the 21st Ohio were captured by Trigg's ubiquitous brigade of Preston's division, which got in their rear and surprised them. *O.R.,* XXX, pt. 2, 432.

[38] In his report, Hindman stated that "between 7:30 and 8 p.m. the enemy was driven from his position." *Ibid.,* 305.

[39] On the morning of the 21st, Forrest, with some 400 troopers, pushed forward to the vicinity of Rossville and routed a detachment of Federal cavalry which fled in

the direction of Chattanooga. It was in this action that Forrest's horse was wounded by a Minie ball which severed an artery in its neck. Seeing the blood spurt from the wound, Forrest leaned forward and inserted his index finger, staunching the flow until the field was cleared of the enemy. Only then did Forrest remove his finger and dismount. Whereupon, the wounded beast sank to the ground and expired. Shortly thereafter, on a spur of Missionary Ridge, Forrest captured a group of Federal lookouts perched on small platforms in a clump of oak trees. Taking the place of one of them, he obtained a panoramic view of Chattanooga, the river and the surrounding country below and at once dictated the celebrated dispatch to Polk in which he said, "The enemy trains are leaving, going around the point of Lookout Mountain. The prisoners captured report two pontoons thrown across for the purpose of retreating. I think they are evacuating as hard as they can go...I think we ought to press forward as rapidly as possible." At the bottom of the note were penned these words: "Please forward to Gen. Bragg." They fell on deaf ears. John A. Wyeth, *Life of General Nathan Bedford Forrest*, (New York and London, 1899), 259-261.

[40] Manigault's understanding of the Confederate losses at Chickamauga as a little over 17,000 men is very close to the mark. Stanley Horn in *The Army of Tennessee* estimated them at 17,800 and Livermore in *Numbers and Losses in the Civil War* put them at 16,986 killed and wounded and 1,468 missing. On the other hand, Manigault's estimate of Federal casualties is too high. Rosecrans' losses were officially reported as 16,170 of whom 4,757 were listed as captured or missing (*O.R.*, XXX, pt. 1, 179). In regard to the capture of artillery by the Confederates, Manigault hit it almost on the nose. The exact figure was 51 pieces (*Ibid.*). Among the impedimenta taken by the Southerners, as receipted for by Capt. O.T. Gibbes, C.S. Artillery, Ordnance Officer, Army of Tennessee, one finds, in addition to the more conventional weapons and equipment of war, the following: 3 bass drums, 1 kettle drum, 3 copper bugles (damaged), 7 halters, 33 pounds of picket rope and 365 shoulder straps. *O.R.*, XXX, pt. 2, 40-43.

[41] These are the figures given by Hindman in his report dated Oct. 25, 1863. *O.R.*, XXX, pt. 2, 302.

[42] In his official report, Manigault wrote: "We have to deplore the loss of many brave officers and men who fell on that bloody field. The loss of no one will be felt more keenly than that of Capt. D.E. Huger, assistant inspector-general, of my staff, who fell about half an hour before sunset, pierced through the heart by a rifle ball and expiring immediately. Earnest and zealous in the discharge of his duty, he had made himself respected and beloved in the command by his gentlemanly manners, his impartial and consistent discharge of the duties of his department, and by his great courage, coolness and judgment in action" (*O.R.*, XXX, pt. 2, 344). Col. John C. Reid, commanding the 28th Alabama in Manigault's brigade, referred to Capt. Huger in these words: "Never did an officer display more gallantry on a field. In the discharge of his duties as a soldier he fell. His memory will be cherished and his service never forgotten" (*Ibid.*, 350). And this tribute from Maj. John N. Slaughter, who led the 34th Alabama: "Riding fearlessly amid the shower of canister and Minie balls, waving his sword and calling on the men to rally, and encouraging them by his heroic daring, he fell pierced through the heart and died almost instantly. We rejoice to know that he died as the patriot and soldier would wish to die...in the stern performance of duty...yet we mourn that one so young, so gallant, so full of promise, should be cut off in the morning of life and at the threshold of his usefulness and be lost to his family, and his invaluable services lost to his country in this her hour of peril" (*Ibid.*, 353). Capt. Huger typified the

young men of the best blood of the South who gave their lives gladly for a cause they regarded as sacred. Although their memory was kept green by those who survived the war, their loss was a blow from which the South suffered for generations.

[43] Although Manigault refers to the severity of the fire to which the brigade was exposed, "when first we became engaged in the morning," his official report, as well as those of his regimental commanders, leads one to believe that the heaviest fighting occurred, as seems most likely, during the assaults on Horeshoe Ridge in the late afternoon when Capt. Huger lost his life and the final victory was won. Col. Reid of the 28th Alabama stated in this connection: "About 4 o'clock the brigade...became furiously engaged with the enemy; and this was the most desperate and hotly contested field of the day." *O.R.*, XXX, pt. 2, 348.

[44] PERSONNE is in error here. As previously noted, the Federal troops in McLemore's Cove were Baird's and Negley's divisions of Thomas' corps. McCook was located farther to the south in the vicinity of Alpine.

[45] A rather charitable glossing over of Bragg's failure to bring Thomas' isolated divisions to battle in McLemore's Cove!

[46] This, of course, was the beginning of the final victorious assault on Horseshoe Ridge.

[47] Cpl. E.B. Glisson of Company F, killed in action. He was selected by his comrades for the Roll of Honor as most conspicuous for gallantry and good conduct in the battle. *O.R.*, XXX, pt. 2, 540.

[48] This refers to the capture of the 22nd Michigan, the 89th Ohio and a portion of the 21st Ohio by Trigg's brigade of Preston's division.

[49] Manigault reported the brigade losses as 540 killed or wounded, severely, dangerously or mortally; 69 slightly wounded; 47 prisoners — total 656 out of 2,025 carried into action.

[50] C. Irvine Walker, who later commanded the regiment and after the war wrote a history of the 10th South Carolina, published in Charleston in 1881.

[51] Perhaps out of modesty, Manigault does not dwell on this narrow escape.

[52] PERSONNE was the nom de plume of Felix G. de Fontaine, army correspondent of the *Charleston Daily Courier* from 1861 to 1865. In 1864 he published *Marginalia; or, Gleanings From An Army Notebook,* (Columbia, S.C., 1864), and subsequently, in 1896, began the publication of *Army Letters of Personne 1861-1865, News From The Front.* These letters were intended to be issued monthly, price 10 cents, but sales must have been disappointing, since only Nos. 1 and 2 of Vol. 1 ever appeared. Both *Marginalia* and the *Army Letters* are today (1981) collectors' items.

6

THE SIEGE OF CHATTANOOGA

And

MISSIONARY RIDGE

(Editor's Preface)

Despite Thomas's stubborn stand on Horseshoe Ridge, by dark of Sept. 20 the Army of Tennessee, in its greatest victory, had driven its adversary in disarray from the field. The way to Chattanooga lay open, and a vigorous pursuit might have changed the course of the war. Certainly it was the last great Confederate opportunity in the West. But Bragg seemed paralyzed. Just as he had been unable to grasp the significance of Longstreet's breakthrough, so now he hesitated, vacillated and in the end did nothing.

That the condition of the Northern army was critical was plain to see. At 5 p.m. on the 20th, Rosecrans telegraphed Halleck in Washington, "We have met with a serious disaster; extent not yet ascertained. Enemy overwhelmed us, drove our right, pierced our center...Every available reserve was used when the men stampeded." And to President Lincoln at 9 o'clock the next morning: "After two days of the severest fighting I have ever witnessed our right and center were beaten. The left held its position until sunset...We have no certainty of holding our position here *(at Chattanooga)*." Although on the 22nd Rosecrans' courage had returned to some extent, and he maintained the disaster was not as great as he had anticipated, the best he could say was: "I think we can hold out several days...Our transportation is mostly across the river." Hardly the words of a commander confident of his ability to turn back a determined pursuit.

Although the disorganization and exhaustion of the Southern troops after the bitter struggle of the 20th may, as Longstreet believed, have made pursuit that night impractical, on the morrow almost every one, with the exception of Braxton Bragg, looked forward to following up the victory won at such terrible cost. That morning Forrest pushed forward to within a mile of Rossville and sent a dispatch to Polk with the request that it be forwarded to Bragg. "Can see Chattanooga and everything around. The enemy's trains are leaving...I think they are evacuating as hard as they can go...I think we ought to press forward as rapidly as possible."

And a few weeks later, in a bitter letter to President Davis, Polk wrote, "If the commanding general, under a delusion he took no pains to dispel, thought the troops were fatigued and chose to put off pursuit until the morning, why did he not attempt it then? Was it because he had made the discovery that the enemy had made his retreat into Chattanooga in good order and that he was secure behind ample fortifications? No, sir; General Bragg did not know what had happened, and allowed the whole fruits of this great victory to pass from him by the most criminal negligence, or, rather, incapacity, for there are positions in which weakness is wickedness. If there is a man in the public service who should be held to a more rigid accounting for failures, and upon the largest scale, than another, that man is General Bragg."

Longstreet was more circumspect. He urged Bragg to cross the Tennessee north of Chattanooga and force Rosecrans to retreat from the city, an idea generally endorsed by Robert E. Lee, who, however, favored crossing downstream below the Federal army. Longstreet thought Bragg had agreed, but nothing came of it. In his official report the latter dismissed such a movement as "utterly impossible for want of transportation," referring to it as a "visionary scheme" of no military propriety and added that "It is hardly necessary to say the proposition was not even entertained." So much for Longstreet's ideas!

In his exhaustive and definitive work, *The Truth About Chickamauga,* Archibald Gracie wrote in 1911 of Bragg's dereliction in not following up the victory at Chickamauga: "The halt to Confederate pursuit from a military standpoint was the most stupendous blunder of the war."

Unlike the Chickamauga campaign, with its intricate maneuvering, the story of the siege of Chattanooga and its aftermath is a straight-forward account of ineptitude and poor judgment on the part of Bragg in the face of the hard, cold efficiency that was to characterize the career of U.S. Grant.

After Rosecrans had retreated into the fortifications around Chattanooga, which he lost no time in strengthening, Bragg established his army in a semi-circle of some six miles, stretching from Lookout Mountain on his left across Chattanooga Creek and along the northwest face of Missionary Ridge to Chickamauga Creek at a point about two miles south of its confluence with the Tennessee above the city. This enabled him to control the Nashville and Chattanooga Railroad from Bridgeport, Ala., to the southwest, as it squeezed through the narrow passage between the northern tip of Lookout Mountain and the river. Furthermore, the wagon road following the north bank of the Tennessee was rendered untenable by the Southern artillery and the sharpshooters posted on Raccoon Mountain. Thus, Rosecrans was compelled to bring in his supplies by a circuitous route of some 60 miles well to the north of the river, through Jasper and across the Sequatchie Valley and Walden's Ridge. It was Bragg's strategy to starve him out.

This plan might well have succeeded had the cautious and unenterprising Rosecrans been retained at the head of the Northern army, but such was not to be. On Oct. 17, U.S. Grant was given command of all operations east of the Mississippi and south of the Ohio. He promptly established his headquarters at Chattanooga and replaced Rosecrans with Thomas, who had proved his mettle at Chickamauga.

Grant lost no time in reinforcing the Union army. Sherman was ordered up from Mississippi with his Army of the Tennessee, some 25,000 men, and "Fighting Joe" Hooker had come from the Army of the Potomac with portions of two corps aggregating 16,000 troops. In the end, Grant would have more than 80,000 men present for duty.

He recognized that his first priority was to open up a new line of supply. Hooker was ordered to cross to the south bank of the Tennessee at Bridgeport and to march east and northeast, down Lookout Valley, to Brown's Ferry. There he was to link up with 1,800 men floated down the river from Chattanooga, under cover of night, in 60 pontoon boats. Still a third detachment was to bring material for a bridge, overland by roads north of the river. This somewhat intricate maneuver was carried out with precision and success. The Southern pickets were driven off, the pontoon bridge laid and the so-called "cracker line," by river from Bridgeport to the Ferry and thence by road to the beleaguered city, was opened. it was in the nick of time, for rations in Chattanooga had been reduced to four cakes of hard bread and a quarter pound of pork for three days, and in the commissary warehouses only four boxes of hard bread remained. Bragg reacted to Grant's move with too little too late, and the threat of starvation that had hung over the Northern troops was lifted.

In the meantime, President Davis had visited the Army of Tennessee in an effort to smooth over what had come close to rebellion in the high command against Bragg for his failure to follow up the victory won at Chickamauga. In this he was unsuccessful, with the result that Polk, Hill, Buckner, Forrest and Hindman were transferred elsewhere. Still, incredibly, he clung to Braxton Bragg. Then, as if to seal his doom and make disaster certain, the latter, with Davis' approval, sent Longstreet, with whom his relations had soured, on a wild goose chase against Burnside in Knoxville, a move that deprived the army of close to 15,000 of its best troops and the services of its most experienced lieutenant general.

Bragg did not have to wait long to pay the price of his folly. Grant's strategic plan was to have Sherman, with his four divisions, subsequently reinforced by two of Howard's, make the main attack against Bragg's right at the northern end of Missionary Ridge, while Hooker, with three divisions, was to move against the Confederate left on Lookout Mountain.

To Thomas was given the job of demonstrating against Bragg's center. However, when Grant received information from a deserter to the effect that Bragg was about to evacuate his lines, he decided to pin him down by having Thomas go beyond a mere demonstration and make a pretense of attacking the Ridge. This the latter did Nov. 23 by pushing forward about a mile in full view of Bragg's men on the crest.

On the 24th, according to plan and in a dense fog, Hooker assailed the Confederate left, seizing Lookout Mountain from the thin gray line posted there to defend it. Much was made by the press of this colorful encounter, dubbed "The Battle Above the Clouds," and so it has gone down in the history books. Later, with his customary bluntness, Grant was to write: "The Battle of Lookout Mountain is one of the romances of the war. There was...no action even worthy to be called a battle...It is all poetry."

Next day, in a major attack, Sherman assaulted the Confederate right on the northern end of Missionary Ridge, only to be hurled back by that redoubtable fighting unit, Cleburne's division. Dismayed by this check to his plans, Grant, in order to take the pressure off Sherman, directed Thomas in the center to occupy the rifle pits at the bottom of the Ridge. This was soon accomplished, but Thomas' men, their blood up, did not stop there. On their own initiative, they surged foward up the slope in the face of a galling fire and broke the Confederate line on the crest wide open. With Hooker now moving against the Confederate left, panic ensued and, for the first time, a major portion of the Army of Tennessee abandoned the field in utter rout.

His center and left crushed, Bragg, to save his army from destruction, ordered a general retreat. He had no option. Narrowly missing capture himself, he rushed about, vainly attempting to rally his panic-stricken troops, crying out: "Here is your commander!" A private in the First Tennessee later wrote: "I felt sorry for General Bragg. The army was routed and Bragg looked so scared. Poor fellow, he looked so hacked and whipped and mortified and chagrined at defeat and all along the line the soldiers would raise the yell: 'Here's your mule! Bully for Bragg, he's h..l on retreat!'"

In his desperation, the Confederate commander called on Cleburne to stem the rout, and nobly did that intrepid leader and his division play their part that evening and the following day at Ringgold Gap, enabling Bragg's battered army to make good its retreat. It had been a close call. Pat Cleburne, born to a Protestant family in County Cork, Ireland, former corporal of Her Majesty's 41st regiment of foot, was well known as the "Stonewall Jackson of the West," and richly did he deserve this accolade for his courage and fighting qualities. Of him, after the war, Hardee would write: "When Cleburne's division defended, no odds broke its lines; where it attacked no numbers resisted its onslaught, save only once, and there *(at Franklin)* is the grave of Cleburne." Cleburne had saved

Bragg's bacon, but it was to be for the last time for that ill-starred nemesis of the Army of Tennessee was approaching the end of his career as its commander.

Chattanooga was unique as the only battle of the war in which all four of the most able Union generals participated — Grant, Sherman, Sheridan and Thomas. "No wonder," commented John Fiske, "there was litle left of Braxton Bragg!"

R.L.T.

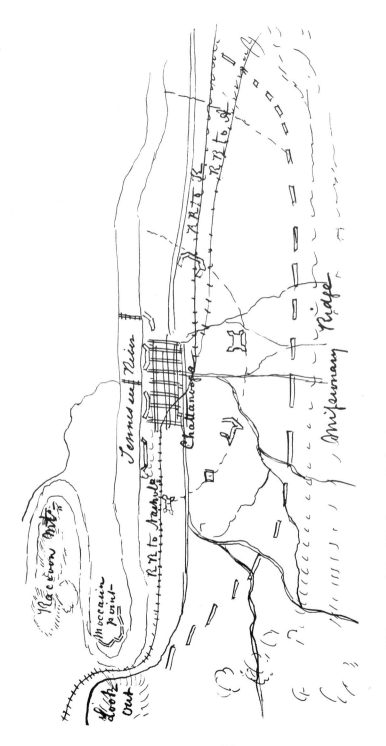

This map of the Missionary Ridge battlefield apparently was drawn by Gen. Manigault. It was not in The Narrative, but was found with his papers accompanying the manuscript.

SIEGE OF CHATTANOOGA

And

MISSIONARY RIDGE

(The Narrative)

I have inferred that General Bragg was dilatory in his movements after gaining his victory, and did not reap all the fruits of success, which he should have done, but the great error did not rest here, and I will try to explain in what it consisted. It will be remembered that the order had been issued on the night of the 19th to attack at daylight. I do not think that this could well have been done at so early an hour, for our formation had to be rectified and some alterations in the line made, and gaps filled, which occupied the first hour or so of daylight, but there was no reason why, at 7 o'clock the action should not have commenced. For the failure to do so, General Polk, commanding the right wing of the Army,* must be held responsible. He defended himself by saying that to General D.H. Hill, commanding the right corps, the order had been issued in proper time, that he fully expected a prompt and ready compliance with it, and was himself in the saddle at the appointed time, expecting momentarily to hear the battle commence on the right. As time wore on, and it did not begin, a staff officer was despatched to learn the cause of the delay, and to hurry General Hill in his movements. After some time he returned, announcing that General Hill's reply was that he had been unavoidably delayed, but would soon commence. A long period again elapsing, and still everything remaining quiet, General Polk rode himself to General Hill's headquarters, and found that officer — who, by the bye, had always borne the unenviable reputation, in a military phase, of having his own way and doing things only as pleased him, and, were it otherwise, throwing obstacles in the way — entirely unprepared to make his advance, and his men, whose rations had just come up, busily at work cooking them. Upon being reproached by General Polk for disobedience and non-compliance with orders, his excuse was that his men were hungry, were without anything to eat, and must be fed before going to battle, or words to that effect. A peremptory order to desist from their present occupation was then issued by General Polk, which I am inclined to think, was sulkily and unwillingly obeyed, and much valuable time

*General Longstreet commanded the left, in which we were. — A.M.M.

123

was lost, through the tardiness of the officers and men, prompt to catch the spirit of their immediate commander, and no doubt much preferring to finish cooking and making a comfortable meal before going into an affair, far from being as palatable. In this manner, four precious hours or more were lost, any one of which was of more value at that time than two or perhaps three at a later period of the day.[1] General Rosecrans's report of that battle has been published all over the country, and I only regret the loss of my copy and my inability to lay my hands upon one, but it is easily remembered that he states therein that a considerable number of his troops did not arrive until just before the battle — some came up just in time to take part — that he was himself employed for hours in altering and correcting his lines, in which many mistakes had been made. Some gross blunders had also been committed by some of his commanders, who had placed their troops in such positions as to render them of little use as they then stood. He moreover lays great stress upon the fortunate delay in the attack made upon him, and makes other admissions of such a character that the opinion may reasonably be expressed, based upon his own report and the great success which attended us afterwards, even when they were prepared to receive us, that had General Bragg's orders been obeyed, as they should have been, and had the battle commenced at 6:00, 6:30, or 7 o'clock, instead 10:30, that it would in all probability have been over by 12 M., a complete victory gained, the enemy routed, scattered, and demoralized, and in fact, the armed power of the Union in the west crippled for many months, perhaps never again to have obtained the mastery, and how may it not have affected the result of the war and perhaps the independence of the South. It is sad to look back and recall all these errors and failures, faults of our own, and committed by those, too, who, however they may have erred or failed, cannot be charged with any lack of patriotism or the deepest interest in the success of our cause.[2]

General Polk was relieved a few days after by General Bragg, from his command, placed under arrest and sent to the rear.[3] Hill also met with like treatment, Hindman also for his failure at McLemore's Cove, like the other two, retired to Atlanta, to await his trial by Court Martial.

I may as well mention that neither of these officers was ever tried. President Davis interfered, and through his instrumentality, proceedings were delayed, and the matter finally compromised. General Polk was sent to Mississippi; Hill, I do not remember what became of him,[4] but Hindman returned after an absence of two or three months to the command of his division.

On the 21st, the troops employed the morning in burying the dead, and collecting arms, artillery, and other military stores which fell into our hands. Late in the afternoon we moved some eight or ten miles to our right and nearer to Chattanooga. On the following day we remained where we rested the night before, and the day after, advanced towards Chattanooga, crossing the Missionary Ridge about 10 A.M. From this ridge, about three miles from the town, we could see the enemy at work like beavers upon their defences. Our lines were soon extended around the place, pickets and videttes thrown out, and the investment of

Chattanooga was begun, our forces reaching from the river west of the town to the same stream east and above it, the enemy having the river at their rear and the country opposite in their possession. We were not strong enough to encircle it completely, or to divide our army by sending a portion of it across the river, a wide, deep, and rapid one.[5] For many days it was confidently expected that the enemy would be forced to evacuate the place, and it was not believed that he could possibly supply and sustain himself there, as he had no railroad, that being in our possession, and the difficulty of hauling provisions a distance of eighty miles over a miserable road, forty miles of which was through the mountains and over them, was deemed impracticable,[6] but still they held on. On several occasions, strong reconnoitring parties felt their position, but found their works fully manned and very complete. Unfortunately, we had done most of it for them. Morning after morning, our skirmish line advanced, hoping to find the enemy gone during the night, but no, there he was still ready to receive us. After a week or two, our pickets ceased firing at each other. Occasionally artillery on either side would open, but the sharpshooters sat down or walked their posts within three or four hundred yards of each other, perfectly exposed to view and offering a most tempting target; but the understanding between them was that as the siege, investment, or whatever it may be termed, promised to be a long one, and as no really active operations were going on on either side, there was no use to make themselves uncomfortable, and it would be more agreeable to watch each other without trying to kill, than to be incessantly engaged in that disagreeable duty, where one invariably ran a great risk of never getting back to his messmates again; so that for very nearly two months, an officer might inspect his lines and discharge his regular duty on the outposts without any misgivings or disagreeable apprehensions.

The garrison in Chattanooga must have suffered much. Rations were reduced to the smallest possible amount that could preserve the soldier in a reasonable state of efficiency for duty. The weather was very cold and inclement for the season, and they soon cut away all the wood within their reach, or pulled down and used for fuel such buildings as were not carefully guarded. Their horses and mules died, I doubt if it will be any exaggeration to say, by thousands. A good many wandered into our lines, mere skeletons. Most of this information was derived from deserters and an occasional prisoner, and was, for some time at least, true — perhaps even worse than I have represented it.[7] Our own troops were comparatively comfortable and well provided for. Tents they had none, but as there was a plenty of timber on the ridge, boards were soon split, and comfortable shanties erected.

In order to secure our own position in case of an attack, a line of defenses consisting of earthworks for artillery and breastworks for the infantry, was thrown up at the foot of the ridge, some 300 yards from the summit and just a little above the plain. They were, however, of very inferior character, owing to the great deficiency of implements and the rough and rocky character of the ground. It took us about two weeks to make ours, as we had to borrow implements for the purpose, and I would have undertaken eight months after, with the same men, to have built a better in four hours; but at this later period they were experts at it, and no mole could have made himself more secure in a like period of time.

Sometime during the early part of the month of November or late in October,* President Davis paid the army a visit, and remained for four or five days, the guest of General Bragg.[8] He reviewed the army, or rather passed along the lines, the men being under arms, and expressed himself much pleased with the appearance of things. He also visited the battlefield of Chickamauga, and complimented the army on the success they had obtained in spite of the difficulties they had to contend against and the superior advantages of position held by the enemy on that occasion. Whilst at General Bragg's, together with several other Generals, I called upon him, to make some representation of an official character. Having finished our business, we arose to take our leave, but he was very pressing that we should remain longer as he had nothing to occupy him then, and expressed a desire to converse on other matters. We again took our seats, and he opened the conversation, speaking fully and freely of many matters — amongst them, several topics of national interest and of vital importance to us as a nation. I was much surprised at his freedom of speech and expressions of opinions on subjects which I had supposed he would rather have avoided. I was much pleased with his manner and the ease and dignity of his demeanour. There was not the slightest affectation or pedantry about him but he conversed easily and cleverly and with the air of a polished and highly educated gentleman.

I was much impressed by him, and the hour that we spent with him was one the most agreeable of the kind that I ever remember. It struck me also that he singled me out and that his attention to me was marked, and I thought that in doing so, I could detect on his part the desire to make the amends for his previous injustice to me, in the matter of my promotion. All this, however, may only have been a mistaken fancy on my part.

I have since been told, and believe it to be so, that on occasions as the one referred to, Mr. Davis is seen to the greatest advantage. He knows his power in this respect, and frequently brings it into play, when in a good humor, and with persons that have never offended him.

This second visit of the President to the Army of Tennessee, like his first, was doomed to bring misfortune on us, for whilst here, he inaugurated a plan of operations for which I believe him to be responsible, which was to send General Longstreet with his corps, together with a considerable force, into East Tennessee, to make a diversion there, and if possible, to take Knoxville, thus reducing the Army of Tennessee, already scarcely equal to the task imposed upon it, to a point far below what it ought to have been, and rendering them utterly unable to cope with the enemy should he receive any reinforcements, which in all probability, would be the case.[9]

*It was between the 12th and 15th of October. — A.M.M.

Previous to General Longstreet's setting out for this new field of action, he had been entrusted with the command of the line on Lookout Mountain and in the valley beyond, extending to the river, and at this last point the country is hilly, almost mountainous, indeed the ridge is known as the Raccoon Mountains. The river washes the foot of them, and here we had complete command of almost the only road by which the enemy could draw their supplies from a distant point on the railroad[10] to feed their troops in Chattanooga, and replace the ammunition expended, or such stores as were necessary to the army. The road on the opposite side was near the margin of the river with mountains towering above it. There was no avoiding this exposed place, except by a circuit of many miles, and this with the reduced condition of the enemy's transportation and the half-starved condition of their animals, they could not do. Here it was the habit to keep one or more batteries of artillery and a considerable number of riflemen, who kept up a heavy fire on the road from across the river, frequently blocking it up with wagons, whose teams were either killed or disabled by our fire. The necessity of keeping this road open on the part of the enemy must be apparent to anyone on reflection, and it was reasonable to suppose that they would make every effort to do so.

Rosecrans, who, from his failure and defeat at Chickamauga, had now got into bad odor with the U.S. government, had been relieved, and General Grant had taken command of the army.[11] With the eye of a soldier, he soon saw the necessity of securing the free use of this road, and a little beyond that too. He made arrangements accordingly, and they were carried out with such secrecy and despatch, that before General Bragg or Longstreet knew anything of his plans he had crossed the river in force, surprised the troops at that point on the left bank, and immediately intrenching themselves, in a position naturally strong, defied all efforts to retake it. Reinforcements were now coming to him rapidly and increasing his forces in his new position, he finally got possession of the valley, and our troops were driven back to Lookout Mountain. This gave him the control of the Nashville R.R. to within ten miles of Chattanooga, establishing a pontoon bridge near the Raccoon Mountains.[12] It was no longer a question as to whether the enemy could be starved out in Chattanooga, but rather a cause for apprehension as to whether we dared remain where we were. Unless heavily reinforced, in the same proportion as the enemy was being strengthened, it would be a problem easily solved. In the face of all this, Longstreet, after making a vain attempt to surprise the enemy,* and to recover that which he had been responsible for and had lost, set out on or about the 4th of November for Knoxville, and closed his career with the Western Army.[13] In Virginia, General Longstreet's reputation stood very high. I do not think that the impression he made in the West was a very favorable one. It was very generally thought also, that he leagued himself with several officers of high rank in Bragg's Army for the purpose of having that General

*On the night of the 28th of October. — A.M.M.

127

removed, and it was also believed that he expected, or hoped, to be advanced by the change.[14]

It is much to be regretted now that with this favorable turn of the scale in the enemy's favour, which I have just described, that General Bragg did not at once retire from the dangerous* position he was occupying in front of Chattanooga, as an investing army.[15]

From about the 10th of November, it began to appear that the enemy was receiving supplies. He began now to open with his artillery whenever a favorable opportunity offered, and it became unsafe to expose a regiment or company on dress parade or inspection, as we had formerly done. His batteries at Moccasin Point kept up a constant fire on the troops and working parties on Lookout Mountain and in that vicinity. Moccasin Point was across the river, and where it made a sharp turn, forming a long and narrow peninsula, known by that name. Many of their guns were mounted on platforms, and threw their shells from the point below across the river, and to *(the)* tableland on the summit or over the mountain. They were so well protected that our batteries could make no impression on them, although having the advantage of a plunging fire. At this portion of the line, the skirmishing was at times very sharp, also on our extreme right, when the line was lengthened to the river by a body of cavalry, there not being a sufficient number of infantry for the purpose; but all along the centre, there was no infantry firing. Although they frequently cannonaded us, our guns seldom replied. They did us very little harm. Such prisoners as we from time to time captured, gave a much worse account of matters for us than was agreeable to hear. They represented their supplies as ample, and the quality of their subsistance good,[16] acknowledging at the same time that their sufferings, occasioned by a deficiency of food, during the earlier part of the investment had been very great; and they also gave the much more alarming intelligence that reinforcements were daily arriving. This was evident to all, for new encampments were almost daily visible, even without a glass, not only on our side, but also across the river.[17] Their works had long since been completed, and were of a most formidable character. From the crest of the Missionary Ridge, the eye commanded a full view of Chattanooga and of the country surrounding it. The enemy's works, lines, and the troops defending them, were plainly visible, and the sight of their army became as familiar to us as that of our own, but two miles off.

Most of the timber on the ridge had been, by this time, cut away, used for fuel, building purposes, and breastworks at the foot of the hill. Such trees as were left standing had completely lost their leaves, and in the valley or level land below, the same conditions of things existed, so that our view was uninterrupted, and at one glance you could take in the position of both armies, numbering perhaps from 120,000 to 130,000 men.

At night just after dark, when all the camp fires were lighted, the effect was very grand and imposing, and such a one as had seldom, I take it,

*Walker crossed out "false" and wrote in "dangerous." — **Editor**.

been witnessed. Over and over again I have spent an hour or more in the quiet of the evening on a large, prominent rock that jutted out from the face of the ridge, and one of its highest points (the place is as familiar to me now as though it were but yesterday) admiring this grand illumination, thinking of home, family, and friends, or speculating as to the future.

The encampment of the troops was generally a short distance in rear of our works. The Quartermasters and Commissaries, with their trains, were located in rear of the ridge, and all brigade commanders or officers of higher rank had their quarters on the top, or a little withdrawn from the crest, on the back slope of the ridge, still within a short distance of their commands, which they could reach in case of necessity in a very few minutes. Upon the whole, were all very comfortably located, and our duties, everything considered, were not hard or irksome.

By the 20th of November, many things betokened that our then existing state of comparative inactivity would not continue much longer, and it was believed by many that the enemy would in a short time assume the offensive and make some effort to force or manoeuver us out of our position; but as a general thing, no anxiety was felt as to our own security, and the desire was very commonly expressed that the enemy would come out and attack us. It was not known by ourselves how weak we were, or the great strength of the enemy, and though our position was really a strong one, yet we had not men enough to make it secure, or even to fill up the lines we purposed holding, even without leaving a regiment in reserve, and our commander trusted too much to the natural advantage of the ground he occupied, or was not fully informed as to the strength of the army he had opposed to him. Perhaps he underrated his adversaries.[18]

I think it was about the middle of October that General Wheeler, commanding the cavalry attached to our army, was sent with almost his entire command, to reach the enemy's rear, and to inflict what damage he could on him by cutting off his supply trains, damaging the railroad, and destroying such depots as he could reach.[19] Crossing the river at some point higher up, I forget the name of the place but distant from Chattanooga some 70 or 80 miles,[20] and making a considerable circuit, he succeeded in reaching their rear, and surprised and captured two trains of loaded wagons, numbering, according to his report, 800. These he burned and destroyed, killing or crippling the mules. If the report be correct — and I know no reason to doubt — this injury to the enemy must have been a very serious one, and well worth risking the enterprise, but somehow or other, it had not the effect of starving the enemy out of Chattanooga.[21] Wheeler's success, however, ended here. His men, never remarkable for discipline, and the officers on a par with the men, seeing so much booty and plunder within their grasp, could not be controlled, but fell to work to secure for themselves as much as they could carry off. There being also a large quantity of whiskey and brandy in some of the wagons (probably for hospital purposes) the men and officers drank large quantities, and the consequence was a great amount of drunkenness. Hard to control at any time, they now became almost entirely unmanageable. Much time was lost before he could get his command away, and then in a greatly disorganized state. The enemy became apprised of the movement and of the disaster. The opportunity for further enterprises was lost, and a counter movement to check or capture him, immediately started in pursuit. He was overtaken or headed off, had to fight his way through, and finally recrossed the river many miles below Chattanooga, where he was safe from pursuit. Several hundred of his men were killed or wounded, a good many captured, and a much larger number straggled or were cut off from their commands, and returned to their homes without leave, to return at their convenience, a not unusual thing with our cavalry. I am inclined to think that this raid, like a great many others, did us more harm than the enemy.[22]

A Lieutenant Lee, of Alabama, a Cavalry officer,[23] and for a long time in Wheeler's command, afterwards temporarily attached to my staff gave me a full account of this raid, and also furnished me with much information as to matters and things connected with this arm of the service. Without repeating what he told me, it will be sufficient to say that, according to his account, such a state of demoralization existed in this corps, owing to the utter disregard of discipline on the part of the men and most of the officers, that it is no wonder that they were not only inefficient as soldiers, but unable to give that assistance to our Generals, in the way of valuable information, so much needed in the field, and one of the most important duties devolving upon them.

Early in November, a large detail had been made from my Brigade, which was sent up the river about seven or eight miles, and was employed in making rafts, cutting logs, and attaching torpedoes to them, and then setting them adrift with the current with the expectation that they would damage or destroy the pontoon bridges at or near Chattanooga; but the result of their labour and experiments was not very encouraging. The draft on my command, however, was so heavy as to reduce it to about 1,500 fighting men. The Brigade had been increased since the battle of Chickamauga by the return of many convalescents and some conscripts for the different regiments.

In spite of this extra duty imposed upon us, we were not relieved a corresponding amount of picket or outpost duty, and the length of line intrusted to our keeping remained undiminished.

On the afternoon of the 23rd of November, whilst sitting in my tent, occupied with some duty in connection with the Brigade, an officer from the picket line came to be in a great hurry to inform me that movements of a most threatening character had been observed in the enemy's lines. Repairing at once to the top of the ridge with my glass, I soon found that his report was correct. All within the hostile lines seemed alive with men, and large masses of troops were pouring out into the space between their works and the lines occupied by their pickets. There must have been at least 50,000 (fifty thousand) men of the enemy under arms. [24]

The Division Commander not being present, and it happening that I was the senior Brigadier in camp, I immediately ordered the division under arms, and the artillery in position. As the movement was visible to the whole army, in a short time the entire force was in the trenches, prepared for an assault.

The Division Commander, Brigadier General Patton Anderson, who commanded during the absence of Major General Hindman, at that time under arrest at Atlanta, soon, however, made his appearance and relieved me. Many were the conjectures as to what were the intentions of the enemy, but we quietly awaited their development. No alteration whatever was made in the disposition of our forces, but, everything was prepared to resist an attack.

At that time my picket line occupied a front of about 800 yards, and a high and commanding eminence known as "The Cedar Hill" was a part of the ground held. It was the most prominent point between the Ridge and Chattanooga, and one of much importance.[25] The 24th and 28th Alabama regiments were on duty that day, and held the picket line. They numbered together about 600 men on duty, both of them being small regiments. The picket line was entrenched with a shallow ditch and low earthwork, with rifle pits a little in advance.

About 4:30 o'clock the enemy formed two lines of battle with a skirmish line in front, and began to move forward. About five o'clock, their skirmishers came within range of ours, and the fight commenced. Our advanced troops were soon driven in by their line of battle, who moved steadily to the attack. Their first line was checked by our fire, but the second line coming to their assistance, together they moved forward in spite of our fire, which was not heavy enough to deter them, and came in contact with the reserve line of skirmishers. Both regiments behaved well, particularly the 28th, which resisted obstinately, and with great gallantry, many of them fighting hand to hand; but the odds against them were irresistible, and Lieut. Col. Butler, 28th Ala., Commanding, in order to save his Regiment, was forced to give the order to retire. The other regiment, 24th Alabama, had already given way. Had they contended much longer, they would have been killed or captured to a man, as the lines to their right and left had broken, and the enemy were getting to their rear. The 28th lost a good many, the 24th fewer — in all about 175 men.[26]

Having obtained possession of our picket line and the hill mentioned, the enemy seemed satisfied, and pushed forward no further. Our skirmishers retired about 350 or 400 yards and halted. Whilst the enemy advanced large numbers immediately in front of the hill to protect and hold it, he set large parties to work upon it, building breastworks and batteries for their artillery. In rear also was a large reserve force, and for the security of this point to which they seemed to attach much importance, they must have held in front at least 6,000 men, exclusive of the two lines in front.

Whilst this combat was going on, all remained silent spectators. No effort to reinforce our advance posts was made, and as our lines were very weak and we had not men enough to man them, and not knowing what was the ulterior intention of the enemy, I do not know that it would have been wise to risk more men to the front. Our skirmish line was lost and to recover it a general engagement would have to be fought.

It would be hard for anyone to imagine my surprise when, about dusk, I received an order to report to General Anderson to receive instructions about retaking the Cedar Hill with my Brigade. I immediately rode to his quarters, and was informed by him that I must at once make an attack, and recover the hill which my picket force had lost — as if I only had lost ground, and the line for a mile on each side had not also been driven in. I must say that I have seldom been more taken aback. On my asking what troops would support me, the reply was, "My own brigade (a Mississippi one, Col. Tucker commanding) on your left, and Gen. Deas on your right, and the orders have been given them to advance with you and to conform to your movements. They are in readiness, and as soon as you are, communicate with them, and then move forward." Of course I had nothing else to do but to obey the orders of my commander, but thought it strange that he did not propose to give the order for an advance himself, but supposed that when ready to execute the order, that I would find him also on the ground to superintend and direct matters. This conversation occurred in front of his tent, and as I mounted and was about to return to my brigade, he went into his tent to supper. Reaching my command in less than five minutes, I gave the necessary orders, and instructed my regimental commanders as to what was expected of us, and how they were to guide themselves, and, everthing being in readiness, I sent word to the two brigade commanders on my right and left that I was ready to advance, and would do so as soon as I received an intimation from them that they also were ready. It was now dark, and only a few prominent objects visible against the gray sky, but the country was familiar to us, and I doubted not but that I could conduct our centre straight to the point indicated. As to our ability to recover it, that was another matter, and I had a good many forebodings as to the result of our effort, but with that I had nothing to do. My orders, whatever I may have thought of them, were imperative.

Shortly after dispatching my messengers, one returned with Col. Tucker, commanding the left brigade, and the other brought a message from Gen. Deas, each reporting that their orders had just been changed, and that instead of their brigades advancing, only their skirmish lines were to do so, and that these were awaiting my orders. Thinking that there must be some mistake about it, so contradictory were the instructions issued, I determined to see General Anderson again, scarcely believing it possible that he intended to sacrifice my brigade, as would assuredly be the case if I was sent forward with 1,400 or 1,500 men, alone against certainly not less than six or eight thousand, supported by many pieces of artillery, already crowning the hill. I thought it folly as originally planned, but as the arrangement now stood, I regarded it as madness and the most reckless stupidity. On my reaching Division Headquarters, I found the Commander still at supper. At my appearing, he came out, and I stated the cause of my delay in advancing, and desired to know what the orders were that really existed. He informed me that he had changed his original plan since my leaving him, and had sent a staff officer to communicate with me, whom I had missed in the dark, and that I would immediately make the attack alone. I then said, "General Anderson, are you aware that my command does not exceed fifteen hundred men, and that in endeavoring to carry out your orders, I must, with such a force, necessarily come in conflict with certainly not less than six, possibly eight, thousand, men, and that under such circumstances it is beyond all reasonable ground of hope that the venture can result in success, whilst the great likelihood is that my brigade will be annihilated or captured?" He replied that I exaggerated the numbers of the enemy, and seemed to insinuate a backwardness on my part, not very creditable to me. It was now time to talk plainly, and I told him that I intended to obey his order as far as it lay in my power to do, and that as I did not expect ever to return myself, as also the greater part of my brigade, that I protested in the presence of one or two officers standing near, against the rashness and recklessness of his order, which would cost so many lives and men, to no purpose, and which I regarded as perfectly impracticable. Just at this moment, Col. Barr, a Mississippian,[27] who was acting as the Division officer of the day, rode up and joined us. He had been in the fight in the afternoon, had had the greatest advantages for seeing and knowing the enemy's strength and the disposition of his forces, and had just come from the advanced posts of the new line to which our pickets had been driven. He was a cool, active, and brave officer, and had seen much service.

I had turned away abruptly, and in a state of high indignation, mounted my horse to ride off, and whilst doing so caught the fragments of a conversation between Colonel Barr and General Anderson.

The latter asked, I think, what Colonel Barr estimated the Yankee force at, which General M. (myself) was about to attack. I caught the answer, "Not less than ten thousand", then a few disconnected sentences, but to the effect that the whole division would be an inadequate force to attempt what one brigade had been required to do. Galloping back to my command, the men were resting in line with their arms in their hands, awaiting my return. I had just called the command to attention, and was giving some last instructions to several officers, preparatory to giving the order, "Forward!" when General Anderson's Adjutant General rode up in great haste, and informed me that the General countermanded the order, and that the troops would return to their quarters. There was a general sigh of relief, and many a "Thank God!" coming from the heart, as the order was extended, and the different regiments were dismissed for the night. There was scarcely an officer or man who did not regard himself as saved, most unexpectedly, from death, injury, or a Yankee prison. They knew the danger which threatened, and regarded themselves as lost men. I have never been able to explain to myself satisfactorily General Anderson's object, purpose, or apparent ignorance of the enemy's force and position, which he, as well as several other hundred officers, had an opportunity of seeing from a prominent position, with scarcely an obstacle to prevent. There can be but little doubt that but for the timely appearance of Colonel Barr, as related, that on that night our brigade would have pretty much ceased to exist. Four or five hundred might possibly have returned, but a large proportion would have been killed, wounded, or captured, and their commander, for one, fully made up his mind that that night was to be his last.[28]

Such evidences of want of generalship, recklessness, and utter disregard for human life, did more on many occasions to weaken and impair the efficiency of our army than any losses inflicted by the enemy; and yet General Anderson stood well in the army, was generally regarded as a clever and efficient officer, and finally was promoted a Major General.[29] Several subsequent events only confirmed me in the opinion I formed of his ability as an officer, on that night of the 23rd of November, 1863, when Colonel Barr was the instrument used to save us. Poor Colonel Barr was afterwards desperately wounded at a battle near Marietta, on the 22nd of June, 1864, when Hood's corps attacked the Yankee right (another affair not very creditable to the military genius of Hood), where he, Barr, lost an arm. Some weeks afterwards, whilst being transported from one hospital to another, or to the railroad, the horses took fright, and, dashing the ambulance against a tree, upset it, breaking it to pieces, and killing that officer.

During the night of the 23rd, orders came to construct a line of defences on the crest of the Missionary Ridge, and such artillery as was in position in the lines at the foot was brought away. On the morning of the 24th, it was cold, cloudy, and misty. Lookout Mountain, five miles off, was completely hidden from our view by the mist, but a continued and heavy cannonade in that direction and the rattle of small arms, barely perceptible, gave us warning that a battle was going on there, and that the enemy were endeavoring to wrest it from us.[30] Throughout the day this lasted, and an incessant fire was also kept up from all of the enemy's batteries on our line. "Cedar Hill", during the night, had been converted into a position of great strength, manned with many guns and a large number of infantry, in breastworks constructed in a succession of curved lines, one above the other, with reserves in their rear. The firing on our picket line was sharp and incessant. During the day we laboured on our new line, but owing to the great deficiency of proper implements, the rocky character of the ground, and the want of material, we made but slow progress. This new line was run out by an engineer officer, whose name I have forgotten. He appeared to be in a great hurry, and said that he had much to do. Not liking the line that he proposed laying out for me, I suggested that if he would leave it to me, I would relieve him of the trouble, and as I was to be responsible for the defence of a certain amount of front, it might reasonably be expected that I would lay it out to the greatest advantage. This he agreed to do, and seemed much pleased at being relieved of some portion of his work, but at the same time told me that his instructions were to run the line on the highest point or outline of the hill. This was just what I wanted to avoid doing, for by doing so, I noticed that at many points, an intervening projection or irregularity of the downward slope prevented the fire of the defenders from playing on the enemy, after their reaching the foot of the ridge and when they ascended. The same obstacle protected them until within 15, 20, or 30 yards of our works. The only way in which this difficulty could be obviated was by selecting the ground when such was the case, below the crest, but whenever it was practicable and could be done, to make use of the highest ground. This defect I noticed in the line of the other brigades, and called attention to it, but it was not deemed worthy of notice, and we paid dearly for it on the day after. I was determined to avoid the error if possible, and though I ran some risk of censure for deviating from instructions, I determined to do so at all hazards.[31]

By four o'clock in the afternoon, rumors began to reach us that the enemy had possession of the Lookout Mountain, our extreme left. It was not credited at first, but in a short time the conviction gradually forced itself upon us that it was a fact.

The force that held it was entirely inadequate to its defense, and though from the precipitous nature of the mountain, the position that our troops occupied was one of no ordinary strength, still, the enemy, by great efforts and in large numbers, having scaled its north face far beyond where our lines extended, were enabled to take our works in flank, and finally possessed themselves of them. My recollection is that there were not more than three brigades on the mountain, perhaps about 4,500 or 5,000 men,[32] and although these might have made good their position against five or six times their number assailing them in front, yet, before attacking, the enemy by ascending far to the west of our line, when they did attack, did so, with everything nearly as favorable for them as for ourselves. It was a most fortunate thing for us that our entire force at that point was not captured but during the night they were extricated, and our entire army was drawn up along the line of the Missionary Ridge, the right resting near the railroad cut, the left a considerable distance from the road to Lafayette, which crosses the mountain near McFarland's Springs.

I little dreamed of our weakness in numbers when a day or two afterwards I was told by good authority that on the day of the battle General Bragg's army consisted of but 27,000 men (twenty-seven thousand), but from other sources and means of getting information, I have little doubt as to the accuracy of the statement. There were many, I take it, who were as much surprised as myself at learning what our strength was, and many more even at this day would be as astonished at this statement. It was known to the army generally that the enemy had been heavily reinforced, but I do not think that they were estimated at more than 60,000 men. When we saw them arrayed against us, we were forced to change our opinion. The army of General Grant on that day could not have been less than 80,000 strong, and I think that General Bragg afterwards put down their numbers at 90,000. General Johnston also in one of his reports alludes to the strength of this army as being 90,000.[33]

The position of our division on the 25th of November was, I think, about the right of the centre of the line. Our brigade was the 3rd in line, having Deas on the right, and Anderson's, General Tucker[34] commanding, on the left,[35] and our front (brigade) occupied a space between the Shallow

Ford road on the left, and another road crossing the ridge and running into the same road a half-mile in our rear. The ridge was lower between these two points than elsewhere *along the division line.* [*] In each of the two right and left brigades were two very high and prominent points, on each of which there was a battery of four guns.

In the centre of our brigade was the highest point in our line, the ground rising gradually from the two extremes to the centre, where for the space of fifty or sixty yards it was quite level, and here was posted Dent's Battery (two sections) of four 12-pound Napoleon guns. The infantry breastworks ran below, some 15 or 20 yards in front. The men in the works were not visible to each other for more than one-half of the distance of the front occupied by them. The works themselves were of very inferior character, owing to the deficiencies before mentioned, were low, and only afforded protection to the lower part of the body, and against the fire of artillery were rather a disadvantage than otherwise, when struck by a solid shot or unexploded shell.

I have many reasons for believing that it was General Bragg's intention to retire on the night of the 24th from Missionary Ridge, but was prevented from some cause unknown to me, and that if the battle had not been forced on by General Grant on the 25th, that he would have done so that night; but I have no authority whatever for saying so, and only judge of his intentions from the movements of our trains, and the tenor of several orders I received, which, to one familiar with the movements of an army, tended to confirm me in my opinion.[36] His report of this battle I have never seen, or indeed the report of any of the generals who took part in it.[37]

On the morning of the 25th November, the sun rose bright and clear, a strong north-west wind blowing, and the weather very cold. The men were under arms at daylight, but there being no indication of an attack, they were about sunrise permitted to break ranks. One half of the brigade was stationed in the old works at the foot of the hill, the other half in the works on the crest. This disposition of troops existed throughout the division, and I believe also in one or two other divisions of the army.

The instructions given to the officers commanding the lower line were, if attacked by lines of battle, to await the approach of the enemy to within two hundred yards, deliver their fire, and then to retire to the works above, a most unwise and injudicious disposition of the forces, and the orders by which they were to be governed of a like character. Only the superior officers were made aware of the plan to be pursued, and the men were kept in ignorance of it. These two separate and distinct lines were occupied by the men in one rank, with an interval of about a pace between each soldier. General Deas commanded the lower line of the division, Colonel Pressley, the 10th S.C., that portion of the brigade so situated.

Words in italics were added to the manuscript by Walker. — Editor.

Gen. Manigault's father and mother. The miniature of Joseph Manigault (1763-1843) was painted by Edward Greene Malbone. The portrait of Charlotte Drayton Manigault (1781-1855) is by an unidentified artist. They were married in 1800.

Mary Proctor Huger Manigault, painted from a photograph. Born in New Orleans, she married A.M. Manigault April 18, 1850.

Gen. Manigault, painted from a photograph believed taken during the war.

Arthur M. Manigault and
A.M. Manigault II, about 1851.
From a photograph. The baby
was born in 1850.

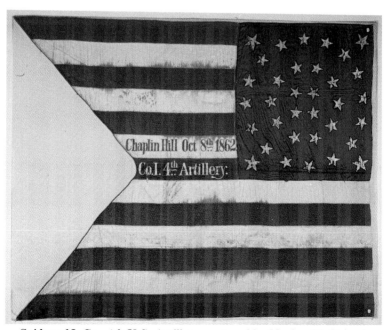

Guidon of I. Co., 4th U.S. Artillery, captured by Manigault's Brigade
at Chickamauga.—Photo by William A. Jordan.

Fighting around the Hurt House during the Battle of Atlanta, 1864. This scene, showing Manigault's Brigade entrenched behind cotton bales, is a prominent feature of the Cyclorama at Atlanta, Ga. —Photo by Eric David Loring.

Gen. Manigault's uniform coat—gray, with buttons and lace of a Confederate general officer. Now in the Confederate Museum, Charleston —Photo by William A. Jordan.

A pistol owned by Gen. Manigault. It is a Colt "Navy" model 1851, believed to be one he carried in the war —Photo by William A. Jordan.

Confederate Monument, Georgetown, S.C. Dedicated to the memory of the Georgetown Rifle Guards, A. Co., 10th South Carolina Volunteers. The relationship between Gen. Manigault and the Guards was one of mutual esteem reflected in the inscriptions. They fought through the war together until he was wounded at Franklin—Photo by Warren Ripley.

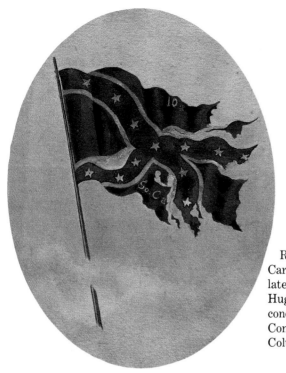

Regimental colors of the 10th South Carolina. A water color painted in the late 19th century by Lelia Garnett Huger. The flag, in much the same condition as shown here, is in the Confederate Relic Room and Museum, Columbia, S.C.

White Oak, Gen. Manigault's rice plantation on the North Santee River in Georgetown County. Painted by Charlotte Drayton Manigault about 1830. It was built by his father, Joseph, in the early 19th century and torn down after the earthquake of 1886.

BATTLE OF MISSIONARY RIDGE
25th OF NOVEMBER, 1863

(The Narrative)

At about eleven o'clock in the morning, heavy firing began on our right, and continued for about two hours with slight intermission, until it finally ceased. The enemy, in heavy force, had, during the previous night and at an early hour in the morning, moved round to our extreme right, and in heavy masses, had made an attack on our front. Cleburne's Division came in for the brunt of it, and repulsed the assault again and again, and the enemy failed in all his efforts to break through there. Our line there was very strong, and had been heavily reinforced at the expense of other portions. I was told that in one or two places there were two supporting lines.[38]

At about 12 M. the enemy began to mass in front of our position, distant about two miles. Shortly after the firing ceased on our right. Several columns of the enemy moved apparently from that direction (the battle there, owing to the configuration of the ridge, had not been visible from any portion of our division) and joined the troops in our front.[39] At about two o'clock these masses deployed and formed two lines of battle with a front of at least two and a half miles, and after completing their arrangements, moved forward to within a mile of our lower works and halted. In rear of these two lines, a reserve force, apparently equal in number to the first or second line, but in close column, by regiments, followed some three hundred yards in rear, as an additional support, and ready to be deployed at short notice. This splendid array of force was preceded by a line of skirmishers, deployed apparently at half distance. I estimate the number of men, open to our view, at not less than fifty thousand (50,000). The sight was grand and imposing in the extreme, and I was much struck by the order and regularity of their movements, the ease with which they preserved their line, and the completeness of all arrangements. Such a sight I never saw either before or after, and I trust under the same circumstances never to see again; and yet I felt no fear for the result, even though the arrangements to repel the attack were not such as I liked. Neither did I know at the time that a column of the enemy was at moment on our left flank and rear,[40] or that our army numbered so few men. I think, however, that I noticed some nervousness amongst my men as they beheld this grand military spectacle, and heard remarks which showed that some uneasiness existed amongst them, and that they magnified the force in their view to at least double their actual number. [41] For some time after this last halt of the enemy, a complete lull and stillness reigned, broken only now and then by a cannon shot. Even our pickets ceased firing. There seemed to be a tacit understanding, that, until the grand conflict, which was momentarily expected, began, that they would leave each other alone.

About four or four-thirty o'clock, I was walking in rear of my line, talking with and encouraging the soldiers, when a rapid succession of shots from the artillery on Cedar Hill, some ten or twelve pieces, gave the signal for the enemy to advance.[42] It was followed by all their artillery in different works, and to a man, on both sides, I will venture to say that the meaning of it was perfectly understood. Our own artillery now commenced to play on the enemy's dark masses, as they moved steadily forward, but not with the effect that I expected. A plunging fire against infantry is far less effectual than over a level plain or slightly undulating ground.

I watched with much anxiety the line below me. They stood firm, and when the enemy had arrived within about 200 yd., gave them their volley, and a well-directed and fatal one it proved; but then followed a scene of confusion rarely witnessed, and only equaled at a later hour on that day. The order had been issued to retire, but many did not hear it in the excitement of the fight, and owing to the reports of their own pieces, and the deafening roar of artillery. Others supposed their comrades flying, and refused to do likewise. Some few feared to make the attempt to retire up the hill,* exposed as they would be to a heavy fire in their rear, and as their movements would necessarily be slow, owing to the great steepness of the hillside, they felt certain that they would be killed or wounded before reaching their comrades above. All order was soon lost, and each, striving to save himself, took the shortest direction for the summit. The enemy seeing the confusion and retreat, moved up their first line at a double quick, and went over the breastworks, but I could see some of our brave fellows fighting to the last, firing into the enemy's faces, and at last fall, overpowered by numbers. Here the enemy opened heavily on our retreating forces, and did some execution, but they soon got beyond their reach, and then they began to reform their line, preparatory to an advance on our second line of works. During this delay, our men opened a steady fire on them from their works above, and did much execution, delaying them some time in their movement by the confusion caused. The distance must have been about three or four hundred yards, varying according to the configuration of the ground. Our artillery could not be depressed sufficiently to strike the foot of the ridge, and could only be used in firing to the right or left, where the ground admitted of it, and harassing the enemy in front of some other portion of the line.

The troops from below at length reached the works, exhausted and breathless, much the greater portion so demoralized, that, breaking through their friends, they rushed to the rear, bent on placing the ridge itself between them and the enemy. It required the utmost efforts of myself, staff, and other officers, to prevent this, which we finally succeeded in doing. Many threw themselves on the ground, broken down from over-exertion, and became deathly sick, or fainted. I noticed several instances of slight hemorrhage, and it was fifteen minutes before

*Missionary Ridge must have been at its highest point 180 or 200 feet high, and must have averaged 160 or 170 feet. The ascent was very steep.[43] — A.M.M.

most of these men were so recovered as to be made use of, or their nervous systems so restored as to be able to draw trigger with any steadiness. Soon, however, some order was restored to these regiments, and they were got into position, although here and there the men of different commands were somewhat mixed up. Still, matters had assumed a very tolerable order in time to receive the Federals, who now began to advance against us. A steady fire met them as they began the ascent, and before they reached half-way up, their first line had crumbled and disappeared, and their second much broken and in some disorder. As a regular formation, they did not advance more than fifty yards further, when they ceased to move forward, reeled, and went back. Our men were now firing slowly and steadily, with great coolness and perfect confidence in themselves and in the security of their position. The third line now reached the ground, deployed, and a second effort was made with it, supported by such of the first two as could be got together to storm our works, but with no better success than on the preceding occasion.

I was now perfectly easy in mind as to my own situation, and turned my attention to General Deas's front, noticing that a large number of Yankees had succeeded in reaching a point within a few yards of his centre (perhaps 20 yards) where they were protected from his fire by some overhanging rock. I directed Captain Dent[44] to turn two of his pieces on them, which he did, and also ordered one or two of my right companies to do the same. They were driven from our view, but it appears that beyond a turn of this same rock and beyond our reach, they also had obtained a lodgement in large numbers. I noticed also a short time before this that the enemy had made much progress in their advance on Tucker's brigade (Mississippians) on my left, but as he had sent word to General Anderson that his position was secure, and that the enemy could not move him, I thought little more of it, regarding the danger on my right as being much more imminent. Whilst thus employed, and happening to look towards the road that ran along the ridge, I noticed one of my regiments, the 34th Alabama, moving along it to my right. Surprised at so unexpected a movement, I immediately went to it, and on enquiring the meaning of it, was informed by its commanding officer that by a special order from General Anderson, he had been withdrawn from the works, and had been directed to reinforce General Deas, who was hard pressed and needed assistance. Immediately after, a staff officer reported to me the order of General Anderson, and I permitted the regiment to proceed, but was much annoyed at so unusual a proceeding and the want of courtesy shown me. My line was consequently much weakened, and the troops remaining had to be much stretched out to fill up the vacancy occasioned by the withdrawal of the 34th, by far the largest regiment in the brigade.

Again returning to the right of the command, I was watching with much interest and anxiety the progress of the fight on the right, when Captain Walker, the A.A.G., galloped to me, and informed me that the enemy had broken the Mississippi Brigade on the left, were in possession of a great part of their line, together with the battery in their centre. From where we stood, the intervening rise in my own line prevented my seeing for myself, and going as fast as possible towards the left, I soon found that Walker's report was correct. Two colors were plainly visible, and their troops were gathering in large numbers on the height, near where the battery was located. Tucker's lines as far as I could see, were entirely abandoned, and I saw only the rearmost of the men, making good their escape down the back slope. My own left was now swinging in the air, and with a weakened line and no reserves that I knew of or saw, our position was critical in the extreme, and unless this force could be attacked and driven off at once, the day and our position were lost. I sent Walker with all speed to inform General Anderson of the disaster, and made such arrangements as I could to save my left flank, now completely exposed. General Anderson's reply to Walker, when he informed him of the occurrence, was that it could not be so, the thing was impossible, the brigade was not broken. Walker, much provoked, answered that he had best satisfy himself, and could do so easily by riding a hundred yards to a point, from which he could himself see the Yankees and their colors. This he did, and sent Walker back to me with orders to draw out half my force from the works and drive the Yankees off, but it is much more easy to give an order than to have it executed, and to do so with half a brigade what a whole one had a short time before failed to do — that is, to beat the Yankees under much less favorable circumstances — was not a thing so easily done. At the same time, seeing the success attending their troops on their right, they were evidently preparing for another assault upon me. The incidents that succeeded passed in rapid succession. Deas's brigade now began to give way.[45] The attacking force had obtained a foothold near his centre, and all his efforts to drive them out failed. Whilst endeavoring to draw out a portion of my command with which to execute the orders of the division commander, the Yankees turned two of the captured guns on my line, completely enfilading it for some distance. At the same time they formed two lines of battle across the ridge, and at right angles with our line, at least 3,000 men at that point, and their numbers were momentarily increasing. Our left opened on them vigorously, also two pieces of our artillery, at a range not exceeding 400 yards.

I had but little hopes of being able to hold my position, and knew that nothing could save us but the timely arrival of reinforcements, which, hoping against hope, I trusted would yet make their appearance. I did not know that the division on our left, Breckinridge's, was in pretty much the same condition as our own, and also that the extreme left of our army had been flanked,[46] and that the Yankees in several lines of battle were carrying everything before them, as they struck our lines in the most favorable manner possible for themselves.

I now began to observe a man here and there, sneaking, or going rapidly to the rear, and directed the Officer of the Provost Guard to order his men to shoot down all who attempted to pass to the rear, unless wounded, but in a moment I noticed that instead of an occasional individual, groups of four, five, and ten, were roving in like manner, and they almost all came from the centre, on which the two guns (captured) were playing. The firing was now heavy and furious. Every effort to check the fugitives in their mad flight proved abortive. My right and left, 28th Alabama (left) and 10th South Carolina (right) still stood their ground and were fighting manfully, Lieut. Col. Butler and Col. Pressley, encouraging and setting their men an example, which deterred them from following the bad one set by others. Neither of these regiments from their position could see each other, but acted as though they did, and were emulating one another. Deas's Brigade was now going to the rear, broken and routed. Seeing that all was lost and that to check the fugitives was impossible, I directed the officers to halt and endeavor to rally their men on a ridge some four or five hundred yards in rear, and also sent two staff officers to do the same. I then turned my attention to the battery, with the view of saving it if possible. Captain Dent was already endeavoring to limber up and retire, but, being exposed to a heavy fire, he lost many men and horses. The enemy to our left was now advancing on us, the 28th firing on them as they did so; but still, onward they came, and they, the 28th, finally gave way. Attacked now in front and flank, further resistance was useless, and Colonel Butler was forced to give ground. Pretty much the same state of things existed on the right with Pressley, and the 10th, together with a portion of the 19th; but he too, pressed on all sides, and fast being enclosed, had also to save himself and command as expeditiously as possible. I was endeavoring to have one of the guns, which had become jammed between two trees, extricated, when Captain Dent called to me, "Leave the gun, General, and save yourself! The Yankees are on you!" Looking to the front, I saw them within fifty yards, pouring over the breastwork. Seventy or eighty men, including some artillerists, were scattered around me, some firing. Others had been assisting at the battery. I directed them to retire at once, and calling to Lieutenant Jannisson,[47] Acting Inspector General, told him we must now ride for it. Many of those around me were shot down and the bullets whistled around me like a swarm of bees. I thought my chance of escape doubtful in the extreme, but determined not to be taken if I could possibly help it, and to run every risk to secure my safety. So putting spurs to our horses, and separating from each other, we dashed down the rough and rugged slope at nearly full speed, and at imminent risk of our necks, the balls pattering against the trees and rocks around me like hailstones. Riding as I was, straight from the enemy, I felt certain that I could not do so long without being hit by the many balls fired at me, and although I increased the distance I had to traverse more than one-half, I rendered their aim less certain and thought my chances better by changing my course. I therefore turned slanting to the left, and had the satisfaction, after a ride of 300 or 400 yards, of placing an intervening ridge between myself and bloodthirsty foes. Here I was rejoined by Lieutenant Jannisson, who also had escaped. We literally ran the gauntlet, and as we were the conspicuous target for their fire, and several thousand shots must have been directed at us, it was only by God's mercy that we escaped. Our horses also were unhurt. Had they been killed, a like fate would in all probability have befallen us, or at least a long and wearisome captivity. Of those who were around me when I started in this race, only a few escaped. We saved two of our guns, the other two fell a prize to the conqueror.

After much exertion, we succeeded in rallying about two-thirds of what was left of the brigade, and formed on a ridge about 500 yards from the battlefield. Here, after a short time, we were joined by Deas's and the Mississippi brigade, General Anderson with the right brigade. The one from Tennessee[48] had been cut off from us, and we saw no more of them until midnight.

The battle seemed to have ended, for there was little more firing, except to our right, where the troops held their position until ordered to retire. To our left, we soon learned that the entire line had given way.[49] The best dispositions possible were made for defense, and information was despatched to General Bragg, or such general of superior command as could be found, telling them of our situation and asking for instructions. About sunset, General Deas marched off with his brigade, without informing Colonel Tucker or myself of his intention, and we were left alone. Fortunately the enemy remained contented with their success, and did not advance against us. It was a matter of much importance that the Shallow Ford road, which the two brigades covered, should be held, as our hospitals, many ammunition wagons, and several trains, had to retreat by it across the Chickamauga, and our holding it and showing a front there, enabled them to do so. Such artillery also as had been brought off, made its way to the rear by this road. About dark, Lieutenant F. Parker, General Bragg's aide-de-camp,[50] came to me with an order from General Bragg, directing me as soon as the wagons, artillery, hospital stores, and wounded had been removed, and were well on their way, to retire across the Chickamauga at Shallow Ford, and there to await orders. At about eight o'clock, everything being in readiness, we started for that point, and after a march of five miles, crossed the creek, and shortly after, reunited with the other brigades of the division.

We were beaten at Missionary Ridge because of the great numerical disparity between ourselves and our opponents, and because the disposition of our forces was injudicious in the extreme. General Bragg was overconfident in the strength of his position, and underrated the number of his adversaries, and their fighting qualities. He had not men enough to make himself secure, besides which he was completely outgeneraled by the Yankee commander. Had the corps which he sent around our left flank[51] (a portion of which attacked it, and contributed greatly to their success) succeeded in gaining the bridges and fords crossing the Chickamauga in our rear, in time, as they had been instructed to do, the Army of Tennessee must have been forced to surrender or been destroyed on the following day. Our defeat may also in a great measure be attributed to the error committed in the location of our defensive line on the crest of the ridge.[52]

Deas and Tucker were clearly broken and defeated, owing to the fact that at their most commanding and vital points, after the enemy commenced the ascent, they were not able to reach them with their fire, until they cleared a bulge in the hill, and then they had them under fire for a space not exceeding fifty yards. The Yankees soon discovered this weakness, and after the first repulse, formed a deep column, and then advanced rapidly from below the point protecting them. The troops in the breastworks had only time to pour in a single volley. The first line attacking may have gone down to a man, but those in rear, pressing forward, reached the works with scarcely any loss, before the pieces could be reloaded, and overpowered the defenders. I am satisfied that to this oversight — and it certainly did exist — may be attributed the failure of the division in this fight.

In the front of our brigade, the intrenchments were so placed that there was no limit to the fire of the men. It only depended upon the range of their rifles. The enemy were repulsed again and again with great loss, and with a sufficient supply of ammunition they might have been kept at bay for an indefinite period, and with little loss to ourselves. The greatest part of the casualties occurred in the lower works and whilst retreating to the intrenchments above, from the artillery fire of the enemy and from the attack on our two flanks, after the brigades on either side had given way, and whilst flying from the works.

The loss of the brigade on the 25th was	366.
The loss of the brigade on the 23rd was	175.
	541

The loss of the army in the different engagements on the 23rd, 24th, and 25th, was, I believe, about 5,500; and about forty pieces of artillery.[53]

I have on several occasions been repulsed and driven back when taking part in an attack, but never before or since have I been one of a routed army, where panic seemed to seize upon all, and all order, obedience, and discipline, were for the time forgotten and disregarded. God grant that I may never again take part in another such affair.[54] To stop the men in their mad flight, even after leaving the enemy hundreds of yards in their rear, was almost impossible. The officers generally seemed to lose their presence of mind. Threats and entreaties alike proved unavailing, and I only succeeded by telling them to reach the brow of a hill still further to the rear, and there to throw themselves upon the ground behind the crest, assuring them that in this way only could they be saved. Collecting the most resolute and authorizing them to shoot down all who went beyond that point, I at last succeeded in forming the nucleus of a line. Once having accomplished this, the rest was easy, and in a reasonably short time matters again assumed a respectable appearance. Confidence somewhat restored, and the men again shoulder to shoulder, they moved forward promptly to the word of command and advanced to a point several hundred yards nearer to the enemy, and I believe would have made a creditable resistance if again the Yankees had attacked them.

It was a long time before they got over the mortification of defeat, and the great majority earnestly longed for an opportunity of wiping out the disgrace.

Several valuable officers were killed in this engagement, but no one was more universally lamented and whose loss was a more serious one to the service than that of Lieutenant Colonel Julius Porcher, of the 10th S.C. In the formation of the regiment, he was one of its captains, had risen by regular promotion to his present rank. Although not a senior captain, those above him, recognizing his ability and worth, had waived their claims in his favor when a vacancy in the majority had existed. He was a brave, sagacious, and industrious officer. Fully alive to the responsibilities of his position, he never spared himself, and labored to perfect himself in all that pertained to the duty of a soldier, and made for himself an enviable reputation. Intelligent, highly educated, and with most pleasing manners, he was with all this the most humble and consistent Christian that I ever met with. Previous to the war, I had not known him but by sight and reputation. I afterwards became intimately associated with him and much attached to him. He was wounded a few moments before the line broke, and unfortunately no litter was nearby at the time on which to remove him. During the confusion which soon after took place he was lost sight of, and fell into the hands of the enemy. Nothing more was ever heard of him or of his fate. Inquiries by flag of truce failed to give any tidings of him, and his fate was for a long time uncertain. I do not doubt but that his wound was mortal, and that he died within an hour after receiving it. The badges denoting his rank removed by some Union soldier as a trophy,* his corpse remained unnoticed as an officer of rank, he was rudely interred amongst the dead left by us on the field, and all traces of him lost to his family and friends.

*A very common habit on both sides. — A.M.M.

NOTES TO CHAPTER 6

[1] The controversy over Hill's delay in initiating the Confederate attack at Chickamauga on the morning of Sept. 20 raged for years after the war. Since the general assault was intended to begin with Hill's troops on the extreme right, and to be taken up successively by divisions from right to left, everything depended on his opening the action. In a circular dated near Alexander's Bridge, Sept. 19, 1863, 11:30 p.m., Hill was directed by Polk, his wing commander, "to attack the enemy with his corps tomorrow morning at daylight" (*O.R., XXX*, pt. 2, 52). Unfortunately, through a series of misunderstandings and misadventures, abetted by inadequate staff work, Hill never received this crucial order. The story of how this came about, as it unfolded in all its drama, challenges the imagination even in retrospect. Surely the evil genius that plagued the Confederacy was at work that night.

After the close of the fighting late in the evening of Sept. 19, Hill, in order to receive instructions for the next day, sought out Bragg about midnight at Tedford's Ford, where the latter said his headquarters would be. There, somewhat earlier that night, Polk and Longstreet had been informed by Bragg of the reorganization of the army into a right and a left wing commanded respectively by these two senior lieutenant generals. This was a risky change in organization in the face of the enemy and one which slighted Hill, who, although a lieutenant general, appears to have been out of favor with Bragg, perhaps for his alleged failure to cooperate with Hindman in McLemore's Cove. Furthermore, Polk had been given verbal orders to attack at daylight, with Breckinridge's division of Hill's corps leading off on the extreme right.

When Longstreet had arrived at Bragg's headquarters shortly before 11 p.m., he had found the army commander asleep in his ambulance. Their conference lasted about an hour, and it is reasonable to assume that Bragg returned to bed at its termination. While only conjecture, it may be that the ambulance was then moved to a quieter location to insure Bragg's sleep. In any case, Hill failed to find the commanding general.

Shortly after his fruitless search had ended, Hill received from his chief of staff, who had met Polk on the road, a message from the commander of the right wing informing him that his corps had been put under Polk's command and that the latter wished to see him at his headquarters at Alexander's Bridge. It was then that Hill made a fateful decision. Exhausted from having been in the saddle from dawn until midnight, he decided to rest for a few hours before proceeding to Polk's headquarters in compliance with the latter's instructions. This was to have tragic consequences.

When Hill arrived at Alexander's Bridge shortly before 4 a.m., the courier who had been detailed to guide him to Polk had left his post and Hill was unable to find his wing commander. He, therefore, left word with one of the latter's aides that he could be found on the line of battle, which he reached a little after daylight. There is no firm evidence, however, that Polk ever received this message.

The courier who had been intrusted with delivering Polk's order of 11:30 p.m. directing Hill to attack at daylight, after searching for the latter for four hours, gave it up as a bad job and returned to headquarters. Learning of this, Polk, at 5:30 a.m. instructed his adjutant-general to send the following message direct to Hill's division commanders, Cleburne and Breckinridge:

> "The lieutenant-general commanding, having sought in vain for Gen. Hill, gives you directly the following order: Move upon and attack the enemy as soon as you are in position."

This order was delivered to Cleburne and Breckinridge in the presence of Hill, who had joined them on the line of battle as cooked rations were being distributed to the men, many of whom, according to Hill, had not had anything to eat for 24 hours. Hill later stated unequivocally that neither of his division commanders had heard anything up until then of an early attack. This seems hard to believe, especially in the case of Breckinridge, who had spent some time at Polk's campfire during the night while his troops were resting after their march to the far right of the line. Yet, in his official report, Breckinridge merely states that "during the night, General Polk informed me that I was to prolong the line of battle upon the right of Major-General Cleburne."

In any case, Hill replied to Polk that his divisions were getting their rations and would not be ready to move for an hour or more, that the line of battle needed rectifying and that the Yankees had been felling trees all night and now occupied a position too strong to be taken by assault, and asked for instructions. Arriving on the line about 7:25 a.m., Polk made no objection to the delay or the reasons therefore and discussed with Hill the alignment of the troops.

When Bragg finally arrived on the scene about 8 o'clock, he sought out Hill and demanded to know why he had not attacked at daylight. In reply, Hill said that that was the first he had heard of such an order. Infuriated, Bragg lashed out at Polk, telling Hill that he had found Polk "after sunrise sitting down reading a newspaper at Alexander's Bridge, two miles from the line of battle where he ought to have been fighting," a charge he repeated in substance in a letter to his wife and again in 1873, with the gratuitous further comment that Polk had said he was waiting for his breakfast, this "about an hour after sunrise."

This accusation of Polk's dereliction that morning was denied by William H. Polk in his biography of his father. He pointed out that both Gen. Cheatham and his aide-de-camp, Maj. Frank McNairy, testified they saw Polk on the line of battle about sunrise, which was at 5:47 a.m. that day. Furthermore, Lt. Col. Thomas M. Jack, assistant adjutant-general of Polk's corps, testified that immediately after Polk's order of 5:30 a.m. had been dispatched in duplicate, "the General then rode to the front accompanied by his staff." In addition, Bragg in 1873 conceded that he had not personally seen Polk after sunrise in a rocking chair reading the newspaper but that the staff officer sent by him to Gen. Polk had so reported. All in all, the weight of evidence appears to sustain Polk's position.

Be that as it may, the net result was that the attack Bragg had intended to take place at daylight did not get under way until about 9:30 a.m. Hill later maintained that this was unavoidable in any case, as the position of the enemy had not been reconnoitered nor the battle line rectified. Also, no cavalry had been posted on the flanks, and the strength and position of the reserves had not been fixed — all this in addition to the necessity of feeding the men before sending them into action.

All things considered, it seems clear that the responsibility for the delay was divided. Bragg failed to take personal command on his right or even be present at the critical hour of dawn. Polk's staff work was inadequate and he is certainly open to criticism for failing to send back-up couriers with the 11:30 p.m. order to attack at daylight, as he subsequently did with the order issued at 5:30 a.m. directly to Cleburne and Breckinridge. Furthermore, he was negligent in not making certain that the guides at his headquarters at Alexander's Bridge were kept on duty throughout the night. As for Hill, regardless of his fatigue, he never should have rested for those three critical hours during the night without first making sure that Polk was informed of his failure to find Bragg. *Battles and Leaders,* III, 653; Horn, *The Army of Tennessee,* 240, 260-261; *Polk,* II, 238-252; *Seitz,* 359-360; Hall Bridges, *Lee's Maverick General: Daniel Harvey Hill,* (New York, 1961), 207-217, (hereafter cited as *Bridges*); *O.R. Atlas,* Series I, Vol. XXX, Sheet 2; Dr. Y.R. Lemonnier, "Gen. Leonidas Polk at Chickamauga," *Confederate Veteran,* XXIV, 17-19.

[2] Rosecrans' report (*O.R., XXX,* pt. 1, 54-64) does not bear out Manigault's recollection to the effect that Rosecrans stated that a considerable number of his troops did not arrive until just before the battle. Had the attack been launched earlier, however, the Northern commander would have had less time to bring reinforcements to Thomas's hard pressed men on the left. Still more important, there would have been several more hours of daylight available to complete the destruction of the Federal army.

[3] The charges against Polk were first, disobedience of the lawful command of his superior in connection with his failure to attack at daylight on Sept. 20; second, neglect of duty to the prejudice of good order and military discipline as evidenced by his failure to report non-compliance with his orders and to take proper or prompt measures to ascertain the causes thereof and, further, not joining his command at daylight and remaining at his field headquarters, two miles from his troops, until and after the arrival of a staff officer of Bragg's (Maj. P.B. Lee) at 7 a.m. and at that time failing to ascertain the cause of his troops not making the attack ordered at daylight. As stated by Manigault, Polk was suspended from command and sent to Atlanta, where on Oct. 6, he demanded a court of inquiry. On the same day, he wrote a long letter to President Davis, throwing the onus on Bragg for his failure to follow up the decisive victory at Chickamauga, either on the evening of the 20th or the morning of the 21st, and urging his removal from command and replacement by Robert E. Lee. Davis, who was a friend and supporter of Polk as well as Bragg, denied Polk's application for a court of inquiry, stating that he had reached the conclusion that a court-martial was not justified. *O.R., XXX,* pt. 2, 55-70.

[4] Hill was not suspended from command, as were Polk and Hindman, but he incurred Bragg's displeasure by criticism of his commander and joining with Longstreet, Polk, Buckner, Cleburne and others in urging Bragg's removal from command. Writing to Davis Sept. 25, Bragg characterized Hill as "despondent, dull, slow...always in a state of apprehension. His open and constant croaking would demoralize any command in the world. He does not hesitate at all times and in all places to declare our cause lost." On Oct. 11, Bragg requested that Hill be relieved from duty with the army, and two days later Davis authorized the move. The formal order relieving Hill came on the 15th and he was directed to report with his staff to Gen. S. Cooper, adjutant and inspector general, at Richmond.

Feeling that he had unjustly been made a scapegoat for Bragg's failures (Polk and Hindman were restored to command), Hill vainly demanded a court of inquiry. There ensued a long and bitter vendetta with Jefferson Davis, who rather spitefully refused to send Hill's promotion to lieutenant general to the senate for confirmation. This resulted in his reverting to his previous rank of major general. Hill then demanded "an unequivocal expression of undiminished confidence in my capacity, gallantry and fidelity" before he would accept further duty, but Davis would not even concede that. Notwithstanding, Hill, unselfish patriot that he was, served effectively, though technically on informal rather than active service, under Beauregard in the operations against Butler south of Richmond in May 1864 and under Early in the repulse of Hunter before Lynchburg in June of that year. Following that, he did a stint as Beauregard's inspector of trenches at Petersburg. In February 1865, as the end approached, Hill was ordered to the field in his native North Carolina and, at Bentonville, joined his old enemy, Bragg, and his friend, Joe Johnston, in the final battle against Sherman's overwhelming forces on their way north to join Grant.

Hill had a caustic tongue which he often used at the expense of others. His testy disposition may have been exacerbated by his indifferent health. Like Bragg, he suffered from what in those days was called "dyspepsia". Bragg referred to him as a "querulous and insubordinate spirit in general," and Stanley Horn in his *Army of Tennessee* says that Hill was "jealous and sensitive and regarded as 'peculiar', a sort of stormy petrel and for some reason a misfit officer." But for all his problems of personality, Harvey Hill was a brave and unselfish man, and no one ever questioned his devotion to the cause of the South. *O.R.,* XXX, pt. 2, 148-149; *Bridges,* 226-272; Freeman, *Lee's Lieutenants,* III, 317-322, 462-464, 490-493, 526; Horn, *The Army of Tennessee,* 240.

[5] The Confederate line reached from the foot of Lookout Mountain on the west, where the railroad from Bridgeport to Chattanooga squeezed between the mountain and the river, to Chickamauga Creek on the east about two miles from its confluence with the Tennessee above the city. Horn, *The Army of Tennessee,* 281.

[6] This route stretched from Bridgeport through Jasper, across the Sequatchie Valley and Walden's Ridge, well to the north of the Tennessee, a distance of more than 60 miles. *Battles and Leaders,* III, 683-687.

[7] Grant, who was not given to exaggeration, described the condition of the garrison in these words: "The men had been on half rations of hard bread for some time, with but few other supplies except...'beef dried on the hoof'...The troops were without shoes or other clothing suitable for the advancing season, what they had was well worn. The fuel within the Federal lines was exhausted, even to the stumps of trees. There was not enough ammunition for a day's fighting." Of the country north of the river, Grant said that it afforded little food for animals "nearly ten thousand of which had already starved, and none were left to draw a single piece of artillery or even the ambulances to convey the sick." *Ibid.*

[8] Davis arrived Oct. 9 and left for Atlanta on the 13th. *O.R.,* XXX, pt. 4, 742.

[9] Davis wrote Bragg from Atlanta on Oct. 29, "It has occured to me that...you might advantageously assign General Longstreet with his two divisions to the task of expelling Burnside *(from Knoxville)* and thus place him in position...to hasten or delay his return to the army of General Lee." To this Bragg replied on the 31st: "The Virginia troops (i.e. Longstreet's) will move in the direction indicated as soon as practicable." He added: "This will be great relief to me" — presumably, that is, to get Longstreet, whose suggestions both strategic and tactical he appeared to resent, out of his hair. (*O.R.,* LII, pt. 2, 554-557). Longstreet warned Bragg that the movement to East Tennessee would give Grant the opportunity to break Bragg's lines around Chattanooga before Longstreet could return. With a "sardonic smile which seemed to say that I knew little of his army or himself in assuming such a possibility," Bragg "intimated that further talk was out of order." *Longstreet,* 481-482.

[10] Bridgeport.

[11] Grant was given command Oct. 17 of the newly organized Military Division of the Mississippi, and it was left up to him whether he should retain Rosecrans as commander of the Army of the Cumberland or replace him with Thomas. He opted for the latter alternative. *Battles and Leaders,* III, 682.

[12] At Brown's Ferry.

[13] Longstreet maintained that Bragg repeatedly discredited information supplied him by Longstreet's signal service and that, in any case, the position at Brown's Ferry and west of Lookout Mountain was indefensible. A look at the map and the force available would seem to support Longstreet's contention. Manigault's partiality for Bragg is once more here evident. *Longstreet,* 471-477.

[14] That Longstreet was ambitious and had an inordinate idea of his abilities as an independent army commander cannot be denied. In this instance, however, Manigault's comment hardly appears justified. In his memoirs, written more than 30 years after the war, Longstreet states that in August Gen. Lee, while discussing affairs in the West, asked him if he was willing to go and take charge, to which Longstreet says he consented provided time was given him to gain the confidence of the troops and "means could be arranged for further aggressive march in case of success." No further discussion of giving Longstreet command of the Army of Tennessee occurred until Davis broached the subject during his visit to the army in October. But by that time, Longstreet said, it was too late, since in his judgment the last opportunity had been lost when Bragg failed to follow up the victory at Chickamauga. He then made the mistake of suggesting Joseph E. Johnston for the command, which only served to annoy Davis, who had a strong antipathy for that able officer. (*Longstreet,* 434-436, 466). On the other hand, it is true that Longstreet joined with Polk, Hill, Cleburne, Buckner and others in urging Bragg's removal. On Sept. 26 he wrote to the Secretary of War: "I am convinced that nothing but the hand of God can save us or help us as long as we have our present commander." *O.R.,* XXX, pt. 4, 706.

[15] Such a withdrawal was urged by Longstreet, and even Bragg himself, and approved by Davis. But heavy rain set in and Bragg used the muddy roads as an excuse not to act. *Longstreet,* 468-470.

[16] This, of course, was so since the opening of the "cracker line" Oct. 30.

[17] The reinforcements consisted chiefly of Sherman's Army of the Tennessee, which had been made available by the fall of Vicksburg. The returns for Nov. 20 showed 16,965 officers and men present for duty. (*O.R.,* XXXI, pt. 2, 13). In addition, "Fighting Joe" Hooker had arrived with portions of the Eleventh and Twelfth corps of the Army of the Potomac and crossed the river at Bridgeport to threaten Bragg's left flank from the west. In passing, it is of interest to note that Hooker's sobriquet of "Fighting Joe" is said to have originated from his predilection for fisticuffs while a cadet at West Point, rather than from any prowess in the field. His most lasting legacy to the American scene may be the alleged application of his name to ladies of the street, a connection presumably derived from the non-bellicose diversions it was rumored took place at his headquarters. Now, seated on his bronze charger in front of the State House in Boston, he stares out over the Common and St. Gaudens' celebrated memorial to Robert Gould Shaw leading the 54th Massachusetts against Fort Wagner in

Charleston Harbor, with a look of power and determination for which he would doubtless prefer to be remembered by posterity.

[18] The Confederate force, depleted by the departure for East Tennessee of Longstreet, followed by Buckner, was heavily outnumbered. Grant stated that the Union army taking part in the Battle of Chattanooga amounted in round figures to about 60,000 men, while Bragg's strength was in the neighborhood of 37,000. *Battles and Leaders,* III, 711; Horn, *The Army of Tennessee,* 301.

[19] Wheeler's orders were issued Sept. 29 and he moved at once to carry them out. *O.R.,* XXX, pt. 2, 722-723.

[20] The crossing took place at Cottonport, sometimes written Cotton Port.

[21] With about 4,000 troopers, Wheeler, in this so-called Sequatchie raid, made a wide swing around the Northern army and inflicted serious damage on Rosecrans' line of supply. His major exploit was the capture and destruction, near Anderson's Cross Roads, of a train of some 800 six-mule government wagons, loaded with quartermaster, commissary, ordnance and medical stores. Including a large number of additional sutlers' wagons, this enormous train, stretching as far as the eye could reach, fell prey to Wheeler's horsemen. In his official report he wrote: "After selecting such mules and wagons as we needed, we then destroyed the train by burning the wagons and sabering or shooting the mules," some 4,000 in number. (*O.R.,* XXX, pt. 2, 722-725). "The destruction of the ordnance trains...presented a fearful spectacle. The noise of bursting shells and boxes of ammunition so resembled the sound of battle as to astonish and alarm the enemy in Chattanooga, who were in doubt as to the cause, until the ascending columns of smoke told them the food and ammunition upon which almost the vitality of their army depended were actually destroyed" (*Wheeler and His Cavalry,* 122-123). Wheeler went on to McMinnville and spread his path of destruction all the way back to the Tennessee River, which he recrossed at Muscle Shoals, ripping up railroad tracks, burning bridges and destroying vast quantities of stores, as well as capturing between 1,500 and 2,000 prisoners. For his exploits he received the thanks of President Davis and the compliments of Bragg in General Orders. All the same, the enemy in Chattanooga, as Manigault points out, did not succumb to starvation, thanks to Grant and the opening of the "cracker line." *Wheeler and His Cavalry,* 117-142; *DuBose,* 206-214.

[22] Dodson reports Wheeler's entire loss during the raid, according to the reports of the several regiments, as three officers and 29 privates killed, 13 officers and 93 privates wounded, and nine officers and 171 privates captured. *Op. cit.,* 128.

[23] W.J. Lee of Lenoir's Independent Company Alabama Cavalry, which served as escort at General Withers' and subsequently Gen. Hindman's headquarters. *O.R.,* XXIII, pt. 2, 945, 948; XXXII, pt.3, 873.

[24] Manigault here refers to Thomas' advance of the 23rd. It was a sight worth remembering. A Northern eyewitness described the scene. "At half-past twelve, Wood's division supported by Sheridan marched out on the plain in front of the fort. It was an inspiring sight. Flags were flying; the quick, earnest steps of thousands beat equal time. The sharp commands of hundreds of company officers, the sound of drums, the ringing notes of the bugle, companies wheeling and countermarching and regiments getting into line, the bright sun lighting up ten thousand polished bayonets till they glistened and flashed like a flying shower of electric sparks...and

all looked like preparations for a peaceful pageant, rather than the bloody work of death." *Battles and Leaders,* III, 721.

²⁵ It seems evident that what Manigault referred to as "The Cedar Hill" was Orchard Knob (also referred to as Orchard Knoll or Hill), which was seized by Gen. Thomas Wood on Nov. 23. *Battles and Leaders,* III, 721.

²⁶ In his report, Thomas says: "The formation being completed about 2 p.m, the troops advanced steadily and with rapidity directly to the front, driving before them first the rebel pickets, then their reserves, and falling upon their grand guards stationed in their first line of rifle pits, captured something over 200 men, and secured themselves in their new position before the enemy had sufficiently recovered from his surprise to attempt to send reinforcements from his main camp" (*O.R.,* XXXI, pt. 2, 94-95). Brig. Gen. Thomas J. Wood, commanding the Third Division, Fourth Army Corps, of Thomas' command reported: "The Twenty-Eighth Alabama, with its flag, was captured almost entire."(*O.R.,* XXXI, pt. 2, 256). One of his brigade commanders, Brig. Gen. Hazen, stated that Corp. G.A. Kraemer, Co. I, Forty-first Ohio, "alone ordered and received the surrender of 20 men with the colors of the Twenty-eighth Alabama." *Ibid.,* 282-283.

²⁷ Col. James Barr, Jr., commanding the 10th Mississippi.

²⁸ Not surprisingly, there is no mention of this episode in the *Official Records.*

²⁹ A native of Tennessee, James Patton Anderson, with the rank of lieutenant colonel, commanded the 1st Battalion Mississippi Rifles in the Mexican War. Subsequently, he served a term in the Mississippi legislature and was later elected a delegate from the Washington Territory. Appointed colonel of the 1st Florida Infantry when the war broke out, he was made a brigadier general Feb. 10, 1862, and fought at Shiloh, Perryville, Murfreesboro, Chickamauga and Missionary Ridge. Having been promoted major general, he was severely wounded in the Battle of Jonesboro outside of Atlanta in the summer of 1864. Recovering, he rejoined the army in North Carolina in the spring of 1865 and surrendered with it at Greensboro. *Generals in Gray,* 7-8.

³⁰ Reference here is to Hooker's successful attack on Lookout Mountain, the so-called "Battle Above the Clouds."

³¹ The error of the Confederate engineers in locating the main line on the "topographical" rather than the "military" crest, the latter referring to the highest line from which the enemy could be seen and fired on, has often been cited as one of principal causes of the Confederate disaster that ensued. Horn, *The Army of Tennessee,* 300; Shelby Foote, *The Civil War: A Narrative,* 4 vols., (New York, 1958, 1974), 855-856. Hereafter cited as *Foote.*

³² This is an accurate estimate. The troops involved were Walthall's, Moore's and Jackson's brigades of Cheatham's division and a portion of Pettus' of Stevenson's, under the command of the latter. Livermore, *Numbers and Losses in the Civil War,* 107; *O.R.,* XXXI, pt. 2, 656-664.

³³ Authorities differ widely as to the numbers involved in the Battle of Missionary Ridge. As noted previously, Grant placed the strength of the Northern army actually engaged in the operations at Chattanooga at about 60,000, while

Stanley Horn estimated the Confederate force at approximately 37,000. However, in the *Southern Historical Society Papers,* Vol. XXXIX, 13, P.D. Stephenson of the 13th Arkansas in Cleburne's division asserts that the Confederate army had been seriously reduced by illness caused by the heavy rains. "We had about 25,000 or 26,000 enfeebled men, thinned out to such attenuation that there was but one 'rank' of us, and in places this single rank was made up of men five to seven or eight feet apart. Such was the picture when morning broke into a lovely winter day."

[34] William T. Tucker, at that time colonel of the 41st Mississippi, commanding Anderson's brigade. He was made a brigadier general Mar. 1, 1864, and was so severely wounded at Resaca on May 14 that he was henceforth incapacitated for field duty. He was assassinated in 1881 allegedly by a man hired for the deed by one Shaw, against whom Gen. Tucker had a case pending for misappropriation of guardianship funds. *Generals in Gray,* 311.

[35] Vaughan's brigade was on the right of the division, so that the brigade order from right to left was Vaughan, Deas, Manigault, Anderson (Tucker). This is what Manigault had in mind when he wrote that "our brigade was the 3rd in line." (ie. from right to left). E.T. Sykes *Walthall's Brigade,* (Columbus, Miss., 1905), 609. Hereafter cited as *Sykes.*

[36] There appears to be no evidence that Bragg intended at this time to withdraw from Missionary Ridge. To the contrary, in his official report he stated: "The position was one which ought to have been held by a line of skirmishers against any assaulting column, and wherever resistance was made the enemy fled after suffering heavy loss." (*O.R.,* XXXI, pt. 2, 666). Nevertheless, there were others who shared Manigault's belief that Bragg would retire. Captain Irving A. Buck, assistant adjutant general of Cleburne's division, wrote: "Based upon the reduction of Bragg's forces by the detachments referred to (Longstreet and Buckner), the increase of Grant's by reinforcements by Hooker and Sherman, coupled with the loss of Lookout Mountain and consequent exposure on his left flank, Cleburne was impressed with the belief that General Bragg, with his slim force, would fall back behind the Chickamauga, and not attempt to hold the extended line of Missionary Ridge." Irving A. Buck, *Cleburne and his Command,* (Jackson, Tenn., 1958), 166. Hereafter cited as *Buck.*

[37] Although Bragg's brief report, along with those of Cleburne, Bate and others, appears in the *Official Records,* the latter do not contain reports from Hardee, Manigault's corps commander, Patton Anderson, his division commander, nor from Manigault himself or any of his fellow brigade commanders, Deas, Vaughan and Tucker. There is a paucity of information from the Southern side on the details of Missionary Ridge and little was written by participants after the war. Evidently they preferred to forget and understandably so, as Missionary Ridge was one of only two occasions during the war when a major Confederate army was driven from the field in panic and rout. The other was Nashville.

[38] The abortive attack on the Confederate right was led by Sherman with a force of six divisions.

[39] In this, Manigault was in error. The attack on Missionary Ridge in the center was made by Thomas' Army of the Cumberland, some 25,000 men, with no support from Sherman on the Federal left.

[40] These were Hooker's troops, fresh from their triumph at Lookout Mountain on the previous day.

[41] As, indeed, Manigault himself appears to have done.

[42] At 20 minutes before four o'clock, six guns, the agreed on signal, were fired in rapid succession (*Battles and Leaders,* III, 725; *O.R.,* XXXI, pt.2, 132). Shelby Foote describes the scene: "The first of the six signal guns was fired under the personal direction of the ebullient and high-strung Gordon Granger, who stood on the Orchard Knob parapet, lifting and lowering his right arm in rapid sequence as he shouted: 'Number One, fire! Number Two, fire! Number Three, fire! Number Four, fire! Number Five, fire!' Before the sixth gun roared, the leading elements were off. 'Forward, guide center, march!' regimental commanders shouted, and the 25,000 infantry in the four blue divisions began their plunge of nearly a mile across the wooded, hilly plain. 'Number Six, fire!' Granger cried." *Foote,* II, 853.

[43] Manigault underestimates the height of Missionary Ridge. At Bragg's headquarters it was over 400 feet. *Official Records, Atlas,* Plate L, Map No. 3.

[44] Captain S.H. Dent, commanding an Alabama battery in the artillery battalion attached to Anderson's division. *O.R.,* XXXI, pt. 2, 659.

[45] Gen. Cheatham, in a letter written Nov. 16, 1883, said: "It was Dea's (sic) Brigade that broke first." (*Sykes,* 609). The description of the battle on his division front given by Manigault is corroborated in a contemporary article in the *Atlanta Register* correcting a previous report that his brigade, along with Deas', had been the first to fail to maintain its position on the Confederate left at Missionary Ridge. The article concludes: "Thus it happened that Manigault's brigade was *not* the first to give way, but the *last* in that portion of the line."

[46] By Hooker's troops.

[47] George A. Jennison, adjutant of the 24th Alabama, who had been praised for gallant conduct at Chickamauga by Manigault and by Col. N.N. Davis, his regimental commander. *O.R.,* XXXI, pt. 2, 344, 347; *List of Staff Officers of the Confederate States Army,* (Washington, 1891), 85.

[48] Vaughan's brigade, made up of the 11th, 12th and 47th, 13th and 154th, and 29th Tennessee regiments. *O.R.,* XXXI, pt. 2, 659.

[49] Breckinridge's and Stewart's divisions.

[50] F.S. Parker, Jr., a.d.c. to Gen. Bragg, later promoted to major and assistant adjutant general. *Confederate Staff Officers,* 125.

[51] Hooker's command.

[52] To the factors listed by Manigault as contributing to the Confederate disaster at Missionary Ridge, Bragg added two others. The first he pointed out in his official report, somewhat unconvincingly. The troops, he said, "had for two days confronted the enemy, marshalling his immense forces in plain view, and exhibiting to their sight such a superiority in numbers as may have intimidated weak-minded and untried soldiers." The second was whiskey. To President Davis,

a week after the battle, Bragg wrote: "Breckinridge was totally unfit for any duty from the 23rd to the 27th — during all our trials — from drunkenness...General Hardee will assure you that Cheatham is equally dangerous...I can bear to be sacrificed myself, but not to see my country and my friends ruined by the vices of a few profligate men" (*O.R., LII*, pt. 2, 475). And in a letter to his friend, Gen. Marcus Wright, "I candidly confess my inability to command an army when its senior generals can with impunity remain drunk for five successive days, as Cheatham and Breckinridge about the time of our retreat from Missionary Ridge. It is folly to talk of troops having confidence in a man they know to be drunk whenever any emergency arises...On this occasion it was so bad I had to order a Brigade Comdr. not to obey Breckinridge, but to follow my instructions and his own judgment." (Letter from Bragg to Marcus Wright, Warm Springs, Ga., 29 Dec. '63). One wonders, under the circumstances, why Bragg did not prefer charges against Breckinridge.

The latter's reputation as a two-fisted drinker was well known. In *The End of an Era,* (Boston, 1899), 450-453, John S. Wise relates an amusing incident of the surrender negotiations between Sherman and Joseph E. Johnston as told to him by the Confederate commander. "You know how fond of his liquor Breckinridge was?" Johnston said. "Well, nearly everything to drink had been absorbed. For several days Breckinridge had found it difficult, if not impossible to procure liquor. He showed the effects of his forced abstinence. He was rather dull and heavy that morning. That is, until Sherman suggested a drink." General Johnston watched the expression of Breckinridge at this announcement "...and it was beatific...When the bottle and glass were passed to him, he poured out a tremendous drink, which he swallowed with great satisfaction...Breckinridge never shone more brilliantly than he did in the discussions that followed until Sherman blurted out: 'See here, gentlemen, who is doing this surrendering anyhow? If this goes on, you'll have me sending a letter of apology to Jeff Davis.'" Time passed and Sherman poured himself a second drink but absent-mindly did not offer one to the others. "From pleasant hope and expectation the expression on Breckinridge's face changed successively to uncertainty, disgust and deep depression. He took little part in the remainder of the interview." On the way back to camp, Johnston asked Breckinridge what he thought of Sherman. "He is a bright man, and a man of force," Breckinridge replied, his voice rising, "but General Johnston, General Sherman is a hog! Yes, sir, a hog! Did you see him take that drink by himself?" Johnston, rather unsuccessfully, attempted to assure Breckinridge that Sherman was royal good fellow but absent-minded. "Ah!" protested the big Kentuckian, half sighing, half grieving, "no Kentucky gentleman would ever have taken away that bottle. He knew we needed it and needed it badly."

[53] As reported by Hardee on Dec.26, the losses in Bragg's command in the engagements before Chattanooga and at Ringgold Gap amounted to 361 killed, 2,180 wounded and 4,146 missing or a total of 6,667 (*O.R., XXXI*, pt. 2, 684). The Federal Chief of Ordnance, Department of the Cumberland, listed as captured from the enemy a total of 40 field guns and howitzers, the precise figure mentioned by Manigault. *Ibid.,* 619.

[54] As a result of a severe wound, received at the Battle of Franklin, Manigault was spared the Confederate disaster at Nashville in December 1864, of which Hood wrote, "I beheld for the first and only time a Confederate army abandon the field in confusion." (Hood was not present at Missionary Ridge). *Hood,* 303.

7

WINTER QUARTERS

At

DALTON, GEORGIA

(Editor's Preface)

The retreat from Chattanooga had ended at Dalton, Ga., not because that place had any particular advantages of position of defense, but simply because it was there that Bragg's army came to a halt after the disaster on Missionary Ridge, the Northern pursuit having been checked by Cleburne's stubborn rear-guard at Ringgold Gap. Realizing, at last, that the jig was up, Bragg resigned his command and was replaced — after much soul-searching and many misgivings on the part of Jefferson Davis and his cabinet — by Joseph E. Johnston.

Despite his natural inclination for the defensive, Johnston was well received by the troops. Stanley Horn, in his *Army of Tennessee,* describes his arrival: "When he first came to Dalton, a body of troops, with a band, marched to his headquarters to serenade him and called loudly for him to come out and show himself. He came to the front door, accompanied by the well-loved General Cheatham, who introduced him by patting him affectionately on his bald head and saying, 'Boys, this is Old Joe.' And 'Old Joe' he was to the Army of Tennessee forever after."

During the winter the army was strengthened by the return of stragglers and the many absent with or without leave. Furloughs were granted in rotation so that most of the men were able to visit their homes. This gave a boost to morale, as did a noticeable improvement in rations, clothing and equipment. Rigorous training, including a comprehensive program of target practice, brought the troops to a high state of proficiency.

Notwithstanding his accomplishments and his popularity with the men, all was not serene for Joe Johnston. By nature somewhat disputatious and extremely touchy when he considered his honor or reputation at stake, he was nettled by Davis' constant needling as to the necessity for taking the offensive. He felt, and with good reason, that he knew more than the president did about the condition of the army and its capabilities, and he did not hesitate to imply as much. The relationship between the two men, never close, could be described at best as "correct." As time went on, Johnston tended to take Davis less and less into his confidence, which in the end was to lead to his downfall.

In rejecting an offensive strategy, although giving lip service to it, Johnston had persuasive arguments on his side. The Army of Tennessee was outnumbered roughly two to one and, while the South was scraping the bottom of its manpower barrel, no such problem faced Sherman who, in addition, had the virtually endless material resources of the North behind him. Under the circumstances, to stand on the defensive, give ground grudgingly, keep his army intact, draw Sherman further and further from his base of supplies, inflict as much damage as he could and await an opportunity to strike back, was a policy that was not only realistic but offered the greatest prospect of tangible results. Certainly Grant thought so. "For my own part," he wrote, "I think that Johnston's tactics were right. Anything that could have prolonged the war a year beyond the time that it did finally close, would probably have exhausted the North to such an extent that they might have abandoned the contest and agreed to a separation."

R.L.T.

WINTER QUARTERS

At

DALTON, GEORGIA

(The Narrative)

T he entire army having made good their retreat across the Chickamauga during the night of the 25th, rested on the bank several hours,
during which time order was restored as far as practicable, and our
trains pushed forward on the different roads leading towards Dalton. A
couple of hours before day the retreat began in good earnest. Reaching
Ringgold on the afternoon of the 26th, we encamped there that night, and
on the following day arrived at Dalton, from Chattanooga about 38 miles.

Our Division was one of those in advance, and we consequently saw
nothing more of the enemy. There was, however, some hard fighting
between our rear guard and the advance of the enemy who pursued with
only a small portion of his army. At Ringgold General Cleburne with his
Division, and one or two other brigades, had been left in rear with
instructions to hold the enemy in check, until the advance with the wagon
trains could gain some distance. This skillful and brave officer selected
with much judgment a strong position on some ridges, between which the
road from Chattanooga to Dalton ran, a mile or two south of Ringgold.
Carefully screening his men from view, he allowed the enemy to advance
into the defile, which most imprudently they did, and then unmasking his
batteries at the further end, opened a most destructive and heavy fire on
their ranks, killing and wounding a good many, and driving them back in
utter confusion and dismay. After holding his position sufficiently long to
effect the purpose of the Commanding General, he retired unmolested,
the Yankees declining to follow any further, and here ended the pursuit.[1]

At the end of four or five days, it being evident that for the present at least, the Federal commander did not intend to carry on any further operations, his army having returned to the vicinity of Chattanooga, and preparing winter quarters, we also commenced like preparations, and set to work making ourselves as comfortable as possible.

It was well for us that General Grant had not the means to follow up his successes. Had he been provided with the means of taking the field and pursuing vigorously and to a distance, the fate of the Confederacy must have been sealed in a few months.[2]

General Bragg, immediately after his arrival at Dalton, applied to be relieved of the command of the Army of Tennessee, and his request was granted.[3] Within a fortnight he took his leave of us, Lieutenant General Hardee temporarily supplying his place. Here my military connection with this officer ceased. Since that time I have never met him. I have always regarded him as one of the best organizers of an army and disciplinarians that I ever met with, and he possessed many of the qualities essential to a commander. Full of energy, indefatigable in his labors, firm and impartial as an administrative officer, he was no respecter of person or rank, and punished a delinquent, be he the general next below him, or the meanest soldier in the ranks, the one with as little hesitation as the other. A terror to all quarter-masters and commissaries, no trains ever stopped the way, or were out of place, and seldom was there any grumbling about the quantity or quality of food. And in like manner from the Lieutenant General down to the company subaltern, all knew that to disobey an order or to be a delinquent in any way, was sure to bring the iron hand down upon his head. I think that the army under his command, all things considered, was in a higher state of efficiency whilst he ruled than ever before or after. At first he was an exceedingly unpopular officer; all feared, none liked him, but it was not long before they found him out. Leaving out the higher grades of officers, such as held prominent commands, with whose electioneering plans for political capital and other sinister ambitious views he interfered with or exposed, he was as a general thing much more loved than any other in like position. The rank and file of the army became much attached to him, and in spite of his misfortune parted from him with regret.[4] He was not, however, a great general; made many mistakes, some of which he was not responsible for; was always overmatched in numbers, and when pitted against Grant, his inferiority was too evident. His campaign around Chattanooga, after the victory of Chickamauga, showed great deficiency both as a tactician and strategist. The least said about it, the better for his reputation. Personally, I learned to like him, although at first much prejudiced against him; but he certainly was excited by the purist patriotism, and one of the most honest and unselfish officers of our army.[5]

The press of the country did him great injustice, and I think was the cause, to a considerable extent, of impairing his efficiency as a commander. Their hostility towards him, expressed in animadversions on his character and ability, of the bitterest character, was chiefly owing to the fact that he did not like newspaper correspondents, and these gentlemen, on several occasions having by his orders been ejected from the army and forbidden to come within its lines — very properly for the injudicious character of the information they conveyed in their letters to the public prints — turned their letter-writing abilities against him in a spirit of spite and pique, and in a great measure formed the public opinion, creating difficulties and animosities, which, it can be easily understood, cramped and interfered much with his usefulness. As a chief of staff, his services would have been invaluable in an army. As a commander, I do not think that he was up to the charge of a large army, against such odds as he had to contend with. Yet I rank him fourth in merit and ability amongst our Confederate generals.[6]

For the first two weeks after our arrival in Dalton, the weather was bitterly cold, and all hands were busily employed in the construction of winter quarters, and by the end of that time, or about the middle of December, the entire army was comfortably housed, in rough cabins of logs or boards, each with a large chimney and fireplace attached, and the sides arranged with bunks, like the berths of a vessel, to raise the men from the damp ground. The ground for our camps was selected with great care, much room allowed and laid out with regularity. The positions chosen, were, as may be supposed, with a view to our protection, each division being responsible for some road, gap, or other strategic point. Comfortable shelters, such as could keep out rain, sleet, or snow, were built for the horses and mules, with the sides, especially that one to the south, carefully screened with brush to protect the animals from the cold winds. Large lots surrounding them were enclosed, so that on a fine day, they might walk about and sun themselves. The encampment of each brigade was like a village, or independent municipality, and everything went on with a regularity and order that made it an easy task for each chief to rule. Some admirable orders were issued as to our camp arrangements, and the discipline and police arrangements were as near perfection as could be. The wives, families, and friends, of many of the soldiers came to see them, bringing with them many good things from home. Our picket duty was light, and the outposts had little to do, and were seldom annoyed. The hardest work in which the men were employed, after completing their houses, buildings for the quarter masters' and commissary's stores, as well as the shelter for the stock, was the labor upon the roads, which required constant work to preserve them in a fit condition for our wagons to travel over. General Johnston, who succeeded General Bragg, adopted the wise and reasonable policy of furloughing a certain per centum of men, thereby giving all the hope of short visit to their homes, to which they looked forward with great pleasure,[7] and although the winter proved to be a very cold one with much rain and little sunshine, everything bore a bright and cheerful aspect, the winter passing quickly and pleasantly; our food reasonably good and sufficient, our houses comfortable with roaring fires, kept constantly supplied by large quantities of most excellent fire wood.

I remember on our arrival in Corinth in '62 with my regiment, all of the men being from the low country of South Carolina, where pine or lightwood is an essential to a good fire, and without it, it was almost impossible to make a decent one, that, being conducted to our camping ground on a cold, rainy day in April, the men looked round them in despair at the poor prospect for a good blaze, in live trees,* already coming out with their thick, green foliage, and I heard many exclamations of disgust expressed towards a country in which no lightwood could be found, or other kindling. To their surprise, however, they soon found that with the material before them, and a few dry branches with which every tree was supplied, a large and more comfortable fire could be more easily obtained than in their own country of pine trees and scrub oaks. So surprised were they at the success of this, their first effort, under such discouraging circumstances, that I never after heard any complaints of a like nature.

Whilst on the subject of firewood, I will mention here, though rather out of place, having forgotten to do so in the earlier part of this narrative, that whilst in Tennessee I was much struck on many occasions with the character of some of their forests, consisting entirely of cedar trees in every stage of growth and size, and as far as I was able to judge, covering at times several thousand acres. It always indicated land of the poorest quality, totally unfit for agricultural purposes. The surface always showed much rock and loose stones, cropping out in every direction, with the coating of soil or earth very shallow. Many of these trees grew to an enormous size, compared with any that I had ever seen in Carolina. In height they equaled our larger yellow, or long-leaf pine; and the trunk, at the height of a man's shoulder from the ground, decidedly larger. From these forests, all of the farms in the vicinity are supplied with the material for fencing, rails, posts, etc., and many farmers haul it for this purpose from a long distance. All the bridges also are built of this material. The great advantage that it possesses over almost all other wood, is that it never rots, or at least will last as a fence for several generations. An old farmer told me on one occasion, when asking him about it, and referring to his fence, a worm one, near which we were standing, that his father had put it up before he could remember, and that he himself had owned the farm nearly fifty years. Another one stated that his fence had been put up fifty years ago. Both these fences were in an excellent state of repair, and were what would be regarded in S.C. as remarkably strong and efficient. After a good many years it became necessary to replace a rail on top to preserve the height, the lower one possibly having disappeared, but only so trifling a repair is necessary at long intervals. Their bridges, made of the same material, have for their flooring pieces perhaps six by three, the narrow edge up. They are worn through by the wheels constantly travelling over them, but never require repair on account of decay. A farm once enclosed by such a fence, if

*These trees were for the most part red oak, post oak, with a few tupelo and hickory. — A.M.M.

160

not destroyed by fire, will last a man a lifetime, and that of his son after him. I often thought what a blessing a few such forests would be to us in S.C., where the annoyance and expense of keeping up our fences is a matter of yearly anxiety, and costs us much more than our planters and economists generally have any idea of.

About the 15th of November I applied for a furlough, and was promised one so soon as several generals should return, a large number being then absent, enjoying that privilege. During the period of Gen. Bragg's rule I had been several times offered one, but I was unwilling to take advantage of the opportunity which my position gave me over others, who were just as anxious as I was to visit their homes and families, and indeed it was much more important that they should do so. The dissatisfaction had been very great amongst the men, seeing how easily and frequently many officers of high rank obtained them; and, thinking that they had good grounds for complaint, I had no idea of adding to it. But now there was a fair prospect of everyone being gratified in the course of a short time, and as I thought that I could be better spared now and less missed than a later period, I determined to ask for one, and on the 22nd of December received it, and left the same evening for Columbia, where the family were then living, as refugees. I arrived on the night of the 24th, after an absence from the state of very nearly twenty-one months.

It may easily be imagined how agreeable the change was to me, and how I enjoyed the quiet of home, the partial relief from anxiety, and the happiness of once more being with my family. And yet what changes had taken place! Our home was amongst strangers, our circumstances strangely altered, the comfort and happiness that we had enjoyed at dear old "White Oak"[8] was a thing of the past, and although we still looked forward to happy days there, we little dreamed that our hopes would meet with a bitter disappointment. Grief too had made its mark on some of the faces that welcomed us. Dan and Stenie[9] had both passed away, the latter dying from disease contracted whilst with me in Mississippi, and after his return home, where we all hoped, that by careful nursing and change of diet, he would again recover his health; but it was not to be so, and the sad countenances of their parents told too plainly how great was their bereavement.

During my short stay, for my leave of absence was limited to twenty days, I made a visit to Charleston to see my brothers, Henry and Edward,[10] and remained there forty-eight hours. My leave at last drew to its close, and on the 11th of January, 1864, I started on my return to the army. Willie had accompanied me on this visit, and with his younger brother, Joe, we took our leave of the family, and left Columbia on the evening train.[11] At Branchville we parted from Joe, then on his way to Charleston, where he was to enter service for the first time, at the early age of seventeen, as a private in the signal corps. I thought at the time, "Will we ever meet again?" but my apprehensions were not for him. One short month elapsed, when I received the sad intelligence from Mary that her brother, whilst in the discharge of his duty at Fort Sumter, in Charleston Harbor, had been instantly killed by a shell fired from one of the enemy's batteries, on the...of February.* Joe was an affectionate promising lad of fine personal appearance, intelligent and amiable; and had a few months before been confirmed, and had become a communicant of the Episcopal Church.

Seldom have a family ever had more cause to mourn, or parents been more grief-stricken — three sons lost in the service of their country in the brief period of a twelvemonth, one from disease caused by exposure, privation, and fatigue; another killed almost instantly in the closing scene of a great battle; the third and youngest of them struck down, scarcely knowing what it was that hurt him, on the walls of that fortress, the glorious defence of which has been a matter of pride to us, and a subject for history, as illustrating what courage, perseverance, and skill can accomplish under the most adverse circumstances. The three brothers lie side by side in "Magnolia"[12] in their undisturbed rest, only to be awakened "At that last trump" on that "dreadful day".

After a pleasant and rapid journey, we reached the army at Dalton, on the night of the fourteenth, and shortly after, our brigade, where we were welcomed by our comrades most heartily, and before a blazing fire. All the incidents which had taken place in the army of any moment, during our absence, were recounted, and many questions answered by ourselves.

Very little worthy of mention took place during the winter and spring that we lay around Dalton. In the month of February, Gen. Thomas, temporarily commanding the Federal army, advanced against our position, and leaving our winter quarters, the army was drawn up in line of battle to the north of the town, and awaited the approach of the enemy. Some heavy skirmishing took place, and artillery duels. The cavalry also were several times seriously engaged. Gen. Thomas found our position too strong for him, and after three days retired, retracing his steps to Chattanooga. I do not think he ever intended any serious attack, but hoped by his demonstration to maneuver Gen. Johnston out of his position. On the third day after making his appearance, he retired with his whole army to the vicinity of Chattanooga, and a short time after

*Gen. Manigault was mistaken about the date. Records at Magnolia Cemetery state that Pvt. Joseph Proctor Huger, Signal Corps, CSA, was born Oct. 16, 1846, and was killed by an enemy shell at Fort Sumter April 13, 1864. John Johnson, in his "The Defense of Charleston Harbor" (Walker, Evans & Cogswell Co., 1890) states in a footnote on page 206: "On the 13th of April (1864) during some practice between the Federal batteries on Cummings Point and the Confederate works on James Island, a promising young member of the Signal Corps, Joseph P. Huger, was looking on from the most conspicuous part of the fort, the south-western angle, and thoughtlessly waved his cap when the Confederate gunners made a hit. The action instantly drew upon him the fire of a 30-pounder Parrott rifle from Cummings Point; the shell exploded with great precision and took off his head." — Editor.

we also returned to our quarters, and nothing interrupted the ordinary routine of our duties for very nearly three months.[13]

At Dalton we were fortunate in having several large open fields, affording sufficient space for drills and reviews, and so large that a corps of twenty thousand men in two lines could go through their evolutions without difficulty or inconvenience. Several sham battles were fought, the exhibitions creating much interest and amusement. On one occasion a review was held by Gen. Johnston, in which 36,000 men (infantry) were under arms, with one hundred and twenty guns. The cavalry was not included, and four or five thousand men with several batteries of artillery were not present, owing to the necessity of some portion of the army being on duty at the front. It was a fine spectacle, and reminded me of a review that I once saw in France, near Paris. The numbers on that occasion were greater, and the effect finer, but our men were far superior physically, of greater height, weight, and showed a much more hardy appearance.

As winter passed and the spring with finer weather set in, we drilled twice daily, in the morning after breakfast for an hour and a half, and in the afternoon; company drill both for heavy and light infantry, at the first named hour; battalion or brigade drill afterwards, with occasionally a drill of the division or corps. On Sunday morning each brigade was reviewed and inspected by its own commander, the division or corps commander frequently being present, when everything was brought out, and wagons, ambulances, forges, and all that appertained to the command underwent a rigid scrutiny. Having little else to do, all our time was devoted to such duties as tended to improve the men as soldiers, and added to the efficiency of the army. General Johnston displayed much zeal and energy, and certainly improved the command in many ways, making some judicious alterations in its organization and interior management, and instituting some most admirable regulations. I will mention several changes which struck me as being advantageous, and the good effect of which was at a later day very perceptible.

Heretofore each brigade had a battery attached to it, which formed as much a part of it as any one of the regiments did. In going into battle the battery would accompany the infantry, and would receive orders from the brigadier commanding. It often happened that a brigade would become engaged on ground, the character of which was entirely unsuited for the use of artillery. The consequence would be that this useful arm would remain idle when it might be doing good service on some other part of the line. There were chiefs of artillery, it is true, and the division or corps commander had full authority to use their discretion in locating the guns, and frequently did so. Still, as they were regarded as a portion of the brigade, and each commander, bent upon protecting himself, even at the expense of the general welfare, or, in other words, was responsible for his command only, and trusted that a favorable opportunity would offer where he might use those weapons to some advantage, they made great difficulty about their removal, laying more stress than was at all necessary for keeping them, and frequently carried their point. Hitherto the position of chief of artillery in time of action was a mere sinecure, and as a general rule, these officers, whether attached to the staff of a corps or division, were very inefficient and of but little use. According to the new arrangement, the artillery was formed into regiments, one attached to each corps, and one in reserve for the use of the army; and when a division was ordered on any special duty, a detail of so many batteries as were thought necessary would be assigned it, under the command of a field officer of the regiment. Such also would be the case when any similar duty would be required of a brigade or smaller force. If a line of battle was selected, the guns would be located without reference to any one brigade.[14]

To each brigade was assigned one or more wagons, according to its strength, to be used for the transportation of tools. A commissioned officer and two assistants, generally some soldiers, who, from wounds or some other cause, were not so well fitted for the line, had charge of these utensils and were responsible for them, as well as for their being always in condition for immediate use.

Immediately on halting for the day after a march, axes would be distributed to each regiment, according to its quota, and turned in by the officer of the regiment on the following morning before starting, that officer receiving back the receipt he had the day before given for them. Were any short, he became responsible. and had to pay for them, provided he could not account properly for their loss. Should it happen that on halting, the troops were ordered to intrench themselves, a general distribution of all the tools took place. It must be remembered that about this time there were no wagons used for the men's baggage, in which the tools could be carried, and were they distributed amongst the different companies, it would not be many weeks before nearly, if not quite, all would be missing.

Such tools as were required were very expensive, scarce, and could hardly be replaced. Our success and means of defense in a great measure depended during the last year of the war in preserving our supply. Soldiers are proverbially careless, and officers of our army, those of the line particularly, were scarcely any more careful than their men. One would suppose that the system would be too complicated to work well, and that it was comparatively too large a detail for the purpose, and that to place it in charge of a commissioned officer was unnecessary. Such, however, was not the case. The arrangement in a short time worked admirably. The service of the officer was necessary, and he was the most useful man of any of the same rank in the command. The tool wagon became an institution and a necessity, nearly as important to us as those used for ammunition. The load for one wagon, generally the best in the train, in our brigade consisted of 100 shovels, 35 picks, 60 axes, 12 froes, 4 wedges, 2 cross cut saws, 3 hand saws, 4 or 5 augers, and a few other tools. These numbers seldom varied, were sometimes more, seldom less. It was a good load for one wagon, and was regarded as a sufficient supply for about 1,500 men. More could have been used to advantage, but ordinarily with such a supply, on reasonably good ground and with all the necessary material handy, that number of men could in the course of a couple of hours build and throw up a very complete and tolerably safe line of defense — always supposing that they are hibituated to that sort of work, and that the enemy are not coming down upon them rapidly.

I should state that in addition to the duties already mentioned, the same officer, generally a 2nd Lieutenant, had charge of the ambulances, the tool wagon almost invariably accompanying them.

The regulations which governed us on the march, the organization of the Infirmary Corps, Provost Guard, and cooking department, differed much from what we had previously been accustomed to, and were decided improvements.

I took much pride in the Infirmary Corps of the brigade. They consisted of a selection of our best men, such as were noted for courage, capable of carrying heavy loads, enduring much fatigue, and intelligent. They were thoroughly drilled and instructed, could put temporary splints on a broken limb, stop a dangerous hemorrhage, and were familiar with many such arrangements as are usually resorted to by surgeons when immediate attention is necessary to prevent a man bleeding to death, or to save him from much agony, which he would have to endure from an ugly fracture whilst being roughly transported to a considerable distance. With the means of doing so each man was provided, being supplied with a simple tourniquet, roll of bandage, and one out of every four carried one or two sets of splints. This in addition to the contents of the hospital knapsacks.

A drill of this corps would startle a spectator a good deal, were he suddenly to find himself a witness to it, and ignorant of what was going on, on hearing an officer in the uniform of a surgeon call out: "Man wounded, bleeding to death, artery injured, right leg, above knee," and immediately see several sets of litter bearers start off on a run in the direction of as many helpless forms a couple of hundred yards off, returning in a few minutes, each litter containing a body, with the limb apparently in the condition mentioned, with the proper precautions taken to prevent a fatal result.

The position of a litter bearer was one of danger, and no sinecure. Many of them were at different times killed. To make a good one, the coolest courage was necessary. Many a man of ordinary bravery, after getting into a fight, will stand his ground and stay there; but it requires a little more than that to go in and come out, again and again, from a place of comparative safety to one of great danger; and as these men are not always under the eye of an officer, only the best and most tried can be relied upon, and should be chosen with great care for that duty. The number of men set apart for this purpose varies according to the size of the command, from four to six per centum of the total effective being allowed; the six men are not too many, allowing three to each litter. One or more commissioned officers, according to the number of men in the corps, with a sergeant from each regiment, control and direct them when in the field.

The Provost Guard, as its name would imply, was strictly a police force, in no manner charged with the protection of the camp, but responsible for the safe keeping of all culprits, carrying out the sentences of Courts Martial, or the infliction of such punishment as the brigade commander authorized, and correcting all breaches of camp orders, a detachment of them being nearly always on duty, scouting around the neighbourhood, arresting all stragglers, marauders, or men absent from their commands without leave. In battle they are most often used, deployed in the rear of the line, to prevent any skulking or passing to the rear without proper authority, although on several such occasions they were attached to some regiment and took part in the fight, or were used to prolong a line, when the space allotted us was rather greater than we could fill with safety, without making use of them. All prisoners captured were turned over to them for safe keeping. On the march they brought up the rear, allowing no one to drop behind without authority, or to straggle on the flanks of the column, into farm houses, orchards, or fields of corn, sugar-cane, or the like. These men, like the litter bearers, were carefully selected, and with a good officer at their head, soon became a terror to all evil-doers and triflers, and assisted much in the preservation of discipline.

As may be supposed, they were not regarded with any very kindly feeling by the men, who never lost an opportunity of sneering at them, or letting off some witticism at their expense. On one occasion, I happened to be near a regiment, standing at ease, or resting, when the Provost Guard was passing near. My attention was attracted by hearing some one call out, "Look out, boys! Anybody with a pocketbook or plug of tobacco in his pocket, put his hand over it, for here come the Provost Guard!" Of course, a number of his comrades immediately pretended to secure the supposed pocketbook, and a succession of remarks and humorous speeches flew along the line, although there was nothing of such a character, or so pointed, as to render it necessary that any officer should interfere. It was very amusing, and I laughed heartily, particularly as I was unobserved; and the scorn and contempt with which the Guard passed by, in the most profound silence, made it still more ludicrous, they not deigning a reply to the jokes which they knew were leveled at them, but looking as though they had mentally resolved to pay off this score whenever an opportunity offered itself of doing so, promising themselves that it would be no laughing matter then.

The Provost Guard in one brigade consisted of 26 privates, 2 corporals, 2 sergeants, and 2 commissioned officers — total 32.

The senior Lieutenant acted somewhat in the capacity of a staff officer, and was usually mounted. Lieutenant Malone,[15] of Mobile, belonging to the 24th Alabama, who for a long time commanded this Guard, was a very efficient and useful chief. He afterwards obtained the command of his company, and was very severely wounded during the latter part of the siege of Atlanta. When I last heard of him, about a year ago, he was still suffering from it. I have never seen him since the day that he received said wound.

The cooking department was under the control and management of the brigade commissary,* assisted by a commissary sergeant from each regiment, and a detail of five men to every two hundred present. Ordinarily this force was sufficient, excepting when three or four days' rations had to be cooked hurriedly, when an extra force would be furnished for a few hours to assist. The commissary was provided with several wagons for the transportation of the cooking utensils, one being able to contain the utensils necessary for about 400 men. He was also allowed two or three wagons, always kept loaded with an additional supply of flour, meal, meat, or other food. This department was thoroughly systematized, worked well, and saved the men much trouble. Their food was better prepared and less wasted.

Major S.E. Lucas was the Brigade commissary, was industrious and efficient, and gave much satisfaction.

It was a great mistake on the part of our commanders to order the issue of more than three days' rations to the men, as was frequently done. I found that even with three days in advance it was rarely that the command had more than a half supply for the last day, and in case of there being four or five days issued, they fell short in an increased proportion.

The explanation is a very simple one. Soldiers, like children, are thoroughly thoughtless, thinking only of to-day, little of to-morrow. Whilst on the march, their appetites were larger, and indeed a greater amount of sustenance is required; but if anything, their supplies are not as large, having no opportunity of providing for themselves. Bent only on satisfying their hunger, they would intrench each day on the provision for the day after, and on the last day find themselves almost without food. The bread ration, consisting of flour baked into biscuits, or corn meal "dodgers", was bulky, giving the haversack an unwieldy and cumberous shape, and adding to the difficulty of carrying it, more so than if a pound or two in weight had been added. The more one ate out of it, the less unwieldly it became, and there was something gained, they thought by that. But the most serious objection to these large issues was that frequently, and particularly in damp, rainy weather, the bread soured and became mouldy, and, not only unpalatable, but really unfit to eat. The corn bread in such weather, after the second day was invariably spoiled, and often had to be thrown away. I never could understand why it was that our Government did not supply our armies to a greater extent with what we know as sailor's biscuits, called by the Yankees "Hard Tack", which I think they might have done, and is far better suited to an army in the field than anything else that I know of. Yet flour was sent us, which we had to cook ourselves, and many soldiers whose proper place was in the ranks with a musket in their hands, had to be detached as a cook.

*Only one commissary to a brigade allowed during the latter part of the war. — A.M.M.

The men, however, selected as cooks, were such as were fit for little else, such as wounded soldiers, convalescent, but perhaps with a stiff arm, leg, loss of several fingers on the right hand, or such like defects, so that really our effective force in the line was not much diminished.

During the latter part of the month of March and the month of April, the army was daily employed practicing at the target, each man in the brigade firing fifteen shots. I took a good deal of pains in endeavoring to carry out the orders in this matter, regarding it as a very important one, and when not necessarily otherwise employed, spent much of my time where the shooting was going on. Each regiment had its own target, a large one not easily missed even at the greatest distance at which we fired (500 yards), laid off in squares and properly numbered and lettered. A company at a time from each regiment would practice, each man firing three shots a day. As one company would get through, another would take its place, and so on, from eight o'clock in the morning until four in the afternoon. Each man was obliged to fire his own rifle, so as to become as familiar with its quality and peculiarities as possible. It took us several weeks to get through, but was regarded rather as a pastime by the men, the greater number taking much interest in it, and I think that they learned much more of their weapons, their capability, and how to handle and direct them, in those few weeks, than they did in the previous two and a half years. I have always regarded it as being quite as necessary that a certain amount of practice in target firing should be required for the soldier, whatsoever his weapon may be, as that he should be thoroughly instructed in all the different schools in the book of tactics.

I am satisfied that the knowledge and comparative familiarity that they attained under this order of General Johnston was of great importance to us in the campaign fast drawing near, and cost the Yankees several thousand additional lives.[16]

Towards the latter part of April, we began to make arrangements for leaving our winter quarters three miles south of Dalton, and about the 1st of May, moved to a line a mile north of it, which had been selected by General Johnston to resist any advance of the enemy.

I believe we all left with regret our old encampment and the surroundings which had become so familiar to us, and where we had spent some very pleasant days. No more exciting games of "base ball", no more races or wrestling matches, in which the different regiments would contend, or desperate contests with a neighbouring brigade, when the snow lay deep upon the ground,[17] all in the most friendly spirit, harmless and healthful amusements, in which it was a common thing for the men to indulge, when their duties for the day were over, or between the intervals of drill, and which I think all officers should encourage; but instead of all this, war, in all its stern reality, was again about to break loose, and one of the most trying and obstinately contested campaigns shortly followed, seldom, I believe, exceeded in the history of wars for the character of the struggle or the hardships and dangers to which all were exposed, day after day, week after week, for the period of four months.

NOTES TO CHAPTER 7

[1] Thus at Ringgold Gap, Cleburne saved the army a second time, for which he received the thanks of Congress. With a force of 4,157 bayonets, he held off a vastly superior enemy and suffered a loss in killed, wounded and missing (there were only 11 of the latter) of 221. (*O.R.,* XXXI, pt. 2, 753-758). Cleburne's brother, Christopher, still in his teens, took part in the defense of the gap during which, when ammunition ran low, the men resorted to hurling stones down the hill at the enemy, as they had done two days previously on the right at Missionary Ridge. "The General was much diverted and pleased when told that one of the prisoners, an Irishman, who was disabled by one of the missiles, upon seeing Christopher — 'Kit' as his comrades called him — said, 'Ah, you are the little devil who smashed me jaw with a rock!'" *Buck,* 185.

[2] It was the relief of Knoxville, where Burnside was besieged by Longstreet, that drew Grant's attention. In his report on the Chattanooga campaign, Grant wrote: "Had it not been for the imperative necessity of relieving Burnside, I would have pursued the broken and demoralized retreating enemy as long as supplies could have been found in the country." *O.R.,* XXXI, pt. 2, 27-37.

[3] That Bragg was crushed by the disaster at Missionary Ridge is plain to see in his correspondence with Jefferson Davis. Although charging Breckinridge and Cheatham with drunkenness and the troops where the lines were broken with shameful conduct, in his innermost soul Braxton Bragg knew where the responsibility lay. On Dec. 1 he wrote: "The disaster admits of no palliation, and is justly disparaging to me as a commander," although, in extenuation, he added that the fault was not entirely his. (*O.R.,* LII, pt. 2, 745). The next day he was more contrite: "No one estimates the disaster more seriously than I do, and the whole responsibility and disgrace rest on my humble head." *Ibid.,* 568.

[4] This is not the conventional view of Bragg. Grant described him as a man of the highest moral character, remarkably intelligent and well informed, thoroughly upright, but naturally disputatious and possessed of an irascible temper (*Battles and Leaders,* III, 710). "None of General Bragg's soldiers ever loved him," a private of the First Tennessee wrote after the war. "They had no faith in his ability as a general. He was looked upon as a merciless tyrant." Yet when Bragg was relieved, even this observer, who was given to hyperbole, was a bit more charitable. "We had followed General Bragg all through the long war. We had got sorter used to his ways, but he was never popular with his troops. I felt sorry for him. Bragg's troops would have loved him, if he had allowed them to do so; for many a word was spoken in his behalf, after he had been relieved of the command." (Sam R. Watkins, *Co. Aytch, Maury Grays, First Tennessee Regiment,* (Nashville, 1882), 71, 131. Hereafter cited as *Co. Aytch*). On the other hand, some testimony tends to bear out Manigault's assessment of Bragg. "He was endeared to the men," wrote a member of the Nineteenth Tennessee, "by sharing with them the hardships and toils of army life, the long marches by day and night, through rain and sunshine, heat and cold...The army was loathe to give him up, the only censure...was in not pressing pressing forward and reaping a full harvest of victory after his battles." W. J. Worsham, *The Old Nineteenth Tennessee Regiment, C.S.A.* (Knoxville, 1902), 104. Hereafter cited as *Worsham.*

[5] Neither friend nor foe ever questioned Bragg's unselfish devotion to his country's cause.

[6] It is interesting to speculate on the identity of the three generals Manigault ranked above Bragg. Probably Robert E. Lee and Stonewall Jackson and quite possibly Bedford Forrest.

[7] Johnston instituted a "system of furloughs by which the entire army, in detachments, was able to visit home on leave of absence, and this vastly improved the morale" (Horn, *The Army of Tennessee*, 312). "He gave furloughs to one-third of his army at a time, until the whole had been furloughed. A new era had dawned." *Co. Aytch,* 132.

[8] Manigault's plantation on the north bank of the North Santee near Georgetown.

[9] Dan and Stenie (Stephen) were brothers of Manigault's wife, Mary Proctor Huger. Dan had been killed in action the previous September at Chickamauga.

[10] Maj. Edward Manigault was commander of the Siege Train, an organization of siege artillery which manned several batteries in the defenses of James Island immediately south of Charleston. He was severely wounded and captured in February 1865 when the city was evacuated and Northern troops moved in. *Transactions No. 4, Huguenot Society of South Carolina.*

[11] Willie and Joe also were brothers of Mrs. Manigault.

[12] Magnolia Cemetery, of which Henry Timrod wrote on the occasion of the decorating of the graves of the Confederate dead by the ladies of Charleston on Memorial Day, April 1867:

> "Stoop, angels, hither from the skies!
> There is no holier spot of ground
> Than where defeated valor lies,
> By mourning beauty crowned."

[13] Under orders from Grant, Thomas moved out from Chattanooga with four divisions, the object being to gain possession of Dalton and the territory as far south of there as possible. Finding Johnston's army in greater strength and more strongly posted than he had anticipated, however, Thomas gave it up as a bad job, after heavy skirmishing and an action at Buzzard Roost on Feb. 24 and 25 that resulted in losses of 17 killed and 272 wounded. Nevertheless, Thomas considered the movement a success in that he believed it caused Johnston to recall Hardee's corps, which had previously been dispatched to Mississippi to aid Polk in repelling Sherman's expedition against Meridian. In point of fact, Hardee's troops, consisting of the divisions of Cheatham, Cleburne and Walker, were on their way back to the army at Dalton quite independently of Thomas's threat. *O.R.,* XXXII, pt. 1, 8-14, 477; LII, pt. 2, 627; Joseph E. Johnston, *Narrative of Military Operations,* (New York, 1874), 286. Hereafter cited as *Johnston.*

[14] This, of course, permitted the massing of batteries and was far superior to the old system.

[15] Lt. Edward Malone, appointed provost marshal to Gen. A.M. Manigault Sept. 20, 1863 (*Staff Officers of the Confederate Army,* 102). Manigault singled him out for praise in his report on Chickamauga: "Lieutenant Malone, brigade provost-marshal, was active in the discharge of his duty, and rendered efficient service in

the prevention of straggling, forcing many who were unwilling to face the heavy fire to which they had been exposed back into their proper positions." *O.R.,* XXX, pt. 2, 344.

[16] The details of this target practice as related by Manigault are corroborated by Sam Watkins of the First Tennessee, who told an amusing story reflecting the efficacy of this training. As the troops were returning to camp after a session of firing, he relates, "a buck rabbit jumped up, and was streaking it as fast as he could make tracks, all the boys whooping and yelling as hard as they could, when Jimmy Webster raised his gun and pulled down on him, and cut the rabbit's head entirely off with a minie right back of the ears. He was about two hundred and fifty yards off" (*Co. Aytch,* 140). Cleburne, whose division was probably the best fighting outfit in the army, organized an elite corps of sharpshooters, equipped with Whitworth and Kerr rifles brought through the blockade from England. These rifles were described as of beautiful finish and workmanship and of long range. The Whitworth was fitted with telescopic sights and had an accurate range of 2,000 yards. This corps of sharpshooters was particularly effective in picking off artillerymen and silencing or reducing the fire of their batteries. Although it suffered 60% casualities in the Atlanta campaign, its ranks were quickly filled by volunteers anxious to be transferred to this service. *Buck,* 201-202.

[17] These snowball battles were entered into with great enthusiasm by the troops. A member of the Nineteenth Tennessee described one such encounter: "Finally the greater part of the two divisions (*Cheatham's and Walker's*) were engaged in one of the biggest snowballing of the world's history. Generals, Colonels and company officers were engaged. Regular military maneuvers were observed, two lines of battle and more than a mile long, lasting three and a half or four hours. There were about five thousand engaged in it" (*Worsham,* 108). A private in the First Tennessee gave a more personal account: "The snow balls would begin to fly hither and thither, with an occasional knock down, and sometimes an ugly wound, where some mean fellow had enclosed a rock in his snow ball. It was fun while it lasted, but after it was over the soldiers were wet, cold and uncomfortable...It was a general knock down and drag out affair." *Co. Aytch,* 135.

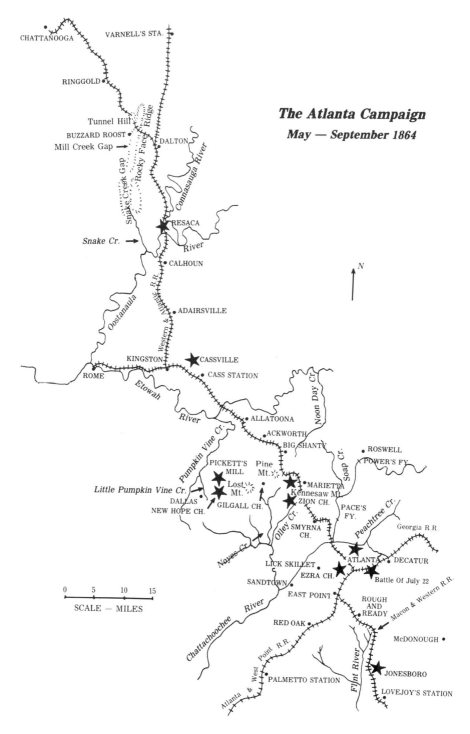

CHATTANOOGA
VARNELL'S STA.

RINGGOLD

Tunnel Hill
Rocky Face Ridge
BUZZARD ROOST
DALTON
Mill Creek Gap →

Snake Creek Gap
Conasauga River

RESACA
Snake Cr. →
River

CALHOUN

Oostanaula
Western & Atlantic R.R.

ADAIRSVILLE

KINGSTON
CASSVILLE
ROME
CASS STATION
Etowah
River
Noon Day Cr.

ALLATOONA

ACKWORTH

BIG SHANTY
ROSWELL
POWER'S FY.

PICKETT'S MILL
Pine Mt.
Soap Cr.

Little Pumpkin Vine Cr.
Lost Mt.
MARIETTA
Kennesaw Mt.
ZION CH.

DALLAS
NEW HOPE CH.
GILGALL CH.
PACE'S FY.

Pumpkin Vine Cr.
Olley Cr.
SMYRNA CH.
Peachtree Cr.
Georgia R.R.

Noyes Cr.
ATLANTA
DECATUR
LICK SKILLET
EZRA CH.
Battle Of July 22

SANDTOWN
EAST POINT
ROUGH AND READY
Macon & Western R.R.

RED OAK
McDONOUGH

Chattachoochee River

Atlanta & West Point R.R.
PALMETTO STATION
Flint River
JONESBORO
LOVEJOY'S STATION

The Atlanta Campaign
May — September 1864

N

0   5   10   15
SCALE — MILES

172

8

JOHNSTON'S CAMPAIGN

From

DALTON TO ATLANTA — 1864

(Editor's Preface)

Under instructions from Grant, now in overall Union command, "to move against Johnston's army, break it up, and to get into the interior of the enemy's country as far as you can, inflicting all the damage against their war resources you can," Sherman launched the Atlanta campaign May 5, 1864, as the Army of the Potomac in the East crossed the Rapidan and closed with Lee and the Army of Northern Virginia.

Just to the west of Dalton, where Johnston's army lay encamped, Rocky Face Ridge, or Mountain, stretches roughly 25 miles in a generally north-south direction, its northern end terminating some three miles above Mill Creek Gap, through which the railroad from Chattanooga ran. Opposite Resaca, 10 or 12 miles south of Dalton, lies Snake Creek Gap.

Rejecting the alternative of marching around the northern end of Rocky Face and engaging Johnston in the open ground about Dalton, Sherman advanced to the western face of the ridge, pushing back Wheeler's dismounted cavalry, which, in the gratuitous words of a Northern newspaper correspondent, "fought our advance with an abandon and desperation worthy of a better cause." Finding Mill Creek Gap heavily fortified, Sherman, while maintaining pressure there, dispatched McPherson and his 23,000 men of the Army of the Tennessee in a wide flanking movement to the south under orders to march through Snake Creek Gap and cut the railroad at Resaca in Johnston's rear. This was to be the first of many such maneuvers wherein Sherman, putting to good use his great numerical superiority, was able to leave an army of about the same size as Johnston's in the latter's front, while throwing an equal force on his flank.

In compliance with his instructions, McPherson marched southward and passed through Snake Creek Gap, only to run up against a Confederate force of three or four thousand entrenched troops guarding the railroad at Resaca. After a sharp action, he withdrew, thereby incurring the displeasure of Sherman, who insisted McPherson had missed a great opportunity by not pressing his attack with more vigor. By the time the rest of Sherman's army had reached Resaca, following the route taken by McPherson, the wily Johnston was there facing him in a strong defensive position, his army well in hand.

Kept informed of his adversary's movements by Wheeler's far-ranging cavalry, and having constructed two military roads from Dalton to facilitate his withdrawal, the Southern commander conducted his retreat in masterly fashion, accurately estimating the time it would take Sherman's large force to pass through the rugged country around Snake Creek Gap. This was Joe Johnston at his best.

The Federal assault at Resaca having been thrown back on May 14 and 15, an attack by Hood on the Union left gave promise of important results. This was referred to by Manigault as the Second Battle of Resaca or Oostanaula. The attack, however, had to be called off when news came that some of McPherson's troops had swung around to their right and crossed the Oostanaula further south and were threatening the railroad near Calhoun in Johnston's rear. Outflanked once again, the Confederates made good their retreat across the river on the night of the 15th and withdrew to Calhoun. Johnston found no suitable defensive position there, nor did he at Adairsville 11 or 12 miles farther south. As a result, the Southern withdrawal was continued to Cassville.

From Adairsville to Cassville two diverging roads led southward, the one on the left proceeding somewhat to the east of south directly to the latter town. That to the west followed the railroad south to Kingston and thence due east some six or seven miles to Cassville, thus forming two sides of a triangle.

Correctly divining that Sherman's army would use both roads, Johnston saw an opportunity to strike the force on the eastern one when the two Federal columns were at the greatest distance one from the other. To take advantage of this opening, he ordered Polk's corps to confront the enemy on the direct or left hand road from Adairsville and contain his advance, while Hood was to swing off to the Confederate right and fall on the exposed left flank of the advancing Northerners. Hardee, meanwhile, was to slow as best he could the other enemy column coming on from Kingston.

The stage seemed set for a decisive blow, when word came from Hood that he was being attacked on his right rear and would have to suspend his advance in order to protect himself. Johnston maintained, then and later, that Hood was misled by false intelligence, and the evidence indicates the troops assaulting Hood were only a detachment of McCook's Federal cavalry, hardly a force of sufficient strength to justify abandonment of the flank movement on which the Confederate plan depended for success. In any case, so much time was lost that Johnston decided it was too late in the day to reorganize and press the attack. Therefore, he reluctantly withdrew his army to a strong defensive position on a ridge to the east and south of Cassville, which he was later to describe as the best he saw occupied during the war.

At a meeting of senior officers that night, however, Hood, joined less enthusiastically by Polk, claimed the line was enfiladed by Northern artillery and that he would be unable to maintain his position the next day. Faced, thus, by an expressed lack of confidence on the part of two of his three corps commanders, Johnston, against his better judgment and in a step he always regretted, abandoned the position and retreated across the Etowah River that night to Allatoona. There, for a few days, the army had an opportunity to rest and refit.

From his knowledge of the country gained as a young officer of the regular army years before the war, Sherman was thoroughly aware of the strength of Allatoona Pass. He decided, therefore, to turn the position by moving south from Kingston, away from the railroad, with his objective Marietta by way of Dallas. Wheeler kept Johnston informed of Sherman's movements and when the Southern leader was satisfied as to his opponent's intentions, he marched his army southwestward to intercept him.

The clash took place near New Hope Church, just northeast of Dallas, and there followed, in execrable weather, four days of bloody fighting during which each side lost about 3,000 men. Repeated Northern assaults were thrown back, but Sherman kept extending his flank, this time to the left or east, until Johnston was compelled to pull his troops back in a downpour of rain and take up once more a position across the railroad. There, at Pine Mountain on June 14, Bishop-General Polk was killed by a Northern artillery shell.

Falling back to the vicinity of Kennesaw Mountain, Johnston took up a new line, which extended on his right across the railroad and on his left to Noyes Creek southwest of Marietta, and awaited Sherman's next move. On June 22, a sharp action took place on the extreme Confederate left near Zion Church between Hood's corps and the troops of Hooker and Schofield, with indecisive results.

Reasoning that he could not with prudence stretch out his army any farther, Sherman, on June 27, assailed the Confederate center at Kennesaw Mountain, only to meet with a bloody repulse in the hardest fighting of the campaign up to that time. His losses were severe, according to his own account, amounting to about 2,500 men killed and wounded, a figure he later revised to 3,000, against a Confederate loss of 630. The ferocity of the struggle at the "Dead Angle" was described by Sam Watkins of the First Tennessee. "The sun beaming down on our uncovered heads, the thermometer being one hundred and ten degrees in the shade, and a solid line of blazing fire right from the muzzles of the Yankee guns being poured right into our faces, singeing our hair and clothes, the hot blood of our dead and wounded spurting on us, the blinding smoke and stifling atmosphere filling our eyes and mouths, and the awful concussion causing the blood to gush out of our noses and ears, and, above all, the roar of battle made it a perfect pandemonium." Little wonder that another soldier remarked: "Hell had broke loose in Georgia, sure enough!"

A member of the Nineteenth Tennessee wrote years later: "The cannons bellowed like so many mad bulls, sent shot and shell plowing the ground, scattering rocks, dirt and everything movable, cutting down trees and felling limbs...Our musketry played upon them cutting them down like grass before the sickle...O what a slaughter was here."

The bulk of the fighting on the Confederate side was done by the divisions of Cheatham and Cleburne of Hardee's corps and French's and Featherston's of Loring's (formerly Polk's). Hood's corps on the Confederate left was not actively engaged.

Recognizing, after this experience, the futility of attacking Johnston's entrenched lines head on, Sherman now resorted to a series of flank movements, which, indeed, he could have done in the first place and saved all the blood spilled at Kennesaw Mountain. His first move was to transfer McPherson from his extreme left to his extreme right, overlapping the Confederate lines there. Then, in order to keep his adversary off balance, he followed this up on July 8 by swinging Schofield in the opposite direction in a wide arc some 10 miles beyond Johnston's right flank. Virtually unopposed, Schofield the next day crossed the Chattahoochee upstream near the mouth of Soap Creek, forcing Johnston to withdraw his army south of the river to the very gates of Atlanta. Thomas, in the meantime, was slugging his way south along the railroad.

For Jefferson Davis back in Richmond, retreat across the Chattahoochee was the last straw. Making one final, but abortive, effort to get Johnston to commit himself to a course of action other than continued withdrawal, the Confederate president, fearful that Atlanta was to be abandoned without a fight, at last took the fateful step of removing Johnston from command of the Army of Tennessee and replacing him with Lt. Gen. Hood, who was given the temporary rank of full general.

Thirty-three years old, six feet two in height, with blondish auburn hair and flowing beard, Hood was a striking figure. On his body he bore the scars of battle. His left arm had been crippled at Gettysburg and he had lost his right leg at Chickamauga. A brilliant, hard-hitting brigade and division commander in the Army of Northern Virginia, his boldness and bravery were never questioned. But did he have the qualities necessary to command an army? Robert E. Lee, his old commander in the East, didn't think so. When asked by Davis for his opinion, Lee hesitated and with his customary tact suggested that Hardee had more experience. Time alone would tell, but there was no doubt that Hood would fight.

R.L.T.

JOHNSTON'S CAMPAIGN

From

DALTON TO ATLANTA — 1864

(The Narrative)

T he infantry and artillery of General Sherman's (Federal) army was estimated by General Johnston at 110,000 men, and about 10,000 cavalry. The army at Missionary Ridge after deducting its losses in that battle must have reached as high as 80,000, and was afterwards reinforced by the "Army of the Ohio", under General McPherson, and Schofield's army from Knoxville and East Tennessee, the two together numbering at least 30,000 men. I think that the estimate of General Johnston was not far from the mark, and if the truth was known, the strength of the Union Army more nearly approximated those figures than the number that General Sherman gives as his grand total, which are as follows:

Infantry	88,188
Artillery	4,460
Cavalry	6,149
Grand aggregate number of troops	98,797[1]
Guns	254

This grand army of Sherman's was composed of three separate and distinct armies:

Army of the Cumberland — Infantry, C.& A.	60,773
Maj. Gen. Thomas Comdg. — Guns	130
Army of the Tennessee — I., A., C.	24,465
Maj. Gen. McPherson Comdg. — Guns	96
Army of the Ohio — I., A., C.	13,559
Maj. Gen. Schofield Comdg. — Guns	28

On the 1st of May, the effective total of the Army of Tennessee* was:

Infantry and Artillery	40,900
Cavalry	4,000
By General Johnston's own report, number of troops	44,900[2]

My own estimate of the number of guns, I put down at 130[2]

He was afterwards joined by a large force of cavalry, after the campaign had opened several weeks, probably as many as	3,000[3]

With this force General Johnston had to contend against more than double his numbers, splendidly equipped, and with an almost inexhaustible magazine of supplies from which to draw, and with reinforcements constantly coming to him, in such numbers by his own admission (see his report) that in spite of the heavy losses he met with, "These figures have been maintained during the campaign."[4]

THE BRIGADE at the commencement of the campaign numbered as follows:

Total effective rifles	1,666
Officers — Brigade, Field, Line, & Staff	172
Total number of combatants	1,838
Litter bearers & Infirmary Corps	71
Cooks	54
Total strength of Brigade	1,963

Our trains and means of transportation were reduced to the lowest limit, and as well as I can remember consisted of the following:

Brigade commander and staff	1	wagon
For Officer's baggage	5	"
Ammunition	5	"
Arms	1	"
Cooking Department	4	"
Ambulances	6	"
Forage	1	"
Ambulance for Brigade Comdr. & Staff	1	"
Forge	1	"
Medical wagon	1	"

Making in all, 18 wagons, 7 ambulances, 1 forge.

*Composed of Hardee's Corps   4 Divisions
Composed of Hood's Corps   3   "
       and
Cavalry under Wheeler   2   "[5]   — A.M.M.

Everything was now sent to the rear, but such as was absolutely necessary for our operations in the field. I did not see my wagon train again, or my baggage, excepting for three or four days early in July, for four months. A pot, a frying pan, a few plates, knives, forks, and cups, with a blanket, and a change of underclothing, I placed in my ambulance, and was dependent upon the driver and orderly, during the whole of that period, for our cooking, washing, and such other conveniences as we stood in need of. Our servants with the baggage went far to the rear, and when it so happened that we were near enough to communicate with them, we were under so continuous and heavy a fire that it would have been dangerous to them, and unfeeling on my part, to order them in attendance upon me.

The condition of our army was excellent. They were well equipped and armed, the interior organization was good. The men, for the most part, had seen much service, and might be called veterans. Their spirits were high, health fine — the sick list not exceeding one per cent of the total present.

On the 6th of May, I think it was, that Sherman began his advance,[6] and on the evening of the seventh his advance was within a few miles of us. On the same afternoon, some of our most advanced infantry outposts came in contact with them exchanging shots before retiring. Our cavalry gradually fell back that afternoon and the following day. On the 8th, skirmishing and partial combats took place at many points along the line, and the enemy began to develop themselves in our front. Our line of battle was strongly posted on some high ridges, one of which, known as the Rocky Face,[7] the enemy assailed with great impetuosity on the 9th, and was several times repulsed by a portion of Hood's corps.[8] Our division was on the extreme right of the corps, but did not become seriously engaged, although the enemy's rifle bullets and shells searched every point of the line. On the same afternoon the enemy were reported in Snake Creek Gap, about 8 or 9 miles from Resaca, the latter place distant from Dalton about 18 miles. McPherson's army having moved towards that point in our rear by a road running parallel with the one we protected,[9] but separated by a high ridge of mountains, the gaps in which were in our possession, Hood's corps was during the night detached and sent to Resaca to assist a small force[10] and a large body of cavalry already there, to check such a move; but before our arrival, information reached us that after some hard fighting, the enemy had drawn off. On the following day we returned to Dalton.[11] On the 12th, the enemy appeared to have retired, and his movements looked mysterious. The division was sent out in the direction of Red Clay, on the road known by that name. After moving cautiously about five miles, we came up with a brigade of our calvary which was then engaged with the enemy. A portion of my brigade and Tucker's (formerly Colonel, now General Tucker, he having succeeded to the command of Anderson's brigade, that General having been likewise promoted and sent to Florida) Mississippi Brigade, were ordered to their assistance, as the enemy were driving them. The tables were soon turned, and the enemy withdrew.[12] Returning late that evening to Dalton, we found the place being evacuated, the army falling back. Sherman, finding it impossible to drive Johnston from his position, and failing in his attacks to find a weak point or force an opening, had suddenly during the night of the 11th and day of the 12th, withdrawn the greater part of his army, leaving a corps[13] to hide his movements; and, moving towards Snake Creek Gap, was endeavoring to strike for his rear at Resaca, hoping to capture it before Johnston could himself reach it, and thus cut him off; but the latter, always wary, and thoroughly up to his business, was not long in detecting the move, and, divining his intention, hastily withdrew from in front of Dalton, and on the appearance of Sherman and his army before Resaca, was in line and ready to receive him.

On the morning of the 14th of May, our lines drawn up in battle, and having hastily thrown up some rude breastworks, the enemy began to show himself, his columns gradually hemming us in, and shortly after eleven o'clock commenced —

THE BATTLE OF RESACA

(The Narrative)

The Army of Tennessee was drawn up in two lines, and in the following order — Hood's Corps on the right, with *(his)* right resting on the Connasauga River, the Corps consisting of three divisions, posted from right to left as follows: Stewart's Division, Stevenson's Division, Hindman's Division; then came Hardee's Corps, of four divisions, and on their left, Polk's command, only a portion of which had arrived from Mississippi, and joined us here. The remainder came up a few days after, consisting of about 2,000 cavalry, and two divisions of infantry, perhaps 12,000 men in all. General Polk's left rested on the Oostanaula.[14]

Resaca lay about two miles in our rear, and was thus encircled by our forces. The Oostanaula bounded it on its south side, which river, a short distance east of the town, branched. The one to the left, or running in a N.E. direction, was known as the Connasauga.

The position of our Brigade was in the second line on the brow of a hill, with a scattering growth of timber on it. In our front, about one hundred and fifty yards distant, was Deas's Brigade, on lower ground, very nearly at the foot of the slope, and in his front the ground was comparatively level, and, for a half-mile, open, and appeared to be an old field that had been thrown out, unplanted for several years. Directly in the centre of his line, a high ridge ran out at right angles from our line, and on this height, eight pieces of our artillery were planted. The Yankees evidently expected to find us unprepared to receive them, and no doubt hoped that all our forces had not arrived. They gave us very little time to speculate as to their intentions. An hour could scarcely have elapsed before they came on us with their lines of battle. Deas and Walthall[15] repulsed them cleverly; but they were not to be refused, and made two other attempts, with a like want of success. In these attempts, they must have suffered heavily and lost many men.

Their fire was at one time very severe, especially that of their artillery, which came up in beautiful style, unlimbered and plied us with their shot and shell unceasingly. Our own guns, being largely outnumbered, were almost silenced, and could make no impression on them; but in spite of this superiority, the deadly fire of our front line forced them back, the infantry whipped, the artillery obliged to fall back out of range; but with their rifle cannon, they reached us at every point, and several of their batteries succeeded in enfilading my line at different points; tho in rear of General Deas, from our elevated position, we were a better mark for them, and, taking advantage of it, they gave us no rest during the day, causing us a considerable loss. During one of these attacks, whilst standing on the brow of the ridge, I was struck on the hand by a rifle ball and slightly wounded. After retiring for a short time to have the injury examined and the wound dressed, I returned to the command, and remained with it during the remainder of the fight.[16]

Failing in their efforts on this portion of Hood's line, the Yankees transferred their offensive operations against Stevenson's and Stewart's divisions, and some desperate fighting occurred there, the brunt of it falling on Stevenson.[17] An advanced work in his line, somewhat detached, was carried by the enemy, and a battery of four guns fell into their hands;[18] but the main line proved impregnable, and after three or four determined assaults, each time repulsed with heavy loss, the enemy gave it up and withdrew from the contest. With a view, I supposed, of preventing any reinforcements being sent to the assistance of Hood's corps, threatening demonstrations were made against our entire front (of the army) and for hours the rattle of small arms and roar of artillery was nearly equal to anything that I ever heard. Late in the afternoon, Stewart and Stevenson advanced and gained some ground to the front, forcing the enemy back some distance. The loss in Hood's corps this day was severe, but the enemy must have lost four or five to our one. This disproportion must certainly have existed in front of Hindman's division.[19] General Tucker's, the supporting brigade on my left, lost more men than the brigade which did the fighting in their front — Walthall's.

Poor Tucker had his left arm shattered. The operation of "resection" was performed, but (he) never recovered the use of his arm and unfortunately he had, at the battle of Perryville, been severely wounded in the right arm, leaving it so stiff as to be of very little service to him. His condition was such after his recovery that he was obliged to retire from active service. He was a good officer, and a serious loss to the army.[20]

The loss in the brigade on the 14th was about (110) one hundred and ten men, and 8 or 9 officers, several of them very good ones. A captain of the 28th Alabama, whose name I regret having forgotten, one of the best of the officers the line, was killed.[21]

SECOND BATTLE OF RESACA

OR OOSTANAULA — May 15th, 1864

(The Narrative)

During the night of the 14th, the enemy worked up to within five hundred yards of our line, and at some points, to within 350 or 400 yards. Firing commenced at daylight, both infantry and artillery, but we were now better protected, having on the previous night materially strengthened and increased the height of our breastworks. Our batteries were also well protected and in a better condition to cope with those of the enemy.

They, like ourselves, had not been idle during the night, and morning revealed them to us, almost as secure as ourselves from attack. Late in the forenoon, we were all made aware by the heavy firing far to the left, that sharp work was going on in that quarter. It turned out that the enemy was making an effort on General Polk's position and a part of General Hardee's. They succeeded in getting possession of a high ridge overlooking the town of Resaca, and there planted several batteries, which commanded the place, the Rail Road Depot, and bridge, as well as several other important points.

I have always understood that it was desired to bring this ridge within our lines, but that in doing so, it increased them beyond our ability to defend. For this reason, the line had been run nearer to Resaca. General Johnston thought best to make an effort to retain possession of this point, and a comparatively weak force was placed there, in advance, and somewhat detached from the main body, he trusting that the enemy would be deterred from attack by the great natural strength of the position, and their ignorance of the size of the force holding it. In the event of their being driven from it, there was very little doubt that the men could be extricated, or that they would do so themselves. The enemy must have become informed of this state of things, attacked, and finally got possession of it.[22] Not satisfied with their success, they pushed on to break through what they supposed to be the second line, and the fighting became severe, extending along the greater part of our front. They were kept back at all points, and finally gave it up. With the exception of a heavy fire of artillery from both sides, for a short space the men remained inactive.

About four o'clock in the afternoon, Hood's corps was ordered to advance and assail (the Federal left), the movement to commence on the right with Stewart. A few minutes before the hour designated, the order was countermanded, but unfortunately for that division, its commander did not receive it until after he had engaged.[23] Meeting with much success at first, Stewart's men drove the enemy before them for some distance, but being unsupported in consequence of the other troops not advancing, in obedience to the last order, and the enemy seeing themselves assailed by comparatively so small a force, rallied, and, fresh troops coming to their support, Stewart was in turn forced to give way, and his command and original line was for some time in great danger.

This state of affairs to some extent involved Stevenson in the fight, who had to advance to his assistance. Other troops were hurried there, amongst them, our brigade.

The division was at last extricated and fell back to their former line, order being restored at all points.[24]

At dark I was relieved by General Stewart, and was on my way back to rejoin my own division, when one of its staff officers came to me with orders to halt where I was, and to await the arrival of the division, which would pass along that road at nine o'clock, giving me also the information that the army would fall back, and cross the Oostanaula that night. At the appointed time the division reached us. The whole army, with the exception of the skirmish line, left to cover our movements, which fell back at a later hour, was now in motion, the heads of the different columns converging towards the two bridges at Resaca.[25] Our corps crossed on the railroad bridge, in much confusion, owing to the darkness of the night, and some few mistakes or misunderstandings. General Bragg would have managed much better. The enemy had become aware of our retreat, the artillery was thundering on our lines, and throwing their shells almost into Resaca itself, whilst our skirmishers and rear guard were giving away slowly. The enemy, fortunately for us, advanced with too great caution. The whole army, with its artillery,* and other material, crossed in safety, with only a small loss. I never could understand why it was that the batteries on the ridge before spoken of, did not open fire on the bridges, during the night, and whilst they were choked up with troops. They had the range of the bridges and had been practicing on it all the afternoon, and I think it very likely that they must have known what was going on. Had they done so, although it is not likely that many would have been killed or wounded with their shells, the demoralization and confusion they would have caused might have been serious in their consequences.[27]

I soon learned the necessity which existed for this movement on the part of General Johnston was in consequence of Sherman's detaching a considerable force with all his cavalry, with instructions to cross the Oostanaula, near Lay's Ferry, capture Calhoun, and destroy the railroad.[28] They succeeded in a measure, but a counter movement having been made by General Johnston, Calhoun remained in our possession until the army passed, and the railroad was not so injured but that it

---

*The artillery, as well as everything on wheels, crossed at a third bridge, in the Connasauga, and rejoined us a day after.[26] — A.M.M.

could be repaired, and all the trains, loaded with army stores, made good their escape.[29] With a pontoon bridge across the river in his rear,[30] the enemy also having effected a lodgement on the opposite side within a short distance of the railroad, General Johnston could not, without incurring great peril, remain longer at Resaca, with a river in his rear, his communications in danger, the enemy having it in their power as soon as their dispositions were completed, to cut him off, and either force him to surrender, or to fight a battle under the most disadvantageous circumstances.

Johnston stayed at Resaca just as long as he should have done, retired at the right time, fought a battle pretty much on his own terms, punishing the enemy heavily, for it must have cost them ten or twelve thousand men,[31] with a loss to himself not exceeding four thousand, the greater part of which caused by one of those accidents, or miscarriages, that can not always be provided against.[32]

Whilst the fight on the 15th was going on, a regiment of Federal cavalry crossed the Connesauga, got within our lines, but fortunately did no greater harm than to fall in with our Brigade hospital, distant two miles from us, capturing some hospital attendants, the leader and several members of the band, destroyed some public property and carried off several mules and horses. Before they could get further, or do more harm, they were set upon by some of our own cavalry, and driven back across the river.[33]

The temporary disarrangement of our band was a great deprivation to us, but in the course of four months, we had procured the services of another and a better leader, and our music was far better than it had ever been before.

It was always the custom, when an action was expected, and as soon as a general Field Hospital was established, to send the musicians of the band to that place to assist the surgeons and attend upon the wounded until they could be properly taken care of. By using them a detail of effective men was avoided, for the services of every man that could pull a trigger were required, and we ran no risk of losing a good musician, a most serious loss, were it to happen. The habit was a very good one, and worked well. On such occasions as an engagement, our band was of no use to us, for at such a time I doubt if a regular step could have been preserved, and I am certain that the band could not have played in time for any one to march by — and why run the risk of spoiling fine music?

By daylight on the 16th, the last man had crossed the river, and the bridges in a blaze, the army moving by two different roads, falling back in the direction of Cassville.

The staff officers present with me in these battles were Lieut. W.E. Huger, A.D.C.; Lieut. Jennison, Actg. A.A.G.; in place of Capt. Walker, in the rear, sick; and Capt. Dean, 19th S.C., Actg. Inspctr. Gnl.

Falling back from Resaca by easy marches, on the 17th at about one o'clock we reached Adairsville. At this point we were joined by French's Division, which made the junction with us of General Polk's army corps complete. I have before stated that I thought his entire force amounted to 12,000 men. On reflection, I am inclined to believe that I overestimated his strength. 10,000 men must have been quite as many as they numbered. They consisted of two divisions, French's and Loring's, with several batteries of artillery and some cavalry.[34]

We had not been in our camp near Adairsville more than two hours, when the quick discharge of several pieces of artillery startled us from the meal that we were preparing to eat. In the course of half an hour the firing drew much nearer, and the discharge became more frequent. The rattle of musketry could be heard plainly, and we were ordered under arms.[35] Our division marched to the right. Walthall's and Sharp's* Brigades, under General Hindman, took some position in the line, where exactly, I do not know. The third brigade was sent a mile or two on our right flank, to hold some cavalry in check that were reported coming in that direction, and my own was ordered to occupy a high and abrupt hill on the extreme right of our line. We were only for a short time under a trifling fire. From our prominent position, I got a fine view of what was going on below me. As we faced the enemy, the country in our front was very pretty. The land was of excellent quality, fertile and much cleared, with the green crops of wheat, oats, and young corn covering it like a carpet. The village of Adairsville looked very prettily in the distance, and there was just wood enough, with the distant mountains, to make a very interesting landscape. The alarm was caused by the advance guard of the enemy, cavalry and infantry, driving in our cavalry and outposts. These meeting a check in the shape of two corps, awaited the arrival of their main column, and immediately as they came up, began to form a line of battle. About a mile and a half distant, sharp skirmishing and a slow but steady cannonade continued until dark, but the enemy made no other serious demonstration.[37] From my position I could see the greater part of our own force, and here and there that of the enemy. The evening was still and calm, with all the freshness of spring after a gentle shower. The martial array was very imposing, and the indications of an impending contest just sufficient to excite the imagination without causing too much anxiety.

During the night, we received orders to move at daylight, and a couple of hours before day I was instructed to meet the division at a certain point, to take my place in the column. Whilst lying on the top of our ridge, we could hear the movements of our troops, as they marched off during the night, and when the time came for us to start, everything from that part of the field had departed. A thick fog had risen during the night, and it was with much difficulty that I could find my way out to the road to join the division, which was that day to be the rear guard.

The enemy did not follow us as promptly as we expected, so that we were unmolested, and at an early hour in the morning we reached Cassville, going into camp about two miles from the town. Here we had a good rest for nearly twenty-four hours.[38]

On the 19th, we were under arms by eight o'clock, and were marched several miles east of the town, for the purpose of finding out something

---

*Late Tucker's Brigade, but known hereafter as Sharp's.[36] — A.M.M.

about the enemy in that direction. A part of the division came in contact with a large body of cavalry,[39] and before we were aware of it a battery of artillery opened on us, doing some mischief. This cavalry covered the movement of some portion of the Federal army, who were soon afterwards discovered in force. The purpose for which we had been sent being accomplished, we retired to the line of battle selected, where it was the purpose of General Johnston to fight. His address to the army, stating his intention, etc., was received by the troops with cheers, and we were soon busily occupied in throwing up a defensive line.[40]

AFFAIR NEAR CASSVILLE

19th May, 1864

(The Narrative)

The ground upon which our army was drawn up, so far as I could see, seemed to me to possess great advantages, comparatively open and well adapted to a battle ground.[41] We occupied the brow of a high range of hills, the ground in our front level and cleared up, consisting mostly of open fields, Cassville lying about a half-mile in our front. General Johnston had determined to fight, having now succeeded in concentrating his whole force, and was stronger on that day than ever before or afterwards, his army numbering, I should judge, full 50,000 men,[42] all of them good soldiers and old ones, full of mettle, and anxious to measure themselves once more with the enemy.

The position had been selected with much judgment, giving us great advantages over the enemy, who, I doubt not, would have been the assailants. Hood's Corps occupied the right, Polk's the centre, and Hardee's the left. By four o'clock, our dispositions were complete. The infantry formed in two lines each, as well as the artillery, protected by light field works, hurriedly thrown up. Between that hour and five o'clock, there was much heavy skirmishing, and a sharp cavalry engagement, in which the latter did not show to any advantage, and all our light troops were driven in by the steady advance of the enemy. At several points, the enemy's line came so near before halting that the men on either side exchanged shots. As our artillery opened on them, that of the enemy came into action in beautiful style, and selecting their positions with great skill, opened fire on ours, and soon showed an almost overwhelming superiority. It must be remembered that they had two guns to our one, and a greater number of rifled pieces, which also gave a great advantage in range and accuracy. I saw one battery of ours knocked to pieces, and the gunners driven from their guns in less than fifteen minutes. I was told of another instance of the same kind that occurred in our division front, and I think it likely there may have been others.[43]

It soon became evident that the enemy did not intend to bring on a general engagement that evening, however much we may have desired it, and as dark approached and the firing gradually ceased, we began to raise and strengthen our defences, preparing in this and other ways to give the enemy a warm reception on the following morning, believing that battle was inevitable, and trusting that the day would terminate in success for our arms.

To our great surprise, and to the disgust of many, at midnight, we received the order to retire, and at two o'clock, our division drew out as noiselessly as possible, and, bringing up the rear of our corps, took up the line of march for the railroad crossing at the Etowah River.

It was a delicate piece of business to get away without the enemy discovering our intentions. They certainly had a suspicion of it, and felt for us with their skirmishers, but ours did their duty well, driving back the forces that had been sent to make the discovery as to whether our lines were occupied or not. After having accomplished their purpose, our rear guard, composed entirely of the picket line, fell back from the breastworks, and soon after overtook us.

General Johnston says in his report that it was his intention to fight at Cassville, but that during the earlier part of the evening of the 19th, Generals Polk and Hood, in a conference with him, had expressed an opinion adverse to such a course, and stated that the positions held by their respective corps were untenable.

This surprised and annoyed him, as he was of the opinion that the portion of the line occupied by the command of those officers, was by far the strongest of what he regarded as a very strong position, the more so as General Hardee, whose position on the left was much weaker, was of opinion that he could make good his, and was for fighting. With two out of his three corps commanders so unwilling to risk an engagement, and making so unfavorable a representation of matters, he reluctantly gave the order for the army to retire that night, a step, as he says, he afterwards regretted. I can not help but think that the council of those two officers was unfortunate.[44]

After crossing the Etowah River and destroying the bridges, the army encamped on the left bank and were undisturbed for several days. Sherman appears to have rested his men for two or three days previous to his next move.[45]

After crossing his army near (Kingston), General Sherman moved to our left, and in the direction of Dallas, making a wide circuit and leaving the railroad on his left. He must have had a very large amount of transportation as the country into which he was about to operate, was a very poor one, and could not contribute in any way to their wants, and he must have carried a wagon train with from fifteen to twenty days' rations for his entire army.[46] His purpose in not crossing in our front or vicinity was to avoid the Alatoona pass, which Johnston held, and which, from the character of the country, was in a position thro which he could not in all probability have forced his way, and the only thing left for him to do was to turn it.[47] General Johnston was not long in discovering his movements, and on the 24th of May a portion of his army was near Dallas, and the remainder fast concentrating near that place. On the 25th, at about midday, our division arrived in the vicinity of New Hope Church, the rest of the corps coming up a few hours later. We were just in time to form our line of battle, but had thrown up no works, when the enemy began to make his appearance, and the pickets became engaged.

BATTLE OF NEW HOPE CHURCH

May 25th, 1864

(The Narrative)

Our skirmishers had hardly become engaged before the enemy opened upon us with his artillery, throwing his shot and shell around and over us, doing but little damage, as, owing to the dense woods and the few roads that existed in this country, it was mostly guess work with them, tho their shots did come unpleasantly near. This point was quite an important one, for besides the necessity that existed for carrying out General Johnston's plan of battle, three important roads leading from Dallas, Ackworth, and Marietta,[48] came together at this point, and it was necessary that we should retain them, and the enemy were as anxious as we were to get possession of them.

As soon as the firing began, which was a surprise to us, for we did not expect to meet the enemy so soon, the order was given to the men to raise a temporary breastwork at once. Retaining one half of the command in line, the rest were set to work constructing them, and in a space of time not exceeding ten minutes a very respectable breastwork of logs, limbs of trees, mixed in with stones and rocks, was erected, giving the men much protection from rifle balls, and the fragments of shells after bursting. I never saw men work so hard or so expeditiously. The tools had not been distributed, and they had to rely alone upon the material they could find on the ground, near the line, but no log was too big or stone too heavy for their purpose. All seemed to be endowed with superhuman strength, and the pile seemed to grow out of the ground.

Apprehension, to a great extent, and the knowledge gained by experience, made them work in a style and with an energy that I have never seen equaled at any time.

General Thomas's command were the assailants, and Hooker's corps bore the brunt of it. Their chief attack was against that portion of the line held by General Stewart's division. Our brigade, which was in the front line and on the right of our division, was immediately on Stewart's left, but we had very little to do in the fight. Only our extreme right was at all engaged, and then only for a short time.[49]

The country was so thickly wooded that we could not see over one hundred yards in our front, and we had not been allowed sufficient time to remove the underbrush.

Although the attack reached to within one hundred and fifty yards of our right flank, what with the growth and dense smoke it was almost impossible to make out anything. Still the fire on us was at times severe, though not directed particularly towards us. I have seldom known the Yankees so pertinacious as they were on this occasion.

I could not see much of it myself for the reasons mentioned, but I was told by others of the character of the conflict, and could judge pretty well from the firing on both sides, that although the contest was limited to a short space, that it was a desperate one. The enemy seemed determined to break through at that point, and made repeated efforts to do so, coming up in so many lines that the attack may almost be said to have been made in column. Much anxiety was felt as to whether Stewart could continue to resist, and apprehension felt that he would finally be forced to give way to the repeated and almost overwhelming assaults; but he was heavily reinforced by additional troops in his rear, one of our brigades being sent for that purpose. All these necessary precautions, however, proved unnecessary, and he repulsed his adversaries in brilliant style, with terrible slaughter, and without being shaken, or his line in danger for one moment. Only two batteries could be used advantageously, and they did great execution. A section of two 12-pound howitzers, old style, were the most effective of all the pieces. Being light, easily handled, and the range short, they were just the guns for the occasion. This was one of the very few instances that I ever knew of that description of ordnance being of much use in any of our campaigns in the west. The fight must have lasted about an hour and a half, when the enemy gave it up, and night soon coming on, the firing ceased entirely. The loss to our forces was comparatively trifling, whilst the enemy suffered very heavily.[50]

———————

At about ten o'clock on the night of this last battle, we were removed to another point in the line, which was being extended to our right. At an early hour in the morning, we were again removed to support some other division, where an attack was threatened, and for several hours were under a pretty sharp fire. Later in the day, it becoming evident that the enemy were gaining ground to our right to outflank us, we were withdrawn, and marching some two miles in that direction, got in position just in time to defeat their purposes. All this afternoon and the day following, the fighting on our skirmish lines was very severe. The pickets were once or twice driven in, and their line lost, rendering it necessary with additional troops to become the attackers ourselves, and recover it.[51]

On the 28th, Hood was ordered with his corps to move upon the left flank of the enemy, and attack.

We went out for this purpose, marched some eight miles or ten miles, and then returned, Hood reporting, I believe, that he found the enemy too strong, and too securely protected by his intrenchments. I had no means of forming an opinion in regard to this matter, not being in a position to make any observations for myself.[52] After our return, we lay in rear of the line of battle, but quite near enough for their cannon balls and rifle bullets to annoy us a good deal, having no works to protect us. A couple of hours before day we moved again to the extreme right, and my brigade relieved that of a General Granbury,* who, two days before, had had a severe fight on the same ground, with two divisions of the enemy, whose object had been to get on our flank at that point, and had attacked a brigade of dismounted cavalry, which had been charged with its defence. It had not been threatened before, and was deemed secure, when the enemy, finding out our weakness there, had detached a corps to secure this position on our flank. Johnston, always with his wits about him, detected the movement, and frustrated it. Granbury's brigade, the most advanced of the force sent for this purpose, arrived on the ground just as the cavalry were giving way, charged the enemy, driving them back. The position he held was a very strong one, and the enemy wanted it, but a short time elapsed before they reappeared, and assailed him with great impetuosity, but were repulsed over and over again.[54] Two howitzers were again distinguished for the execution they did in this fight. They were so placed as to take the enemy in flank, as they marched to the assault, and raked them as they descended a hill and got into a gorge, which separated the first hill from the one on which the Confederate troops were standing. I was told that one of them had been discharged two hundred times during the fight, but this I am inclined to doubt. Still, I could easily understand that from the position they occupied relative to the attacking lines, they must have told with fearful effect, at a distance not exceeding three hundred yards, on the enemy's ranks, and the evidence left on the ground told plainly that the service they had rendered was most important. Many of the dead Yankees had been buried before our arrival, but I have seldom seen so many dead bodies lying over so

---

*General Granbury commanded a Texas brigade, one of the best fighting ones in the army, but they were more slovenly and looked less like soldiers than almost any other. General Granbury was afterwards killed at the battle of Franklin.[53] — A.M.M.

small a space as where this partial engagement took place.[55]

We remained in this last position until the night of the 4th of June. During that interval much fighting took place, but nothing that could be called a battle. The contests were generally for the picket line, or demonstrations on one side or the other to discover the enemy's strength. We were daily under fire, not a day passing that our list of casualties was not added to. A part of Hardee's corps was seriously engaged, I think on the 26th, driving back the enemy, who had attacked, with heavy loss.[56] On the 24th also, General Wheeler, with a portion of the cavalry, passed to the enemy's rear, beat the enemy's cavalry, and burned two hundred and fifty wagons.[57] The continued effort of General Sherman seemed to be to envelop our right, and he was constantly gaining ground to his left. We consequently had to make a corresponding movement, and after several days, instead of our being on the right of the army, we were in the centre.[58] On the 4th, orders were received to prepare for a move, and after dark, in a torrent of rain, we abandoned our works, and retired to a stronger and new line, some 9 or 10 miles in our rear. On the 5th of June, the army rested with its left on Lost Mountain, its centre at Gilgal Church, the right near the railroad.[59] Our positions were constantly changing, gaining ground on the right daily to meet and check the enemy, so that on the 9th our right rested on what was known as Noon Day Creek. Heavy skirmishing daily, the enemy moving up to us by successive lines of intrenchments.

On the 14th of June, Lieut. Gen. Polk was killed on Pine Mountain, whilst making a reconnaissance.[60] On the 18th, Hindman's division was sent to reinforce General Hardee, on the left of the line, who appeared to be threatened. In spite of the rain which poured in torrents nearly all day, on arriving at his position on the left, we found matters looking very serious, and I fully expected that we were in for another battle. The firing was very heavy, only a little short of what it usually was during a general engagement. The enemy had now changed their tactics, and were covering a movement to our left.

After remaining exposed several hours in momentary expection of being ordered to go in, we were relieved, and ordered back to the right, it being evident that no general action would take place that day. The new change in the plans of the enemy necessitated a corresponding one on our own. A portion of our line was abandoned, and on the 19th the army was nearer to Marietta, distant about two miles, our lines forming very nearly a half circle around it, with the right, Hood's corps, its right resting on the Marietta and Canton road, Loring's (late Polk's) corps on Kennessaw Mountain, with Hardee's left extending across the Lost Mountain and Marietta Road.

On the 20th, Wheeler with his command routed the Federal cavalry on our right.[61] On the evening of the 20th, our corps, (Hood's) was transferred from the right to the left, the cavalry occupying the position that we left. Found the enemy gradually working round in this direction, and his position opposite our front a very formidable one.

BATTLE OF THE 22nd JUNE, 1864

NEAR MARIETTA, GA. SOMETIMES CALLED

BATTLE OF ZION CHURCH [62]

(The Narrative)

This engagement, spoken of by General Sherman, as the *"Affair of the Kulp House"*, was a disgrace to the officer who planned it, and showed an amount of ignorance of the enemy's position, and the difficulties to be overcome before he could be reached, for which there could be no excuse. The ground had been ridden over by many officers the day before, at latest, and ought to have been thoroughly understood by General Hood, the greater part of his staff, and particularly his engineers.

I formed my estimate of him on this occasion for the first time, and subsequent events only confirmed me in the opinion that he was totally unfit for the command of a corps, altho he might have deserved the reputation he had acquired as the best division commander in the "Army of Northern Virginia."

About one o'clock in the afternoon of the 22nd, Hindman's division was ordered under arms, and shortly after moved in the direction of our picket lines, taking care to screen our movement from observation by keeping some woods between ourselves and the enemy, and halting behind the brow of a hill out of view. Here we were joined shortly after by the other two divisions of the corps, Stewart's and Stevenson's.[63] The instructions issued were as follows: My brigade was to advance alone for the purpose of getting possession of a belt of woods, between ourselves and the enemy, to hold it to the last man, resisting any effort on their part to take it. A battery of artillery was sent along with us. It was apprehended that from the direction of the enemy's lines and the position of the wood relative to it, that they could occupy it to great advantage, and endanger our right flank, either whilst attacking or after attaining *(our)* object. I could never see how it was to effect us in the latter event.

A second brigade of our division was also ordered on detached duty somewhere to the left, and the remaining brigades, with Stewart and Stevenson, in two lines of battle, were to assail, the guide being to the left; and it was supposed that in the advance and as they neared the breastworks, the right of our line would clear the wood which I held, some 3 or 400 yards.

I had just taken possession of the said wood, driving the enemy's skirmishers from our front, and a portion of the men were hard at work throwing up a protection of logs and rails, when the rear attack commenced. The greater part of our men, after clearing the brow of the hill behind which they had been formed, were exposed to a fire of both artillery and infantry for a full half-mile; but they swept boldy forward, regardless of the withering fire directed against them by the enemy from behind their well-constructed works. I have no doubt but that the entire line would have carried the works and driven the enemy out, but no one expected to find, as two-thirds of the attacking force did, on nearing the works, that they were located on the opposite side of a creek, with a boggy, miry margin on each side.[64] The delay caused by the difficulty in crossing gave the attacked great advantages, and produced so much confusion and disorder, that the whole impetus of the charge was lost, and the formation was not sufficiently compact to effect any good result, and we were driven back and forced to retire. In the meantime, the greater part of Stevenson's Division, on the extreme left, had struck the enemy at a point where the works had crossed the creek, it making at that point a bend to the rear, and running in a different direction, and had carried them, but their comrades having failed in their effort, owing to the difficulty mentioned, and the enemy having nothing further to fear in that direction, turning their entire attention to them, and bringing fresh troops into the contest, they in turn were forced to give way, falling back under a galling fire. Hindman, who never led his division, but left it entirely to his brigadiers, after receiving his instructions to manage their own commands, was so entirely ignorant of the ground, having made no observation of it previous to the commencement of that attack, that they, acting under his orders and directions, found themselves, soon after getting under fire, clashing with each other, and in an almost inextricable jumble. From the beginning of the affair to the end, the enemy opened a steady fire on our position in the wood.

Fortunately for us, the slight breastwork that we had hurriedly constructed, gave us much protection. Besides the fire from their small arms, there must have been at least twenty guns playing on us, the shot and shell tearing through the timber, cutting down trees and large branches, which fell in our midst. It was a terrific fire, and lasted until dark. As our line was somewhat withdrawn from the skirt of the wood, the enemy could not very well see our exact position, altho we could generally see them, and had a full view of the narrow open space that separated us. This also contributed much to our safety, and our loss was comparatively small.

The affair was a miserable failure, and must have cost us 1,500 or 2,000 men, to no purpose.[65]

Hindman knew about the existence of the creek, for he had mentioned it to me only the day before. I can scarcely suppose that General Hood was ignorant of its existence, and as I have mentioned before, the ground had previously been inspected two days before by officers of the corps, previous to the enemy's extending their line so far to our left. The most ordinary recognizance should have revealed the fact as to which side of the creek the enemy's lines were on.

But the strangest part of the whole affair is that General Johnston in his report, alluding to this engagement, says that on the 22nd the enemy attacked Hood in his breastworks, and were repulsed with loss. The only explanation that I can give for this strange and incorrect statement is that General Hood fought on this occasion on his own responsibility, was ashamed of the result, and did not give a correct statement. At the same time, it must be admitted that if my supposition be correct, how was it possible for General Johnston to remain for any length of time so completely deceived as to the true nature of this fight.[66]

From this time until the 2nd of July, our Division occupied the same position, heavy skirmishing going on daily, and constant cannonading, the enemy working up to us by successive lines of intrenchments, and gaining ground to our left, so that at last his extreme right was nearer to the Chattahoochie River and Atlanta than we were. On the night of the 2nd, General Johnston evacuated his lines around Marietta, and fell back five miles from Marietta to Smyrna Church camp ground. Before this took place, however, General Johnston had had an opportunity of punishing the enemy severely. On the 27th of June, General Sherman assaulted our lines at two points, the attacks falling upon portions of Hardee's and Loring's Corps.[67] They were both repulsed with great loss to the assailants. This is the only instance in which Sherman in his report of this campaign admits that he was defeated, and that it cost him a heavy loss, altho the number that he gives falls far short of what it actually was. Our own loss did not, I believe, exceed 6 or 700 men.[68]

At about one o'clock on the morning of the 3rd, we reached our new position near the Smyrna camp ground. The night was a very dark one, and part of our line running thro a thick wood, it was impossible to get to work before daylight. The men threw themselves on the ground in rear of their stacks of arms, and slept until daybreak. As soon as it was light enough to see, the ground was laid out, and the labor of constructing breastworks and batteries was commenced. In a few hours the lines were in a condition to resist an attack, and by midday the enemy were upon us. The rattle of musketry gave us warning that our outposts were engaged, and shortly after their dark lines could be seen drawing towards us. Steadily and warily they felt their way onwards, until, arriving at a proper distance, they halted, going to work immediately to secure themselves in the same way that we had done. During the 3rd and 4th we were employed in strengthening our works, clearing out the woods in our front, where they existed, and constructing "abatis" and "palisades", fighting between the pickets going on all the time, as well as a steady artillery fire. I do not think that the position selected here was a very strong one. The line selected was a very irregular one, many salient points occurring in it. The consequence was that with the long-range weapons of the present day, many of the projectiles fired at a certain point that missed and passed over the works, would strike some poor fellow in the back, on duty in the other face of the salient.

At this place I saw two Yankee batteries, a mile and a half apart, engage each other with great spirit, firing round after round, each one under the impression that he was engaged with a rebel battery. Our line was so tortuous that I am not surprised at the mistake being made, and just at that point and from the position that these two batteries had taken up, I daresay that each had the appearance to the other of being located in our line of defense. It was a very ludicrous sight, causing much merriment and shouts of laughter for the space of ten or fifteen minutes, until the two combatants found out their error.

Whilst occupying Johnston's attention, the enemy detached a corps from their army,[69] pushing it forward towards the Chattahoochie, with a view to get possession of several crossings on that river of great importance to us. There was only a small force at those places for their protection, consisting of Major General G.W. Smith's Division of Georgia Militia, numbering 1,500 men.[70] General Johnston, fearing that he might lose the important lines of works on the Chattahoochie, a sort of tete-du-pont which he had had the foresight to prepare, whilst the later operations of the last two weeks were going on, using Negro labor under the direction of the engineer corps, fell back to these works, abandoning his lines at Smyrna camp ground on the night of the 4th. I think the distance between the two points was about eight miles. We reached the river at about 8 A.M. on the morning of the 5th, and were immediately assigned our position, which was with the left of the division, about a half mile from the river, General Smith's militia filling up that space. My brigade was 2nd from the left. Our works had been completed, but we immediately set to work to improve them. They consisted of ditch and embankment earth thrown forward. At intervals of 400 yards came substantially built works for our guns, with an occasional "blockhouse", or rather, what was intended to serve as such.

I will mention here that General Hindman on the night of the 3rd, injured his eye in some manner. He himself was anxious to get away, and everybody else equally so to get rid of him. The accident furnished a very good excuse, and we never saw him again during the war.[71] He was afterwards sent to the Trans-Mississippi Dptmt. and the last I heard of him, he had been placed under arrest by General Kirby Smith, and charges preferred against him, for improperly appropriating the Government transportation under his charge, and using it to haul a large quantity of tobacco from one point to another, the same being the property of private parties, and a speculation in which he was interested. The abrupt termination of the war, I believe, put a stop to the investigation. I will now take leave of him, and will refrain from expressing any further opinion of him, for I have nothing to say in his favor, and was only too glad to get rid of him.[72] Brigadier General J.C. Brown, of Tennessee, a favorite of General Hood's, and an officer whose promotion as a Major General was daily expected, was ordered temporarily to the command of the division, until his promotion could be heard of. He was at the time the senior Brigadier in the Army of Tennessee.[73]

By 12 o'clock, the Union Army like bloodhounds on the trail, made their appearance, commencing operations immediately, the fighting soon becoming severe.

I saw four batteries go into position in front of our line, and, concentrating their fire on one point, opened on a very strong earthwork, in which was a battery of four rifled pieces, two of which were 20 pounders. The fire from those of the enemy was so rapid and well directed, throwing many of their shot through the embrasures, or just striking the inner edge of the parapet, that the artillerists, officers well as men, lost their nerve, and almost abandoned their guns, seeking shelter close under the works. It was not the first instance in which I had seen evidence of our artillery giving up too easily, and they began about this time to show too great dread of the superiority which the enemy possessed over us in this arm, and to use a vulgar but very expressive phrase, were considerably "under the hack". To some extent this state of things was owing to the order which had been issued restricting the fire of artillery on account of the short supply of ammunition, only permitting them to open in cases where it was necessary to do so.[74] Often when the time arrived for bringing the guns into play, those of the Yankees having had the advantage of long practice and unlimited supply of ammunition, had attained the range with such precision as to render it a most dangerous matter to attempt the working of our guns. The men became unnerved, and fired with little accuracy, and having to contend against more than double their number of guns, superior in weight of metal and in range, felt that they were whipped before the order, "Commence firing" was given. As a general rule, I think that our artillery was deficient. Many batteries were commanded by officers quite unfit for so important a command as a battery of light artillery, the management of which required great attention, much experience, and versatility of knowledge.

The Yankees, if they excelled us in anything, did so in this branch, and their generals certainly seemed better to understand the uses of this weapon than ours did. It always bore a conspicuous part on their side, whilst the part taken by ours contributed little to our successes or any successes in which I was a participant. In justice, however, to some, I must state that there was a very respectable number of batteries that were fully equal to the best in the Yankee army, and on all occasions when not too heavily overmatched, proved too much for their opponents, forcing them to withdraw from the conflict, frequently leaving a piece or two behind, or driving the men from their pieces. Amongst this class, were the batteries of Dent, Robinson, and Garrity, of whom I saw a good deal, and never saw them yield or give way, unless fully authorized by the condition of affairs to do so.[75]

About five o'clock on the evening of the 5th, my brigade having a short time previously been withdrawn from the breastworks, to be used as a reserve, another command taking its place, I received an order to hurry with all speed towards the left of the line to reinforce some command there where the line was weak, and the troops, mostly militia, were not regarded as the most reliable. Some movements of the enemy indicated an assault, and the point was regarded as a most important one. To reach my destination I had the choice of two routes, one immediately in rear of the works, where at one point we had to cross a high, bare hill, entirely exposed to the enemy, for the space of about two hundred yards; the other a safer but less direct way, which, if taken, would have increased the distance near a quarter of a mile, taking ten minutes longer to make our appearance at the point of danger. Not knowing how great the urgency might be for our immediate presence, and receiving two orders in quick succession to hurry up and lose no time, I determined after a very slight hesitation to take the shortest direction, tho the most exposed, knowing full well that it would cost us something to run the gauntlet. Closing the command well up to the brink of the point where the danger commenced, the order was then given to double-quick, each regiment following the one that preceded it, the moment it had gained the proper distance. No sooner did the head of the column show itself than four Yankee batteries opened on us, and firing with the greatest rapidity, shrapnel and spherical case all bursting with admirable regularity, over, under, and around us, threatened to destroy or sweep us away. They had been firing at everything which showed itself on this hill during the day, and had the range of it. When I saw the storm that we had created, I trembled with anxiety for my poor men, a little perhaps for myself, and deeply regretted not having taken the other road, but it was too late now to make a change. The only thing to be done was to go by with all speed. This was an occasion when there was no necessity to hurry the men. However averse they usually were to double quicking, they did it this time at a pace for which no authority can be found in Hardee's Tactics.[76] In six or eight minutes we had passed the danger, and found ourselves in a position of comparative safety, with a loss of only eleven men killed or desperately wounded. I think that for the short space of time that we were exposed, that this was the severest artillery fire that I have ever been exposed to. The air seemed alive with shells, bursting, it seemed to me, within only a few feet of my head. I was the only officer mounted, and have no doubt that they used me to some extent as their principal target. Both myself and my horse passed through unscathed, tho covered with dust, and struck in many places by clods of dirt, small pebbles, etc. The poor animal seemed almost paralyzed by fear, and would at times shrink down under me, so as to induce me to believe once or twice that she had been wounded.*

I was much surprised at the smallness of the loss that we had sustained. Fully three hundred shot must have been fired at us, and I have frequently seen two or three balls kill as many or more men than we lost; but the fire of artillery is generally more demoralizing than destructive, and the losses that it inflicts are generally caused by one or two well-directed, or as frequently as not, accidental shots.

After all, the enemy made no assault; were in all probability deterred from doing so by noticing the arrival of reinforcements, other troops

---

*This mare, after having been through many fights, was afterwards killed in the battle of the 22nd July, near Atlanta, Lieut. W.E. Huger, A.D.C., riding her at the time. — A.M.M.

coming up as well as my command, but no one else tried that short cut over the hill.

The army remained in possession of these lines, confronting the enemy, until the 9th. It would be tiresome to repeat the occurrences of every day even if I could remember them.

Our occupations and employments were only a repetition of events that had now been going on for more than two months, altho perhaps during the last day or two of our stay, the fighting may have been a little more severe than ordinarily, our loss amounting to from five to fifteen men.

Sherman failing in all his efforts to force Johnston out of this strong position, again resorted to his old system of flanking, and determined to cross the river above our position. His large army and great excess of men enabling him to detach a force for this purpose, whilst the greater part of his army threatened us in our position, we had not the means of thwarting him, and on the 8th he succeeded in effecting a lodgement on the east bank, many miles above our right flank;[77] and on the night of the 9th, General Johnston retired across the Chattahoochie. The enemy at the time at many points being within a very short distance of our lines, the men exchanging shots from the breastworks.

To retire without giving any alarm or bringing on an attack was a very delicate operation, but every precaution being taken by wrapping the wheels of our artillery with such material as would muffle and deaden the sound, and by strewing the pontoon bridges with green corn stalks, etc., the result was that the whole army drew out, saving everything in the way of material and without the loss of a man. Everything having crossed to the left bank, the pontoon bridges, of which there was three, were removed and safely in rear before the enemy began to make his appearance on the opposite side.[78] Leaving about a fourth of our force on picket or outpost duty near the river, the remainder retired towards Atlanta, distant from the river about eight miles, and, encamping around the city about three miles from it, made the most of the few days of comparative quiet which succeeded.

From the morning of the 10th of July to that of the 17th, the brigade and Army remained in a state of comparative quiet, and undisturbed rest.[79] The clothing of the men stood greatly in need of careful washing and cleaning, and the rest that all obtained during this short respite was much needed and enjoyed. Still the time was not passed in idleness. Rigid inspections were made, and as far as practicable, many deficiencies were supplied, and everything got in a state of readiness for future action. During this period, we performed as a brigade, one tour of picket duty, lasting forty-eight hours. It was by no means arduous, and but little picket firing took place. The stream separated us from the enemy, who were similarly posted on the opposite bank of the river. I do not believe that we lost a single man on this occasion.

On the morning of the 17th, Sunday, riding into Atlanta for the purpose of going to church, and to hear Bishop Ley, of Arkansas, at that time accompanying the army as a missionary, I noticed an unusual stir amongst the train of wagons, and the movement of considerable bodies of troops, which attracted my attention.[80] Returning to camp later in the day, I found that orders had been received a short time before to hold ourselves in readiness to march at any moment. All our transportation, which had here rejoined us, with the exception of those containing the ammunition, tools, and the ambulances, had been sent away at short notice. The surgeons looked mysterious, and had received orders to prepare for the reception in Atlanta of a large number of wounded. As the day wore on, the passage of troops in larger numbers, their dusty faces and uniforms indicating that they had come from some position far to our left, could be observed.

The men, from long familiarity with such matters, and naturally shrewd and observant, had also been struck by these signs, speaking freely amongst themselves, remarking that Old Johnston was waking up again, and that before many hours had passed, they would again be grappling with the foe. At last the rumor that the enemy had crossed the Chattahoochie, was whispered about and an hour or two afterwards, it was asserted with authority.[81]

About 5 P.M., the bugles sounded for the men to fall in, and in less than fifteen minutes after, the division had taken the route step, moving in a north-easterly direction.

All this, together with the information we had received as to the enemy, now known to have crossed at a point between Roswell and Power's Ferry,[82] with the Peach Tree Creek between them and ourselves, looked ominous. I made up my mind that within twenty-four hours or, at farthest, forty-eight, a battle would be fought, perhaps the battle of the war, and that Johnston intended now to deliver his blow suddenly, and with the determination of saving Atlanta, and bringing the campaign to a final issue. I did not know then as much about the country as I afterwards learned, and of course could only conjecture how and where the attack would be made, but I am perfectly satisfied now from all I heard and the observations I made that day, that General Johnston truly stated his intention when he says in his report, that at Peach Tree Creek he purposed attacking as soon as a considerable portion of Sherman's army had crossed that stream. Owing to the shallowness of the river and ease with which it could be forded many miles above Atlanta at various points, it was impossible for him to prevent the enemy crossing the Chattahoochie, but correctly divining that, after having made the passage of the river, they would move upon him, having yet the Peach Tree Creek to cross, a large and deep stream, before they could reach him, that the proper time to bring on an engagement was after a portion of the army had crossed the latter stream, hoping to defeat and cut them off before the remainder could get over, and if successful, and Sherman forced to retreat, there would have been two streams in his rear. instead of one.[83] By almost all to whom I spoke, whose opinion was worth anything, no doubt was entertained but that within two days a fight would have been brought about. The army on that day was as strong as when the campaign began. The infantry and artillery amounted to 41,000 men, the cavalry about 10,000, the arrival of Polk's Corps, and other reinforcements fully covering its losses.[84] The men were in fine spirits and admirable condition, confident in their own ability and in the ability and skill of their commander, to whom they were much attached. They moved on cheerfully, and with high hopes.

A little before dark, we were halted and went into bivouac on the side of the road, having come in contact with one of our columns, marching in the same direction, whose orders were to precede us. At the same time, several heavy clouds of dust, distant several miles, indicated that the army was moving as a whole, all the different columns tending in the same direction.

The command, on being dismissed, were instructed to be in readiness to march at a later hour during the night, as our stay there depended somewhat on the movements of others; but the hours of darkness passed, one after the other, without any sign of our leaving. Some time after sunrise, an officer brought me the intelligence that General Johnston had been removed from the command of the army, by an order received the preceding night from Richmond, and that General Hood had been placed in command. I soon found on inquiry that the information was too true. The news had flown through the different camps, and was in the possession of everyone. The effect of it was visible on the countenances of all, and altho little was said openly, it was very evident that the change was regarded, not only unfavorably, but as a calamity.

The removal of General Johnston from the command of the Army of Tennessee, was one of those hasty and ill-judged steps on the part of Mr. Davis, which, I believe, contributed materially to the downfall of the Confederacy, and possibly it caused it.[85]

I have always thought that had General Johnston been permitted to retain the command, Sherman never would have gained Atlanta. I believe that Johnston would finally have defeated him and driven him across the river.[86] Hood very nearly succeeded on two occasions in doing so, and only failed when Victory was in his grasp, because he could not profit by his successes, not knowing how to handle or use his men, fighting on both occasions only a portion of his army, the remainder looking on, silent spectators. The opportunity of defeating the enemy at Peach Tree Creek was delayed too long, and then undertaken with an inadequate force. Johnston, with his superior generalship, would have converted these affairs into brilliant triumphs. His foresight as to the enemy's movements proved correct in every point. Had he lost the opportunity, or the enemy not have laid themselves open as they did at P.T.C., his intention was to have gathered his entire force on one of the enemy's flanks, and attacked, leaving only the militia, which Governor Brown was sending him to hold the works around Atlanta.[87]

The troops in the subsequent engagements, without confidence in Hood, did their part nobly. They failed to obtain any permanent advantage, not from any fault of theirs, but because the head which directed them, was incompetent, and entirely unfit for the responsible position he occupied.[88]

Even had Johnston lost Atlanta, Sherman never could have marched through Georgia and South Carolina, as he afterwards did. Neither could he by any possibility have committed the egregious error of undertaking the Tennessee campaign a few months after, leaving a large army in his rear to destroy and lay waste some of the most valuable region of country in the Confederacy, interrupting our railroad and other communications from one end of the Republic to the other. Great as is the praise due the troops who fought under Hood, with Johnston they would have deserved still greater, for they would have fought even better.

From the 17th day of July, 1864, when General Joseph E. Johnston was removed from the command of the Western Army, events disastrous in the extreme, many of them the result of mismanagement of military affairs in Georgia and the West, followed each other in rapid succession. From bad to worse we hurried to our ruin. I do not mean to claim for General Johnston that, but for his removal, our cause would have been triumphant, for the country was rotten at the core, and the people were fast wearying of the war; but I do think that the war might have been protracted for at least a year, and that eventually we might have obtained terms, such, it is true, as at an earlier period we would have scorned, but which would have left us in a far better condition than that to which we have since been reduced.

On the 18th, General Hood assumed command of the army, General Johnston turning over to him,

Infantry and artillery	41,000 men
Cavalry about	10,000 ”
Johnston had lost, killed and wounded	10,000 ”
And from all other causes	4,700 ”
Received by reinforcements, I.& A.	15,000 ”
He states that the effective strength had been increased during the campaign	2,000 ”

The losses sustained by the cavalry he does not give. In the report that I take these figures from, he also states that of the 10,000 cavalry, 4,000 joined him during the campaign.

He estimates the enemy's loss as being five to one on our part, and in the instances where we held the ground and had an opportunity of accurately comparing the loss on both sides, it varies in our favor from 7 to 1 to 90 to 1, all these instances together giving an average of 13 to 1.[89]

But for the two unfortunate occasions, the first at Resaca, where Stewart's division attacked, the order directing them not to do so having miscarried or failed to reach them in time, and the stupid affair on the 22nd of June near Zion Church, for which I take it Hood alone was responsible, the disproportion of the loss sustained by the two armies would have been still greater. We always fought to great advantage behind breastworks. Even our picket lines were carefully prepared for the protection of the riflemen with pits, and a shallow ditch connecting one with the other. Whenever the enemy took them from us, it required a line of battle to do so, preceded by their skirmishers. The latter never could make any impression on them. On such occasions, the loss to the enemy would be quite severe, whilst to us it was trifling. Our men had learned to shoot with great accuracy, and in the skirmishes and picket fights, killed many of their adversaries. From my own experience, I do not think General Johnston's estimate of five to one by any means extravagant.[90]

NOTES TO CHAPTER 8

[1] This is one of the rare instances in which Manigault to some extent confuses the facts. As has been previously pointed out, estimating the strength of armies engaged in a campaign is complicated by differing definitions of "present for duty," "effectives," etc., not to mention the natural inclination on both sides to maximize the strength of an opponent and minimize one's own. Manigault's estimate of 80,000 for the Northern army after the Battle of Missionary Ridge is probably pretty close to the mark. However, it should be noted that this includes the Army of the Tennessee, then commanded by Sherman and subsequently assigned to McPherson when the former, in March 1864, assumed Grant's job as overall commander in the area. McPherson never did command the Army of the Ohio, which was under John M. Schofield and included the troops from Knoxville and East Tennessee. For general purposes of comparison, Sherman's army at the commencement of the Atlanta campaign can be taken at roughly 100,000 men and 254 guns, opposed by Johnston with about 50,000 troops, including cavalry, and 144 guns. *O.R.*, XXXII, pt. 1, 2-5; XXXVIII, pt. 3, 12-14, 676; XXXVIII, pt. 1, 62-63, 115; *Battles and Leaders*, IV, 281-283, 293.

[2] These figures are given by Johnston in his official report of the campaign as the "effective" strength of the Army of Tennessee (*O.R.*, XXXVIII, pt. 3, 614). However, the return for the army as of April 30 showed 4,589 officers and 49,911 men "present for duty" and 144 guns (*Ibid.*, 676). It was generally the Confederate practice not to include officers in "effectives."

[3] Presumably Manigault refers here to Brig. Gen. William H. Jackson's division that joined the army May 17. The return for June 10 showed 4,537 effectives present in the division. *O.R.*, XXXVIII, pt. 3, 615, 677.

[4] Manigault fails to mention that Johnston was substantially reinforced by the transfer to his army of Polk's corps from Mississippi. With some 15,000 infantry, Polk joined Johnston at Resaca. *Ibid.*, 677; *Battles and Leaders*, IV, 281-283.

[5] Wheeler's command consisted of three small divisions under Maj. Gen. William T. Martin and Brig. Gens. John H. Kelley and William Y. C. Humes. *O.R.* XXXVIII, pt. 3, 642.

[6] Sherman wrote in his memoirs: "On the 5th (*of May*) I rode out to Ringgold, and on the very day appointed by General Grant from his headquarters in Virginia, the great campaign was begun." William T. Sherman, *Memoirs*, 2 vols., (New York, 1875), II, 31. Hereafter cited as *Sherman*.

[7] Bate's, Stewart's and Cheatham's divisions were posted, from right to left, on Rocky Face Ridge covering Mill Creek Gap through which the railroad from Chattanooga approached Dalton. Stevenson's division was formed across the valley east of the ridge, his left connecting with Cheatham's right. Hindman's division, of which Manigault's brigade was a part, was placed in line with Stevenson on the latter's right. Cleburne's and Walker's divisions were in reserve. *Battles and Leaders*, IV, 263.

[8] Stewart's division, that was holding Mill Creek Gap.

[9] It was Sherman's plan to demonstrate against the gaps in Rocky Face Ridge but to make his decisive move by pushing McPherson's Army of the Tennessee through Snake Creek Gap to the south to cut the railroad at Resaca in Johnston's rear and force him to withdraw. In his report of the campaign, Sherman wrote, referring to Mill Creek Gap: "The position was very strong, and I knew that such a general as was my antagonist, who had been there six months, had fortified it to the maximum. Therefore I had no intention to attack the position seriously in the front, but depended on McPherson to capture and hold the railroad to its rear" and force the Confederate army to evacuate Dalton. (*Sherman*, II, 32). The respect with which Sherman regarded his wily opponent increased as the campaign progressed. Of him he wrote after the war: "No officer or soldier who ever served under me will question the generalship of Joseph E. Johnston." *Battles and Leaders*, IV, 253.

[10] Two brigades of Brig. Gen. James Cantey's division, which had just arrived from Maury's District of the Gulf (*Buck*, 208; *Polk*, II, 324; *Johnston*, 307). These troops were the vanguard of the reinforcements brought by Polk from the Department of Alabama, Mississippi and East Louisiana, made up of the infantry divisions of Cantey, Loring and French and the cavalry division of Brig. Gen. W.H. "Red" Jackson, some 19,000 men in all. Well entrenched, Cantey, with a force of between three and four thousand, threw back McPherson's advance through Snake Creek Gap and prevented the latter from cutting the railroad in Johnston's rear (*O.R.*, XXXVIII, pt. 3, 677; *DuBose*, 285). There is no evidence in the records of "a large body of cavalry" in addition to Cantey's infantry. Wheeler was busy to the north and Jackson's troopers did not arrive on the scene until a week later. *Battles and Leaders*, IV, 281.

[11] Hood, with the divisions of Cleburne, Walker and Hindman, had been dispatched on May 9 to Resaca to meet the threat of McPherson's advance, but on the following morning, learning of the latter's repulse by Cantey, was recalled. *O.R.*, XXXVIII, pt. 3, 614; *Battles and Leaders*, IV, 263; *Wheeler and his Cavalry*, 176; *Johnston*, 307-308.

[12] In his terse account of this action, Wheeler does not mention the part played by Manigault and Tucker. He merely states, "May 12, attacked Stoneman's corps near Varnell's Station and drove it to Rocky Face Ridge, killing, wounding, and capturing fully 150 of the enemy." *O.R.*, XXXVIII, pt. 3, 944; *Battles and Leaders*, IV, 265.

[13] Howard's Fourth Corps of the Army of the Cumberland. *O.R.*, XXXVIII, pt. 1, 64.

[14] As noted previously, Cantey's division had already arrived. It was followed May 10-12 by Loring's, and they were joined a few days later by French's infantry division and Jackson's cavalry. These troops, which formerly constituted the Army of Mississippi, became Polk's Corps of the Army of Tennessee. The return for June 10, 1864, showed an effective total of 19,245. *O.R.*, XXXVIII, pt. 3, 677.

[15] Brig. Gen. Edward C. Walthall's Mississippi brigade, recently transferred to Hindman's division to replace Vaughan's Tennessee brigade, was posted in the front line to the left of Deas, forming the extreme left of Hood's corps. In support of Walthall was Tucker's brigade on Manigault's left. *Ibid.*, 798.

[16] In describing this action, Johnston wrote, "On the 14th spirited fighting was maintained by the enemy on the whole front, a very vigorous attack being made on Hindman's division of Hood's corps, which was handsomely repulsed." *Battles and Leaders*, IV, 265.

[17] Stevenson's division was posted on Hindman's right and Stewart on the right of Stevenson. *O.R.*, XXXVIII, pt. 3, 811-813.

[18] This was Corput's Georgia Battery of Major J.W. Johnston's battalion, the capture of which actually took place the following day, May 15. (*Ibid.*, 812, 861; *Johnston*, 313). In reference to this Gen. Johnston wrote: "No material was lost by us in the campaign *(from Dalton to Atlanta)* but the four field pieces exposed and abandoned at Resaca by General Hood." (*Johnston*, 351). To this statement the latter strenuously objected, saying that it just wasn't so and, somewhat illogically, that anyway he had more guns than he needed and the four abandoned ones were old iron pieces and not worth the sacrifice of one man to reclaim, to say nothing of the 100 to 200 men he contended would be needed to accomplish that purpose. *Hood*, 95-98.

[19] Neither the *Official Records* nor Johnston's *Narrative* gives a break-down of Confederate casualities by specific battle in this campaign. As a result, Manigault's figures cannot be verified, but almost certainly his estimate of Northern losses in this instance is grossly exaggerated.

[20] In the closing weeks of the war, Gen. Tucker filled an administrative post as commander of the District of Southern Mississippi and East Louisiana. *Generals in Gray*, 311.

[21] This was Capt. H.G. Loller. *C.M.H.*, VII, 147.

[22] The enemy seizure of the ridge referred to by Manigault occurred the evening before, Gen. Cantey having been driven from a position that commanded the railroad bridge. Efforts to retake it on the 15th were unavailing. (*Johnston*, 311-312; *Polk*, II, 327). Johnston made light of the affair stating that on the night of the 14th, Polk's advance troops, some 40 or 50 skirmishers, had been driven from a hill in front of his left which commanded at short range the bridges over the Oostanaula, but that no attempt was made to retake it. Northern participants described it differently. Gen. Cox, commanding the Twenty-third Corps, stated: "The height held by Polk was carried, and the position intrenched under a galling artillery and musketry fire from the enemy's principal lines. During the evening Polk made a vigorous effort to retake the position, but was repulsed...The hill thus carried commanded the railroad and wagon bridges crossing the Oostanaula, and Johnston, upon learning of Polk's failure to retake the lost ground, ordered a road to be cut during the night, and a pontoon bridge to be laid across the river a mile above the town, and out of range of fire." Jacob D. Cox, *Atlanta*, (New York, 1882), 45-46. Hereafter referred to as *Cox*. Johnston confirmed this. *Johnston*, 312.

[23] The reason for countermanding Hood's attack on the 15th was that word had come that Federal troops were crossing the Oostanaula near Calhoun, threatening Johnston's communications and rendering the continued occupation of Resaca too hazardous. *Johnston*, 311-315.

[24] Four brigades were sent as reinforcements to support Hood's attack on the Federal left. Two from Walker's division took part in Hood's first assault on the

evening of the 14th, and the other two, one from Hardee's and one from Polk's corps, were to support the renewal of the attack on the 15th. This was countermanded. however, when, as indicated, word was received that the enemy was crossing the river in Johnston's rear near Calhoun. Unfortunately Stewart's division did not receive the order in time, attacked and was roughly handled. *O.R.,* XXXVIII, pt. 3, 615; *Johnston,* 311-315.

[25] That is to say, the railroad bridge and the wagon road bridge on trestles near it.

[26] This was the pontoon bridge laid by Johnston's order, on which Hood's corps also crossed the river. *Johnston,* 314.

[27] Just why the enemy did not open up on the bridges as Polk's and Hardee's corps were crossing the river has never been adequately explained. In referring to what he described as "the miraculous escape of *(the)* army at Resaca," Hood said that he would "always believe that the attack of Stevenson's and Stewart's division *(on the 14th)*...together with our return to our original position on the following day, saved us from utter destruction by creating the impression on the Federals that the contest was to be renewed the next morning. *(the 16th.)* They were thus lulled into quiet during the eventful night of our deliverance." (*Hood,* 97-98). While this explanation strikes one as contrived, it may have merit in view of the lack of urgency with which the Northern troops prepared to make use of the position they had seized. Brig. Gen. Charles R. Woods, commanding the First Brigade of the First Division of the Fifteenth Army Corps, declared in his report: "The advantage gained by this position was that it gave a fair view of the bridges in the rear of the enemy's position and at short range, so that they could be destroyed, by a vigorous cannonading, in an hour. During the night of the 15th, embrasures were put up and two 20-pounder Parrots and two Napoleon guns were put in position to destroy the bridges, but during the night the enemy evacuated the works, and our troops marched in on the morning of the 16th, by which time, it may be noted, Johnston's army was safely across the Oostenaula." *O.R.,* XXXVIII, pt. 3, 143.

[28] The force so dispatched was McPherson's army of the Tennessee, some 23,000 men, which was ordered to support Garrard's cavalry division sent on the 14th to attack or threaten the railroad between Calhoun and Kingston. *Sherman,* II, 35-37.

[29] Failing to find a suitable defensive position near Calhoun, Johnston rested his men for 15 or 18 hours and then continued his withdrawal southward. *Johnston,* 319.

[30] At Lay's Ferry. Actually, Sherman had had two pontoon bridges laid there. *Sherman,* II, 35.

[31] Once again, Manigault appears to have greatly overestimated Northern casualties. Sherman stated that his losses during the campaign up to the time he entered Resaca amounted to about 600 dead and 3,375 wounded. *Sherman,* II, 36.

[32] Reference is evidently to Stewart's costly attack on the Federal left on the 15th, when the countermanding order failed to reach him in time.

[33] This attack by Stoneman's cavalry is described by Johnston. "About noon a large body of Federal cavalry captured the hospitals of Hood's corps, which were in an exposed situation east of the Connasauga. Major-General Wheeler, who

was sent to the spot with Allen's and Hume's brigades, drove off the enemy and pressed them two miles, taking two standards, and capturing forty prisoners." *Johnston,* 312.

[34] The returns of the Army of Tennessee for June 10, 1864, showed Polk's corps with an "effective total present" of 14,708, consisting of Loring's division (5,239), French's division (4,127), Cantey's division (4,150), and artillery, 50 guns, (1,192). In addition, Jackson's division of cavalry had joined with 4,537 effectives, bringing the total of reinforcements from the Army of Mississippi, formerly commanded by Polk, to 19,245. *O.R.,* XXXVIII, pt. 3, 677.

[35] "Troops who had not been in line, but massed in bivouac, quickly formed, while the firing was going on." Journal of Lt. T.B. Mackall, aide-de-camp to Brig. Gen. W.W. Mackall, chief of staff. *Ibid.,* 982.

[36] Now commanded by Brig. Gen. Jacob H. Sharp, formerly colonel of the 44th Mississippi.

[37] "That our troops might not be disturbed in their bivouacs...Cheatham's division...and Wheeler's troops together kept the head of the Federal column at a convenient distance, by sharp skirmishing, until nightfall." *Johnston,* 319.

[38] It will be recalled that when Sherman followed Johnston south from Adairsville, his army marched by two diverging roads, which, at their greatest distance, one from the other, were some eight or nine miles apart. Determined to seize the opportunity thus offered, Johnston, on the morning of May 19, issued orders for an attack on the eastern column.

Leaving Polk's corps on the Adairsville Road to hold up the Federal advance, the Southern commander directed Hood to swing around to the east and fall on the Union left flank. After proceeding two or three miles, the latter received word from a member of his staff that his right rear was threatened, and he consequently abandoned his march and fell back to deal with the enemy threat. Johnston maintained that the information on which Hood based this decision was manifestly untrue and castigated him for acting on his own, without informing his commanding officer.

Writing later, Hood hotly denied that he had ever received orders for the flank attack in the first place and said that he had advanced on his own initiative with, however, Johnston's consent. He insisted that he had, in fact, been attacked in flank and rear and produced witnesses to attest to it. He learned later, he said, that the Federal troops involved were a portion of Maj. Gen. Daniel Butterfield's Third Division of Hooker's Twentieth Corps, an explanation accepted by both Stanley Horn and Shelby Foote in their works previously quoted, though neither referred to any specific authority in confirmation. (Horn, *The Army of Tennessee,* 328; *Foote,* III, 342). Presumably, they relied on Hood's statement on page 104 of his *Advance and Retreat.* More persuasive are Govan and Livingood, who said that the troops that attacked Hood's right and rear were a unit of McCook's Federal cavalry, a force hardly of sufficient strength to justify Hood in abandoning the assault on the Union left flank, which was the key to Johnston's strategy for striking Sherman's army a telling blow. (Gilbert E. Govan and James W. Livingood, *A Different Valor: The Story of General Joseph E. Johnston, C.S.A.,* (Indianapolis, 1965), 274-275. Hereafter cited as *A Different Valor*).

Justified or not, Hood's action caused Johnston to give up his hope of taking the offensive and to order a retrograde movement to a defensive position east and south of Cassville. *Hood,* 98-104; *Johnston,* 330-322; *O.R.,* XXXVIII, pt. 2, 751-752; *Ibid,* pt. 3, 616, 621-622, 634-635, 985.

[39] McCook's First Cavalry Division of Sherman's army. *O.R.,* XXXVIII, pt. 2, 751-722.

[40] This congratulatory General Order was written about 7 or 8 o'clock on the morning of May 19 and issued to the troops during the day. "Soldiers of the Army of Tennessee," it read, "you have displayed the highest quality of the soldier — firmness in combat, patience under toil. By your courage and skill, you have repulsed every assault of the enemy...You will now turn and march to meet his advancing columns...I lead you to battle. We may confidently trust that the Almighty Father will still reward the patriot's toils and bless the patriot's banners." Johnston, at his wife's urgent request, had recently been baptized by Bishop-General Polk, which doubtless added to the ardor of his appeal to the Almighty, although such language was pretty much standard fare in those days.

This ringing call to arms was received with enthusiasm by the troops, who were tired of retreating and wanted to turn and come to grips with the enemy. Sam Watkins, who could pour it on, wrote, "I never saw our troops happier or more certain of success. A sort of grand halo illuminated every soldier's face...Joy was welling up in every heart. We were going to whip and rout the Yankees...Every soldier had faith enough in old Joe to have charged Sherman's whole army. When 'Halt!' 'Retreat!' What is the matter? General Hood says that they are enfilading his line, and are decimating his men, and he can't hold position...The same old story repeats itself." (*Co. Aytch,* 166). Adjutant George Guild of the Fourth Tennessee Cavalry wrote in like vein: "This order...was received with the wildest enthusiasm. The bright reflection from the long lines of the enemy's guns across the open space was an inspiration for the troops to move upon them at once." Then delay, word from Hood that he was being enfiladed and could not hold his lines. "That night Johnston retired and it was not surprising that some soldiers dropped out of line, to be picked up by the enemy." George B. Guild, *Fourth Tennessee Cavalry Regiment,* (Nashville, 1913), 61-62.

[41] Johnston described it as "the best position I saw occupied during the war." *Johnston,* 332.

[42] Again Manigault is on the low side. The army return for June 10 showed 60,564 effective total present. *O.R.,* XXXVIII, pt. 3, 677.

[43] The damage inflicted by the superior Northern artillery tends to support the conviction of Hood and Polk that their lines were untenable in the face of the enfilading fire of the enemy's guns.

[44] For years afterwards, the causes of the retreat from Cassville were argued back and forth and became a bitter bone of contention between Johnston and Hood. The former held to the position that he reluctantly withdrew only after both Hood and Polk had expressed the opinion that they could not hold their lines after the Federal artillery opened on them. Hood, with the backing of Polk's son and aide-de-camp (Polk himself was killed in action shortly thereafter before he had an opportunity to leave a written statement on the matter), equally vehemently

insisted that he and Polk were ready and willing to take offensive action to improve their position and recommended retreat only if that were not done. Hood wrote, prior to his death from yellow fever in 1879, "I do at this day and hour, in the name of truth, honor and justice, in the name of the departed soul of the Christian and noble Polk, and in the presence of my creator, most solemnly deny that General Polk or I recommended General Johnston, at Cassville, to retreat when he intended to give battle; and affirm that the recommendation made by us to change his position, was throughout the discussion coupled with the proviso: *If he did not intend to force a pitched battle.*

Hood maintained that his and Polk's positions on the ridge at Cassville were untenable due to the enfilading fire of the Federal artillery. The preponderance of evidence would appear to bear him out. Certainly the statement of Capt. Walter Morris, chief engineer of Polk's corps, who made a detailed examination of the ground, supported Hood's contention, as did the testimony of Gen. F.A. Shoup, chief of artillery of the Army of Tennessee. As to whether Hood and Polk recommended offensive action, there is no consensus. In any case, in the face of their lack of confidence in their ability to hold their lines and despite the fact that Hardee was all for standing and fighting, Johnston ordered the withdrawal of the army across the Etowah that night. *O.R.*, XXXVIII, pt. 3, 616, 685, 983-984; *Battles and Leaders,* IV, 268-269; *S.H.S.P.,* XXI, 314-321; *ibid.,* XXII, 1-9; *Johnston,* 322-325; *Hood,* 104-116; *Polk,* II, 330-333, 351-357; *A Different Valor,* 276-278, 428; Samuel G. French, *Two Wars: An Autobiography,* (Nashville, 1901), 196-198, Hereafter cited as *French.*

[45] "We were well in advance of our railroad trains, on which we depended for supplies, so I determined to pause for a few days to repair the railroad...and then to go on." *Sherman,* II, 38-39.

[46] Sherman wrote in his memoirs: "The movement contemplated leaving the railroad, and to depend for twenty days on the contents of our wagons." *Ibid.,* II, 42.

[47] While on duty as a lieutenant of the Third Artillery in 1844, Sherman had become familiar with the topography of the region and was aware of the strength of Allatoona Pass on the railroad. He therefore decided to turn the position. *Ibid.,* II, 42.

[48] By air-line, Dallas was four miles southwest of New Hope Church, Ackworth some 10 miles northeast and Marietta 13 miles due east. The latter two were on the railroad.

[49] The Confederate line stretched from east of New Hope Church on the right to Dallas on the left, with Hardee again on the left, Polk in the center and Hood on the right. Horn, *The Army of Tennessee,* 329.

[50] In his report, Stewart wrote: "The entire line received the attack with great steadiness and firmness, every man standing at his post...The enemy was repulsed at all points, and it is believed with heavy loss...Eldridge's battalion of artillery ...was admirably posted, well served, and did great execution. They had 48 men and 44 horses killed or wounded...No more persistent attack or determined resistance has anywhere been made." Stewart estimated his losses at between 300 and 400, while Hooker reported his as 1,665 (*O.R.,* XXXVIII, pt. 3, 818; pt. 2, 14). "This engagement was one of the most spectacular of the whole war. In the midst

of it a severe thunderstorm came on with blinding downpour of rain...The booming thunder kept pace with the roar of the artillery and the lightning vied with the flashes of the guns as the rain pelted down on the men struggling in the thick underbrush." (Horn, *The Army of Tennessee,* 330). Due to the severity of the fighting, the Northern soldiers changed the name of the place from New Hope to "Hell-Hole." *Sherman,* II, 44.

[51] During the 26th and 27th Sherman kept extending his line to the left, toward the railroad, and Johnston countered by shifting troops to the right. "On the morning of the 26th...Hindman's division was withdrawn from my left, and placed in position on my right, the enemy countinuing to extend his left." *O.R.,* XXXVIII, pt. 3, 761; *Hood,* 119.

[52] Hood explained that "the Federals had during the night drawn back their left flank, recrossed Little Pumpkin-vine Creek, and were entrenched...thereby placing between the opposing forces a swamp and difficult stream to cross, in addition to entrenchments on the opposite bank...An attack would have been extreme rashness...I reported these facts to General Johnston and was ordered to return." (*Hood,* 117-124). The latter was critical of Hood's assessment and this became another bone of contention between the two men. *Johnston,* 333-334; *Battles and Leaders,* IV, 270.

[53] Brig. Gen. Hiram B. Granbury's brigade consisted of the 6th, 7th and 10th Texas infantry and the 15th, 17th, 18th, 24th and 25th Texas cavalry (dismounted). *O.R.,* XXXVIII, pt. 3, 639.

[54] On May 26, Cleburne's division had been detached from Hardee's corps and sent to the extreme right of the army beyond Hood. The action on the 27th, in which Cleburne, supported by Wheeler's cavalry, threw back an assault by the Federal Fourth Corps (Howard's) and one division of the Fourteenth (Palmer's), was known as the Battle of Pickett's Mill. A night attack by Granbury completed the Federal repulse and cleared the Confederate front. Describing the action, Cleburne wrote, "The Texans, their bayonets fixed, plunged into the darkness with a terrific yell, and with one bound were upon the enemy. Surprised and panic-stricken, many fled, escaping in the darkness; others surrendered...It needed but the brilliancy of this night attack to add luster to the achievements of Granbury and his brigade in the afternoon. I am deeply indebted to them both." *Ibid.,* 720-726; *Buck,* 218-221; *Battles and Leaders,* IV, 269-270.

[55] "During the progress of the battle the howitzers were used with deadly effect by an oblique fire upon the masses of the enemy, several lines deep" (*Buck,* 219). Cleburne said the lowest estimate of the enemy dead was 500. *O.R.,* XXXVIII, pt. 3, 726.

[56] Hardee's corps was not engaged in any general action on the 26th, spending the day skirmishing and maneuvering for position. *Ibid.,* 705.

[57] Under orders to ascertain in which direction the Federal army was moving and to inflict such damage as he could, Wheeler crossed the Etowah on the 22nd and, on the 24th, at Cass Station captured 350 wagons and their teams loaded with supplies for Sherman's flank movement to Dallas, the majority of which he burned. When he returned to the army he brought with him 70 loaded wagons and their teams, 300 equipped horses and mules, not to mention 182 prisoners, for which exploit, along with other accomplishments, he was congratulated by

Johnston in General Orders. *Johnston,* 325; *DuBose,* 304-305; *O.R.,* XXXVIII, pt. 3, 949.

[58] Polk's corps had been moved to the right of Hood's to extend the line in that direction, so that the formation temporarily became Hardee's corps on the left, Hood's in the center and Polk's on the right. In the series of actions around New Hope Church, the two armies slugged it out in miserable weather in vicious fighting. Sam Watkins described the scene: "The trees looked as if they had been cut down for new ground, being mutilated and shivered by musket and cannon balls...The stench and sickening odor of dead men and horses were terrible. We had to breathe the putrid atmosphere." *Co. Aytch,* 163-164.

[59] When it became obvious that Sherman, constantly outflanking Johnston's right, was moving to the railroad, the latter, on the night of the 4th, pulled his troops out of their lines and moved to take up a defensive position there. "The night set in with drizzling rain and fog...the line began to move at 11 P.M...groping its way through mud and water over narrow and difficult roads... (I) rode back and forth along the line, splashing through the mud, plunging through the water, drenched with rain, keeping the column on its march." *Polk,* II, 335-336.

[60] On the morning of June 14, Polk, along with Johnston and Hardee, rode with their staffs to the top of Pine Mountain to have a look at the enemy. Although warned by the artillerists there — one of whom was Beauregard's son, Rene' — of a Federal battery of Parrott rifled guns about half a mile to the front that had been firing on any one showing himself, Johnston and some of the others went to the parapet for observation. In a few moments "there was a flash, a puff of smoke, a sharp report, and in an instant fragments of splintered rock and flying earth scattered around them, as a shot was buried in the parapet." Johnston and Polk withdrew to the left, conferred for a few moments behind a parapet, and, as they were retracing their steps, a shell struck Polk, tearing through his chest, and killing him instantly. With very few exceptions, the bishop-general was much beloved by officers and men. In his grief, Johnston issued a heart-felt message to his troops: "You are called to mourn your first captain, your oldest companion in arms...We have lost the most courteous of gentlemen, the most gallant of soldiers. The Christian, patriot, soldier has neither lived nor died in vain. His example is before you; his mantle rests with you." On Polk's body were found four copies of Dr. Quintard's little work, *Balm for the Weary and Wounded,* inscribed with the names of Joseph E. Johnston, Lt. Gen. Hardee and Lt. Gen. Hood, with the "compliments of Lieut. Gen. Leonidas Polk, June 12, 1864." All were saturated with his blood. *O.R.,* XXXVIII, pt. 4, 776; *Polk,* II, 347-350; *Buck,* 222-224.

[61] At Noonday Creek on June 20 Wheeler came in contact with the "enemy with three of his brigades, charged and drove them, capturing 120 prisoners, 150 horses and 2 stands of colors." (*DuBose,* 332.) Johnston called this the most considerable cavalry affair of the campaign. *Johnston,* 339.

[62] The Battle of Zion Church receives comparatively little attention in the *Official Records* and other primary sources, quite possibly because it brought discredit on both commanders involved. The action took place on the Confederate left, some three miles to the southwest of Marietta, when two divisions of Hooker's Twentieth Federal corps and two of Hood's — Hindman's and Stevenson's — clashed head on. Reporting promptly to headquarters at 9:50 that night, Hood said he was attacked but "drove the enemy back, taking one entire line of breastworks and a portion of a second on his right." He reported Stevenson's division mainly

engaged and Hindman's slightly, with a few prisoners taken from Hooker and Schofield. Pursuit was stopped, he continued, "because of encountering an enfilading fire from a bald hill in front of Hardee of sixteen pieces." In his official report he mentioned only the attack, ignoring his repulse. *O.R.*, XXXVIII, pt. 3, 760, 762.

[63] Stewart's division was not actively engaged in the fighting.

[64] This was Noyes Creek.

[65] Stevenson reported his loss at 870, of whom 807 were killed or wounded. *Ibid.*, 815.

[66] In his report, Johnston did not say, as Manigault contends, that the enemy attacked Hood "in his breastworks" and was repulsed with loss. What he did say was: "On the 22nd Lieutenant-General Hood reported that Hindman's and Stevenson's divisions, of his corps, being attacked, drove back the enemy, taking a line of breastworks, but were compelled to withdraw by the fire of fortified artillery" (*Ibid.*, 617). Two days after the fight, he telegraphed Bragg in Richmond to the same effect, namely that Hood had driven the enemy back and taken one entire line of breastworks, the pursuit being stopped by exposure to fire of fixed batteries. (*O.R.*, XXXVIII, pt. 4, 788). When he came to write his memoirs some 10 years later, however, he reached a more damaging conclusion, saying that, instead of achieving a success, "we had suffered a reverse." Hood, he explained, in attacking the entrenched artillery, had subjected his two divisions to a loss so severe that the attempt was soon abandoned with casualities of about a thousand men (*Johnston*, 340; *Battles and Leaders*, IV, 271-272; *O.R.*, XXXVIII, pt. 3, 814-815). By that time, of course, Johnston and Hood were at loggerheads.
On the Federal side, Sherman was highly critical of Hooker, who was in the habit of striking out on his own from Thomas' army to which his corps belonged, and then, when he came in contact with the other wing commanders, McPherson and Schofield, pulling his rank on them. This time, to make matters worse, he went over Thomas' head in appealing to Sherman for reinforcements and, to boot, gave the latter false information when he claimed Johnston's three corps were all in his front, a contention the army commander knew not to be true. Sherman gave Hooker a good dressing down and from then on relations between the two went from bad to worse, until Hooker resigned from the army. *Sherman*, II, 57-59.

[67] Manigault is here referring to Sherman's costly frontal assault against the Confederate lines at Kennesaw Mountain.

[68] Johnston admitted a loss of 808, attributing Sherman's repulse to the fact that the latter had encountered intrenched infantry "unsurpassed by that of Napoleon's Old Guard, or that which followed Wellington into France, out of Spain." *Johnston*, 343.

[69] Dodge's corps of McPherson's Army of the Tennessee. *Cox*, 133.

[70] This was the same General Smith (Gustavus W.) who, in the spring of 1862, as senior major general present, commanded for a few hours the main Confederate army in Virginia between the wounding of Joseph E. Johnston at Seven Pines and the appointment of Robert E. Lee to succeed him. Piqued at being passed over for promotion to lieutenant general in October 1862, when Longstreet, Kirby Smith and Stonewall Jackson understandably got the nod, along with Hardee, Polk,

Holmes and Pemberton, this one-time street commissioner of the City of New York resigned his commission in the Confederate army and in June 1864, accepted an appointment from Gov. Joseph E. Brown to command the Georgia State Militia (Gustavus W. Smith, *Confederate War Papers,* New York, 1884, 255-263; Freeman, *R.E. Lee,* II, 71-76; *Generals in Gray,* 281). Smith states that the militia numbered a little over 3,000 men at this time, but Johnston put their effective strength at about 1,500 (*O.R., XXXVIII, pt. 3, 617, 970*). Stanley Horn described these troops as "those unique Confederate soldiers who, by the dictum of Governor Joe Brown, were permitted to fight only when an enemy had actually crossed the state line to invade the sovereign soil of Georgia...They were mostly young boys under seventeen or elderly men outside the age limit of Confederate conscription. As soldiers they were better than nothing — but not much better." (Horn, *The Army of Tennessee,* 338). Johnston, however, said they "rendered good service." *Johnston,* 344.

[71] "Hindman...was struck, in riding, by the branch of a tree across his eye, which became inflamed and rendered him unfit for duty." *C.M.H.,* X, 293.

[72] Hindman's subsequent career, after leaving the Army of Tennessee, is something of an enigma. Evans says, in one reference, that after the Atlanta campaign he served in the District of Northern Mississippi, and, in another, that he was granted a furlough and finally settled in Mexico. (*Ibid.,* 293, 404). References to him in the *Official Records,* for the period in question, are fragmentary. Nevertheless, the following facts can be established. Sometime in July 1864, he wrote to Adjutant-General Cooper in Richmond, requesting a transfer to the Trans-Mississippi Department, where he had previously served in command of the then district from May 26 to Aug. 20, 1862, and later as a major general commanding a corps in the Trans-Mississippi army. His letter was referred to Secretary of War Seddon, who took it up with the President. Davis, going by the book as usual, said a transfer could be made only if there were a suitable opening to which an officer of Hindman's rank could be properly assigned. He added that he "would be pleased to relieve General Hindman of the embarrassment described in any practicable manner," going on to hint at a leave of absence for physical disability. Seddon took it from there, telling Hindman there was no suitable opening and expressing the very serious regret of the Department at his physical disability and "other causes that induce you to desire a transfer" and leaving the idea of a leave of absence up to him. (*O.R., XXXVIII, pt. 5, 926; LI, pt. 2, 1,031*).

Word of Hindman's possible return to the Trans-Mississippi got around and prompted a letter, dated Aug. 5, 1864, from A.H. Garland, a member of the Confederate House of Representatives from Arkansas, to Seddon. Garland pulled no punches and told the Secretary of War in blunt terms what he thought of the idea. "His coming here will be productive of evil I greatly fear. His course when here *(Hindman in 1862 had imposed martial law and resorted to conscription and impressment in Arkansas)*...will not be forgotten soon and I am satisfied his transfer will revive bad and evil feelings, that to some extent have passed away. I hope, therefore, the Department...will leave us with those we have." (*O.R., LI, pt. 2, 1,042*). These warnings appear to have fallen on deaf ears, for in a letter to Seddon dated Aug. 10, Hood referred to Hindman as "having left for the Trans-Mississippi Department." (*O.R., XXXVIII, pt. 5, 953*).

The trail then becomes faint, at least in the *Offical Records.* There is evidence that Hindman was involved, legitimately or otherwise, in the shipment of tobacco to the Trans-Mississippi Department in October 1864. In correspondence relating to it, such suggestive phrases as "if the tobacco is for the troops" or "if government tobacco" keep cropping up, along with clear indications that Hindman was in charge of the shipment. That there was doubt as to the ownership of the tobacco is indicated by the following statement in a communication of the Assistant Adjutant General of the District of Arkansas: "Should the tobacco prove to be the private property of any one, no wagons or other public means will, under any circumstances whatever, be used in its transporation." And "Prince John" Magruder, commanding the District, only added to the confusion by saying, "I presume the tobacco is for the army, though I know nothing about it." (*O.R.*, XLI, pt. 3, 1,007-1,008; XLI, pt. 4, 998). So, in an atmosphere of suspicion and doubt, one takes leave of that rather unsavory character, Hindman, the object of Manigault's undisguised contempt.

[73] John C. Brown was commissioned major general to rank from Aug. 4, 1864. (*Generals in Gray*, 36). Manigault's statement that Brown was the senior brigadier in the army is not correct. He was, in fact, junior to the following officers of that rank then serving with the Army of Tennessee: Hugh W. Mercer, John K. Jackson, Winfield S. Featherston, William W. Mackall (Johnston's chief of staff), States Rights Gist, George Maney and Matthew D. Ector, listed in order of seniority. Brown was, however, the ranking brigadier in Hood's corps. Marcus J. Wright, *General Officers of the Confederate Army*, (New York, 1911), 49-89.

[74] Johnston wrote that the supply of artillery ammunition was so inadequate that it could be used only to repel assaults or in serious engagements. *Johnston*, 345-346.

[75] The batteries commanded by Capt. Staunton H. Dent and Capt. James Garrity were from Alabama and attached to Hood's corps. The other battery Manigault singles out for praise was probably Howell's Georgia Battery, attached to Hardee's corps and commanded at the time by Lt. W.G. Robson. *O.R.*, XXXVIII, pt. 3, 643.

[76] Hardee's *Tactics* was the standard training manual used by both sides. Originally composed by Lt. Gen. Hardee, C.S.A., when he was a brevet lieutenant colonel in the old army (U.S.), it was adopted by the Confederacy and reprinted there during the war in several editions. Its full and rather imposing title was *Rifle and Light Infantry Tactics; for the Exercise and Manoeuvers of Troops When Acting as Light Infantry or Riflemen.*

[77] Sherman made up his mind, while feinting opposite Hood on his right, to cross the Chattahoochee upstream on his left. To accomplish this, he swung Schofield around from his position in reserve on the right and forded the river just below the mouth of Soap Creek, some 10 miles beyond the Confederate right. *Sherman*, II, 68-70; *O.R.*, XXXVIII, pt. 2, 515-516.

[78] The country bridges, along with that of the railway and his pontoons, afforded Johnston two crossings for each of his three corps. *Cox*, 141.

[79] During this time Sherman was regrouping, moving the remainder of his army across the Chattahoochee upstream and preparing for the final move on Atlanta, now a scant 10 miles from the nearest Northern troops. *Sherman*, II, 70-71.

[80] It was on this day that Sherman ordered the general advance against Atlanta. *O.R.*, XXXVIII, pt. 1, 71.

[81] The crossing of the Chattahoochee by Sherman had begun with Schofield on July 8, followed a few days later by McPherson, but it was not until the 17th that Thomas, with his Army of the Cumberland, completed the movement with over half of Sherman's troops, and it was doubtless to this that Manigault refers. *Sherman*, II, 70-71.

[82] Manigault is in error here. Thomas' crossing took place at Powers' Ferry and Pace's Ferry to the south farther downstream. *O.R.*, XXXVIII, pt. 1, 71.

[83] That is to say, Peachtree Creek and the Chattahoochee.

[84] Hood acknowledged that the effective strength of the army at the time it was turned over to him was: Infantry, 33,750, artillery 3,500, cavalry 10,000, plus 1,500 Georgia militia, or a total of 48,750 — only moderately below Manigault's figure of 51,000, which was evidently taken from Johnston's official report. *Ibid.*, pt. 3, 619, 630.

[85] The removal of Johnston and his replacement by Hood, as well as its effect on the future course of the war, constitutes one of the most controversial issues in the history of the Confederacy. Johnston had no lack of admirers, Sherman and Governor Brown of Georgia among them, and, considering the discrepancy in numbers and material resources between the two armies, it is difficult to argue with his basic strategy of forcing Sherman to attack him in intrenched positions, inflict as much damage as he could and await an opportunity to strike his opponent a decisive blow should he make a mistake and expose a portion of his army to attack. It should be added in Johnston's defense that he repeatedly, but unsuccessfully, urged that Bedford Forrest's cavalry in the West and John Morgan's in the East be combined to attack and break Sherman's 300-mile-long supply line back to Nashville and force his withdrawal.

But Davis in Richmond saw things differently — constant retreat, the abandonment of territory, and no assurance from Johnston as to how or when he could halt Sherman's advance. Certainly, also, the mutual antipathy of the two men, not to mention their peculiarities of character, made co-operation doubly difficult. Most observers, particularly those on the scene, agreed that the morale of Johnston's troops remained high and their confidence in him as a leader unimpaired. In the end, however, Davis took counsel of his fears and prejudices and, in a telegram dated July 17, removed Johnston from command. It was a fateful step.

The effect on the soldier in the ranks was one of shock and dismay. "The news came like a clap of thunder from a clear sky...This was a death knell to the Army of Tennessee" (*Worsham*, 125). "Great stalwart, sunburnt soldiers by the thousands would be seen falling out of line, squatting down by a tree or in a fence corner, weeping like children. This act of the War Department threw a damper over this army from which it never recovered, for 'Old Joe', as we called him, was our idol!" (W.J. McMurray, *History of the Twentieth Tennessee Regiment Volunteer Infantry, C.S.A.*, Nashville, 1904, 319). And the irrepressible Sam Watkins summed it up in these words: "The most terrible and disastrous blow that the South ever received was when Hon. Jefferson Davis placed General Hood in command of the Army of Tennessee." *Co. Aytch*, 174. For a detailed discussion of Johnston's removal, see *A Different Valor*, 308-338.

[86] Presumably the Chattahoochee.

[87] This is what Johnston said he had in mind doing, both in his official report

(*O.R.*, XXXVIII, pt. 3, 618), and later in his memoirs (*Johnston,* 350). Critics have pointed out that it is unlikely the untrained militia, composed of old men and boys, could have successfully carried out the role assigned to it in the face of Sherman's veterans, an assessment fully shared by the commander of the militia, Gen. Smith. *Hood,* 147.

[88] When President Davis was considering Hood for the command of the Army of Tennessee, he sought the opinion of Robert E. Lee. The latter replied by wire on July 12, with his accustomed tact, "It is a bad time to relieve the commander of an army situated as that of Tenne. We may lose Atlanta and the army too. Hood is a bold fighter. I am doubtful as to other qualities necessary." In a letter later that day Lee went into more detail. "Hood is a good fighter, very industrious on the battle field, careless off & I have had no opportunity of judging his action, when the whole responsibility rested upon him. I have a high opinion of his gallantry, earnestness and zeal. Gen. Hardee has more experience in managing an army." Davis should have known Lee well enough to have been able to read between the lines. (Douglas Southall Freeman, ed., *Lee's Dispatches,* New York, 1915, 282-284.) With the wisdom of hindsight, Sam Watkins had no reservations regarding Hood. "As a soldier, he was brave, good, noble and gallant...but as a commanding general he was a failure in every particular." *Co. Aytch,* 226.

A Kentuckian by birth, Hood graduated from West Point in 1853 near the bottom of his class, having come within an ace of being thrown out for bad conduct. The most serious charge against him was being absent from quarters one evening — presumably at Benny Havens', the local tavern — for which he was broken as a cadet officer and received a public reprimand from the Superintendent of the Academy, Col. Robert E. Lee. He also was given demerits for such derelictions as being late at church, chewing tobacco, not cutting his hair, making unnecessary noise and dancing on a piazza.

After graduation, Hood served for two years in California with the 4th Infantry, following which he was tranferred to Texas. There he joined the crack 2nd Cavalry of which Albert Sydney Johnston was colonel and Robert E. Lee lieutenant colonel. In a skirmish with the Comanches he narrowly missed death and received his first wound, an Indian arrow piercing his left hand and pinning it to his saddle.

In the spring of 1861, he resigned his commission in the old army and reported to Richmond for assignment. After a stint with the cavalry under Magruder on the peninsula between the York and the James Rivers, he was appointed that summer, by President Davis, colonel of the 4th Texas Infantry.

March 2, 1862, he was made a brigadier general and was given command of the Texas Brigade. With that celebrated fighting outfit, he distinguished himself at Gaines' Mill, breaking the Union line at the critical moment, and subsequently at Second Manassas and Sharpsburg. Promotion to major general came in October and at Gettysburg, the next summer, he led a division in Longstreet's corps in the bitter fighting on the second day. The following September he joined the Army of Tennessee at Chickamauga. *Hood,* 5-16; *Generals in Gray,* 142-143; *Dictionary of American Biography,* IX, 193-194; John P. Dyer, *The Gallant Hood,* Indianapolis, 1950, 27-49.

[89] In attempting to put the best face on it, Johnston quite clearly grossly inflated the losses in Sherman's army. For Johnston's official report of the Atlanta campaign, from which Manigault evidently took these figures, see *O.R.,* XXXVIII, pt. 3, 619.

[90] Johnston admitted a loss of 9,972 killed and wounded in the campaign from Dalton to Atlanta, while Sherman put his casualties for the same period at 16,829. *Johnston,* 356; *Sherman,* II, 47, 63.

9

THE STRUGGLE FOR ATLANTA

(Editor's Preface)

North of Atlanta the Chattahoochee flows in a southwesterly direction, crossed by the Western & Atlantic Railway some six miles northwest of the city. Just above the railroad bridge Peachtree Creek joins the river, flowing almost due west.

Sherman decided the best way to get at the city was to transfer the remainder of his army to the left bank of the Chattahoochee north of the bridge and hook up with Schofield who was already across. Then he would execute a grand right wheel, with McPherson on the left, Schofield in the center and Thomas on the right, the latter taking position on the north bank of Peachtree Creek. McPherson was to make a wide sweep, strike the Georgia Railroad from Augusta some seven miles east of Decatur, then turn west and follow the tracks to the latter town where he would be joined by Schofield.

On July 19, the three Northern armies were converging on Atlanta, Thomas crossing Peachtree Creek and McPherson and Schofield approaching from the west along the railroad and just to the north of it. Between Thomas and Schofield a gap of several miles existed, and Hood determined to take advantage of this and strike Thomas a decisive blow as he was in the act of crossing the creek. For this purpose he would use Stewart's (formerly Polk's) and Hardee's corps, leaving Cheatham, now in command of his own old corps, to hold off Schofield and McPherson.

The attack was set for one o'clock, but a delay of some three hours ensued as the Confederate line was shifted to the right to permit Cheatham to confront McPherson. This gave Thomas time to complete the crossing of the creek and to throw up some earthworks, so that when the assault, which Sherman described as a "furious sally," was finally delivered, it met, despite some initial success, a bloody repulse in what came to be known as The Battle of Peachtree Creek.

Hood blamed Hardee, somewhat unfairly, for not pressing the attack; and the latter, in justification, pointed out that Cleburne's division had been taken from him to reinforce Cheatham just as it was to join in the assault.

Far from discouraged by the costly failure of his attack at Peachtree Creek, Hood lost no time in taking the offensive once more. In a brilliantly conceived move that evoked memories of Stonewall Jackson at Chancellorsville and Second Manassas, he left Stewart and Cheatham to hold the defensive lines around the city and sent Hardee's corps, notwithstanding his previous criticism of its leader, on a night flank march around to the southeast to strike McPherson's unprotected left. That Sherman was caught by surprise is made clear by his later confession that he thought the Confederates were giving up the city.

When Hardee, after a gruelling night march, was in position, he launched the attack with determination and apparently every prospect of success, as he had effectively turned McPherson's left and was assaulting it at a 45 degree angle from the rear. Jabbing his finger at the map, Hood exclaimed to his chief of staff, "Hardee is just where I wanted him."

Then occurred one of those tricks of fate that, at times, decide the outcome of battles, even, perhaps, the destiny of nations. By pure happenstance the Federal Sixteenth Corps, on its way to reinforce McPherson's left, found itself precisely in the spot where it could fall on Hardee's exposed right flank as he moved to the attack. The full force of Hardee's assault was blunted. Too late, Hood threw Cheatham's corps, spearheaded by Manigault's brigade, eastward along the Georgia Railroad in an advance that tore a hole in the Federal left center. By then, however, Hardee had shot his bolt, and a counterattack by the Fifteenth Corps and Col. Mersy's brigade of the Sixteenth restored the Federal line.

In this bloody Battle of Atlanta, Northern casualities were severe. Particularly, Sherman mourned the loss of his friend James B. McPherson, commander of the Army of the Tennessee. It was this officer that Sherman counted on to take over the army should anything happen to him. And yet, as the attacking party, the Army of Tennessee lost better than two to one, men they could ill afford to lose, and Hood's dream of emulating Stonewall Jackson went up in smoke.

After a few days of inactivity following the bitter fighting of the 20th and 22nd of July, Sherman made his next move. He swung the Army of the Tennessee, now under Maj. Gen. O.O. Howard, whose corps had been routed the year before by Stonewall Jackson at Chancellorsville, from the left of the Federal line around in back of Schofield and Thomas to the extreme right. This was west of the city, which by this time was under steady bombardment. There, Howard's force faced to the east, with its right reaching out toward the railroads coming up from the south and southwest that formed Hood's life-line.

To meet this threat, the Southern commander, whom Howard referred to as "indomitable," contrived a flank movement of his own. Gen. Stephen D. Lee, now in command of Hood's old corps of which Manigault's brigade was a part, was ordered westward through Atlanta and out the Lick Skillet Road to check the extension to the south of the Federal right under Howard. It was then Hood's intention to have Stewart and his corps sweep around Lee to the south and fall on the Federal rear. But things didn't work out that way. Lee was so hard pressed in his effort to throw Howard back on the 28th, that Stewart had to be sent directly to his aid, abandoning the proposed flank attack. Even this proved of no avail and the Confederate assault on Howard failed to attain its objective in this, the Battle of Ezra Church, known also, as Manigault points out, as the Battle of the Poor House (there was one nearby) or Lick Skillet Road.

Embittered by the repeated failure of his attacks, Hood, to his discredit, now began to criticize the morale and fighting spirit of his troops in order to explain away his lack of success. His reflections were not only ungenerous but, with few exceptions, untrue. If anyone were to blame for an occasional show of caution in charging breastworks, it was clearly Hood himself for throwing his exhausted men, time after time, against entrenched positions held by superior numbers. As Stanley Horn observed in referring to the Southern troops at the Battle of Ezra Church, coming as it did so soon after Peachtree Creek and the Battle of Atlanta on the 22nd, "The spirit, indeed, was willing, but the flesh was weak." Small wonder!

While keeping up the bombardment of the city, Sherman now settled down to the process of generally extending his intrenched line to the right, or south, nearer and nearer to the vital railroads. Every move on his part, however, was met by a corresponding one by Hood, so that the two armies spent the month of August facing each other from heavily fortified positions. Patton Anderson described the scene: "Firing between...the two picket lines was constant during the day, and not infrequently during the night...The main line was constantly being strengthened, the trenches were enlarged, the breastworks were made wider and stronger in every particular, while every available obstruction...was resorted to...Abatis of the most substantial kind, chevaux-de-frise, and palisades of approved style bristled along our whole front, giving confidence to our troops and speaking defiance to the foe."

In praising the spirit and determination of his officers and men, Anderson had this to say: "To the brigade commanders *(Deas, Brantley, Sharp and Manigault)* I am especially indebted for their prompt obedience to every order and cheerful cooperation in everything tending to promote the efficiency of the command and the good of the service. Their sympathy, counsel and hearty cooperation lightened my burden of responsibility and contributed to the esprit de corps, discipline and good feeling which happily pervaded the division, and without which the bravest troops in the world cannot be relied on."

By Aug. 25, the two armies had reached the vicinity of East Point, where the railroad running south from Atlanta branched, the line to the southeast continuing on to Macon and that to the southwest to Montgomery.

During the past month the cavalry on both sides had been active. Hood had sent Wheeler with about 4,500 men against Sherman's communcations in a brilliant raid that reached to the outskirts of Nashville. Such was the capacity of the North, however, with its virtually unlimited resources and men, to repair the damage inflicted, that the effect was only temporary and did not play an important role in the outcome of the campaign. On the other side, McCook, Stoneman and Kilpatrick were given a crack at the railroad south of Atlanta, but they were all beaten back, and Sherman came to the conclusion that only the infantry itself could do the job and make it stick.

Leaving the Twentieth Corps to guard the railroad bridge over the Chattahoochee north of the city, Sherman pulled the rest of his troops out of the lines on the 26th and started them on a major offensive against the Macon railroad in the vicinity of Jonesboro.

Misled by reports from his cavalry and from Union prisoners as to the amount of damage inflicted by Wheeler on the Atlantic & Western Railroad, Hood became convinced that the main Federal line of supply had been effectively cut and that in consequence, Sherman was being compelled to fall back across the Chattahoochee. How long Hood held to this erroneous belief is debatable, as is the extent of his subsequent confusion as to where, and in what strength, Sherman's main thrust against the railroads would fall. Finally, and only in the nick of time, he sent Hardee's and Lee's corps south to Jonesboro, with orders to attack on August 31st and throw the Northern troops back from the railroad, westward across the Flint River.

This was a pretty tall order for two small corps in the face of virtually the whole Federal army. Predictably, the attack failed. Any glimmering hope of success was dashed by a lack of coordination between the two corps, for which Lee blamed Hardee, a contention in which Manigault appears to have joined. Always on the lookout for an opportunity to run Hardee down, Hood characterized the attack as "rather feeble," only 1,400 men having been killed and wounded. Thus, to Hood's failures at Peachtree Creek, Atlanta and Ezra Church was added the abortive attack at Jonesboro.

That night, still harboring the illusion that Sherman was threatening to attack the city, Hood ordered Lee's corps to return to Atlanta. Later on, he tried to make it appear that he was pulling Lee back to join Stewart, who was at Atlanta, in another of his fanciful flank attacks, but now the game was up.

With Sherman in full control of the railroad between Jonesboro and Rough and Ready, some 12 or 13 miles up the line, it was obvious that Atlanta's time had come. Bowing to the inevitable, Hood abandoned the city on Sept. 1 and concentrated his weakened and exhausted army the next day at Lovejoy's Station, about six miles south of Jonesboro, Stewart marching down from Atlanta and Lee from near Rough and Ready, where he had halted on his way back to the city. Hardee joined the other two corps from Jonesboro after a final stubborn rear-guard action against Sherman at that point.

At 6 a.m. Sept. 3, Sherman telegraphed Gen. Halleck, chief of staff, in Washington: "So Atlanta is ours, and fairly won." On the 6th, to Hood's relief, the Northern commander drew his army back from Lovejoy's to the city and the Atlanta campaign, begun four months ago to the day at Dalton far to the north, was over.

R.L.T.

THE STRUGGLE FOR ATLANTA

And

BATTLE OF PEACH TREE CREEK

(The Narrative)

O n the 18th, our division moved during the night towards the Peach Tree Creek, and on the following morning entrenched ourselves, some skirmishing going on in our front, but in which we took no part. On the evening of the 19th, we were withdrawn from that point, and moved to our right, and to the east of Atlanta about two miles from the city, holding the two roads, known as the Peach Tree Creek Road and the Decatur Road, which ran parallel alongside of the railroad going to Augusta, and the country lying between, my brigade on the right, connecting with a division of cavalry, which continued the line some distance further. On the 20th we had constructed a very strong set of works, with our artillery behind earthworks and in good positions. The enemy began to show himself towards midday, and the light infantry soon became engaged.[1]

On the afternoon of this day, at about three o'clock, General Hood attacked the enemy at Peach Tree Creek, falling upon their right centre. Hardee's corps and a portion of Loring's[2] being the force he used for that purpose. I never could learn much regarding this battle. Our own corps was distant about three or three and a half miles. We could only see the smoke rising from the battlefield, and hear the discharges of musketry and artillery.

I heard many expressions of censure from the officers engaged bestowed equally on Hood and Hardee. It appeared to me that from what I could gather, that in the earlier part of the engagement the attack was most successful, and that the enemy were driven a considerable distance. Hardee, satisfied with his success, halted, and did not push on as he should have done. The other portion of our troops continued to fight and gain ground, but, being unsupported, were eventually checked and finally driven back.[3]

Had Hardee done as it was said he should have done, continued to move forward, he would not only have divided the Federal Army, cutting them in two, but he would also have captured a large number of guns, in rear of which the enemy had been driven back in confusion, and from which the gunners had all fled. There was no greater obstacle to prevent his gaining more ground than presented itself to the other two divisions, who, being left alone to continue the fight, were finally checked in their course by an accumulation of forces against them, and forced to retire. General Sherman, in a conversation six weeks afterwards with a General Govan,[4] who, with a portion of his brigade had been captured at Jonesboro, and was at the time his prisoner, told that general, when speaking of this engagement, that nothing saved him on that occasion but the unaccountable remissness or deficiency of our commanding officers, who, after having broken his lines, and with a large number of pieces within his grasp, failed to take advantage of the favorable opportunity, halted their column, and remaining stationary, gave him time to rally his men, bring up help, and finally to recover his ground, his artillery, and a complete restoration of his line. He admitted that he had been wholly unprepared for an attack, but one division was entrenched, the others were uncovered, and the horses of his artillery were at some distance from the guns. Had the attack been a determined one, and well led, the consequence to him would have been disastrous in the extreme.

How much truth there was in his statement is a matter for others to make up their minds about, but it certainly coincided with the accounts given by several officers of rank, who took part in the affair. Sherman, in his conversations with General Govan, which were repeated to me, and much of it I heard directly from that officer, must have spoken very freely and fully as to the events of the campaign, which at that time had ended. I remember that he also said to General Govan that at Resaca he made sure that Johnston and his army were in his grasp, and that he, Johnston, only saved himself by a few hours. Had he delayed six hours longer, he would have been forced to surrender, or have had his army destroyed. There were other points on which he spoke, that will be mentioned in the course of this narrative.[5]

This battle of the 20th proved a complete failure, altho a success as far as mere fighting was concerned. We lost more men than the enemy did, and gained no substantial advantage. It did not delay the enemy twelve hours, but only made him more cautious, and caused him to be in a better state of preparation for any occurrence of a like nature.

Sherman states that he got possession of the field of battle, and found upon it 500 dead and 1,000 wounded, and claims to have captured seven stands of colors. The last assertion was a lie, for no colors were lost. His figures as to the killed and wounded who fell into his hands were also incorrect, altho I have no doubt that it cost us fully 4,000 men.[6]

Amongst the killed on this day was Brigadier General Clement Stevens, of S.C., one of the best officers in our army.[7]

After nightfall, Hardee with his command and the other troops engaged, fell back to their works, abandoning the ground they had engaged.

On the 21st, severe skirmishing went on in front of our position, and the enemy cannonaded us incessantly. To our right, a sharp engagement took place between the division of General Cleburne and the enemy, in which our troops were completely victorious.[8]

A little after dark on the night of the 21st, our lines were abandoned, and the army fell back to the works surrounding Atlanta, which had been fortified previously by the engineers.

At daylight on the morning of the 22nd, we fell to work, fortifying and strengthening our works. By 10 o'clock the enemy's lines drew round us, covering our front, which formed something like a half circle around the city. They had not men enough completely to invest us, and our own lines covered on three of the four sides of the town, the flanks or extremities extending out for a considerable distance further than the other portions of the works.

During the whole of this morning, we had sharp work. Our artillery was placed in strong works, prepared with much labor, and judiciously located, and on this occasion, owing to the advantages they possessed, proved a little too strong for the enemy.

Whilst marching in from our abandoned works on the preceding night, we came in contact with a column on the route going out on a road leading south from Atlanta, which proved to be Hardee's corps, and one or two divisions temporarily attached to it.[9] We soon learned that some expedition was on foot, but no one could tell its purpose, or whither bound.

At about two o'clock on the 22nd, we were all startled to hear heavy firing on our right, distant from two or three miles, which gradually drew nearer and increased in volume, as the engagement became general.[10] At first there were many conjectures as to what it meant, but soon recollecting the movement of troops which we had seen the night before, we were not long at a loss to account for it.

BATTLE OF JULY 22, 1864

NEAR ATLANTA

(The Narrative)

General Hardee, with his corps and additional force on the night of the 21st and morning of the 22nd, under instructions from the commanding general, made a wide circuit, south and east, falling upon the enemy's left flank, at some distance south of the Augusta railroad, at about 12:30 o'clock. He found them somewhat unprepared for his attack, altho their left had been strongly intrenched, on a high and commanding hill, where they had collected a considerable number of guns.[11] As on a previous occasion he at first met with a great deal of success, catching the enemy at great disadvantage. He routed and drove them a considerable distance, capturing and killing a large number.

When the enemy had somewhat recovered from the surprise and confusion created by so sudden and unexpected an assault, and had been enabled by the opportune arrival of a fresh corps[12] to form a new line, and offer some resistance, he ceased his efforts to push further, contenting himself with his success, and holding the ground which he had gained with the spoils that were left in his hands. At four o'clock the firing in that direction ceased. Everything being screened from our view excepting the smoke which rose from the battlefield, we, that is, those of us that were in the breastworks, were of course unaware of the result of the fight, or of the success that had attended the effort. The division had been ordered to hold itself in readiness for action when the firing first began, and the brigade commanders shortly after received their instructions as to the movements contemplated. At about four o'clock, or a little after,[13] the division was ordered to advance,[14] and did so, springing over the breastworks in the following order: Deas's brigade, commanded by Colonel Coltart,[15] on the right, with its left resting on the railroad, supported by Brantley's*[16] and my own on the left, its right on the railroad, (to which line we both threw our guides) and supported by the brigade of General Sharp.[17] Our orders were to move on until we found the enemy, and then to attack and drive him out of his works, which we were to hold until further orders. It was expected that we would find him prepared for our reception, in our own old line of works that we had abandoned the night before about a mile in our front.[19] The ground for a half mile after leaving our position was comparatively open; so that we could move along without difficulty. A skirmish line preceded us. The enemy who had considerable force with a battery of artillery,[20] in advance of their main line, were easily driven back, and during our progress we captured over a hundred prisoners. Still moving forward, we passed through a belt of woods, which screened the brigade, excepting the right regiment, the 10th S.C., which was exposed to view from the time it left the breastworks, and consequently suffered severely. The nearer we approached the enemy, the more severe became their fire, particularly that of the artillery, which caused us the loss of a good many men. The country fortunately was gently undulating, so that for a great portion of the time we could not be seen by them. I had several times to check the movement of the line, as it got in advance somewhat of the brigade on our right.[21] At length, we reached a hollow between two hills, which ran almost parallel with the front of the position occupied by the Yankees, where we halted to rectify the alignment, and close up any gaps that had occurred during our advance.

Everything being in readiness, we were about to move forward, when General Brown ordered me, through a staff officer, not to do so until

*Formerly Walthall's, who had lately received the promotion of "Temporary Major General."[18] — A.M.M.

Colonel Coltart was also ready. What delayed them, I do not know, but it caused us to remain inactive for at least five minutes, the shot and shell annoying us much, the fragments from the shell and bullets from the spherical case falling amongst us incessantly. Seeing at last that the other brigade on my right appeared to be in readiness, the order to move forward was given, and on clearing the brow of the hill, there stood the enemy in their brestworks, not over two hundred and fifty yards from us. Their flags fluttering lazily in the breeze indicated the length of line occupied by each regiment, and the numbers opposed to us. I saw and noticed all this only for a moment, and thought it looked very pretty, but in the next instant the whole scene was shut out, everything enveloped in smoke. A deafening roar smote upon the ear, and a storm of bullets and cannister tore through our ranks and around us. The men by this time were well under way, and altho the line staggered and reeled for a moment, it quickly recovered and went forward. The space that separated us being half cleared, or perhaps as much as two-thirds of it cleared, the fire became more deadly and alarming. The pace at which the men were moving slackened; large gaps were visible here and there. The line had lost its regularity, warbling like the movements of a serpent, and things looked ugly, but our supports were coming up in capital style, not more than one hundred yards in rear. The men saw them, and gathered confidence. All the field and most of the line officers played their part well at this crisis. Conspicuous amongst them was Lieutenant William Huger, A.D.C. The gallant examples set by so many overcame all hesitation, excepting in small portions of two regiments, and the brigade nearly as a whole, dashed forward and over the works, rifles and artillery flashing in their faces.

At the last rush, most of the enemy broke and fled. Still a goodly number fought on, until they saw that further resistance was useless or were killed or overpowered. Many of our men were killed or wounded in the work itself, amongst the latter, Colonel Pressley, shot through the shoulder with a rifle ball, fighting hand to hand with several Federal soldiers.*[22]

We had scarcely secured our positions before our supports were up to us, and as the enemy on our right and left gave way, seeing their line broken, the two brigades, Sharp's and my own, gained ground on the two flanks, occupying a space equal to their entire front. On examination we found that in the line that we had carried were sixteen (16) pieces of artillery. Four of these were 20 pounder Parrott guns. The other twelve consisted of Napoleon 12 pounder and three inch rifle guns.[23] We also recognized that the works from which we had driven the enemy, were the same that we had thrown up on the 20th and 21st, but had been much strengthened and altered to fight inwards. The abattis which we had covered our front with had been reversed, and had presented itself as an obstacle to us, but so impetuous was the last rush that many officers

*His wound proved most serious, from which he did not recover in time to rejoin his regiment before the final surrender of the Army. — A.M.M.

and men declared that they were not aware of its existence until some minutes after the contest had ended. Owing to the fact of their being two ditches to the work, one cut by ourselves and the other the enemy to suit them, and the heavy fire that they kept upon us, having rallied and formed a new line about five hundred yards off, it was almost impossible to save the guns we had captured. Six pieces were with much difficulty removed, but it was impossible to do anything with the others just then.

It must have been about fifteen minutes after we had taken the works, when an order was brought me to retire at once. Reluctantly we were compelled to obey it, and in a few minutes commenced to fall back. We had abandoned the works and retreated about a quarter of a mile when we were halted, the order was countermanded, and we were directed to return and reoccupy them.[24]

We found the enemy moving up to take possession, they seeing that we had retired. A few of their men were already in. They were again driven back, this time with little difficulty, and we again took possession. Preparations had by this time been completed by the enemy to recover and restore their line. In a few minutes we were hotly engaged, and succeeded in driving back our assailants, but we were much annoyed by two batteries on our flanks, which enfiladed our lines, to which we could not reply, no artillery having having accompanied us.[25]

It appears that the brigades of Deas and Brantley, who had somehow or other got too far to the right, could make no impression on the enemy and accomplished nothing. After sustaining the heavy fire and cannonade from the enemy for some time, and seeing only my own and Sharp's brigade fighting, I felt certain that unless supported and our force increased, we must eventually be overcome by numbers and be forced to relinquish our prize. I therefore sent several messages asking for assistance, and giving notice of the condition of things. Other troops must have been sent for before my request was received, as those which finally came to our assistance were brought out from our own line, and much time was lost. They should have been at hand for any emergency. Two brigades finally made their appearance, one of which was sent to the right to General Sharp,[26] the other to me on the left. I forget whose brigade it was that reported to me, or the name of the colonel who commanded it, but he was one of the coolest fellows I ever saw, handling his command with great ease and judgement.[27] As they came up to me, not knowing where they were wanted, their formation was unsuited for the occasion, and they were compelled to change front under a heavy fire. The artillery practice of the enemy was splendid, and that of a battery on our left under the supervision of General Sherman himself (see his report) was accurate in the extreme.[28] Their shells tore through the lines or exploded in the faces of the men with unerring regularity; but the new front was speedily obtained, and they moved to the position designated without flinching. Their left regiment sometime after gave way, but the others stood their ground to the last. It must now have been three hours since we had left our own works to bear our part in the battle, and we had been fighting steadily for fully two hours, with but slight interruption, repulsing every effort of the enemy to drive us out. The sun had set, and a message had been sent to the Division Commander from both Sharp and myself, to say that we could make our positions good and could hold them, when an order came to us to retire quickly, as the enemy was moving in large masses on our left flank and rear, and to delay would cause the loss or capture of the forces engaged. There was nothing left for us to do but to obey, and I never saw men obey an order so unwillingly. They were fully conscious of having distinguished themselves, and wanted to bring off the artillery which they had so gallantly captured. They believed that the place could be held, and that as soon as dark set in, the guns could be moved with little difficulty.[29] They did not seem to understand the purpose for which they had been fighting, or the strategy of their general. Much disgust was expressed at the time and afterwards, when all the events of the day were known, and it was believed that had a competent commander been present, the result of the day's work would have been far different. Instead of ten or twelve pieces of artillery, a few colors, and a figuring up of the comparative loss of both sides, in which, in proportion to our strength, we suffered much more severely,[30] had a proper use been made even of the forces engaged, had the attacks been simultaneous, had reinforcements been ready to lend their assistance, it might have culminated in a brilliant victory. One third of Sherman's army would have been cut off, and with a force in its front, rear, and flank, must have been destroyed or captured. Sherman himself remarks in his report, "but fortunately their attacks were not simultaneous", and to all intents and purposes admits that he was taken by surprise.[31]

We fell back from the positions we had gained, leaving our much coveted prizes, and many of our dead on the field. The enemy immediately took possession of the ground we had relinquished, opening a scattering fire on us as we retired, but not daring to follow us. I saw no enemy on our flank except those with whom we had been contending. My orderly, Sam Neysmith, was wounded by my side as we were returning, which laid him up for several months. Soon after we regained our defensive line around Atlanta, and counting up our losses, found that the division had lost over 1,000 men, out of which number a little over 400 killed or wounded, and thirty missing, fell upon our brigade. We had captured about 400 prisoners, six pieces of artillery, several ambulances, one color, and about seventy or eighty artillery or officer's horses. We carried into the fight about 1,400 combatants. Three out of the six field officers were severely wounded, and 32 others of various ranks either K or W.

Lieutenant G.A. Janisson, A.A.G., and Lieutenant W.E. Huger, A.D.C., were the only staff officers present. Both behaved admirably, and were uninjured. The latter had two horses killed under him.

Captain Walker, formerly the Adjutant General, had lately been promoted to the Lieutenant Colonelcy of the 10th S.C., and served with his regiment. During the remainder of the war he commanded it, Colonel Pressley never being able in consequence of his wound, received that day, to return to duty with it.

Take it all in all, this was one of the most spirited and dashing contests that the brigade ever fought, and they won much praise for their obstinacy and valor. I do not remember any instance during the war when so small a force captured so many pieces of artillery in one fight (16), the same being protected by works.[32]

I will mention a touching incident of the battle told me by one of our officers, Captain Oliver (afterwards Lieutenant Colonel, 24th Ala., a gentleman and a soldier, every inch of him).[33] He was amongst the first in the breastworks, when his regiment struck it, and near one of their batteries, a moment or two after getting in, he noticed a captain of artillery, evidently the commander of the battery, a few paces in rear, leaning with his unsheathed sword in his hand against a tree. He described him as a handsome young man of fine figure, gazing sadly on the scene around him, and apparently in abstracted thought. He immediately approached him, ordering him to surrender. The officer seemed startled and surprised, as though suddenly interrupted in some reverie, but, immediately collecting himself, in a graceful, gentlemanly manner, complied with his demand. He then ordered him to the rear, and received the reply that he was wounded, and unable to walk, pointing at the same time to his stomach, with one hand. Captain O. then noticed what he had not done before, that the skirt of his coat partly concealed a terrible wound, by which the apron of the stomach had been laid open, as tho done by some sharp instrument, permitting a portion of his bowels to fall outwards, which with his left forearm and hand he was supporting. Perceiving his helpless condition, with the assistance of a soldier, he carried him from the exposed position where he was standing, over the breastwork, laying him in the ditch, and making him as comfortable as circumstances would permit. The poor fellow, however, was sinking fast, and died a short time before we retired from the works. Any effort of mine to relate the incident would fail to create the interest and sympathy which Captain Oliver excited for this poor sufferer in the account he gave to some of us.

Our position in the works around Atlanta remained unchanged until midday of the 27th, the usual fighting going on. On the 26th, the enemy began to withdraw from our right, transferring their forces gradually to our left.[34] The division was withdrawn from the point they had been occupying on the 27th, moving in rear of our lines and towards our left. After dark we passed through Atlanta, moving out on what was known as the Poor House, or Lickskillet, Road, in a direction a little south of west from Atlanta, bivouacking about two and a half miles from the city.

NOTE — *Major General McPherson, Union Army, and Major General W.H.T. Walker, of the Confederate S.A., were both killed on the 22nd.* — **A.M.M.**

Several unimportant movements were made during the earlier part of the morning of the 28th. Finally at about 11:30 o'clock, the line of march was taken up, and with the division of Clayton (formerly Stewart's, lately promoted Lt. Gen'l, and a corps commander) and Loring's, now returned to his division, Stewart having assumed command of General Polk's old corps, we marched beyond our line of defences, in the direction of the Poor House. We could distinctly hear heavy skirmishing, accompanied by some artillery, which seemed to come from that point. Most of us came to the conclusion that the day would not pass over without an action, and our apprehensions were soon verified.

BATTLE OF JULY 28 NEAR ATLANTA

Known By Many As

BATTLE OF THE POOR HOUSE

Or

LICKSKILLET ROAD

(The Narrative)

During the nights of the 26th and 27th, General Sherman had withdrawn three of his corps, composing what was known in the Federal Army as the "Army of *(the)* Tennessee", formerly commanded by General McPherson, but since his death on the 22nd, commanded by Major General Howard[35] — from his extreme left, and moving them in rear of his army, they were passed round to the right, extending his line in that direction due south. Discovering this movement, General Hood determined to check it, hoping to find the enemy unprepared for an attack, and assailing them on the flank, to do them much injury, and check their movements towards our left. As it turned out, he was too late, the enemy having completed their movement, and gained their object. Lieutenant General Stephen D. Lee, who, a day or two previously, had reported to General Hood for duty, and had been assigned to the command of his, Hood's, old corps,[36] was entrusted with the execution of his plans, the force at his disposal for the accomplishment of his purpose consisting of three (3) divisions, our own, Clayton's, and Loring's.[37] Other troops were brought up afterwards, as the battle bid fair to be more serious than was at first apprehended.

At about noon, or a little later, our line of battle was formed, the division being on the left. Three brigades of our division formed our front line. My own drawn up in rear constituted the second line, or reserve force. I do not remember the order of the other divisions on our right, but think that Clayton's came next.[38] The skirmishing, which was confined entirely to the cavalry, which had followed the enemy in his movements, was going on in front, at least a half mile to our right. Our original formation must have been at least three-quarters of a mile from the position occupied by the Federals, or what was supposed to be their position, on a well-wooded ridge, the ascent of which was very steep, commanding a partial view of some open fields which lay between us.[39] After moving forward some distance, my command was ordered to halt in rear of a belt of woods about a half mile from the enemy, there to remain in readiness until wanted. The other brigades moved on, and in a few minutes we were made aware, by the rapid and steady discharges that the action had commenced. I learned shortly after, that Deas's brigade, Colonel Johnston commanding, and Sharp's, advanced against the ridge in their front,[40] whilst Brantley's, separating itself, and going more to the left, attacked what it was supposed would turn out to be the extreme right flank of the enemy. He, however, came full upon their front in line of battle, and protected by temporary breastworks, their right extending far beyond his left. The division next on our right only threatened, but did not go in, consequently Johnston and Sharp found themselves, similarly situated as Brantley, assailing two lines of battle, protected in some measure by works hastily constructed, themselves being in one line only. The result may easily be imagined.[41]

I suppose I had remained in my position 20 minutes, and the firing had nearly ceased, when an order came for me to advance straight to the front. After clearing the wood, and going some distance through an open field, we were halted by General Lee, with whom was our Division Commander, General Brown; and by the former I was directed to place the Brigade in such a position that the front would be exactly parallel with that of the ridge, and pointing out to me the highest portion of it, directly in our front, which seemed for the distance of 300 yards to exceed by fifteen or twenty feet the height of any other portion, was ordered by him to carry it and establish myself there, remarking at the same time that I would find little difficulty in doing so, as the enemy were not in force, and only held it with a few light troops. General Brown also remarked by way of encouragement, I suppose, to myself, and the line near which we were standing, that General Sharp with his brigade had found no difficulty in executing a like order. I never yet have been able to explain to myself how it was that those officers so unblushingly made such a statement, knowing, as they must have done, that it was totally incorrect. Johnston, Brantley, and Sharp, had been repulsed in great confusion, and with much loss, and the latter officer was at the moment sitting on horseback near them. I did not know anything about the result of the fight so far. The thick belt of woods before mentioned, behind which the brigade had been standing, shut out everything from our view. Arriving upon ground that had not been fought on, and at an intermediate point between the two previous attacks, there were no signs of a repulse or of disorder, and seeing General Sharp present, I concluded that he had merely come to make a report of his success.[42] Altho exposed to a slight fire, where we were standing, or rather, sitting on our horses, slightly protected by a rise of the ground in front of us, from the ridge which was distant about six hundred yards, (600), I regarded it as being nothing more than a fire from their sharp shooters, and no suspicions whatever arose in my mind as to what was really the true state of affairs. Carefully inspecting the ridge, nothing whatever could be seen of any works or lines of battle, owing to the dense foliage with which it was shrouded from the foot to the very summit. The men, I believe, had as little apprehension as myself as to the result, and when everything was ready, moved forward at the order, steadily and like veterans. Clearing the brow of the only intervening hill, we had a space of about 350 yards of perfectly open ground, excepting at one point, where lay a small wood, covering about 4 or 5 acres of ground, but which terminated within two hundred yards of the enemy's position, where the ground became again open. As we advanced, the balls began to tell more and more rapidly, but we did not experience the fire of their first line until just before reaching the wooded portion of the field, when it tore loose on us with intense severity; but the pace was accelerated, the wood gained, anu the men rushed on the enemy behind their piles of rails, logs and rocks, now plainly visible, and distant about seventy-five yards from our centre. The greater part of each regiment got over, and broke the line. On the right and left they were not so successful.. The fire on the flanks was too heavy, and several companies at each end crumbled and gave way, yielding towards the centre, and falling in rear of their comrades, now in advance. Tho the enemy were now driven out, and forced to abandon their first line throughout almost the entire space where we struck them, the obstacles before them were more serious still. Half way up the height, another line of defense and another line of battle showed itself, pouring into us a steady and deadly fire. At the summit was still a third line. It was but for a short time that the men were able to hold what they had gained. They knew that no assistance was coming and that it was impossible, in their shattered condition, under such a fire, to carry the second line. The construction of the works was such as gave them little protection on the outside, and on the other side it was completely exposed to the fire of the enemy's second line. It was evident that retreat could only be delayed a few minutes, unless reinforcements were sent forward to our assistance. No such arrangements appear to have been contemplated.[43]

The enemy, however, soon saved us any hesitation; for, seeing how contemptible a force had assailed them, and that, to all appearances, they had been left to their fate or own resources, they sallied from behind their timber piles on the right and left, attacking simultaneously. There was no resisting it. Beginning at the two flanks, the line crumbled towards the centre, and the rest was flight and confusion, until we reached the ground from which we had started to make the assault. Here the order to halt and reform was promptly obeyed, and in less than five minutes the brigade was in line again, every regiment and company in its proper place, with but few stragglers missing, only our dead and wounded absent. Ten minutes had not elapsed after order had been restored, when we were again directed to attack, and the same instructions repeated. A second time we advanced, and tried to do over again with diminished numbers, against an enemy fully as strong as he was before, their confidence increased by the result of our last attack, what we had failed previously to accomplish. The order to advance was promptly obeyed, but only a few reached the breastworks. The line generally gave way within fifteen or twenty yards, under the severity of the fire, and fell back, rallying again almost as readily, and with as few skulkers, as after the first attack.

Artillery was now brought up, which opened heavily upon the enemy for fifteen minutes or more, doing, it is said, great execution (this we got from prisoners taken afterwards), altho the artillerists and gunners could only guess at the position occupied by the hostile lines. I had withdrawn the brigade about one hundred yards from the point where they had been rallied and reformed, to the cover of a road running parallel with the field of battle, which, having been partly excavated on the hillside, gave good shelter to the men, whilst resting and recovering from their fatigue and protected from the many bullets which were sweeping the ground in every direction. Twenty minutes may have elapsed since our last failure when an aid of General Brown's came to me with repetition of the old order, again to attack and carry the height, alone, unsupported, after two failures, and with the command reduced to seven hundred men. I could scarcely credit my senses. I had made my report as to the cause of our failure, and the position and strength of the enemy, and I thought the Corps and Division commanders had seen enough for themselves to give assurance of the utter impracticability of obtaining any success, but by using a very heavy force, with a formation of at least two lines of battle. First extending the order to the command to be in readiness, I galloped to the spot where General Brown was standing. Pretty much the same scene took place as occurred between myself and General Anderson at Missionary Ridge, excepting that I had a very different person to deal with, and in every way a better soldier and more reasonable officer. He almost immediately replied to my remarks that the order was not his own. He disapproved of it, and was satisfied that the brigade had done all that it was possible for them to do, and that we had just ground for regarding ourselves as being unjustly and ungenerously dealt with. Such were the orders given him by General Lee, which he could not do otherwise than extend. He seemed much annoyed and excited as I turned to leave him. I had no choice left me now, and started to return and execute the order, making up my mind that fail we must.* I had not passed over one half the distance that separated me from the brigade, when I heard my name called. Looking round, I saw

*The original manuscript reads: "Whatever the result of our effort, I for one would not return." This was crossed out and "fail we must" substituted. — Editor.

General Brown trying to overtake me. On his coming up, he said that he intended to disobey General Lee's order, and would abide the consequences, at the same time withdrawing the instructions that he had previously sent me.[44] Our artillery continued for some time to cannonade the enemy in their position, which was feebly responded to by theirs, either because their guns had not arrived, or they found much difficulty in getting them in position. After an interval of a half hour from our last attack, I saw preparations being made for a new one, and soon learned that Walthall's division was about to make an effort against the position which I had assaulted twice before. I saw the arrangements completed, which consisted of two lines of battle, three brigades in the first, two in the second line, the whole commanded by Major General Walthall, and the troops fresh, not having previously taken part in the engagement.[45] Feeling much interest in the result, I determined to watch the assault, and moved forward with them to the edge of the small patch of woods already spoken of, which at one point lay between ourselves and the enemy. On the edge of this wood, I took position behind a large tree, comparatively safe from the many balls which were flying in every direction, and awaited the result. The attacking force moved forward in a style much to be admired, regardless of the severe fire which greeted them from the moment they came within view, and looked as tho they would sweep everything before them. As they neared the wood, the discharges doubled in intensity. Nevertheless, they continued to advance, and finally disappeared amidst the trees and underbrush. The rattle of musketry at that moment and for several successive minutes almost exceeded anything that I had ever heard before. For a short time, I thought they had succeeded, but it was not to be so. After a short interval, I saw groups of five or six going to the rear at a rate that told plainly they were not wounded men. These were almost immediately succeeded by squads of ten or a dozen, then by scores, and finally the entire force in utter confusion and rout. All efforts on the part of their officers to preserve something like order proved unavailing, and the division which a few minutes before had shown to such advantage, exciting the admiration of all who beheld their compact and steady advance, was seeking in dismay and confusion the nearest point that afforded protection and cover from the storm of bullets which scattered death and destruction on all sides. I hugged my tree closely, and trembled when I thought of my escape from the same danger to which I had been exposed only a short time before.[46]

Thus had five brigades failed to accomplish the task imposed upon one. Twice had the latter gallantly responded to the order of their superior. Twice had they been driven back discomfited, the odds against them proving far beyond their ability to overcome. A third time they had been called upon, and would again have gone to the slaughter, knowing full well beforehand what the result would be, had it not been for the action of the Division Commander, who took upon himself the responsibility of disobeying an order given to him by his superior, believing that the circumstances warranted his doing so.[47]

There was no more serious fighting that day. The enemy in turn threatened to advance upon us, but our own troops were coming up in large numbers, which fact they becoming aware of, deterred them. We were afterwards shifted about from one position to another, but were not again seriously engaged.

Of the three divisions that General Stephen D. Lee carried out for the purpose of fighting the enemy, only one, (our own) came in actual contact with the enemy,[48] and that one attacked by brigades at three separate points, in neither instance having any supports whatever. Walthall's Division, which had been sent to his assistance, he did make use of as a whole, but it was too late when he did so. The enemy were too well prepared. In no instance did any part of that division succeed in reaching the enemy's breastworks even. What he, General Stephen D. Lee, ended by doing, he should have commenced by doing. Success might under those circumstances have attended his efforts. It was one of the many miserable exhibitions of generalship, this whole affair, which was characteristic of the officers of the Army of Tennessee, and one of the numerous instances of which I was a witness and a sufferer. All that Sherman had to do was to keep on the defensive. His enemies were fast consuming themselves. The mismanagement in this affair was so patent to the dullest spectator or combatant, that the men lost all confidence in their leaders, and were much dispirited in consequence.[49]

Sherman, in his report, makes the following remarks, which show how the rank and file performed their part on this occasion: "His advance was magnificent, but founded in an error that cost him sadly, for our men coolly and deliberately cut down his men, and, spite of the efforts of the rebel officers, ranks broke and fled; but they were rallied again and again, as often as six times at some points, and a few of the rebel officers and men reached our lines of rail piles, only to be killed or hauled over as prisoners."[50] General Sherman was himself present in the field, and altho not very accurate in his statement, was evidently impressed by the fighting qualities of our men exhibited in this action. The fighting done on our part was confined to between 8 and 9 thousand men, whilst there must have been on the ground from fifteen to eighteen thousand men, one-half of which never discharged a musket or took the offensive during the whole day. I think I have said enough to give some idea of the ability of many of our generals to handle troops in an engagement.[51]

Our losses were heavy, particularly in officers, and, as may be supposed from the account given, was heavier in our brigade than any other.[52] After this action there was but one field officer left.[53] Three regiments were commanded by junior captains, one by a lieutenant.[54] My staff were all wounded, and I was left alone. Lieutenant Huger, A.D.C. was severely wounded through the thigh in the first charge. Unwilling to leave the field, nothing but a peremptory order from me could force him to do so. Lieutenant G.A. Jennison, A.A.A.G., was struck from his horse, and lost an eye. I was much indebted to a Lieutenant Lee, belonging to (a) company of cavalry attached to the division as an escort, and doing the duty of couriers, for the proffer of his services to act as aid during the fight. His services were very valuable, and during the remainder of the war, he was detached from his command, doing duty on the brigade staff.

There were 34 officers killed or severely wounded in the brigade on this day.[55] The division also suffered heavily, losing some of its most efficient field and line officers.

Lieutenant General Stewart and Major General Loring were amongst the several wounded, also General Brown slightly.[56]

There was not much artillery used in this fight on either side, being confined almost entirely to our rifles.

During the night, we withdrew, retiring within the lines of defense, leaving the greater part of our dead and wounded in the hands of the enemy.

Tho unsuccessful and hardly used, the brigade acted on this day with great spirit and bravery, and tho twice beaten off with heavy loss, were rallied, reformed, again ready for duty, without difficulty or loss of time, promptly obeying all orders extended to them. I was much pleased and perfectly satisfied with the manner in which they bore themselves, but it was a sad sight to see the shattered remnant of this fine body of men as they withdrew from the contest, to think what had become of the rest of them, and how uselessly and foolishly they had been butchered.

THE SIEGE OF ATLANTA

(The Narrative)

No more efforts were made on the part of General Hood to check the flank movements of General Sherman, who gradually extended his lines to our left, in a southerly direction towards East Point, a station on the Macon R.R.;[57] and he remained entirely on the defensive, meeting the enemy as he gradually gained ground, by a series of works, consisting of well-constructed forts, breastworks, and rifle pits, between the enemy and the railroad.[58]

For several days after the battle of the 28th, we were shifted about from one position to another, hard at work all the time on intrenchments. On the fourth day, we became settled in a position which we retained during the remainder of the siege of Atlanta. It was about three or four miles from Atlanta, in a direction S.W., the Lickskillet Road being about a mile on our right, the *(Sandtown)* road half a mile to our left. Ours was the left brigade of the division, having on our left a Georgia brigade belonging to Clayton's Division, and a very mean one it was.[59] The space for which we were responsible extended a distance of about 450 yards, the line running across a high bald hill, the two flanks reaching to some low ground on each side of it. The parapet and a redoubt for a battery of three guns ran along the outward slope towards the enemy, about 100 yards from the highest part of the hill, the ground rocky and covered with loose stones and broken rock. In front of us for about 200 yards, the country was open and generally meadow land. Beyond this it was open, and another hill not quite as high as the one we were on, fronted us. I am somewhat particular in my description, not that it is of much consequence, but because every feature and nook of that location is indelibly fixed on my mind, and I there spent four weeks, the most anxious, exhausting, and perilous, of any like period, during the whole course of my experience as a soldier. During the first two or three days after the 28th, much of our work was done in daylight, for altho the enemy were in our front, yet their first lines of intrenchments, as also their picket lines, were at a considerable distance from us. Their fire consequently was not very annoying and but little attention was paid to it. They gradually worked up nearer, however, so that we were forced at last to do all our work after nightfall.

Our works consisted of a ditch for the infantry, with the earth thrown outwards, forming an embankment of sufficient thickness to resist even the three-inch rifle shot, or solid shot from the 12-pounder Napoleon guns of the enemy, provided it struck below the exterior crest of the work. Head logs protected the men whilst firing. A double row of palisades covered our entire front, and beyond these an almost impenetrable "abattis", varying in width from fifty to one hundred feet. In addition to this, for the last week of the time we spent there, a substantial and well-constructed (bombproof?) gave almost complete security. Owing to the fact that four batteries of guns were almost all the time playing on us, one of them enfilading almost the entire line, another very nearly doing the same, whilst from the other two, we received a direct fire, it was necessary to protect ourselves by traverses, zig-zags, and the like, in which the men showed much ingenuity. The ground in rear of our works was completely honey-combed, making it a matter of much peril for any one to pass within twenty yards of the line after dark, unless pretty familiar with the locality.

Our picket line consisted of rifle pits, with head logs, about fifteen feet long, with various figures, depending altogether on the situation, fifteen paces separating them, but all connected by a ditch from two to three feet deep, and about 2 or 2½ feet wide. By this covered way the officers on duty could pass from post to post in comparative safety, and when necessary, reinforcements could be sent under cover from one threatened point to another. So also, when the fire of several guns was brought to bear on any rifle pit, for the purpose of destroying it, as they, the enemy, frequently did, almost completely demolishing them one after another, the men would abandon them for the time, scattering and spreading themselves along the connecting trench. The labor for the construction of these exposed works was most often furnished by the men who were on duty on the skirmish line, a portion working whilst the others kept watch. As it was for their own protection and to their advantage to make the line as secure as possible, we never experienced much difficulty in getting the work done, altho sometimes working parties were detailed specially for this duty. Of course the labor went on from night to night, always improving, enlarging, and strengthening them, each relief on going out after dark carrying in the hands of every soldier a forked branch of a tree or young sapling, the leaves all trimmed off and points sharpened, so as gradually to form an "abattis". In this manner these skirmish lines presented a formidable obstacle to the enemy, and if sufficient time had elapsed to complete them, they could generally be held against four or five times as many men as occupied them. From two of these lines, we were driven successively, after many severe contests. Our third line was even stronger than either of the two first, and resisted all the efforts of the enemy to possess themselves of it, altho in the brigade on our left, the skirmishers had been driven back to the breastworks, beyond which there were no pickets. On our right also the line was much retired, so that our picket works somewhat represented a salient. This was the case in each of the three instances where we constructed these works.

The fighting on the picket line was incessant, and the ammunition daily expended by our detail, consisting of about one hundred and seventy-five rifles (175) for a long time averaged rather more than six thousand rounds of ammunition daily, or about 35 rounds per man.[60] At times the contest would be desperate, and the enemy frequently repulsed, and I have more than once seen a line of battle in addition to the pickets on duty, driven back and utterly unable to advance. On both sides the shooting was very accurate, the men frequently dropping their balls between the lower part of the head log and the parapet. The slightest carelessness or imprudent exposure of one's person was sure to result in death or a severe wound. This sort of duty coming round as it did nearly every fourth day, was particularly trying to the men, as for twenty-four hours no sleep was to be had. The mind was in a constant state of tension as well as the body, it being necessary to be ready at any moment to repel an attack, and no one knew when to expect it. It must be remembered also that in our main works we were almost as much exposed, the bullets from the sharpshooters and continued fire from the artillery forcing the men to take shelter under the works or in the ditch all day; and even at night the danger was only a little less, excepting for an hour or two immediately after dark, when there was generally a complete cessation.

Our daily loss varied from five men to fifty-five, the two extremes, and would average, I suppose, about ten or eleven. As a general thing more casualities occurred in the main line of works than on the picket line, which can be easily explained from the fact that in the former, owing to the greater distance of the danger, the men would become careless of exposure, and move about as though there was no danger, in spite of the strictest orders to the contrary. An unfortunate cannon ball, or a few well-directed rifle shots, or perhaps accidental ones, would make them keep close for some time, until its effect had worn off, when again they were as indifferent as ever. With the latter (those on picket) each soldier was on the qui vive. He knew full well what would be the consequence of the slightest imprudence on his part, and was constantly being reminded of the danger in which he stood. To judge from the continued firing, the deadliest hate existed between the two opposing lines, yet they would frequently call to each other, asking and answering questions, and from daily contact with each other, they knew the names of the different brigades, regiments, and sometimes individuals, to whom attention had been called by some cause or other, each organization bearing a different reputation. Thus our men would frequently announce the fact during the night that the following would be a hard day, because such a regiment from Indiana, or some other state, was opposed to them. At another time, they would congratulate themselves on the event of some other regiment being on duty, as they were known to be averse to carrying on matters in too deadly a spirit. When the ordinary skirmish firing was going on, and a man on either side happened to be killed or wounded in one of the rifle pits, his comrades would call out, "Cease firing on this pit!", would stick up his ramrod on the front of the embankment, with a piece of white cloth or sheet of paper on the upper end of it. That pit would remain unmolested until the litter bearers made their appearance and carried off the soldier, altho during the time, the rest of the lines would go at it just as ever. The wounded man removed and out of range, the ramrod with its indicator would be removed, and hostilities would recommence. How this understanding was arrived at, no one could ever tell me, and how far it extended throughout the armies I do not know; but it was a very common occurrence along our division front, and was very honorable and creditable to both parties. I know that many a man's life was saved by it. It was only during this period, and on this line, that I ever knew this humane arrangement to exist, and it ought to be a matter of great regret that it is not universal.

Whilst on duty, the men in the rifle pits, exposed as they were to an August sun the whole day, would consume a good deal of water, rendering it necessary that their canteens should be refilled. As a general rule, for any one to leave the line was an undertaking of great peril, but a Confederate soldier must have water, and will run almost any risk to satisfy his thirst. In order to lessen the danger, the following expedient was commonly adopted.

It would fall to the lot of one man to take all the canteens of the others with whom he was posted. Notice would be given to the adjoining pits some distance to the right and left, that a man was going for water from No. 9 or 5, and at a given signal a quick and steady discharge would commence on the opposite rifle pits of the enemy from whom any danger was to be apprehended. The Yankees in them would lower their heads to avoid the flying balls, coming in quick succession, and there being no concert of action of their side, our men would have it all to themselves. The fellow, with a dozen canteens slung around him, would take advantage of the opportunity, spring out, and, running rapidly, in a minute or two reach a place of safety behind some swell of ground, or a thick wood, and at his leisure procure what was wanted. On his return, approaching as near as he could with safety, he would communicate his return by some peculiar cry, which his comrades hearing, they would again open on the enemy, whilst he regained his place, unhurt, and only a little out of breath.

For the first ten days of this period, I occupied with the staff officers a central position in the breastworks, spending the entire time, night and day, in the ditch of the intrenchment, only leaving it to go along the line, keeping under cover, or to attend to such duties as were necessary; and when the exposure could not be avoided, the risk was at all times great, and during the day, even a single individual showing himself for a minute or two would be sure to draw a fire on him, either of artillery, or from the sharpshooters.

I estimated that during those ten days, at least fifteen hundred shot and shell either struck or exploded within twenty paces of where we lay. No shot ever fell immediately in our section of the work, altho the traverses separating *(us)* from the other sections, and not more than fifteen paces apart, received several balls, and men were killed on either side of us. The embankment was frequently struck, the balls either grazing the works, or burying themselves in the bank and exploding, in either instance covering us with dust and dirt, producing a sensation not very pleasant.[61] Many fragments of rock, splinters, and a few fragments of shells fell in our section, but resulting in no serious injury to anyone. Finding our quarters very uncomfortable and far from cleanly, I determined to adopt the same plans and precautions universally followed by all other General officers, whose rank and position required that they should be very near the line, which was to provide what was commonly known as a "bombproof" for headquarters. A point was selected about 150 yards in rear of the intrenchments, a little in rear of the outer edge of a wood which approached the line, and taking advantage of a slight gully worn by heavy rains, with a little additional labor, in a few hours, we were comfortably fixed, and about as secure as in the breastworks. These precautions were absolutely necessary, and were universally adopted by all officers. Without them, no one's life was safe, even for a few hours. The safety, however, was only comparative, and one could not be otherwise than anxious during the continuance of the siege.

On one occasion, Lieutenant General Lee, making a tour of the lines occupied by his corps, on reaching my brigade, sent for me to accompany him along our front. He was attended by an aid, also by Major General Anderson, who had been sent back to the Army of Tennessee, and had been assigned to the command of our Division. After inspecting the works and preparations made for defense, it being his first visit, he expressed a desire, to get in some position where he could more distinctly see the enemy's works and proposed going a little back from the works to where the hill was higher, and a good view could be obtained. The spot he pointed out was a very open and exposed one, and where, if a man showed himself for a moment, not only several rifle balls would be sent at him, but he got off well if a shot or two from a rifle cannon did no more than cover him with dust, or explode within a few feet of him. Being perfectly familiar with the danger myself, and knowing his ignorance of the same, and regarding myself as being somewhat responsible for his safety under the circumstances, I mentioned the danger we would incur, and suggested a point on the edge of the wood in our rear, which offered the same advantages, and where we were not so apt to be seen, or attract attention.

My suggestion was declined, rather brusquely, and off we started. We soon reached the spot, Generals Lee and Anderson using their glasses to observe with greater accuracy the enemy's position. I, knowing full well what to expect, did not view the scene with much complacency, expecting every moment that one or more of us would be struck down.

Several rifle balls hummed ominously by us, and we had not been stationary more than fifteen seconds, when a severe concussion in our midst, accompanied by a cloud of dust and smoke, and the smart in several parts of the body of each of us from small fragments of rock or loose pebbles, gave notice that a shell had burst amongst us. The report of the gun, the bursting of the shell, and the horrid screech which accompanied it, were simultaneous. Fortunately, we had separated from each other a few feet. I turned to see who had fallen, but all were standing. The aid was rubbing his leg, where a stone had struck him. General Anderson was picking up his hat, and General Lee brushing from his face and neck the sand and dirt with which he had been deluged. The shell, a percussion one, had struck and exploded within six or eight feet of us. As no one had been hurt, I was not much put out by the occurrence, and rather pleased than otherwise to notice the disconcerted countenances of my companions, who had rejected my counsel. I was determined to say nothing more, however, on the subject. The first shell was speedily followed by several more, fortunately not so well directed. The place was getting disagreeably hot and uncomfortable. The enemy seemed bent upon hurting somebody, and would certainly have done so in a very short time had not General Lee turned to me and remarked that it would have been better had my advice been taken, and proposed that we should seek some temporary shelter. Nothing loath to do so, I pointed out a position occupied by the infirmary corps of one of the regiments, about twenty yards off, and into it we slid not very ceremoniously. The enemy had very likely recognized the party as consisting of officers of rank, and before we reached the excavation, three batteries were firing away at us, and continued pounding away at our miserable little place of refuge for full fifteen minutes, much to our annoyance, and that of the infirmary men, who evidently did not regard us as welcome visitors.

At the end of that time, the firing slackened, and we drew out one by one, Generals Lee and Anderson soon after taking their departure, and so ended the observations of the enemy's position for that day. On the next visit we looked at them from the edge of the wood.

Between the 18th and 22nd, Wheeler, with the larger portion of his cavalry, perhaps 5 or 6,000 men, was sent to the rear of the enemy's lines on a raid, with a view to interrupt Sherman's communications by destroying the railroad, capturing trains with supplies, detached posts, and the like — General Hood trusting that by this means, if properly executed, the enemy would be cut off from their supplies, would soon exhaust that which he had with him, and be forced to fall back and abandon the siege of Atlanta.[62] Sherman could not have desired anything better, for he had well provided against any such contingency. He was well provided with provisions, had an immense supply train with his army, besides accumulating a large quantity, in his magazine 'on the right bank of the Chattahoochie, not more than 8 or 9 miles from Atlanta, which was protected by an intrenched camp and an adequate force of men for its security.[63] This force, being detached, also left him far superior to us in cavalry, with which he could effectually cover his after movements, and the various posts along the R.R. being strongly intrenched and garrisoned, gave him little uneasiness about them, when threatened by such troops as Wheeler commanded.[64]

Wheeler, as usual, effected but little, did some damage to the R.R., captured a few trains, and one or two unimportant posts, secured seven or eight hundred beef cattle, and finally, after a long and circuitous march, rejoined the army, just before the campaign ended — the disastrous result of which may partly be attributed to the error committed in sending away from the army at that time so considerable a body of men, whose services were very important in lengthening our lines, or holding the enemy's cavalry in check, and in breaking through the screen which they presented to cover the later movements of their infantry.[65]

As our cavalry moved to their rear, a similar raid was undertaken by the enemy. Much damage was done to the Macon R.R., the only one of any use to us at that time, and our communications were interrupted for a week or more. Such of our cavalry as had not accompanied General Wheeler, behaved with much credit to themselves in pursuing, overtaking, and, with the assistance of a brigade of infantry, defeating and driving off the raiders.[66]

About the 26th or 27th of August, General Sherman, finding that he could not take Atlanta by a direct attack, or reach the Macon R.R. in our vicinity, our Army presenting an unbroken front and always extending itself so as to meet his as he gained ground to the right, commenced his last and successful maneuvre, and began to draw out from his works, commencing on his right. For three succesive nights, this state of things went on, and I think it was on the morning of the 27th that we found their entire line deserted, and the last army corps gone from our front, altho we were fully aware during the night of what was going on.[67] Many were the surmises as to what had become of the enemy. Our entire army rested near their trenches, glad of the opportunity for a little rest, and entirely ignorant of future movements of either force. The cavalry could furnish no information, were too weak to develop their operations, being kept at bay by the superior numbers of the same branch of the enemy's force, who completely masked the flank march to our rear, which General Sherman immediately commenced.[68] I do not know what General Hood's opinion was, but it was generally believed at the headquarters of the Army and by the generals of higher rank, that Sherman had not only given up all hopes of taking Atlanta, but had been forced by heavy losses, interruptions to his communications, and failure of his supplies, to retreat across the Chattahoochie back again upon Chattanooga, and that the campaign had terminated for him in utter failure; but all these sanguine and cheering hopes were doomed to disappointment, and we learned on the 30th that the enemy was far to our rear, having by a wide circuit made for a small town on the Macon R.R. called Jonesboro, and was fast approaching it.[69]

The steps taken to defeat them in their object and at the same time hold Atlanta, were as follows: Lieutenant General Stewart with his corps and all the Georgia militia, was left in the latter place, whilst Generals Lee and Hardee, with their two corps, were hurried off without delay towards Jonesboro to meet and check the enemy at that point, about twenty-five miles distant.

Hardee moved first, followed by Lee, our Division in rear. They reached Jonesboro during the day and night of the 30th.[70] The enemy soon after made their appearance (three corps), both parties intrenching themselves in full view of each other, a half-mile or possibly a little more separating them. On the following day, the enemy was reinforced by several corps, so that they far outnumbered us.[71]

The Brigade had been left at Atlanta when the Division marched,[72] and placed on duty with General Stewart temporarily, but was to act as a rear guard protecting the artillery and ammunition trains, which, owing to the suddenness of the move, had been left behind, to follow as soon as they could be got ready. About 12 o'clock on the night of the 30th, I received orders to draw in my pickets and outposts, which were far apart and much extended, and to move to East Point, thence to Jonesboro. It was daylight before we got away from East Point, and the last of the batteries were under way, and then commenced a most tedious and annoying march. The roads were bad and narrow, the horses of the guns and mule teams of the wagons, much reduced from the great scarcity of corn and forage, were scarcely able to carry their loads. The day too was excessively hot and no water to be had. My instructions were, in addition to the usual precautions for protecting the train, to bring forward all stragglers, and to give every assistance in pushing forward the artillery, no battery or piece to be permitted to fall in the rear. We had much trouble with stragglers, and could not have brought up less than two thousand of them, from every division and brigade of the two corps in front of us, besides which the men were much exhausted in pushing and assisting the tired and broken-down teams out of mud holes, and up the steeper hills. The enemy also were on our flank, the advance guard of one of their three armies, which was striking for a point between Atlanta and Jonesboro. After accomplishing about half the distance, we were obliged to abandon the road on which we were marching, parallel with and west of the R.R., the enemy having taken possession of it, and cut us off. Here I was joined by another brigade, and some skirmishing took place, but we succeeded, by taking a crossroad, in reaching the R.R., and moving by another which ran near to it, but on the east side. How strong the enemy were at that point where they intercepted us and at the time, I could not tell, but if there had been a couple of thousand or more of them, they certainly lost a fine opportunity of capturing or destroying many guns or wagons. It was a great relief when I found myself within three or four miles of Jonesboro, and again heard the familiar sounds of opposing artillery and the rattle of musketry.[73]

Tired and foot-sore, we rejoined our Division, then in line of battle, about half past two, P.M. The men were allowed a short time to rest, whilst I reported to the Division commander for instructions. He informed me that Generals Hardee and Lee had received orders by telegraph from General Hood, then in Atlanta, to attack the enemy, and that in an half-hour's time it would begin.[74] Sharp skirmishing and a steady cannonade was going on at the time. The enemy were to be plainly seen about three-quarters of a mile from where we were, but strange to say, it was not known on which side of the Flint River they were posted. I soon after rejoined my brigade, and conducted by a staff officer, got into the position assigned me, being one of the supporting brigades of the second line, and covering the left half of the division.[75] Here we remained about half an hour, awaiting the signal to advance. The men were very tired. The long march and loss of rest on the preceding night, the laborious offices which they had been called upon to perform during the day, had completely exhausted them. The long and tedious siege through which they had passed, lying cramped in the trenches, exposed night and day to an harassing fire, badly fed and clothed, added to the fatiguing march, had reduced them to a condition by no means satisfactory, and I thought I saw pretty plainly that there was not much fight in them. The same condition of things existed throughout the army. The troops were weary, dull, sluggish, and entirely without that spirit which had hitherto characterized them on all such occasions as the present. They had long since lost confidence in their leaders, and knew full well what was likely to be the consequence of an attack against superior numbers, protected by a complete set of field works.[76]

BATTLE OF JONESBORO, GEORGIA

AUGUST 31, 1864

(The Narrative)

At about four o'clock P.M., the action commenced on the left in Hardee's corps, and was immediately followed up by Lee's Corps. By some mismanagement on the part of General Anderson, the division did not go well into action. The movement of the three brigades of the front line was not simultaneous. The right brigade must have been engaged at least five or six minutes before the other two. The fourth brigade, belonging to another Division,[77] and in rear of which a part of my brigade was, was also slow in getting off. My instructions had been not to allow a greater interval than 100 yards to exist between myself and the line in front. Almost at the last moment, a different arrangement was made from what had previously existed. Anderson took command of the front line, consisting of three of his own, and one of Major General Clayton's brigades, whilst General Clayton commanded the second line, composed of three of his own and one of Anderson's, my brigade.[78] As the troops advanced from their breastworks, we, the supporting line moved up to them, and awaited orders from General Clayton to advance in turn. In front of the breastworks, a dense growth of timber and brushwood had been felled, for the double purpose of making our fire more deadly in case of an attack from the enemy, as well as to impede their progress, should such an event occur. This obstruction proved a serious inconvenience to our men, creating much irregularity in the line, making the movement for the space of two hundred yards, and until they reached the open ground beyond, very slow. General Clayton kept us back until the first line had gained a distance of some 300 yards, that is to say, until they had passed over 100 yards of the open ground, which, as soon as it was reached, the troops moved over rapidly. As soon as we were directed to advance, we experienced the same difficulty in getting thro the tangled mass of fallen trees, etc., the consequence of which delay was, that instead of our being able to preserve the distance that existed when we started, by the time we got clear of the obstruction, instead of there being 250 yards between ourselves and the advanced troops, it was nearer 500 yards, and, owing to the undulating and hilly character of the country, our comrades were out of view.[79] The brigade on my right was about 100 yards behind me, that on the left I never saw anything of after getting out of the wood. General Clayton did not accompany us. Pushing on, we crossed one or two intervening hills, from the summit of which we could catch for a moment or two, a view of the fight and of our front line. At last we came in full view of the enemy and works, from which they were pouring a continuous and deadly fire. I soon saw that the first line had failed. They had not reached within two hundred yards of the enemy. The line had ceased to advance, had halted, and was returning the fire of the enemy. As we neared them, they began to give way, and just before reaching them, they broke in confusion, creating much disorder amongst my own men, but the regimental and staff officers did their duty well, and altho checked in our impetus for a moment, the line recovered itself, and continued to go on. I could see as well as the smoke would allow, for the country was very open, that the failure was not confined to the troops immediately preceding us. Apparently our whole line had failed, and at several points the second line, which from the direction of the line of the enemy's works, had struck them before we did, was also recoiling in confusion.

The fire was too heavy. The men did not behave as well as on any previous occasion, and all efforts to carry them on, failed. When within eighty or ninety yards of the works, the line gave way. All order was lost, and it was a hopeless task to attempt anything further, just there and then. At a point about three hundred yards from where we had been broken, the brigade was halted and rallied, just behind the brow of a considerable ridge. Here also I was joined by the fragments of several other regiments, with which, and my own brigade, I formed a line, and immediately commenced throwing up a temporary breastwork of rails and such other material as could be found for the purpose; but it was a dangerous operation to construct it under the fire to which we were exposed. We nevertheless succeeded in a measure in doing so.[80] Whilst so engaged, my orderly, Stephen Moore, of Co. K, 10th S.C., a most excellent young man, who had accompanied me in many fights and for whom I had a high regard, was struck down within a couple of feet of me, a rifle ball passing through his head, entering at one temple and passing out at a corresponding point of the other. I thought, of course, that the wound was a fatal one, but as he was still alive, my kindly feelings for him induced me to have him taken to the rear, where at least he might die amongst his friends.

To the surprise of all, he afterwards recovered, and is now alive and hearty, but unfortunately the wound cost him both eyes, and he is hopelessly blind. He was at the time about 19 years old.

My purpose in halting where we did and not retiring to the breastworks, as all the other troops did, so far as I could see, was to enable our commanders, in the event of their determining to renew the attack, to do so from a point nearer to the enemy than at first, and the position was a favorable one for the purpose. With a little management, a considerable column might have been massed in rear of the ridge, without much previous exposure, and as I knew that one of our divisions[81] had not been engaged, and General Hardee's corps to all appearances had done but little fighting, I thought it likely that the attack would be renewed, the more so as it was plain to anyone that if we failed to defeat Sherman here, Atlanta must fall.

At this point, I must have had in all not more than eight hundred men, consisting of my own and portions of other commands. All had been engaged; and were to a certain extent demoralized. I sent two staff officers to the rear to give information of my position, and to ask for orders, also to bring back any stragglers. Shortly after despatching them on this errand, Major General Anderson, commanding the division, rode up with an aid, apparently much excited, and ordered me to advance and attack again. As he rode along the line, he addressed the troops, and urged them on. It certainly was an act of consummate generalship to push forward 7 or 800 men, just defeated, of scattered commands, no other troops to support them within 500 yards, against I do not know how many thousands. The result was as might have been expected. The folly of the order was so evident to all that nothing but the habit of obedience to the orders of their superior officers, carried them forward for a space, but as soon as they again got well under fire, they broke easily, and fell back to the last position.

General Anderson, as the line began to move forward, received a severe wound in the face, shattering the jaw, and producing other serious injuries. His life was for a long time in great danger, but I believe he ultimately recovered.[82]

After this last and feeble effort, we remained about a half-hour in this position, when orders came to me from General Lee to retire to the main

247

line, which we did in good order, altho subjected to a sharp and galling fire, but had the satisfaction of knowing, that altho beaten, we were the last troops in the field, or engaged.

I learned afterwards through General Lee and others that General Hardee had endeavored to throw the whole brunt of the fight, on Lee's Corps, and instead of doing what he had engaged to do, attack the enemy in his intrenchments, he only drove their skirmishers from their rifle pits, and their cavalry from their extreme right, and then, halting, awaiting the result of Lee's attack before proceeding further.

It was not the first time that he had been charged with the same want of faith and unmilitary conduct.[83]

Night soon after closed in on us, and the firing which had been continued at long range, ceased. Most of our killed and wounded fell into the hands of the enemy, and the army certainly gained no credit on this occasion. Altho the loss in killed and wounded in this battle, was, considering all the circumstances, comparatively small, yet it cost us the lives of many valuable officers.

I never saw our men fight with so little spirit as at Jonesboro, but I think that in some measure I have accounted for it in the preceding pages.

During the night of the 31st, our Division received orders, along with the others of Lee's Corps, to return to Atlanta, and to draw out from our position at about two o'clock in the morning. At that hour the troops were under arms, Hardee's Corps extending their front, occupying our works, and facing the enemy in a single line. After some delay, just as day was breaking, we began to get clear of our lines, whilst the enemy, detecting our movement, began shelling the rear of our column severely. My brigade brought up the rear, suffering to some extent from their fire. It had the good effect, however, of keeping the column well closed up, and in a short time we were clear of their missiles. Our route lay by a road which ran nearly parallel with the R.R., and at a distance from it varying from one and a half to three miles.[84]

During the day we had a slight skirmish with the enemy, and for a time there was every reason to expect an attack. After marching about half the distance from Jonesboro to Atlanta, we received orders to halt, and form "line of battle". Our skirmishers were thrown out, and preparations made to resist an attack. None, however, was made, altho but a short distance separated the opposing forces, and, night closing in, the men lay on their arms, and were held in readiness for any emergency.[85]

ATLANTA EVACUATED

(The Narrative)

About midnight, many heavy explosions at a great distance and in a northerly direction, were heard, whilst at the same time the reflected light against the clouds of what appeared to be a considerable conflagration, could be distinctly seen, and the impression soon became general that Atlanta was being evacuated. Our surmises proved correct. The reports we heard were the blowing up of our magazines there, and the burning of several storehouses containing a considerable amount of quartermaster's and commissary's stores, as well as trains of cars, locomotives, etc.[86]

I was told by many persons who were present whilst Atlanta was being evacuated, that they were surprised and astonished see the great amount of supplies, consisting of sugar, bacon, coffee, whiskey, shoes, and clothing of every description, that were given over to the flames and destroyed, whilst they had been under the impression that no such stores existed with the army, and they, as well as most of the officers of the army, knew that for these very articles the rank and file of the army had been much in want, and had suffered greatly, altho requisitions had repeatedly been made for them, and had invariably been returned with the indorsement that the articles wanted were not on hand. On one or two other occasions, I happened myself to be an eye-witness of very nearly the same condition of things as was described to me at that time.

At an early hour on the morning of the 2nd of September, our corps commenced their march, but not now in the direction of Atlanta. Turning off abruptly from the road on which we had been marching the day before, we struck out almost due east, in the direction of the small town called McDonough, in which direction General Stewart also, with his corps and the other troops which he had with him, holding Atlanta, was now also retreating. The Army of Tennessee was now in a most critical position, separated in three distinct bodies, with the enemy between them at two points. The enemy with two-thirds of his force cut us off from Hardee at Jonesboro. The same state of things existed between ourselves and Stewart, whilst a considerable force threatened us in front, following in pursuit as we retired towards McDonough.[87] Sherman had attacked Hardee in his lines before Jonesboro on the afternoon of the 1st of September, the day after our fight there, had broken his line and defeated him. Nothing saved him and the force under his command but the mistakes made by two of the Yankee corps commanders, who, having been sent to gain his rear whilst a general attack was made on his front, took the wrong roads, and only found out their mistake too late to intercept him in his retreat.[88] Hardee is said to have shown much skill in extricating himself from his perilous position, and in the selection of a new one about eight miles in his rear, near Lovejoy's Station, on the Macon R.R., covering the McDonough road, by which the other portions of the army were expected to rejoin him, and again be concentrated.[89] After a long and tedious march, having made a detour of nearly fifty miles, we succeeded in reaching him the evening of the third.

General Sherman lost one of the most favorable opportunities ever offered to a general of destroying his antagonist, with one exception, when the positions were reversed, and General Hood threw away a golden opportunity, at a later period,[90] that ever came under my personal observation during my military life. He seems to have been aware of it also, and to a certain extent acknowledged his error, I have been told; but at the same time attributed his failure to the densely wooded nature of the country in the vicinity of these last operations of the campaign, and to the few roads by which he could move his army.

Altho these excuses are plausible to some extent, yet I can not help thinking that at this time he showed less skill as a commander and general than at any other time during the campaigns he made against us, and with which I happened to be familiar.

Our Division was now commanded by Major General Edward Johnson. He had just been assigned to the Army of Tennessee, and had formerly belonged to the Army of Northern Virginia, where he had served with great credit, but had unfortunately been captured at Spottsylvania Court House early in the summer, and had just been exchanged, at Charleston, a month or two before he joined us in Georgia. The wound of General Patton Anderson at Jonesboro left the command of the Division vacant, and we were most fortunate in having him (Johnson) henceforth as our commander. My association with him was satisfactory in the extreme, and I say without hesitation that he was the best Division commander I ever met with, a thorough soldier and capable officer. I have but little doubt but that as a corps commander he would have proved himself far superior to others that I knew, and it is much to be regretted that our Generals as a general rule were so far inferior to him. Had it been otherwise, the result of our contest might have been different. Under his charge, the Division soon regained its former high character, and was again regarded as the first in the Army of Tennessee.[91]

Again we found ourselves on reaching Lovejoy's Station, with the enemy in our front, and until the evening of the 7th, we were at it again night and day. My brigade occupied the right of the army. Nothing out of the usual course worthy of mention occurred during this short space, excepting that on the last named evening, General Johnson was sent to the extreme left of the enemy's line, with two batteries of artillery and three brigades, to cannonade them in their works. A demonstration without making a regular attack was intended, but for what purpose I never learned. After getting clear of our own right, we advanced quickly, got possession of rather a commanding eminence, and opened heavily with our guns. Two brigades were held in hand near the batteries, whilst my own was pushed forward several hundred yards in advance, to receive any attack made from the Yankee works. The artillery played over our heads, whilst some skirmishing took place, but we could not draw them out, and about dusk we withdrew.[92]

On the following morning, whilst lying on a bed of straw in an old barn, where I had sought shelter from a heavy rain that had been falling during the night, unwilling to get up and leave so luxurious a couch, it suddenly struck me that I missed the regular pattering of the picket firing, and that I had not heard the report of a single piece of artillery. I called the attention of several officers near me to the fact, and as it was then broad daylight, we commented on so unusual a circumstance, and all of us immediately got up. Before we had finished washing, the officer of the day came in and reported the fact that the enemy had disappeared during the night. Further information was soon after received, confirming what we had already heard, and the joyful news was spread along the line that the enemy had retired, that our cavalry, supported by a large body of infantry,[93] was following and watching their movements. All was soon in readiness for any movement that might be ordered, but we were not called upon.

The enemy retreated towards Atlanta, and we were glad enough to let them go unmolested. Sherman's army, as weary and exhausted as ourselves, required rest, re-equipping and re-organizing, and, contented with the result of the campaign, he brought it to an end by retiring from the field, leaving us in our last position near Lovejoy's, whilst he fell back towards Atlanta.[94]

The campaign had lasted four months to a day, during which period scarcely a day had passed without an engagement of some kind, having fought over a space of one hundred and thirty-two miles. There were but twelve days during that period that I had not been under fire, either of their artillery or infantry, the same being the case with nearly the entire command. The brigade had taken part in seven general engagements, had been engaged in many skirmishes, and nearly one-third of the force had done picket duty daily, which alone was a task of great danger and hardship. Night after night, the whole force had lain upon its arms, in constant apprehension of an attack, whilst during the day and the greater part of the night they were engaged in throwing up lines of breastworks, or strengthening and repairing them. The marches, it is true, were generally short ones but were for the most part made at night and conducted with great order and regularity, and the men in constant readiness to make or repel an attack.

When the campaign opened in May, the effective force of brigade officers and men, including "litter bearers", numbered about		1,900
About 100 recruits and 100 convalescents joined during the campaign		200
		2,100
We lost in killed and wounded	1,250	
" " " prisoners and missing	150	
" sent to rear sick	75	
	1,475	1,475
Effective strength 8th of September, 1864		625

As soon as it was positively ascertained that Sherman had retreated to Atlanta, and that in so doing the campaign had come to an end, the troops went into regular encampments, making themselves as comfortable as circumstances would permit, and immediate and active steps were taken to supply an adequate amount of equipments, shoes, clothing, and the like. A few days after the withdrawal of the enemy, an armistice of ten days was agreed upon between the commanding generals, partly to give rest and a breathing spell to the men, to reorganize and recruit, but avowedly for the purpose of exchanging prisoners and removing the citizens of Atlanta whom Sherman had determined to force beyond his lines, as well as many others in the adjacent country who declined to take the oath professing loyalty to the U.S., and a regret for past offences. As may be supposed, there was much suffering occasioned by this forced exodus, and a great part of the transportation of the army was put into requisition to effect the removals.[95]

By the army this respite from active service in the field was hailed with many evidences of satisfaction, as the men stood in great need of rest and refreshment, being nearly worn down by the hardships and heavy duty to which they had been subjected for so long a period. Their numbers were much diminished by the casualties of war. I do not think that men ever enjoyed with a keener relish the delightful repose of the two weeks that succeeded.

The loss of the army during the period from the time that Hood took command until the 8th of September, I have never yet been able to ascertain. It must have greatly exceeded that incurred whilst under the command of Johnston, whilst the loss inflicted on the enemy did not, I believe, equal our own.[96]

Sherman had succeeded in his grand object, the capture of Atlanta, and the destruction of our communications east and west by our most important and direct railroad routes. I believe as before stated that had not Johnston been removed, he would have followed him in his purpose, and not only have driven him back across the Chattahoochie, but would have forced him to retire to Chattanooga, and I think the battle which would have been fought on the 18th, or at the latest, the 19th, of July, would have settled that point. General Hood could neither see nor comprehend the tactics or plans of General Johnston, lost the opportunities, when offered, that the latter had been manouvering for, assumed the offensive in the wrong way and at the wrong time, and instead of adhering to his, Johnston's wise policy, took a directly opposite view of the military situation, the consequence of which was the loss of the campaign and very nearly the whole army.[97]

At this encampment near Lovejoy's Station, on the Macon and Atlanta R.R., the officers of higher rank had at last an opportunity of comparing notes and interchanging opinions on the operations of the past four months. The necessity for continued presence with their commands had kept them too busy, and allowed them no time to visit each other, but now much of their leisure time was passed in this way, and it was surprising to note how the many views and experiences harmonized with one another. I learned more of the events not connected with my own command in these few days than during the entire time occupied by the campaign.

The expertness exhibited by our troops in throwing up a defensive line of works from long habit and much practice was very remarkable. Whenever we halted within reach of the enemy, advanced or fell back from point to point, a line of battle was formed, the ground having been previously selected by the proper officers, and before the command broke ranks, the tool wagon drove up, its contents were distributed, the companies told off into working parties, and immediately after stacking arms, every man would be at work for at least an hour, at the end of which a very respectable and strong obstruction to the enemy would be raised. After that only a sufficient number to keep all the tools in use was employed, parties regularly relieving each other, and the work of enlarging, strengthening, and adding additional defenses, would go on almost as long as we remained there, so that in most instances our works might almost be called formidable, and we were never driven from them. Even our picket lines, being prepared with the same care, tho on a much smaller scale, served to check many an attack made against them in force. This hard labor but very necessary precaution, was always cheerfully performed, and carried on with much spirit and emulation.

To give some idea of the severity of fire between two opposing armies, in the positions occupied by ourselves and the enemy near Atlanta, and during which period no general engagement took place, I will mention the result of some observations made the morning after the Yankees withdrew from our front, and when they moved off towards Jonesboro.[98] I went over much of the ground that had been occupied by them, but have reference chiefly to that portion of it in front of our brigade. The first picket line that we prepared was about six hundred yards from the third and last one from which we were never driven, and that one distant about from 200 to 250 yards from our main works. Over the first named space many sharp contests had taken place, and at all times the firing was incessant. The ground had been densely wooded, the growth being principally small oak and hickory trees. Even our pickets had not been able to descry the main Yankee line, during the earlier part of the three weeks which followed, but for some time before they retired, their entire line and successive works were plainly to be seen from our main works. The growth had been cut away principally by the fire of artillery and rifles from both sides. Saplings as large as a stout man's thigh were so weakened and frayed by bullets from the rifles that they had not in most instances the power of resisting the most ordinary breezes, and had fallen to the ground. Scarcely a shrub or a tree was left standing, and such of the latter, generally large ones, as remained, were much shattered and in a tottering condition. The head logs used to protect the men in the rifle pits were filled with bullets, much splintered, and in shreds. Scarcely a day passed that some of the pits were not filled up by the fire of their artillery, sometimes burying their occupants, who, if not killed or wounded, found it hard to extricate themselves. Finally, the picket lines were about (80) eighty yards apart, and at one point they had a battery only one hundred yards distant, and a space of another hundred yards separated it from their main line. It would be supposed that at so short a distance our sharpshooters could have prevented their gunners from working the pieces, but it must be remembered that the Yankee sharpshooters were also watching for anyone to expose his person by shooting at the artillerists, whilst at the same time, they, the gunners, were protected by iron, bullet-proof shutters, dropping in front of the embrasures, so arranged that the piece could be aimed even when the shutters were lowered. When ready to fire, the contrivance was raised on its hinges by a lanyard, and the piece discharged without exposing anyone in the battery. In spite of all our efforts, we could make no impression on it, or check its fire for a moment. Opposed to a brigade on our right was a battery similarly arranged, distant only eighty yards from its picket lines. We succeeded several times in repulsing serious attacks made for the possession of those advanced works. At some points of our lines, in other portions of the army, the main body of the enemy had worked up to within 100 and 200 yards, so close that, excepting after dark, it was impossible to throw out any skirmishers or videttes. Yet we were so thoroughly secure in our strong works, and there were so many obstacles in the way before they could be reached, in the shape of abattis, fallen trees, and lines of sharpened stakes, that I do not believe that had they come on in thrice their number they could have made any impression on us.

Many and earnest were the hopes expressed that they would try it, and I am assured that the slaughter would have been terrible, and the result most satisfactory, but unfortunately for us, Sherman was too wise and prudent to do so, and afterwards adopted a surer and more effectual method of obtaining possession of Atlanta.

Before the armistice had half expired, it became known to the troops that in a few days our position would be changed. About the 18th of September, the greater part of the army were on the route, marching in a north-westerly direction towards a point on the Atlanta and West Point R.R., called Palmetto Station, and reached it after a three-day's march. I do not know that the terms of the armistice were infringed by this movement, as it had been agreed on that neither army should approach within a certain distance of the other during its continuance, and altho our relative positions were changed by it, yet we were still outside the prescribed limit.[99] Here we threw up a defensive line, and preparations were made for active operations, but what were the objects of this new campaign, no one could determine.[100] President Davis arrived on a visit to the army for a few days on or about the 24th, and on the 26th, the army having been drawn up under arms in rear of their works, were reviewed and inspected by him in that position. His reception was even more than cold.[101] The men still felt sore at the result of the late operations. The press and the country generally had been unjust towards them, and had visited upon their heads the obloquy which should have properly been borne by the President and his advisers and their tool, our Commanding General. Never did men deserve censure less than the rank and file as well as most of the officers of the Army of Tennessee. Comparisons not only unfavorable, but often insulting, were drawn between our own and the Army of Northern Virginia, commanded by General Lee. Under the circumstances, it was very natural that the attention of the people should be more attracted by the operations of the Virginia army than our own. Its great success had brought it into high favor, and men had brought themselves to believe that upon them, and them alone, hinged the fate of the Confederacy. General Lee was popular, and deservedly so, with the masses, but he was not faultless, as many supposed, and it had so become the habit to praise him and his men on all occasions, that even when failure and mistakes were too evident to be controverted, a lenient public would too easily find a loophole to escape by, or some plausible pretext to shield them from censure. Far be it from me to detract one iota from the fame and laurels won by those brave men. Well did they deserve the admiration of their countrymen, and I, for one, most gratefully render it; but that they alone should be encouraged, mistakes and failures forgiven, and be regarded as the only army that deserved commendation, whilst others had endured as great sufferings, contended as frequently with the enemy, against as great odds, perhaps under more adverse circumstances, were not infrequently reproached, or read or heard of unfavorable or detracting comparisons, was neither just nor generous to men who had made as many sacrifices, and had striven as hard to do their duty as the latter had done.

The Government and chiefs in the various supply departments gave by far the greater part of their attention and means to the troops of Virginia. Their clothing was of far better material, more frequently supplied, rations of better quality, whilst coffee, sugar, tea, luxuries unknown amongst us during the last eighteen months of the war, always composed a part of their ration.[102] For our supplies, we were most often dependent upon our own commander, who had to play the Quartermaster and Commissary General as well as attend to his other duties in the field, and it not infrequently happened that supplies and clothing that had been collected by his subordinates for immediate use, by an order from Richmond, instead of being sent to his own army, were transferred to Virginia.

Attention has seldom been called to the fact that whilst General Lee was battling against numbers, it is true, far in excess of his own, as were we also, that the armies opposing him were composed of an inferior class of men, principally freshly imported foreigners, or the sweepings of the great cities of the Northern and Eastern states, whilst the material of the Yankee army of the west was made up almost entirely of hardy, native-born Americans from the Western and Northwestern states, whose habits, mode of life, and familiarity with weapons, made them far more formidable antagonists than their comrades on the seaboard, and had enlisted from very different motives. Of the many hundred prisoners that I came in contact with, I could not help noticing the fact, how few foreigners were among them, certainly not exceeding one in ten.

The untimely end of General A.S. Johnston, when the Battle of Shiloh was just won, whose death saved the Northern Army from destruction or capture; the unpopularity of General Bragg, with some of his political lieutenants, in the Confederacy; and the fatal error in removing General Joseph Johnston on the eve of battle, and at the crisis of the campaign, were unfortunate events, which not only robbed the army of much "eclat" which it would have acquired, but actually turned successes into a reverse, and brought about eventually many disasters.

The cause, however, of the dissatisfaction to which I have alluded, was principally owing to the removal of General Joseph Johnston and the appointment of General Hood to the command. The skill and energy of the former, together with the confidence felt in his ability by all, had given the men a reliance on their own superiority and a certain belief that they would eventually beat the enemy, save Atlanta, and recover the country as far north as Chattanooga.

Hood's exhibition of generalship whilst with the army, and up to the time of his promotion to its command, had proved him unfitted for the command of a corps, so that it is not surprising that as their leader, the army received the announcement with very bad grace, and with no little murmuring. Shortly after assuming the command, and it became evident what his plan of operations was to be, and system of attacks, it was seen that if continued, a very few more engagements would destroy the whole army, and that the lives of men were being thrown away to no purpose, he not having eye or head to take advantage of the successes which the army twice gained by its valor, which Joseph Johnston or Stonewall Jackson would have seized with avidity, and have brought about a very different result.

Owing to its reverses as well as to the other causes which I have mentioned, our army to a certain extent had lost some of its spirit and discipline, during the last two months, and were in no very good humor with the Government, and particularly with Mr. Davis, and they showed it while he passed along the lines. No cheers saluted him, countenances were depressed and sullen. An occasional murmur could be heard, growing more distinct, as he passed from left to right, and a voice here and there would call out, "Give us Johnston! Give us our old Commander!" and other remarks of a similar nature. This happened in many brigades. Arrests and threats of punishment alone prevented the cry from becoming loud and general. Still, in many instances he must have heard them.

Our Brigade, I am glad to say, exhibited no such want of discipline, but remained firm and steady, looking sternly to the front, altho they heartily endorsed the prevalent feeling, and felt every desire to express their disapprobation.

One could not help remarking the expression of President Davis's countenance as he passed by. He looked thin, care-worn, and angry. A scornful expression rested on it. He scarcely deigned to lift his hat from his head as we saluted. General Hood, with the Corps commanders, their staffs, and a large escort, accompanied him. All looked uneasy and apprehensive. I never remember taking part in an affair of the kind so cheerless and unsatisfactory as this one was, where everyone seemed anxious to have it over.

President Davis remained a day or two longer, a guest of the Commanding General. During that time the details and arrangements were no doubt fully discussed and determined on, which resulted in the unfortunate campaign that followed, which speedily brought to an end all our bright hopes of independence, peace, and rest, for which we had been so long and arduously battling, hurrying on the final scene which left us a conquered and enslaved people, at the mercy of a heartless, unscrupulous, and tyrannical enemy.[103]

NOTES TO CHAPTER 9

[1] Having completed the crossing of the Chattahoochee on July 17, Sherman's army advanced on the 18th in what he described as a "general right wheel." Thomas's Army of the Cumberland on the right, facing Peachtree Creek, formed the pivot with Schofield and McPherson making a wide arc to the east and south, the latter striking the railroad from Augusta some seven miles east of Decatur. There he turned west toward Atlanta, breaking up the railroad as he progressed, and that night joined forces with Schofield near Decatur. On the 19th, Thomas was crossing Peachtree Creek, while Schofield and McPherson advanced from the east along the railroad and just to the north of it. The three converging armies met little opposition. Manigault describes the withdrawal of Hood's old corps, now under Cheatham, from the Peachtree Creek line and its transfer to the right to meet the threat posed from that direction by Schofield and McPherson. *Sherman,* II, 71-72.

[2] Formerly Polk's, but now commanded by Lt. Gen. Alexander P. Stewart under whom Loring served as a division commander after temporarily leading the corps.

[3] In this, the Battle of Peachtree Creek, Hood attempted to carry out Johnston's intention of assaulting the enemy as he was crossing the creek, with his forces divided, as indeed they were when Schofield and McPherson marched off on their swing to the east. His object was to drive Thomas into the narrow space between Peachtree Creek and the Chattahoochee, pen him up and crush him. By the time Hood was able to mount the attack with Hardee's and Stewart's corps on the 20th, however, having been delayed by extending his line to the right to protect that threatened flank, Thomas's entire command was over Peachtree Creek, throwing up breastworks, and the opportunity lost of catching him in the act of crossing. Hood had intended to take advantage of the gap of about two miles between Thomas' left and Schofield's right and was initially successful as Bate's division of Hardee's corps poured into the opening. Redoubtable defensive fighter that he was, Thomas brought up his reserves and reestablished his line, aided by a galling artillery fire from the Federal guns north of the creek. On the rest of the front, the fighting was bitter but inconclusive. Just as Cleburne's reserve division of Hardee's corps was about to be thrown into the fray, it was suddenly called off to the right to oppose McPherson's threatening advance along the railroad, a vital fact that Hood failed to mention, when he attempted to make a scapegoat out of Hardee. There was no love lost between the two men, Hardee regarding Hood as incompetent and the latter claiming that Hardee "did nothing more than skirmish with the enemy," a charge not borne out by the facts. The Confederates suffered a bloody repulse, casualties amounting to some 5,000 including prisoners, men they could ill afford to lose. *O.R.,* XXXVIII, pt. 1, 156-157, 290; pt. 3, 630-631, 698, 870-873; *Buck,* 230-232; Horn, *The Army of Tennessee,* 352-353; *Hood,* 165-172; *Sherman,* II, 72-73.

[4] Brig. Gen. Daniel C. Govan, commanding an Arkansas brigade in Cleburne's division of Hardee's corps.

[5] Manigault here lends credence to Hood's assertions regarding the cause of the failure of the Confederate assault on Thomas at Peachtree Creek on July 20. In his official report, Hood says that Hardee "failed to push the attack as ordered...I have every reason to believe that our attack would have been successful had my order been executed. I am strengthened in this opinion by information since obtained through Brigadier General Govan, some time a prisoner in the enemy's hands." Govan was subsequently captured at the Battle of Jonesboro. *Hood*, 323; *O.R.*, XXXVIII, pt. 3, 631.

[6] These statements attributed to Sherman were taken from his official report, in which he put the Confederate loss at not short of 5,000 (*O.R.*, XXXVIII, pt. 1, 71). Writing after the war he was more precise, placing the Confederate casualities at 4,796 and his own at 1,710. *Battles and Leaders*, IV, 253.

[7] A native of Connecticut, whose family had moved to South Carolina, the state of his mother's birth, Clement H. Stevens was a Charleston banker, cashier of the Planters and Mechanics, at the outbreak of the war. Something of an inventor, he was responsible for the construction of the so-called "iron battery" — the wooden structure was faced with railroad iron — which participated in the initial bombardment of Fort Sumter. At first Manassas, while serving as an aide to his brother-in-law, Gen. Barnard E. Bee, who fell there, Stevens was severely wounded. Subsequently elected colonel of the 24th South Carolina, he took part in the action of Secessionville and then was transferred, like Manigault, to the West. Badly wounded again at Chickamauga, he won the praise of his brigade commander, States Rights Gist, a fellow South Carolinian, as the "iron-nerved" and was called by his men "Rock" Stevens. He was promoted brigadier general in January 1864, and served with distinction in the Atlanta campaign, leading a brigade in Walker's division of Hardee's corps. Grievously wounded a third time at Peachtree Creek, he died a few days later in Atlanta on July 25. *Generals in Gray*, 291-292; *O.R.*, XXXVIII, pt. 3, 655.

[8] Cleburne referred to this day's fighting as the "bitterest" of his life. "Surely it was one of the most trying ordeals that men can be subjected to," wrote a member of his staff. "Forced strictly to act upon the defensive, they had to endure the whole day, not only the harassing and deadly fire of small arms from commanding ground, but also that of the enfilade and reverse of powerful artillery, especially that of De Gress' First Illinois Battery of 20-pound Parrotts...To add to the discomforts, the day was fearfully hot, and it seemed that a modern Joshua had appeared and commanded the sun to stand still. Never was its sinking more gladly hailed." (*Buck*, 233-234; *S.H.S.P.*, VIII, 350-351). Gen. J.A. Smith, commanding the Texas brigade on Cheatham's right, described in his report the effect of the overwhelming artillery fire of De Gress' battery: "I have never before witnessed such accurate and destructive cannonading. In a few minutes 40 men were killed and over 100 wounded by this battery alone. In the Eighteenth Texas Cavalry, dismounted, 17 out of 18 men composing one company were placed hors de combat by one shot alone." *O.R.*, XXXVIII, pt. 3, 746.

[9] The flank attack on McPherson was made by Hardee's corps alone, although supported by Wheeler's cavalry. Horn, *The Army of Tennessee*, 354-355; *O.R.*, XXXVIII, pt. 3, 631.

[10] The first clash occurred about noon, when Bate's and Walker's divisions on Hardee's right attacked Dodge's Sixteenth Corps. *Cox*, 168.

[11] This was the bald hill where McPherson's left had been refused and intrenched, at right angles to the main line. Horn, *The Army of Tennessee*, 356.

[12] Dodge's Sixteenth Corps, which had been in reserve and arrived purely by chance just as Hardee's attack was getting under way. *Battles and Leaders*, IV, 326; *S.H.S.P.*, VIII, 360-361.

[13] Establishing the timing of a military action in the 1860's, where large numbers of troops were involved during the excitement and confusion of battle, is difficult at best, depending, as it does, on an individual's memory at a time when his mind is quite obviously on other things. The problem is compounded by the fact that the same orders were not infrequently received and executed by different commanders at differing times. The case at hand is a good example. No less than twenty-one officers from both sides left written accounts of when they believed the advance was ordered or actually began. The estimates range from 1:30 P. M. to a "few minutes after 4:00," with nine placing the time at 3 or thereabouts, and five giving the hour as 4. Robert L. Rodgers, *Capture of the De Gress Battery in the Battle of Atlanta*, (n.p., n.d. — 1898?), 1-11, 19-26; *O.R.*, XXXVIII, pt. 3, 21-29, 58-59, 102-104, 115-117, 139-140, 147-148, 173-174, 179-180, 188-189, 195, 210, 217-218, 223-224, 245-247, 250-251, 260, 262, 265; *Sherman*, II, 80-81.

[14] This was the spearhead of the attack Hood ordered Cheatham to make against the Federal Fifteenth Corps in order to relieve the pressure on Hardee. Unfortunately, the latter had virtually suspended offensive action by the time the advance occurred, and this lack of coordination contributed to Hood's failure to attain his objectives. *Cox*, 173-175; *Battles and Leaders*, IV, 329.

[15] Col. John G. Coltart of the 50th Alabama. *O.R.*, XXXVIII, pt. 3, 648.

[16] Commanded by Col. William F. Brantley of the 29th Mississippi, who was made a brigadier general on July 26. Like Hindman, he was assassinated after the war, apparently the victim of a long-standing personal feud. *Generals in Gray*, 32-33.

[17] Like Brantley, Col. Jacob H. Sharp was promoted brigadier general four days later on July 26. He had replaced Gen. William F. Tucker, disabled by wounds at Resaca, in command of a brigade of Mississippians in Hindman's division, the latter now led by Brig. Gen. John C. Brown. *O.R.*, XXXVIII, pt. 3, 762; *Generals in Gray*, 273, 311.

[18] Edward C. Walthall was promoted major general on June 10 to rank from July 6, 1864. After a distinguished career in the army, he entered public life and served in the United States Senate almost continuously from 1885 until his death in 1898. *Generals in Gray*, 326; *Sykes*, 572.

[19] Lt. Col. Walker, who was to take command of the 10th South Carolina on the wounding of Col.Pressley, estimated the distance as "about three-quarters of a mile." Rodgers, *De Gress Battery*, 8.

[20] This was a section (2 guns) of Battery A of the First Illinois Regiment of Light Artillery. *Ibid.*, 8; *O.R.* XXXVIII, pt. 3, 179, 254.

[21] Deas' brigade, under Col. Coltart. Owing to buildings in its front, impassible fences, and slight curves in the road, this brigade drifted to the right, so that when it reached the picket reserve of the enemy, an empty gap of 150 yards existed between its left and the railroad. *Ibid*, 779-780.

[22] A graduate of the South Carolina Military Academy, Col. James F. Pressley had succeeded Manigault in command of the 10th South Carolina. *C.M.H.* V, 805.

[23] Manigault is in error here. Eight guns were captured by his brigade — Four 20-pounder Parrotts of De Gress' Battery H of the First Illinois Artillery; and four of the six light 12-pounders of Battery A of the same regiment (Rodgers, *De Gress Battery*, 4; *O.R.*, XXXVIII, pt. 3, 58-59). Doubtless, the 16 guns Manigault reported as taken from the enemy included the remaining two guns of Battery A of the First Illinois Artillery and the six pieces of Battery F, located south of the railroad, the caissons of which were, in fact, captured.

[24] The severity of the fighting is indicated by the losses suffered — In De Gress' battery, 14 men and 39 horses; and in Battery A, 32 men and 55 horses. Sherman said in his memoirs that every horse in De Gress' battery was killed. In the Federal counterattack, the latter's four 20-pounder Parrotts were recaptured, as were two of the pieces belonging to Battery A of the First Illinois, leaving a total of four guns of Battery A that Manigault's brigade captured and held (*O.R.*, XXXVIII, pt. 3, 262, 265, 364, 538-539; *Sherman*, II, 80, 83; *Cox*, 175; *Battles and Leaders*, IV, 288). After examining Manigault's account of the capture of the Union guns by his brigade at Atlanta on July 22, 1864, Col. Walker wrote the following memorandum:

"My recollection of this differs somewhat from yours and is as follows:

After taking the works and the battery *(Battery A of the First Illinois)* in front of the 10th Regt having been secured (This Battery I at once moved round by hand to our side of the Breastworks, through a gap, & detailed Co. A to man if need be — But some of our men having secured some of the limbers & others having been sent out from the main line, the Guns were carried in), you determined to cover the other captured guns & bring them off. You formed the line obliquely to the line of works, your left retired & were about to advance, when an attack of the Yankees caused you to retake your position in the breastworks. I do not remember that the 10th Reg't left the works further than this, until the final retreat. The left of the Brigade was certainly retired, but I have always thought with the object stated above & I derived my impression from orders given me by Willie Huger at that time.

I have always felt that Pressley's ordering the left of our Reg't & right of the 19th Reg't into the upper piazza of the wooden house in front of the line, which gave us complete control of the breastworks, contributed largely to the success of the attack. Certainly the attack had failed, until the effect of that fire was felt by the enemy. The credit for this manouver really belongs to me, as I made the suggestion to Pressley as we stood together at the foot of the steps of the house, during the temporary pause in the attack.

You could not have brought off the other guns captured by the Brigade. When we afterwards moved to the left I had skirmishers covering them & myself examined their position with a view to saving them if possible. They were in a thicket cleared only to the breastworks, *with no road or opening leading to the public road* which ran through the works, the gap made by which had been used to bring in the guns captured by the 10th Regt. There was only one possible way of getting them out & that was *over* the breastworks, which only could have been done with *tools* & we had none. I do not think you could have possibly done otherwise even if the enemy had left us undisturbed. You could not have saved those guns." *(Walker refers here to the four 20-pounder Parrotts of De Gress' battery captured just north of the Hurt House)*

[25] After carrying the works in their front, the 10th and the 19th South Carolina had swept to the left, clearing the enemy from the fortifications and taking position to the north of the Hurt house and De Gress' captured battery, where they were exposed to a galling fire on their left from the four guns of the 4th Ohio Battery and two of Battery F of the 2nd Missouri. *O.R.*, XXXVIII, pt. 3, 139, 174.

[26] Stovall's brigade of Clayton's division.

[27] It was Holtzclaw's brigade of Clayton's division (formerly Stewart's), commanded by Col. Bushrod Jones. *Ibid.*, 819.

[28] When Sherman observed the Confederate breakthrough from his headquarters near the Howard house to the northwest, he ordered Schofield to mass his artillery there and open on the enemy's flank. The latter scraped together about 20 pieces and found his mark with telling results, "the smooth guns firing spherical case-shot rapidly, and Cockerell's battery of 3-inch ordnance rifles double-shotting with canister; those admirable little guns proving as useful in a close encounter of this sort as they were in longer range. The advance of Cheatham was checked with terrible carnage." *Cox*, 173; *Sherman*, II, 81; *O.R.*, XXXVIII, pt. 1, 72.

[29] Northern accounts speak of the Fifteenth Federal corps rallying and driving back the enemy "pell mell," retaking the entrenchments and most of the guns in "superb style." (*Cox*, 173; *O.R.*, XXXVIII, pt. 1, 74, 157). It is evident, however, that this occurred *after* the withdrawal of Manigault's brigade, in compliance with the orders to which he took such exception. It was to these orders that Col. Walker referred when he wrote after the war that "Manigault's Brigade was subsequently ordered to our right, and finally, about dark, retired to the main line of works. We had no pressure of the enemy from our front during the occupation of the enemy's works and retired under orders." (Rodgers, *De Gress Battery*, 10).

For a detailed discussion of the attack made by Hindman's and Clayton's divisions of Cheatham's corps, eastward along the line of the Georgia Railroad outside of Atlanta July 22, 1864, see Appendix I. Manigault's brigade, which was a part of Hindman's division, then temporarily under the command of Brig. Gen. John C. Brown, spearheaded the assault that broke the Union line wide open and captured the celebrated De Gress Battery H of the 1st Illinois Light Artillery.

[30] In his official report, Sherman states that his casualties were 3,722 killed, wounded and prisoners and estimates the Confederate loss at "full 8,000 men" (*O.R.*, XXXVIII, pt. 1, 75). Hardee admitted a loss of 3,299 in his corps alone. *S.H.S.P.*, VIII, 367.

[31] "On the morning of the 22nd," Sherman wrote, "somewhat to my surprise the whole line (*along Peachtree Creek*) was found abandoned, and I confess I thought the enemy had resolved to give us Atlanta without further contest." *O.R.*, XXXVIII, pt. 1, 72.

[32] As previously noted, Manigault was under misapprehension as to the number of enemy guns captured on the 22nd. The correct figure was eight, of which four (De Gress' Battery) were subsequently recaptured by the enemy.

[33] Starke H. Oliver, who as a captain later commanded the 24th Alabama. *O.R.*, XXXVIII, pt. 3, 783-784; *C.M.H.*, VII, 132.

[34] The movement began on the morning of the 27th. *Sherman*, II, 88; *Cox*, 181.

[35] After the death of McPherson on July 22, Maj. Gen. John A. Logan, known to his troops as "Black Jack," as senior officer present was put temporarily in command of the Army of the Tennessee. When it came to picking a permanent successor to McPherson, however, Sherman took Thomas' advice and gave the job to a West Pointer, Maj. Gen. Oliver Otis Howard, then commanding the Fourth Corps of the Army of the Cumberland. This put Hooker's nose out of joint, as he not only ranked Howard but Sherman and Thomas as well. "Fighting Joe" promptly applied to be relieved from command of the Twentieth Corps, a request that was heartily approved by Thomas and quickly accepted by Sherman. "General Hooker was offended," the latter wrote in his memoirs, "because he was not chosen to succeed McPherson; but his chances were not even considered." Sherman and Thomas were both glad to get rid of him and he was shipped off to a desk job in the North. *Sherman*, II, 86.

[36] Stephen D. Lee, promoted lieutenant general to rank from July 23, assumed command of Hood's old corps on the 27th. The latter, since Hood's elevation to army command, had been temporarily led by Maj. Gen. Benjamin F. Cheatham of Tennessee. *O.R.*, XXXVIII, pt. 3, 789.

[37] Loring's division was a part of Stewart's corps (formerly Polk's).

[38] Manigault is correct. When Lee, under orders to check the enemy move to his left, marched out on the Lick Skillet Road, he found it in their possession. He at once formed Brown's division, of which Manigault's brigade was a part, on the left obliquely to the road, with Clayton's division on the right, the latter connecting by skirmishers with the main works around the city. *Ibid.*, 762-763.

[39] Sherman describes the Federal position as "well posted and partially covered." *Sherman*, II, 89.

[40] With Johnston (formerly Deas) on the right and Sharp in the center. *O.R.*, pt. 3, 789.

[41] Manigault's statement that the division on his right (i.e. Clayton's) "only threatened but did not go in" is incorrect. In his report, Clayton says that two brigades of his division, Gibson's and Baker's, fought "with gallantry and lost over one-half of their original numbers." *Ibid.*, 763, 821.

[42] To the contrary, Sharp reported that he found his right unable to carry the enemy's position due to an oblique fire too severe to be withstood. On that wing of his brigade "two gallant regiments," he wrote, "never known to falter when the order was to forward, were forced to retire." (*Ibid.*, 789-790). Referring to the Confederate repulse, Brown stated: "In many places the works were carried, but the enemy reinforced so rapidly and with such an immensely superior force, that

263

my troops were driven with great slaughter from them." (*Ibid.,* 767). Lee said much the same, describing how Brown "encountered temporary breastworks, from which he was driven back with considerable loss." (*Ibid.,* 763). These statements obviously cannot be reconciled with Manigault's assertions as to what Brown and Lee said.

[43] Manigault's description of the attack of his brigade is in direct conflict with the damaging testimony of his division commander, who wrote that when Deas' old brigade (Johnston's) was thrown back, he relieved it with his supporting brigade (Manigault's), which behaved badly and whose "demoralization was so great it could not be made effective." *Ibid.,* 763.

[44] Neither Brown nor Lee make any reference to this incident. In his report, Manigault does not elaborate, simply stating that the order for a third effort was countermanded. *Ibid.,* 782.

[45] There were actually three brigades, not five as stated by Manigault, that took part in Walthall's attack — Reynolds' and Cantey's in the first line, supported by Quarles' in the second. *Ibid.,* 927.

[46] No mention is made in Walthall's report or those of his brigade commanders of the "utter confusion and rout" to which Manigault refers. In regard to the attack that cost him 152 officers and almost 1,000 men, considerably more than one-third of his force, Walthall wrote: "If it had been possible for the daring of officers and the desperate fighting of the men to have overcome such odds in numbers and strength of position...the enemy must have been beaten, but double the force could not have accomplished what my division was ordered to undertake." *Ibid.,* 927.

[47] Manigault seems almost to protest too much concerning the conduct of his brigade. That he was not justifying it in his memoirs after the event, however, is made clear by the closing paragraph of his report, written just five days after the Battle of Ezra Church: "For the failure of the command to carry the point that they were ordered against I can scarcely blame either officers or men. They fought as gallantly as I have ever seen them do, but were outnumbered to too great an extent, and the position of the enemy, naturally a strong one, and rendered doubly so by their engineering skill, caused their able and well-sustained efforts to fail in any satisfactory results." (*Ibid.,* 782).

How then does one reconcile these words with those of Brig. Gen. Brown, Manigault's division commander, written only three days after the battle, when, after praising the conduct of his three other brigades, he said: "But justice to these commands which bore their part so nobly compels me to state that the greater portion of Manigault's brigade behaved badly"? (*Ibid.,* 768). The truth, perhaps, lies somewhere in between. In Manigault's defense, it should be pointed out that his brigade suffered casualties comparable to the other three, and that those of his regimental commanders who commented on the conduct of their troops said they "acted very well" or "behaved nobly." (*Ibid.,* 768, 783-784, 785-787). Different observers quite honestly draw conflicting conclusions from the same event and, especially in military reporting, much depends on whose ox is being gored.

[48] While Loring's division was not seriously engaged, Manigault is clearly mistaken in respect to Clayton's, as noted above.

[49] If Jefferson Davis, in getting rid of Johnston, had wanted offensive action,

Hood was certainly giving it to him. But in the process he was bleeding his army white and slowly undermining its faith in eventual victory. Later, in referring to the Battle of Ezra Church, Hardee, no friend of Hood's, would write: "No action of the campaign probably did so much to demoralize and dishearten the troops engaged in it" (*S.H.S.P.*, VIII, 340). Yet, the dogged spirit of the men in the ranks would not die. When a Northern picket called across the lines: "Well, Johnny, how many of you are left?" Back came the reply: "Oh! about enough for another killing." *Cox, 186.*

[50] *O.R.*, XXXVIII, pt. 1, 78.

[51] The bulk of the fighting at Ezra Church was done by Brown's and Walthall's divisions and three brigades of Clayton's. These units reported approximately 8,500 effectives present on July 31. So, allowing for the losses on the 28th of between 2,500 and 3,000, it would appear that Manigault was on the low side in his estimate of those engaged. *O.R.*, XXXVIII, pt. 3, 680, 768, 821, 927.

[52] This statement is not borne out by the *Official Records.* Brown's report listed the brigade losses in his division as follows: Johnston's (Deas'), 269; Sharp's, 214; Manigault's, 198; Brantley's, 126. *Ibid., 768.*

[53] Lt. Col. William L. Butler, commanding the 28th Alabama. *Ibid., 784.*

[54] The 24th Alabama and the 10th and 19th South Carolina were commanded at times by captains. When Adjutant James O. Ferrell of the 19th South Carolina reported that all the captains in his regiment were killed or wounded, Manigault ordered him to take command. Maj. John N. Slaughter led the 34th Alabama at Ezra Church. *Ibid., 768.*

[55] The return of casualities attached to Manigault's report, as compiled from the regimental lists, showed four officers killed and 16 wounded, not including those in the 10th South Carolina. *Ibid., 783.*

[56] Brown makes no mention in his report of being wounded, even slightly. (*Ibid.,* 767-768). Hood, however, confirms Manigault's statement. *Hood, 194.*

[57] At East Point, the railroad forked. The Macon & Western continued on slightly east of south to Macon, and the Atlanta & West Point branched off to the southwest on the way to Montgomery.

[58] Just prior to the Confederate attack on the 28th at Ezra Church, Sherman had decided on an all-out effort by his cavalry to cut the Macon railroad, Hood's main line of supply, south of Atlanta, while his army continued the siege of the city, keeping on the pressure by gradually extending its right flank to the south. For this purpose, he dispatched McCook's division of cavalry on a swing to the west and Stoneman's to the east, with orders to cut the Macon railroad in the vicinity of Jonesboro. Neither expedition accomplished its purpose. McCook did succeed in reaching the tracks at Lovejoy's Station, where he tore up two miles of rails and five of telegraph wire and burned two trains of cars. In addition, he fell upon a Confederate wagon train, and, according to Sherman, burned 500 wagons, killed 800 mules, and captured 72 officers and 350 men. After this considerable success, McCook started back, but was surrounded near Newnan, lost all his prisoners, and was forced to fight his way out, at a cost of more than 900 men killed and captured. On the other flank, Stoneman, although he did destroy 17 locomotives and

more than 100 cars, failed in his hope of liberating the Federal prisoners at Macon and even Andersonville, and ended up surrendering along with more than 500 of his men. As a result of the failure of both of these expeditions, Sherman became convinced that the cavalry alone could not do the job and that the main army itself would have to move against the railroad. *Sherman,* II, 96-98; *Hood,* 193-197.

[59] It was Brig. Gen. Marcellus A. Stovall's brigade, composed of the 1st Georgia State Troops and the 40th, 41st, 42nd, 43rd and 52nd Georgia Infantry. *O.R.,* XXXVIII, pt. 3, 664.

[60] These figures indicating the severity of the fire from the picket line are of much interest, as information of this kind is seldom available in such specific detail.

[61] Manigault refers here, of course, to artillery shell fire.

[62] This, indeed, was Hood's objective, approved by President Davis, who, after all the blood-letting of the 20th, 22nd and 28th of July, was coming around to a better appreciation of Joe Johnston's tactics. He wrote Hood: "The loss consequent on attacking *(the enemy)* in his entrenchments requires you to avoid that if practicable," and he endorsed moving against Sherman's communications (*O.R.,* XXXVIII, pt. 5, 946). Accordingly, Hood ordered Wheeler, with about half his troopers, some 4,500 men, to operate against the 250-odd miles of railroad that supplied Sherman from Nashville. This Wheeler did in a far-reaching raid that carried him north of Knoxville and to within a few miles of Nashville itself. Among the trophies of this, his last such extensive raid behind enemy lines, Wheeler listed the capture of 1,000 horses and mules, 200 wagons, 600 prisoners and 1,700 head of beef cattle. In addition, he said he had destroyed or captured more than 20 trains of cars loaded with supplies, ripped up mile after mile of track, and brought back with him some 3,000 recruits (a claim characterized as "sheer fantasy" by Thomas L. Connelly in his *Autumn of Glory: The Army of Tennessee, 1862-1865*), all at a cost of about 150 men killed, wounded and missing. *O.R.,* XXXVIII, pt. 3, 957-961; *Wheeler and his Cavalry,* 249-255; *DuBose,* 383-387; *Hood,* 198-200.

[63] Sherman had assigned the Twentieth Corps to protect his trains, his hospitals and the railroad bridge across the Chattahoochee. *Sherman,* II, 103.

[64] Despite his exploits, the damage done by Wheeler to Sherman's communications was soon repaired and had no lasting effect on the outcome of the campaign. As Hood later acknowledged: "So vast were the facilities of the Federal commander to reinforce his line ...extending from Nashville to Atlanta...I became convinced...that no sufficiently effective number of cavalry could be assembled in the Confederacy to interrupt the enemy's line of supplies to an extent to compel him to retreat." *Hood,* 200.

[65] Manigault's inclination to belittle the cavalry is once again evident. While the strategic wisdom of the raid may be questioned, it seems less than generous on his part to make light of Wheeler's accomplishments, particularly in view of the latter's recent defeats of McCook and Stoneman. Cox, however, agreed with Manigault, describing the damage done to the railroad by Wheeler as "trifling." (*Cox,* 196.) On the other hand, Hood did not share Manigault's low opinion of the mounted arm, writing after the war: "It becomes my duty, as well as my pleasure, to make acknowledgment of the valuable services of the cavalry of the Army of Tennessee during my operations in Georgia...The Confederacy possessed, in my opinion, no body of cavalry superior to Wheeler and his command." *Hood,* 202.

[66] Reference here is to Gen. Kilpatrick's raid from which he returned on Aug. 22, telling Sherman he had destroyed three miles of the railroad about Jonesboro, which he reckoned it would take 10 days to repair. When, on the following day, Sherman observed trains coming into Atlanta from the south, he "became more than ever convinced that cavalry could not or would not work hard enough to destroy a railroad properly." *Sherman,* II, 104.

[67] The movement began on Aug. 25 and, by the evening of the 27th, Sherman's entire army, except for the Twentieth Corps, was in position along the road from Atlanta to Sandtown, ready to move against the railroads south of the city.

[68] Manigault's picture of the cavalry as being so weak that it could furnish no information appears overdrawn. Cox wrote that the Confederate "horsemen, skirmishing with Garrard on the north and with Kilpatrick on the south, were able to locate the National forces with sufficient accuracy." *Cox,* 197.

[69] Apparently, Hardee was the source of the contention that Hood had been completely taken in and thought Sherman was in full retreat, his lines of supply and communication cut by Wheeler. In his official report Hardee wrote: "General Hood believed the enemy to be retreating for want of supplies. He even ordered Gen. W.H. Jackson, then commanding the cavalry of the army, to harass the rear of the retreating enemy. General Jackson endeavored to convince him of his error, but to no purpose" (*O.R.,* XXXVIII, pt. 3, 700). At the time of Johnston's surrender in North Carolina the following spring, Hardee told Cox that Hood's illusion had been confirmed by the story of an old woman who vainly sought food from some of Schofield's men, only to be told they didn't have enough for themselves. Hardee related that Hood, to whom she had been conducted, seized upon her statement that the Northern forces were short of rations, exclaiming that it corroborated his belief that Sherman was crossing the Chattahoochee at Sandtown. "To this conviction," Cox wrote, "he stubbornly adhered to forty-eight hours longer, when it was quite too late to make new combinations to keep his adversary from the railroad." (*Cox,* 197-198). Understandably Hood, in his report and especially in his memoirs written some 15 years after the war, gave the impression that he was right on top of things all along and made no mention of the idea that Sherman might be in retreat. *O.R.,* XXXVIII, pt. 3, 632-633; *Hood,* 203-204.

[70] It was not until 9 a.m. of the 31st that Cleburne, temporarily commanding Hardee's corps, was in position at Jonesboro; and Lee's corps did not arrive until two hours later. *Cox,* 199; *O.R.,* XXXVIII, pt. 3, 773.

[71] Lee's and Hardee's corps were, in fact, in the presence of Sherman's entire army, with the exception of the Twentieth Corps left behind to guard the railroad bridge across the Chattahoochee. *Cox,* 199; *S.H.S.P.,* VIII, 343.

[72] The division, once again under the command of Patton Anderson, was pulled out of the trenches at 4 a.m. Aug. 30 and started in the direction of East Point. Continuing its march later in the day, it finally reached Jonesboro about 11 a.m. of the 31st. "The darkness of the night, the dense woods through which we frequently marched without roads, the want of shoes by many, and the lack of recent exercise by all, contributed to induce a degree of straggling which I do not remember to have seen exceeded in any former march of the kind," wrote Anderson in his report. *O.R.,* XXXVIII, pt. 3, 772-773.

[73] Manigault's brigade had evidently come in contact with troops of Gen.

Hascall's division of Schofield's Twenty-Third Corps on the extreme left of Sherman's army advancing on Jonesboro. *O.R., XXXVIII,* pt. 2, 514, 518-519; *Sherman,* II, 106.

[74] In the evening of Aug. 30, Hood telegraphed Hardee at Rough and Ready, summoning him to Atlanta, and a railroad engine was sent to carry him there. On his arrival at headquarters, orders were issued for Hardee and Lee to attack the enemy at Jonesboro and, if possible, drive him across the Flint River. That night Hardee returned by rail, reaching Jonesboro before daybreak. *S.H.S.P.,* VIII, 342.

[75] Gen. Anderson states that Sharp's, Deas' and Brantley's brigades were placed from right to left in the front line under his immediate direction, while command of the supporting line was relinquished to Maj. Gen. Clayton, one of the other division leaders in Lee's corps. The second line consisted of Gibson's and Holtzclaw's brigades of Clayton's division and Manigault's of Anderson's, the latter on the far left. *O.R., XXXVIII,* pt. 3, 773, 822.

[76] In extenuation of his own shortcomings, Hood, in his memoirs, twice cites statements by Stephen D. Lee regarding the reluctance of the troops to charge breastworks and their lack of the necessary spirit to ensure success. (*Hood,* 184-185, 195). Small wonder in view of what they had been subjected to since Hood had taken over from "Old Joe"! As Stanley Horn so aptly put it, the men "were tired and worn down — yes, and discouraged. But it was not a matter of the spirit. The spirit, indeed, was willing, but the flesh was weak." Horn, *The Army of Tennessee,* 362.

[77] Stevenson's division. *O.R., XXXVIII,* pt. 3, 824.

[78] A close examination of the *Official Records* indicates, as previously noted, that the front line on the right consisted, from right to left, of Sharp's, Deas' and Brantley's brigades of Anderson's division, and the second line of Holtzclaw's and Gibson's brigades of Clayton's division and Manigault's of Anderson's. The third brigade of Clayton's division, Stovall's, had been sent to the left to support Stevenson's division and had been placed in the second line there, separated from Manigault by Cumming's brigade of Stevenson's division. It would thus appear that the fourth brigade in the front line which Manigault mistakenly refers to as one of Clayton's, was, in fact, Brown's of Stevenson's division. *Ibid.,* 672, 764, 773, 821-822, 824, 835, 857-858; *S.H.S.P.,* VIII, 343.

[79] In his report, Clayton wrote: "Having a considerable quantity of brushwood to go through, and to pass the breastworks, both of which I knew would create confusion in the line, I ordered that it should halt as soon as it should reach the open field beyond, and gave the order to move forward as soon as the first line moved." *O.R., XXXVIII,* pt. 3, 822.

[80] Anderson, who was severely wounded, paints a somewhat brighter picture in his report, saying that the troops advanced with spirit and determination to within pistol-shot of the enemy's works. There, however, they lay down, waiting for reinforcements, and were subjected to a deadly fire from which they suffered heavily and, in the end, were compelled to retire (*Ibid.,* 773-775). Clayton summed it up in these words: "Unfortunately a large portion of the whole command stopped in the rifle-pits of the enemy, behind piles of rails and a fence running nearly parallel to his breast-works, and to this circumstance I attribute the failure to carry the works. Never was a charge begun with such enthusiasm terminated

with accomplishing so little." (*Ibid.*, 822). Stephen D. Lee was less charitable: "The attack was a feeble one and a failure, with a loss to my corps of about 1,300 men in killed and wounded." *Ibid.*, 704.

[81] Manigault apparently here refers to Stevenson's division, which had been engaged less heavily than Anderson's and Clayton's.

[82] Anderson did recover, rejoined the army in North Carolina in the spring of 1865 and surrendered with it at Greensboro. He died in 1872. *Generals in Gray*, 7-8.

[83] This is an injustice to Hardee. Lee, having been ordered to attack when he heard Cleburne open the action on his left, had mistaken the sound of the latter's skirmishers for the guns of the main line and had attacked and been repulsed before Cleburne, temporarily commanding Hardee's corps, became seriously engaged. Learning this, and fearing a counterattack on Lee, who expressed the opinion that his troops were in no condition to renew the offensive, Hardee countermanded the assault Cleburne was about to make on the enemy's works and ordered him to act on the defensive. *S.H.S.P.*, VIII, 342; *Buck*, 252; *O.R.*, XXXVIII, pt. 3, 700-701.

[84] It was not until Aug. 30, Hardee insists, that Hood woke up to the fact that Sherman, far from retreating, was moving against the Macon railroad in the vicinity of Jonesboro. Even then, Hood does not seem to have realized that Sherman had with him virtually his entire army. In fact, as late as 1:20 p.m. Aug. 30, Hood's chief of staff informed Gen. Jackson at Rough and Ready: "General Hood does not think there can be a large force advancing on Jonesborough" (*O.R.*, XXXVIII, pt. 5, 1,005). With what Hardee terms "a marvellous want of information," Hood appears to have thought Sherman was about to attack Atlanta, and it was to its defense that he ordered Lee's corps to return on the night of the 31st (*O.R.*, XXXVIII, pt. 3, 701-702). In his memoirs, with a surprising lack of memory or veracity, Hood attempts to make it appear, in order to justify his move, that he was only withdrawing Lee to Rough and Ready in order to join Stewart for an attack on Sherman's flank. The facts, however, do not bear him out, as the record clearly shows that he ordered Lee to return to Atlanta. *Hood*, 204-206; *S.H.S.P.* VIII, 343; *O.R.*, XXXVIII, pt. 3, 701-702.

[85] The halt was made in the vicinity of Rough and Ready, not for the reason Hood later tried to establish, but because of the evacuation of Atlanta. *French*, 222; *O.R.*, XXXVIII, pt. 3, 765.

[86] Hood wrote that notwithstanding full and positive instructions given in ample time, "the chief quartermaster grossly neglected to send off a train of ordnance stores, and five engines, although they were on the track and in readiness to move. This negligence entailed the unnecessary loss of these stores, engines and about eighty cars...The stores which had been abandoned were blown up at about two o'clock in the morning of the 2d September, and the rear guard soon thereafter marched out of Atlanta." In a dispatch to Bragg a few days later, Hood said he was reliably informed that the quartermaster was "too much addicted to drink of late to attend to his duties." *Hood*, 208-209; *O.R.*, XXXVIII, pt. 5, 1,018.

[87] There is no question that Hardee's corps was cut off from Lee's and Stewart's, but the *Official Records* do not indicate any Federal troops interposed between the latter two, as maintained by Manigault. In any case, neither Lee nor Stewart, in their official reports, mention any interference with their withdrawal to

Lovejoy's, nor do French or Walthall, commanding two of Stewart's divisions. *O.R.,* XXXVIII, pt. 3, 765, 872, 929; *French,* 222.

[88] Not surprisingly, Hardee's account of the action at Jonesboro on Sept. 1 differs radically from Manigault's description. "Through the splendid gallantry of the troops," Hardee wrote, "the position was held against fierce and repeated assaults...It is not too much to say that if the enemy had crushed my corps, or even driven it from its position...no organized body of the other two corps could have escaped destruction." *O.R.,* XXXVIII, pt. 3, 702.

[89] The assistant adjutant-general of Cleburne's division, Capt. Irving Buck, describes Hardee's withdrawal south some four or five miles to Lovejoy's Station in these words: "Towards the close of the day of September 1 the fire from all arms was terrific, and the corps seemed to be in the center of a circle of hissing lead and hurtling iron. It was so surrounded that there literally was no rear, except in a comparatively small opening in the direction of Jonesboro, the passing through which may be likened to emerging between the points of a horseshoe." *Buck,* 256.

[90] Doubtless the reference here is to Hood's failure, in the ensuing invasion of Tennessee, to seize the opportunity to attack and destroy Schofield as the latter retreated through Spring Hill, with the bulk of the Confederate army on his unprotected flank.

[91] Born in Virginia, raised in Kentucky, a graduate of West Point, "Old Allegheny," as he was known to his men, was an officer of wide experience. As a young man, he fought against the Seminoles in Florida and was brevetted major for gallant and meritorious conduct at Chapultepec in the war with Mexico. Later, he served with the "old army" on the frontier in Kansas, Dakota and California, resigning early in 1861 to become colonel of the 12th Georgia. Promoted brigadier general late that year, in the spring of 1862 he served in the celebrated Valley Campaign (whence his nickname) under Stonewall Jackson, who complimented him for "skill, gallantry and presence of mind" at McDowell, where Johnson was severely wounded. After Jackson's death, he commanded Stonewall's old division at Gettysburg and in the Wilderness in May 1864. At Spottsylvania Court House, as Manigault relates, he was taken prisoner. After being exchanged, he was assigned to the command of Anderson's division in the Army of Tennessee. Captured again at Nashville, he spent the remainder of the war in Northern prisons. *C.M.H.,* III, 611-612, *Generals in Gray,* 158-159.

[92] If Manigault is correct that his demonstration took place on Sept. 7, it must have been a probe directed at the rear guard of the Federal army, which by then was completing its withdrawal to Atlanta and its environs. This is indicated by a dispatch from Hood to Bragg in Richmond, dated Lovejoy's Station, Ga., Sept. 6, 1864, 7 a.m.: "The enemy withdrew from my front in the direction of Jonesborough last night." (*O.R.,* XXXVIII, pt. 5, 1,023). No direct reference has been found in either the Northern or the Confederate accounts of this period to the action described by Manigault. See *O.R.,* XXXVIII, pts. 1-5.

[93] Hardee's corps. *O.R.,* XXXVIII, pt. 5, 1,028.

[94] In his memoirs, Sherman wrote: "After due reflection, I resolved not to attempt at that time a further pursuit of Hood's army, but slowly and deliberately to move back, occupy Atlanta, enjoy a short period of rest, and to think well over the next step required in the progress of events." (*Sherman,* II, 110). In his official

report, he had put it somewhat differently: "The object of my movement against the railroad was therefore already reached and concluded, and as it was idle to pursue our enemy in that wooded country with a view to his capture, I gave orders on the 4th for the army to move back slowly to Atlanta" (*O.R.*, XXXVIII, pt. 1, 82-83). Evidently Sherman had more respect for the fighting power of Hood's army than did some of his later critics who thought he had missed a golden opportunity to finish Hood off once and for all. Horn, *The Army of Tennessee*, 367.

[95] The removal of the noncombatants from Atlanta led to a long and acrimonious correspondence, which deteriorated into a free-swinging verbal brawl between the two commanders. After telling Sherman he had no alternative in the matter and must therefore accede to his demands, Hood took off the gloves and ripped into his Northern adversary. "And now, sir," he wrote, "permit me to say that the unprecedented measure you propose transcends, in studied and ingenious cruelty, all acts before brought to my attention in the dark history of war. In the name of God and humanity, I protest." To which Sherman, not to be outdone, replied: "Talk thus to the marines, but not to me." Later, Sherman wrote the mayor of Atlanta, who had joined in Hood's protests: "War is cruelty, and you cannot refine it." Thus, in this gripping correspondence, as good reading now 117 years later, as it must have been the day it was written, we have the equivalent of "Tell it to the marines!" and, apparently, as close as Sherman ever actually came to his celebrated "War is Hell." *Hood*, 229-239; *Sherman*, II, 117-128; Horn, *The Army of Tennessee*, 475.

[96] In the Atlanta campaign, the Confederate loss in killed and wounded amounted to 21,996 men. Of this total, 12,024 was incurred while the army was led by Hood, as compared with 9,972 during the period Johnston was in command. On a comparable basis, Sherman lost 27,245. However, his casualties exceeded those of Johnston by three to two, approximately 15,000 to just under 10,000, while as compared with Hood's they were about a stand-off in killed and wounded. As for prisoners, the figures are conflicting, but it seems fair to say that most of such losses on the Confederate side occurred while Hood was in command. *Sherman*, II, 47, 63, 93, 132-134; *Johnston*, 576-577; *Hood*, 222.

[97] Outnumbered and outgunned as the Confederates were, it is hard in retrospect to quarrel with Johnston's basic strategy. All the same, even if he had held Atlanta and driven Sherman back, it is doubtful that the long-term course of the war would have been materially changed. Yet, as Manigault realistically indicates, the South might have been able to hold out another year and, in the end, obtained better terms.

[98] Manigault here refers to Sherman's move, commencing Aug. 26, when he pulled the bulk of his army out of the lines west and southwest of Atlanta and launched it against the Macon railroad in the vicinity of Jonesboro.

[99] The truce agreed on by Sherman and Hood to facilitate the removal of the citizens from Atlanta was made effective "from daylight of Monday, September 12, until daylight of Thursday, September 22, being ten full days, at the point on the Macon railroad known as Rough and Ready, and the country round about for a circle of two miles' radius, together with the roads leading to and from in the direction of Atlanta and Lovejoy's Station, respectively, for the purpose of affording the people of Atlanta a safe means of removal to points south." (*O.R.*, XXXIX, pt. 2, 356). Clearly, Palmetto Station on the West Point R.R. was outside of the area covered by the terms of the armistice.

[100] Recognizing that the enemy would not long remain idle and had the power to force him to fall back on Alabama for subsistance, Hood saw no hope of maintaining his position at Lovejoy's. Rather than continuing to retreat, he determined on an advance, with two objects in view. One was, by offensive action, to restore the fighting spirit of his men; the other, to cut Sherman's communications, a task he now recognized could not be effectively accomplished by cavalry alone. Therefore, he decided to turn the Federal right flank, attempt to sever the enemy's line of supply and force him to withdraw from Atlanta. The move to Palmetto Station was the first step in this plan.

[101] Accompanied by two of his aides, Davis arrived at Palmetto Station in the afternoon of Sept. 25 and left for Montgomery at 6 p.m. on the 27th. Accounts differ as to the warmth, or lack of it, with which he was greeted by the troops. Perhaps Hood's is the most forthright, for he candidly admits that while "some brigades received the President with enthusiasm; others were seemingly dissatisfied, and inclined to cry out, 'give us General Johnston!'" as later pointed out by Manigault. There were rousing speeches by Davis, Howell Cobb of Georgia and Gov. Harris of Tennessee in an effort to lift the spirits of the troops, but by this time it was pretty late in the game and, anyway, they had heard it all before. While Cobb was laying it on with sweet sounding words, a private of the 19th Tennessee called out loudly: "A shell or two would knock all the sweetness out in less than no time!" Poor Hood — with all his faults, loyal to the core — offered to resign, but Davis, in typical fashion, compromised and appointed Beauregard, whom he disliked almost as much as he did Joe Johnston, head of a new Military Division of the West, with largely advisory powers, retaining Hood under him in immediate command of the long-suffering Army of Tennessee. *Hood*, 253-255; *O.R.*, XXXIX, pt. 1, 805; Horn, *The Army of Tennessee,* 372-374; *Worsham*, 134; Thomas Robson Hay, *Hood's Tennessee Campaign,* (New York, 1929), 27-29.

[102] Lee's men of the Army of Northern Virginia, who suffered and often went hungry in the last year of the war, especially near the end in the trenches around Petersburg, would hardly have agreed with this statement.

[103] At Palmetto Station, Davis and Hood agreed that the latter should move quickly north and endeavour to cut Sherman's communications. If this was successfully accomplished, it was anticipated the Northern commander would withdraw to the north from Atlanta with his army, in which event Hood would give battle, provided he could find a strong position and the morale of his troops warranted it. Otherwise, he would continue on to Gadsden in northeast Alabama and gather supplies. If Sherman declined to pursue, moved back to Atlanta and set out for the sea, Hood was to follow on his heels. No decision to cross the Tennessee River and move on Nashville was apparently discussed, much less adopted, at this time. *Hood*, 254-255; *Hay,* op. cit., 27; Davis, *The Rise and Fall of the Confederate Government,* II, 565.

10

HOOD'S CAMPAIGN INTO TENNESSEE

(Editor's Preface)

Following the fall of Atlanta, Hood, with Davis' approval, decided his best prospect of success lay in operating against Sherman's communications. He, therefore, swung to the west and then north, striking the railroad at points as far distant as Tunnel Hill between Dalton and Chattanooga, ripping up the rails, burning ties and inflicting major damage. Sherman followed with most of his troops and by the middle of October the two armies were back where they had started in May. Surprisingly enough, the Northern commander did not force a show-down pitched battle, and Hood was content to avoid one. It was at this juncture that the two armies separated, Hood going on to invade Tennessee and Sherman to return to Atlanta, whence, after burning the city, he set forth on his celebrated March to the Sea.

The responsibility for the campaign into Tennessee is still a matter of dispute, but it seems probable that the idea was Hood's and that Davis and Beauregard gave their approval. Certainly neither of them opposed it. Ever the dreamer, Hood envisioned a brilliant and far-reaching move that would change the whole course of the war. Advancing rapidly into Tennessee, he would attempt to rout or capture the armies of Thomas and Schofield sent north by Sherman to oppose him, occupy Nashville and there resupply and hopefully reinforce his army. Then he would push on into Kentucky, threaten Cincinnati and swing east over the mountains to attack Grant in the rear at Petersburg. With the latter crushed between his troops and those of Lee, the combined Armies of Tennessee and Northern Virginia would then either march on Washington or turn south and annihilate Sherman. Any chance that this ambitious plan would work out in practice, however, was destroyed when Hood encountered a three weeks' delay in crossing the Tennessee River at Tuscumbia, Ala. This he attributed to lack of supplies, bad weather and the absence of Forrest with his cavalry in West Tennessee. Whatever the cause, it gave Thomas time to reach Nashville and Schofield Columbia, Tenn., on the south bank of the Duck River, where Hood caught up with him.

There, the Southern leader's spirits revived and once more the vision of a decisive blow danced before his eyes. The situation he later wrote, "presented an occasion for one of those interesting and beautiful moves upon the chess-board of war, to perform which I had often desired an opportunity...I had beheld with admiration the noble deeds and grand results achieved by the immortal Jackson in similar maneuvers...and I hoped in this instance to be able to profit by the teaching of my illustrious countryman."

As so often in the past, his plan of action involved a flank movement, this time a swing to the east around Schofield's left, with the objective of seizing Spring Hill on the road to Nashville, thus cutting the Northern army's line of retreat. All seemed to be going well as the Southern troops closed on Spring Hill late in the afternoon of Nov. 29, but then things began to fall apart. By an almost incredible series of misunderstandings and failures on the part of subordinate officers, the way was left open and Schofield's army made good its escape during the night, marching silently northward along the turnpike within sight of the camp fires of the slumbering Army of Tennessee. Despite all the bungling by others, responsibility for the failure to spring the trap lay at Hood's door. Local legend has it that he was drunk that night or drugged by laudanum taken to ease the constant pain from the stump of the leg he had lost at Chickamauga and the withered left arm that resulted from his wound at Gettysburg.

Be that as it may, Spring Hill was the last and perhaps most frustrating of the "lost opportunities" of the Army of Tennessee. Col. Henry Stone of Thomas' staff said: "A single Confederate brigade...planted squarely across the pike, either north or south of Spring Hill, would have effectually prevented Schofield's retreat, and daylight would have found his whole force cut off from every avenue of escape by more than twice its numbers, to assault whom would have been madness and to avoid whom would have been impossible." And Hood, himself, wrote: "Never was a grander opportunity offered to utterly rout and destroy the Federal Army."

Dismayed and distraught by Schofield's escape, Hood gave chase the next day and brought the enemy to bay at Franklin in a strongly entrenched position well supported by artillery. There, without even waiting for two divisions of Lee's corps and most of his guns to come up, and over the protests of Forrest and Cheatham, he, in desperation, impetuously hurled his troops against the well-nigh impregnable breast-works. The result was a disaster, and yet there was something sublime in this last great offensive charge of the long-suffering Army of Tennessee. Surely most of the men in the ranks and their leaders as well must have known the end was in sight and still, with unsurpassed valor, they returned to the attack again and again in desperate fighting. The losses were fearful. Of some 20,000 infantry in action more than 6,000 fell, and more general officers were killed than on any other battlefield of the war. The next morning the bodies of five of them lay side by side in a row on the long back gallery of the McGavock house nearby. A sixth was mortally wounded.

In the final charge in the fading light of day, Manigault was struck down by the minie ball that was to bring an end to his active fighting career. Perhaps it was just as well that he was spared the disaster that was soon to befall the army.

Either unable or unwilling to face reality, Hood, with his battered army, followed Schofield to Nashville and besieged the city. It was his last gasp. Thomas, who outnumbered his Southern opponent more than two to one, bided his time until he was good and ready, then marched out of the fortifications on Dec. 14, turned the Confederate left and on the following day, in one of the few really decisive battles of the war, crushed the Army of Tennessee. There ensued the gruelling retreat in bitter winter weather to Tupelo, Miss. There, Hood resigned his commission and the campaign was over.

In January 1865, the pitiful remnants of the army were transferred to the Carolinas where, under their old commander, Joe Johnston, they took part in the hopeless task of opposing Sherman's march north. The end came at Greensboro, N.C., on April 26, when Johnston surrendered, along with his other troops, what was left of the gallant Army of Tennessee.

R.L.T.

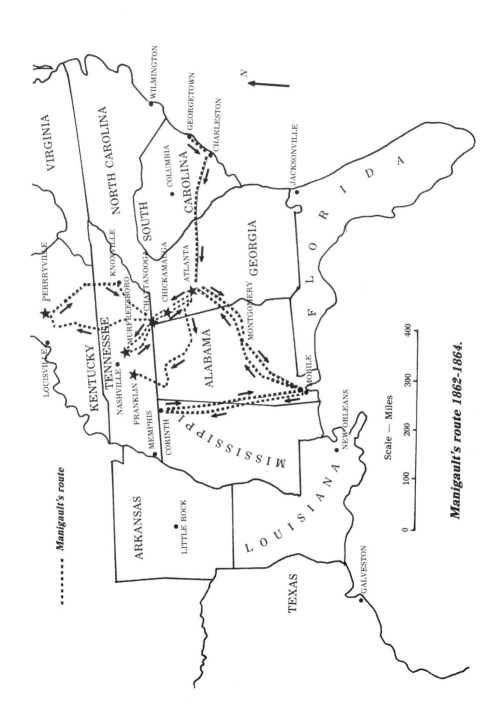

Manigault's route

Manigault's route 1862-1864.

HOOD'S CAMPAIGN INTO TENNESSEE

(The Narrative)

A few days after the departure of President Davis, we broke up our camp, and I think it was on the afternoon of the 30th that our Division, commanded by General Edward Johnson, commenced its march.[1] Our brigade had recruited rapidly, and small as our numbers were, about one thousand (1,000) rank and file, we were one of the strongest in the army.

I can only approximate the strength of the army in its different branches at that time, as I have never seen or heard of any report by General Hood in reference to this period, and excepting to the Commander-in-chief, his staff, and perhaps the Corps Commanders, our real strength was not known to any one.

I should say that the army consisted of about 25,000 infantry, with about one hundred guns, and a cavalry force of 5,000 men, under the command of General Forrest.

It would be safe to say that the army did not exceed 30,000 of all arms of the service. It consisted of eight divisions, forming three Army Corps, with one of cavalry.[2]

The transportation was very much reduced, consisting only of provisions, ordnance, tool, and cooking wagons, with one wagon to each general for themselves and staff, and a limited number of ambulances, and a few medical wagons. All officers below the rank of Brigadier were forced to carry their own baggage and camp equipage, in the best way they could. Such as were able to do so had to use their extra horses for the purpose, or purchased a mule or additional one. In our brigade, there were but two tents, my own, and one belonging to the Medical Department. Each regimental headquarters, the Brigade Commissary and Quartermaster, were supplied with a tent "fly" alone. The officers of the line, for the most part, as well as the men, carried all that they required on their backs.

Altho some issues of clothing had been made, still the men, barring their arms and ammunition, were not in a condition to take the field. It had been found impossible to furnish shoes, uniforms, or blankets, to all who wanted them. This deficiency at such a season of the year, when, in all probability, our operations would be continued far into the winter, ought to have been provided against. Neither was there a sufficient amount of extra wagons or ambulances allowed for the relief of such as happened to be temporarily indisposed, or whose feet would become sore from the long-continued march. Indeed, many walked several thousand miles bare-footed.[3]

The health of the army was admirable. There were no sick, and the men were capable of almost any amount of endurance, had learned to take care of themselves under the most trying circumstances, had seen much of war, and been in many engagements. I doubt if the ranks of any army was ever composed of better material, or could be more relied on in an emergency. It is to be regretted, however, that as much can not be said for the officers. Great deficiencies existed in all ranks, but particularly in the regiments. As a general rule, they were personally brave, but not more than one in five was fit for the commission he held. To the commander of a regiment or brigade who really appreciated the responsibility of his position, the greatest difficulty he had to contend against was the control and management of his subalterns, and the forcing them to comply with the regulations and orders existing for the preservation of discipline and efficiency. It could only be accomplished in a measure, by continued scrutiny, followed by prompt and severe punishment, so soon as any dereliction of duty was detected. Altho for some short time past the spirits of the men were depressed, and discipline had somewhat relaxed, owing to our want of success, and a lack of confidence in our leaders, yet it no sooner became known that we were to assume the offensive, that we were going to the rear of the enemy, and, by adopting a different system of strategy, endeavor to recover much of the ground we had lost, than an immediate and marked change pervaded the whole army. Confidence seemed restored, the officers exerted themselves, and endeavored to discharge their duties as they should have done, the men gave prompt and ready obedience to all orders, countenances became cheerful, whilst all looked forward anxiously for the day to come when we would again be in the field.[4] In spite of General Hood's unpopularity, there seemed to be a tacit understanding amongst us that we would give him one more trial, trusting that he had by his late mistakes and failures learned some valuable lessons in the art of war to his advantage, and that he would now use the means under his command with more discretion, and justify to some extent the high reputation he had gained in the Army of (Northern) Virginia, and the favor with which he was regarded in Richmond.

It was made known by the commanding General to the officers next in rank, and by them successively through the different grades to the men, what his plans were. The information that we received was to the following effect:

General Hood professed to have learned that the army of General Sherman since the occupation of Atlanta had diminished in numbers to a considerable extent, from various causes. The terms of service of many regiments had expired, others nearly so. All such had been sent North to be mustered out.[5] A large force had been sent west to the Trans-Mississippi Department to reinforce some threatened point, as General Kirby Smith (Confederate) had been gaining some important advantages in that quarter.[6] A large number of men had been furloughed, nearly the whole of one corps. It was well known that their losses during the late campaign had been very heavy, and in order to secure the numerous posts in his rear against our cavalry he had been obliged to add largely to their garrisons by drawing men from the army in Atlanta.[7] General Hood therefore conjectured that from the information he possessed, the disparity in numbers between himself and General Sherman was greatly less at that time than at any previous period, and that if he could only succeed in forcing him into an engagement in the open field, that there could be little doubt now as to the result, and that this could be effected, he thought, with everything in our favor, by carrying into execution the plan he had determined on. Having made all the necessary provisions, he intended by a secret and rapid march to move round the enemy's right, reach the railroad some distance in his rear, then following its course, to burn the bridges, tear up and destroy the track for a considerable distance and at many points, at the same time attacking or surprising the isolated garrisons along the line of road, with largely superior numbers, cutting off General Sherman from his base, destroying his communications and means of obtaining subsistence, forcing him to retire from Atlanta, in which it was supposed he had not a sufficient supply to last any great length of time, whilst the country for many miles around that city having been previously swept by ourselves, could not supply any deficiency.[8] He would be forced either by a circuitous route to retreat to Chattanooga, or following us in our movements, hope to overtake, engage, and defeat us, while General Hood could give battle just when and where he pleased, being able to select for himself the most favorable opportunity of doing so. By this unexpected and bold movement, no doubt much uneasiness and alarm would be occasioned, finding themselves with a considerable army in their rear, cut off from their magazines, their railroad communications destroyed, detached posts captured, and starvation staring them in the face. It was thought that much demoralization would ensue at finding the tables thus turned against them. There could be but little doubt as to the result of a battle under such favorable circumstances.[9]

NOTE: At this point, Gen. Manigault's records cease. For information concerning his later military and civilian career, see Pages VII and VIII of the Introduction and the Postscript, Page 282.

NOTES TO CHAPTER 10

[1] Stephen D. Lee's corps, of which Manigault's brigade was a part, left Palmetto Station and crossed the Chattahoochee on Sept. 29. *O.R.*, XXXIX, pt. 1, 810.

[2] A careful examination of the returns of the Army of Tennessee and abstracts from inspection reports, as well as the figures given by Hood in his memoirs, indicates that the strength of the Confederate force on Sept. 20 was approximately 36,500, consisting of about 27,000 infantry, 2,800 artillery and 4,700 cavalry (*Hood*, 218; *O.R.*, XXXVIII, pt. 3, 683; XXXIX, pt. 2, 850-851). The organization of the army when it left Palmetto Station was as follows: Cheatham's corps (formerly Hardee's), consisting of the divisions of Cleburne, Bate, and Brown; Lee's corps, made up of Stevenson's, Johnson's and Clayton's divisions; and Stewart's corps, in which the division commanders were Loring, French and Walthall. (*O.R.*, XXXIX, pt. 2, 851-857). The cavalry division was commanded by Gen. William H. Jackson, Wheeler still being absent on his raid into Tennessee. The latter rejoined the army Oct. 2. *Wheeler and his Cavalry*, 274.

[3] Referring to his arrival at Gadsden, Ala., on Oct. 21, Hood wrote: "I met at this place a thorough supply of shoes and other stores." His chief of staff noted: "On the 21st an issue of shoes and clothing was made to the army." (*O.R.*, XXXIX, pt. 1, 802, 807, 811). That these were insufficient, however, seems clear from the fact that Hood informed Beauregard on the 30th that, in addition to a lack of provisions, "many of his men were again shoeless, or nearly so, and that it would be imprudent to commence a new campaign in that lame condition." Alfred Roman, *The Military Operations of General Beauregard*, 2 vols., (New York, 1884), II, 293.

[4] Describing the scene when the army was told that it was about to return to the soil of Tennessee, Hood later wrote: "The prospect of again entering that State created great enthusiasm, and from the different encampments arose at intervals that genuine Confederate shout so familiar to every Southern soldier", the rebel yell. *Hood*, 270.

[5] In his official report, Sherman spoke of "the expiration of the time of service of many of the regiments." (*O.R.*, XXXIX, pt. 1, 580.). Writing to Grant on Sept. 26, he said: "Our armies are much reduced." (*Sherman*, II, 142). In his memoirs, he noted that the army had undergone many changes since the capture of Atlanta and that the five corps remaining with him when he followed Hood north "were very much reduced in strength, by detachments and discharges, so that for the purposes of fighting Hood I had only about 60,000 infantry and artillery, with two small divisions of cavalry." (*Ibid.*, 145-146). This compared with a peak strength in June of 112,819, and 81,758 at the close of the Atlanta campaign. *Ibid*, 134.

[6] Manigault apparently refers here to the two divisions of the Sixteenth Corps under Maj. Gen. A.J. Smith that were dispatched to Missouri in September to

reinforce the troops confronting Sterling Price, who was then leading a Confederate invasion of that state. *Cox,* 219; Horn, *The Army of Tennessee,* 371.

[7] After the fall of Atlanta, Sherman sent Wagner's division of the Fourth Corps and Morgan's of the Fourteenth back to Chattanooga under Thomas. In addition, Corse's division of the Fifteenth Corps was transferred to Rome, Ga. *O.R.,* XXXIX, pt. 1, 580.

[8] With no hope of reinforcements, Hood came to the conclusion that a move north against Sherman's communications offered the best prospect of favorable results. Not only would an offensive movement restore the morale of his troops, but it would compel Sherman to pull out of Atlanta with the bulk of his force in order to protect his lifeline. Such proved to be the case. On Oct. 4, Stewart struck the railroad between Acworth and Big Shanty, ripping up between 10 and 15 miles of track. "The rebels had struck our railroad a heavy blow," wrote Sherman, "burning every tie, bending the rails for eight miles...so that the estimate for repairs called for 35,000 new ties, and six miles of iron." (*Sherman,* II, 150-151). Having failed to capture Allatoona and the provisions stored there, Hood continued his depredations, tearing up another 20 miles of the railroad between Resaca and Tunnel Hill. (*Hood,* 256-263). Even before this, Sherman had concluded that it would "be a physical impossibility to protect the roads now that Hood, Forrest, Wheeler, and the whole batch of devils are turned loose...I propose that we strike out...for Milledgeville, Millen and Savannah...I can make this march and make Georgia howl!" (Sherman to Grant, *Ibid.,* 152). Thus was hatched the celebrated "March to the Sea."

[9] As matters transpired, Hood's officers unanimously advised him that, although the army was much improved in morale, it was not in condition to risk battle against Sherman. Hood acquiesced, Sherman turned south and the Confederate invasion of Tennessee followed. *Hood,* 263-264.

POSTSCRIPT

The esteem in which Arthur M. Manigault was held by his fellow South Carolianians was made evident in a proclamation by Gov. J.C. Sheppard issued the day following his death near Georgetown in 1886:

"General Manigault was a distinguished soldier, an honorable, incorruptible citizen and patriot, a faithful and efficient public servant...The loss of a citizen so worthy, an officer so useful and much beloved, a gentleman so pure and upright, is a public calamity to be deeply deplored."

All state offices were ordered closed and flags lowered to half mast. But it was in his home district, among those who knew him best, that his loss was to be most deeply felt. The Georgetown Enquirer used these words:

"A gallant soldier and noble gentlemen has gone to his reward...His splendid record as a soldier, under whose command many of Georgetown's sons had bravely marched to death on the battlefields of the Lost Cause, his exalted character, his gentle and considerate disposition, his urbane and courtly manners and his pure and unselfish patriotism had endeared him to every level and condition of society...He was known and loved as an unselfish man and stainless gentleman."

The body was brought from South Island* to Charleston by sea and private services were held at St. Philip's Protestant Episcopal Church. And then — Arthur Middleton Manigault, South Carolinian, Brigadier General C.S.A., was laid to rest in Magnolia Cemetery "only to be awakened 'at the last trump' on that 'dreadful day.'"

R.L.T.

An island on the sea at the entrance of Winyah Bay, about 10 miles from White Oak, where the Manigaults had a summer house. Because of malaria, most planter families did not stay near the flooded rice fields during the mosquito season. — Editor.

BIBLIOGRAPHY

The cornerstone of factual information regarding the War Between the States is the 128 volumes of the *Official Records,* published by the War Department at Washington, and on this monumental and priceless compilation of source material all serious studies of the subject are based. In addition, the Editor is chiefly indebted to the publications listed below.

Adams, Charles Francis   *Lee's Centennial,* An Address...Boston, 1907.

Austin, J.P.   *The Blue and The Gray...*Atlanta, 1899.

Avery, A.C.   *Memorial Address on Life and Character of Lieutenant General D.H. Hill...*Raleigh, 1893.

Barron, S.B.   *The Lone Star Defenders...*New York, 1908.

Black, Robert C. III   *The Railroads of the Confederacy...*Chapel Hill, N.C., 1952.

Boggs, William R.   *Military Reminiscences...*Durham, N.C., 1913.

Brevier, R.S.   *History of the First and Second Missouri Confederate Brigades 1861-1865...*St. Louis, 1879.

Bridges, Hal   *Lee's Maverick General: Daniel Harvey Hill...*New York, 1961.

Buck, Irving A.   *Cleburne and His Command....*Jackson, Tenn., 1958.

Burton, E. Milby   *The Siege of Charleston 1861-1865...*Columbia, S.C., 1971.

Calhoun, W.L.   *History of the 42d Regiment, Georgia Volunteers...*Atlanta, 1900.

Capers, Walter B.   *The Soldier Bishop: Ellison Capers...*New York, 1912.

Cate, Wirt Armistead   *Two Soldiers...*Chapel Hill, N.C., 1938.

Connelly, Thomas Lawrence   *Army of the Heartland: The Army of Tennessee, 1861-1862...*Baton Rouge, 1967.

Connelly, Thomas Lawrence   *Autumn of Glory: The Army of Tennessee, 1862-1865...*Baton Rouge, 1971.

Cox, Jacob D.   *Atlanta...*New York, 1882.

Craven, Avery   *Edmund Ruffin: Southerner...*New York, 1932.

Cumming, Kate   *A Journal of Hospital Life in the Confederate Army of Tennessee...*Louisville, 1886.

Davis, Jefferson   *The Rise and Fall of the Confederate Government...*New York, 1881. 2 vols.

Davis, William C. *Breckinridge: Statesman, Soldier, Symbol*...Baton Rouge, 1974.

Dodson, W.C. (ed.) *Campaigns of Wheeler and his Cavalry 1862-1865*...Atlanta, 1899.

DuBose, John Witherspoon *General Joseph Wheeler and the Army of Tennessee*...New York, 1912.

Duke, Basil W. *Reminiscences of General Basil W. Duke, C.S.A*...New York, 1911.

Duncan, Thomas W. *Recollections of a Confederate Soldier*...Nashville, 1922.

Dyer, John P. *"Fightin' Joe" Wheeler*...Baton Rouge, 1954.

Dyer, John P. *The Gallant Hood*...Indianapolis, 1950.

Emanuel, S. *An Historical Sketch of the Georgetown Rifle Guards*...n.p., 1909.

Fiske, John *The Mississippi Valley in the Civil War*...Boston, 1900.

Foote, Shelby *The Civil War: A Narrative*...New York, 1958-1974. 4 vols.

Freeman, Douglas Southall (ed.) *Lee's Dispatches*...New York, 1915.

Freeman, Douglas Southall *Lee's Lieutenants*...New York, 1942-1944. 3 vols.

Freeman, Douglas Southall *R.E. Lee: A Biography*...New York, 1934-1935. 4 vols.

French, Samuel G. *Two Wars: An Autobiography*...Nashville, 1901.

Govan, Gilbert E. and Livingood, James W. *A Different Valor: The Story of General Joseph E. Johnston, C.S.A*...Indianapolis, 1956.

Gracie, Archibald *The Truth About Chickamauga*...Boston, 1911.

Guild, George B. *Fourth Tennessee Cavalry Regiment*...Nashville, 1901.

Hagan, John W. *Confederate Letters*...Edited by Bell I. Wiley...Athens, 1954.

Hagood, Johnson *Memoirs of the War of Secession*...Columbia, S.C., 1910.

Hancock, R.R. *Second Tennessee Cavalry*...Nashville, 1887.

Hay, Thomas Robson *Braxton Bragg and the Southern Confederacy*...Savannah, 1925.

Hay, Thomas Robson *Hood's Tennessee Campaign*...New York, 1929.

Head, Thomas A. *Campaigns and Battles of the Sixteenth Regiment Tennessee Volunteers*...Nashville, 1885.

Henry, Robert Selph   *The Story of the Confederacy*...New York, 1936.

Hoehling, A.A.   *Last Train from Atlanta*...New York, 1958.

Hood, John B.   *Advance and Retreat*...New Orleans, 1880.

Horn, Stanley F.   *The Army of Tennessee*...Norman, Okla., 1953.

Horn, Stanley F.   *The Decisive Battle of Nashville*...Baton Rouge, 1956.

Jamison, Henry Downs, Jr. (ed.)   *Letters and Recollections of a Confederate Soldier 1860-1865*...Nashville, 1964.

Johnson, Adam R.   *The Partisan Rangers of the Confederate Army*...Louisville, Ky., 1904.

Johnston, Joseph E   *Narrative of Military Operations*...New York, 1874.

Jones, Archer   *Confederate Strategy from Shiloh to Vicksburg*...Baton Rouge, 1961.

Jordan, Thomas and Pryor, J.P.   *The Campaigns of Lieut. Gen. N.B. Forrest*...New Orleans, 1868.

Kirwin, A.D. (ed.)   *Johnny Green of the Orphan Brigade*...University of Kentucky Press, 1956.

Livermore, Thomas L.   *Numbers and Losses in the Civil War in America 1861-1865*...Boston, 1900.

Longstreet, James   *From Manassas to Appomattox*...Philadelphia, 1896.

Mathes, J. Harvey   *The Old Guard in Gray*...Memphis, 1897.

McMorries, Edward Young   *History of the First Regiment Alabama Infantry, C.S.A.*...Nashville, 1904.

McMurray, W.J.   *History of the Twentieth Tennessee Regiment Volunteer Infantry, C.S.A.*...Nashville, 1904.

McWhiney, Grady   *Braxton Bragg and Confederate Defeat, Volume 1: Field Command*...Savannah, 1925.

Nash, Charles E.   *Biographical Sketches of Gen. Pat Cleburne and Gen. T.C. Hindman*...Little Rock, 1898.

Nisbet, James Cooper   *Four Years on the Firing Line*...Jackson, Tenn., 1963.

Noll, Arthur Howard (ed.)   *Doctor Quintard: Chaplain C.S.A. and Second Bishop of Tennessee*...Sewanee, Tenn., 1905.

Noll, Arthur Howard (ed.)   *General Kirby Smith*...Sewanee, Tenn., 1905.

Owsley, Frank Lawrence   *King Cotton Diplomacy*...Chicago, 1931.

Parks, Joseph Howard   *General Edmund Kirby Smith, C.S.A.*...Baton Rouge, 1954.

Polk, William H.   *Leonidas Polk: Bishop and General*...New York, 1894. 2 vols.

Polley, J.B.   *Hood's Texas Brigade*...New York, 1910.

Purdue, Howell and Elizabeth   *Pat Cleburne: Confederate General*...Hillsboro, Texas, 1973.

Ridley, Bromfield L.   *Battles and Sketches of the Army of Tennessee*...Mexico, Mo., 1906.

Rodgers, Robert L.   *Capture of the De Gress Battery, Atlanta, July 22d, 1864*...n.p., 1898.

Roman, Alfred   *The Military Operations of General Beauregard*...New York, 1884. 2 vols.

Seitz, Don C.   *Braxton Bragg: General of the Confederacy*...Columbia, S.C., 1924.

Sherman, William T.   *Memoirs*...New York, 1875.

Simons, James   *Address to the Officers of the Fourth Brigade*...Charleston, S.C., 1861.

Smith, Gustavus W.   *Confederate War Papers*...New York, 1884.

Stevenson, Alexander F.   *The Battle of Stone's River*...Boston, 1884.

Swanberg, W.A.   *First Blood: The Story of Fort Sumter*...New York, 1957.

Sykes, E.T.   *Walthall's Brigade*...Columbus, Miss., 1905.

Thompson, Ed Porter   *History of the Orphan Brigade*...Louisville, 1898.

Toney, Marcus B.   *The Privations of a Private*...Nashville, 1905.

Vaughan, A.J.   *Personal Record of the Thirteenth Regiment, Tennessee Infantry, C.S.A.*...Memphis, 1897.

Walker, C. Irvine   *Historical Sketch of the Tenth Regiment, So. Ca. Volunteers*...Charleston, S.C., 1881.

Watkins, Sam R.   *"Co. Aytch," Maury Grays, First Tennessee Regiment*...Nashville, 1882.

West, John C.   *A Texan in Search of a Fight*...Waco, Texas, 1901.

Wise, John S.   *The End of an Era*...Boston, 1899.

Worsham, W.J.   *The Old Nineteenth Tennessee Regiment, C.S.A.*...Knoxville, 1902.

Wright, Marcus J.   *General Officers of the Confederate Army*...New York, 1911.

Wyeth, John A.   *Life of General Nathan Bedford Forrest*...New York, 1899.

Wyeth, John A.   *With Sabre and Scalpel*...New York, 1914.

Young, Bennett H.   *Confederate Wizards of the Saddle*...Boston, 1914.

Young, J.P.   *The Seventh Tennessee Cavalry*...Nashville, 1890.

Young, L.D.   *Reminiscences of a Soldier of the Orphan Brigade*...Paris, Ky., n.d.

GENERAL WORKS

Battles and Leaders of the Civil War   Robert Underwood Johnson and Clarence Clough Buell (eds.)...New York, 1887. 4 vols.

Confederate Military History   Clement A. Evans (ed.)...Atlanta, 1899. 12 vols.

Confederate Veteran...Nashville, 1893-1932. 40 vols.

Generals in Gray: Lives of the Confederate Commanders   Ezra J. Warner...Louisiana State University Press, 1959.

Journal of the Congress of the Confederate States of America...Washington, 1904-1905. 7 vols.

Southern Historical Society Papers...Richmond, 1876-1953. 52 vols.

Staff Officers of the Confederate States Army...Washington, 1891

The War of the Rebellion: A Compilation of the Official Records of the Union and Confederate Armies...Washington, 1880-1901. 128 vols.

MANUSCRIPTS

Duke University Library, Durham, N.C.

Braxton Bragg Papers.

Confederate Archives: Army of Tennessee Papers, 1862-1865.

Jefferson Davis Papers.

Georgia Portfolio.

Hardee's Murfreesboro Report.

John Bell Hood Letters, 1864.

C.E. Quintard Papers.

Southern Historical Collection, University of North Carolina, Chapel Hill, N.C.

Patton Anderson Papers.

Braxton Bragg Papers.

Benjamin F. Cheatham Papers. (Microfilm of collection at Tennessee State Library and Archives, Nashville, Tenn.)

J.F.H. Claiborne Papers.

Maj. J.B. Cummings Papers.

Gale-Polk Papers.

W.W. Mackall Papers.

NEWSPAPERS

Charleston (S.C.) *Courier.*

Charleston (S.C.) *Mercury.*

Richmond (Va.) *Dispatch.*

Richmond (Va.) *Enquirer.*

Richmond (Va.) *Examiner.*

APPENDIX I

Manigault's Brigade
In The
Battle of Atlanta — July 22, 1864

Scarcely 24 hours after the sounds of battle had died away on Peachtree Creek north of Atlanta on July 20, Hood once more took the offensive. Pulling Hardee's corps out of the lines on the night of the 21st, he dispatched it on a wide swing southeast of the city to attack, from flank and rear, Sherman's extreme left, held by the Seventeenth Corps of McPherson's Army of the Tennessee. At the same time, orders were issued to Cheatham's corps, of which Manigault's brigade was a part, to hold itself in readiness east of Atlanta to assault the Federal Fifteenth Corps, holding the Union line to the north of the Seventeenth.

Hood was confident that, by thus assailing McPherson in front, flank and rear, the latter's destruction would be assured. A strategic conception worthy of Stonewall Jackson at his best, it came within an ace of success. And it was through no fault of his own, but rather as a result of unforseeable circumstance, that Hood, in all probability, was robbed of the decisive triumph he so desperately sought.

The late morning of the 22nd found Hardee in position to launch his attack, and the portents for success were bright. McPherson, and Sherman himself, had been caught by surprise. Both men were convinced that Hood was in retreat and about to abandon Atlanta.

Shortly before noon, Hardee ordered his men forward. In the words of Maj. W.H. Chamberlin of the 81st Ohio, "they came tearing wildly through the woods with the yells of demons."[1] But instead of meeting light opposition and taking the Seventeenth Corps in flank and rear as anticipated, they ran pell-mell into a formidable line of battle, supported by artillery. Who were these enemy troops and how did they get there? The story is an intriguing one, illustrating, as it does, the part good fortune, or the lack of it, plays on the battlefield.

The remaining corps of McPherson's Army of the Tennessee, Dodge's Sixteenth, had been held in reserve near Decatur until the previous day, when it had been ordered forward to support the Seventeenth and extend the latter's left flank. On their way to carry out this assignment, Dodge's men, as luck would have it, found themselves in the path of Hardee's troops as they surged forward against the unprotected flank and rear of the Seventeenth Corps. Despite repeated assaults and prolonged bitter fighting, the Union lines held and the Army of the Tennessee was saved.

Had Dodge's men not been where they were, "there would have been absolutely nothing," wrote Major Chamberlin, "but the hospital tents and the wagon trains to stop Hardee's command from falling unheralded directly upon the rear of the Fifteenth and Seventeenth corps in line. Upon what a slight chance, then, hung the fate of Sherman's army that day."[2] And General Blair, commanding the Seventeenth Corps, had this to say: "The movement of General Hood was a very bold and brilliant one, and was very near being successful...The position taken up accidentally by the Sixteenth Corps prevented the full force of the blow from falling where it was intended to fall. If my command had been driven from its position at the time that the Fifteenth Corps was forced back from its entrenchments, there must have been a general rout of all the troops of the Army of the Tennessee."[3]

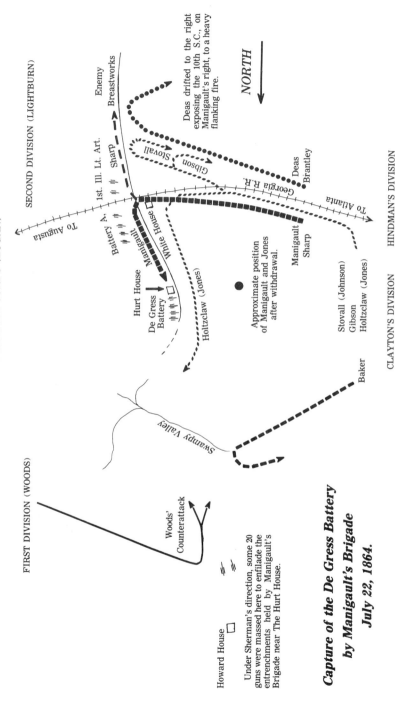

FEDERAL FIFTEENTH CORPS (LOGAN)

SECOND DIVISION (LIGHTBURN)

To Augusta

To Atlanta

Enemy
Breastworks

Deas drifted to the right
exposing the 10th S.C., on
Manigault's right, to a heavy
flanking fire.

NORTH

1st. Ill. Lt. Art.

Sharp

Battery A.

Manigault

White House

Hurt House

De Gress
Battery

Holtzclaw (Jones)

Stovall

Gibson

Georgia R.R.

Deas
Brantley

Manigault
Sharp

Approximate position
of Manigault and Jones
after withdrawal.

HINDMAN'S DIVISION

Stovall (Johnson)
Gibson
Holtzclaw (Jones)

CLAYTON'S DIVISION

CHEATHAM'S CORPS (CONFEDERATE)

Swampy Valley

Baker

FIRST DIVISION (WOODS)

Woods'
Counterattack

Howard House

Under Sherman's direction, some 20
guns were massed here to enfilade the
entrenchments held by Manigault's
Brigade near The Hurt House.

Capture of the De Gress Battery
by Manigault's Brigade
July 22, 1864.

Not to Scale

Now it was Cheatham's turn. In the evening of the 21st and the morning of the 22nd, his corps, consisting of the divisions of Clayton, Hindman and Stevenson, was pulled back to the inner fortifications of Atlanta, abandoning the breastworks thrown up about a mile east of the city limits. These the enemy promptly occupied, reversed and strengthened.

Having early in the afternoon received word that Hardee's attack had, in part, been successful and fearing a concentration of the enemy against him, Hood ordered Cheatham, about 3 p.m., to move out and assault the Federal Fifteenth Corps in his front. The role assigned Hindman's division, now commanded by Brig. Gen. John C. Brown, was to attack eastward along the line of the Georgia Railroad, with Manigault's brigade, supported by Sharp's, advancing on the left, or north, side of the tracks and Deas', supported by Brantley's, on the south.

The terrain over which Manigault's brigade was to go forward was gently undulating, at times wooded and interspersed with narrow swamps, at others comparatively open. Near the railroad, just short of the enemy's line, stood a two-story, frame building, known as the White House. Some 200 yards to the north, on the east or Federal side of the breastworks, was another dwelling, the Hurt House, likewise of two stories but constructed of brick. The De Gress Battery of four 20-pounder Parrotts (Battery H, 1st Illinois Light Artillery) was located just to north of the Hurt House and Battery A of the same regiment (6 guns) at the point where the railroad passed through a deep cut a few yards to the east of the White House.

Shortly after 3 o'clock, Manigault ordered his brigade forward, with the 10th South Carolina on the right, next to the railroad, and, continuing the line to the left or north, the 19th South Carolina and the 24th and 34th Alabama. The 28th Alabama formed the skirmish line, the men of this regiment mixing with those of the other four as the advance progressed.

Clear and strong rang out the voice of Col. Pressley: "'Tenth South Carolina Regiment, prepare to charge the enemy!' To a man, the regiment leaped to the exterior of the works, quickly formed line, and at the command moved forward as steadily as if on practice only. Alec Mathews of Company A, a mere youth, said to those nearest him, 'Boys, put your trust in God and do your duty'...Ere long his pure, brave soul was in the presence of its Maker."[4]

For the first half mile, progress was steady. An advance force of the enemy, made up of the 53rd Ohio and the 111th Illinois, supported by a section of guns from Company A of the 1st Illinois Light Artillery, was easily driven back into the Union lines. Describing this first clash between the two opposing forces, Col. James Martin of the 111th Illinois wrote that his regiment, which had been placed in position half a mile in front of the Federal breastworks to support the picket line, was "attacked by the enemy in heavy force...made a desperate stand, but was compelled by the numbers against them to fall back to the main works."[5] The commander of the 53rd Ohio said: "Finding a superior force of the enemy...about to flank our position, we retired, according to orders, to the line of fortifications (previously) held by the enemy."[6]

Further on, the going became tougher, as the enemy guns began to find their mark. Fortunately, the undulating character of the terrain offered some protection.

To the south of the tracks, things were not going well. Deas' brigade, commanded by Col. Coltart, drifted to the right, exposing the 10th South Carolina to a heavy flanking fire. The cause of this divergence is made clear by Capt. Rouse of the 25th Alabama of Deas' brigade, who stated in his report that his troops were ordered "to keep the left flank within twenty paces of the railroad (Augusta), but owing to buildings, impassable fences, and slight curves of road, when the regiment arrived at the breastworks of the picket reserve of the enemy, the left was about 150 yards from the railroad...There were no troops between our left and the railroad."[7] Although Deas' men subsequently succeeded in taking, and briefly holding, a portion of the enemy's main line, this occurred well to the right, and they, along with Brantley's brigade, accomplished little, remaining separated from Manigault for the rest of the day's action.[8]

Undismayed by the developments on their right, Manigault's troops pushed on in the face of heavy resistance, only to be brought to a halt as they approached the enemy breastworks near the White House, which provided refuge for the left of the 10th and right of the 19th South Carolina regiments. General Sharp, commanding the supporting brigade, offered assistance, but this was declined by Col. Pressley of the 10th, who, at the urging of Lt. Col. C. Irvine Walker, put some of his men and some from the 19th S.C. into the second story of the building, whence they poured a galling fire down into the Union line.[9]

This was too much for the defenders, who began to break. With a final, desperate rush, Manigault's "brigade nearly as a whole, dashed forward and over the works," shooting down or overpowering those of the enemy who had not sought refuge in flight.[10] The gallant Pressley, fighting hand to hand, was shot through the shoulder by a rifle ball and borne from the top of the enemy's fortifications, with a wound that would knock him out of action for the rest of the war. His place at the head of the 10th South Carolina was taken by Col. Walker.[11] The four light 12-pounders of Battery A of the 1st Illinois posted north of the railroad, along with their limbers, fell to the victorious troops and were hauled off to the rear.

Having gained a foothold in the works, Manigault's men swept to the left, turning the flank successively of the 47th, 54th, 37th and 53rd Ohio regiments, which broke in confusion and fled to the rear.[12] Continuing on, they seized the Hurt House and the four 20-pounder Parrotts of De Gress's Battery H of the 1st Illinois Light Artillery, the guns that had thrown the first shells into Atlanta at a range of 2½ miles two days before.[13]

Sharp's brigade, in close support, came up, fanned out to the right and, with Manigault, cleared the fortifications for more than half a mile, seizing the two remaining guns of Battery A south of the railroad.[14] If proof were needed of the bloody character of the fighting, the severity of the Union losses amply affords it. Battery A reported its casualties as 32 men killed, wounded and missing, and 55 horses killed and captured, mostly killed.[15] In his memoirs, Sherman wrote that every horse in De Gress's battery was killed. De Gress, doubtless with greater accuracy, put his losses at 14 men and 39 horses.[16]

Following this stunning success, Manigault's troops were pulled back to regroup, but soon were ordered to return to the captured works, the 10th and 19th South Carolina occupying the trench to the left, or north, of the Hurt House. There they were subjected to a heavy artillery fire from a hill some thousand yards to the north.[17]

Observing the Confederate breakthrough along the Georgia Railroad, Sherman, at his headquarters at the Howard House on "Copenhill," had directed Schofield, commanding the Twenty-third Corps, to mass all the guns he could gather, some 20 in number, and open what the latter described as a "terrible raking fire."[18] Manigault remembered that "the shells tore through the lines or exploded in the faces of the men with unerring regularity."[19]

As soon as Gen. Logan, now in command of the Army of the Tennessee as a result of McPherson's death that morning, learned of the Confederate breakthrough and the capture of the De Gress Battery, he ordered the latter to be "retaken at all hazards."[20]

In compliance with these instructions, Gen. Woods of the First Division of the Fifteenth Corps, who had already opened a heavy artillery fire to prevent the removal of De Gress's guns, ordered his First and Second Brigades, posted in the vicinity of the Howard House, to change front to the left, move out and attack the enemy in flank and rear.

Meanwhile, on the Confederate side. Clayton's division, composed of Stovall's (Col. Abda Johnson), Holtzclaw's (Col. Bushrod Jones), Baker's (Col. John Higley) and Gibson's brigades, had been ordered, about 4 p.m. to shift to the right and support the attack of Hindman's division.[21]

With the 43rd Georgia deployed as skirmishers, Stovall's Brigade, under orders to keep the sun at its back, advanced by the right oblique and crossed to the south side of the Georgia R.R. There it drove the enemy from his works, holding them about 30 minutes in the face of a damaging enfilade fire on its unsupported right flank. Noticing that the enemy was massing and moving up large bodies of fresh men, and the troops on his left being withdrawn, Col. Johnson, commanding the brigade, withdrew it several hundred yards, where he met Gibson's Brigade advancing in line of battle. Assuming that the latter had been sent to his relief and would be thrown in on his unprotected right, Johnson prepared to return to the attack. When Gibson was moved to the rear, however, Johnson was compelled to abandon any thought of renewed offensive action and ordered Stovall's Brigade back to its original position.[22]

Holtzclaw's Brigade, under command of Col. Bushrod Jones, had been ordered to move out in support of Stovall's Brigade, attacking on the latter's left. Dense woods, however, prevented Jones from seeing the movements of Stovall's troops, and, instead of following the latter in their march by the right oblique, he advanced north of the railroad and came in sight of the enemy's works in the vicinity of the White House. There, he encountered Gen. Manigault and Col. Sharp.[23]

It will be recalled that, after the capture of the De Gress Battery and the breastworks north of the railroad, Manigault had been subjected to a punishing enfilade fire from the Union batteries near the Howard House. It was then, seeing only his own and Sharp's brigade fighting, that he had called for reinforcements. "Two brigades finally made their appearance, one of which was sent to the right to General Sharp, the other to me on the left."[24] These were the brigades of Stovall and Holtzclaw.

When Col. Jones came up with Holtzclaw's brigade, Manigault told him the enemy was massed in heavy force on his left flank (presumably Woods' troops moving down from the north in their counterattack to recapture the De Gress Battery), and that he must make a rapid change of front in that direction. This Jones did in fine style, executing the maneuver of change front to rear on the first battalion, which elicited Manigault's praise of Jones as "one of the coolest fellows I ever saw, handling his command with great ease and judgment."[25]

The line of Holtzclaw's brigade now faced generally north, forming nearly a right angle with that of Manigault. Urged on by the latter and Col. Sharp, Jones ordered his men forward. His two right regiments, the 38th and 36th Alabama, charged at a run, seized a portion of the works north of the Hurt House and poured several volleys into the ranks of the fleeing enemy, who abandoned four pieces of artillery, two caissons and a team of four horses.[26]

At this critical juncture, an order came to Manigault and Sharp to retire at once, as the enemy was massing on their left flank and rear and any delay would cause the loss or capture of the forces engaged. There was nothing to do but obey, although Manigault did so with the greatest reluctance, stoutly maintaining that the position could have been held.[27]

The consequences of the withdrawal of Manigault's and Sharp's men were immediate. Jones, his right flank now exposed, was forced to retreat in disorder, losing many prisoners. Clayton pulled back the rest of his division and the way was open for the Federal recapture of the De Gress Battery and the works north and south of the railroad.

Gen. Woods, coming down from the north, reported that "in less than fifteen minutes I had retaken De Gress's battery and driven the enemy from the rifle-pits on their left as far as the railroad. The whole rebel line then fell back, and the works were reoccupied by our troops."[28] But Woods' men were not alone in the recapture of the De Gress battery and the breastworks in its vicinity. Gen. Logan had also called on Gen. Dodge, commanding the Union Sixteenth Corps on the left, for help and had asked him to send the "little Dutchman's brigade" (Col. Mersy's). Logan, himself, conducted this redoubtable outfit — it was to fight three severe, widely separated actions that day — to a point north of the railroad, from which it charged and seized the De Gress battery as Woods' men were coming up on the right.[29]

At the same time, the regiments that had been forced back in confusion by the Confederate assault, reformed and, after repeated counterattacks, played their part in retaking the works from which they had been driven.[30]

That Manigault, without substantial reinforcement, which Hood was in no position to send, could have held his ground, in the face of such a display of force, seems conjectural at best. It is true, nonetheless, that after the Confederate withdrawal, the Union forces failed to pursue — in Manigault's words "not daring to follow us."[31]

The Brigade remained near the front until almost dark (the sun set that day at 6:55)[32] and was then withdrawn to the inner works. It had lost over 400 killed or wounded and some 30 missing, or more than 30 percent of the officers and men who had gone into action, casualties exceeded in its history only by those suffered in the bitter fighting at Chickamauga and Murfreesboro.[33]

R.L.T.

NOTES TO APPENDIX I

[1] *Battles and Leaders,* IV, 326.

[2] *Ibid.*

[3] J.B. Hood, *Advance and Retreat,* 190.

[4] S. Emanuel, *A Historical Sketch of the Georgetown Rifle Guards,* (n.p., 1909), 22.

[5] *O.R.,* XXXVIII, pt. 3, 235.

[6] *Ibid.,* 250.

[7] *Ibid.,* 778.

[8] *Ibid.,* 779-780.

[9] Robert L. Rodgers, *Capture of the De Gress Battery in the Battle of Atlanta,* (n.p., n.d. — 1898?), 9; C.I. Walker, *Rolls and Historical Sketch of the Tenth Regiment, So. Ca. Volunteers in the Confederate Army,* (Charleston, S.C., 1881). 114.

[10] A.M. Manigault, Narrative, 227.

[11] Rodgers, *Capture of the De Gress Battery,* 9; Walker, *Tenth Regiment,* 114.

[12] *O.R.,* XXXVIII, pt. 3, 223, 224, 228, 240-241, 245-246, 250-251, 254, 257, 258, 260.

[13] *Ibid.,* 265.

[14] Rodgers, *Capture of the De Gress Battery,* 9; Walker, *Tenth Regiment,* 115.

[15] *O.R.,* XXXVIII, pt. 3, 262.

[16] W.T. Sherman, *Memoirs,* II, 80; *O.R.,* XXXVIII, pt. 3, 265.

[17] Rodgers, *Capture of the De Gress Battery,* 9-10; *O.R.,* XXXVIII, pt. 3, 789.

[18] J.M. Schofield, *Forty-six Years in the Army,* (New York, 1897), 147.

[19] Manigault, Narrative, 228.

[20] *O.R.,* XXXVIII, pt. 3, 103.

[21] *Ibid.,* 819.

[22] Report of Col. Abda Johnson, commanding Stovall's Brigade in the action of July 22, 1864.*

[23] Report of Col. Bushrod Jones, commanding Holtzclaw's Brigade in the action of July 22, 1864.*

[24] Manigault, Narrative, 228.

[25] Ibid.

[26] Reports of Col. Bushrod Jones, commanding Holtzclaw's Brigade, Lt. Col. Thomas H. Herndon, commanding the 36th Alabama, and, 1st Lt. Jno. C. Dumas of the 38th Alabama.*

[27] Rodgers, Capture of the De Gress Battery, 4; Manigault, Narrative, 229.

[28] O.R., XXXVIII, pt. 3, 139-140.

[29] Ibid., 26, 103, 464; Battles and Leaders, IV, 329-330.

[30] O.R., XXXVIII, pt. 3, 179-180, 189, 201-202, 210, 217-219, 223-224, 240-241, 245-246, 250-251, 254, 257-258.

[31] Ibid., 819; Manigault, Narrative, 229.

[32] The Confederate States Almanac For The Year 1864 (Mobile, Ala.), 15.

[33] O.R., XXXVIII, pt. 3, 789; Manigault, Narrative, 229.

*These reports, which do not appear in the *Official Records* and have never been published or, to my knowledge, cited, are indispensable to an understanding of the part played by Clayton's division in the attack of July 22nd. They were found in the microfilm files of the Southern Historical Collection at the University of North Carolina at Chapel Hill. The originals are in the *Benjamin F. Cheatham Papers* in the Tennessee State Library and Archives in Nashville. Clearly, these reports were not available to Col. Rodgers, when, in 1898, he wrote what was intended to be the definitive account of the capture of the De Gress Battery by Manigault's Brigade. — *Editor.*

APPENDIX II

INTRODUCTION

The Mexican War Service
Of
1st Lt. Arthur Middleton Manigault

Arthur Middleton Manigault, together with many senior commanders on both sides of the Civil War, received his initial combat training during the Mexican War.

In company with such men as Ulysses S. Grant, George B. McClellan and George G. Meade in the North and Robert E. Lee, Braxton Bragg and Jefferson Davis of the Confederacy, he served the apprenticeship which prepared him for higher command in the later, bloodier war.

Few bothered to record their experiences as junior officers. Manigault was an exception. His notes were destroyed during the Civil War, but he wrote from memory a narrative of his service.

That manuscript he kept with his Civil War narrative. It is included here as an appendix. It furthers understanding of the general's character and life as well as knowledge of that largely forgotten conflict — the War with Mexico.

South Carolinians in 1846 held mixed opinions on the advisability of war with Mexico. However, when war came, enthusiasm warmed for the military and the state raised a regiment of volunteers, soon to known as the Palmetto Regiment. Its members included young Manigault who in June 1846 was elected first lieutenant of the Charleston Volunteers. They were mustered into the regiment as Capt. William Blanding's Company F.

The narrative describes Manigault's experiences from the date of his election until the regiment — or what was left of it after heavy casualties from combat and disease — arrived back in this country during the latter part of June 1848, following the end of the war.

It is a vivid account by an intelligent observer, an officer with sufficient knowledge and rank to understand the military situation, but too young for his thoughts to be colored by the political aspirations which so often biased the writings of older and more senior commanders during this war.

This is not to say that Manigault did not exhibit a certain amount of bias in his narrative. He was writing, as he mentioned in the Prologue to the Civil War narrative, *(See Page 1)* not for publication but for the edification of his children. He was a man of strong convictions and his opinions of such men as Gen. Franklin Pierce, later president of the United States, and of the character of the Mexican people in general are often forceful and without equivocation.

However, unlike most officers who wrote for publication after the Mexican War, Manigault's narrative is refreshingly free of braggadocio or snide remarks designed to enhance his own reputation at the expense of others.

Manigault neglected to date the Mexican War manuscript. However, statements in both narratives suggest that he penned it immediately prior to writing his Civil War record, that is to say between the end of the war in 1865 and 1868 *(See Introduction, Page II)*.

It appears to be the work of a man in a hurry to complete a preliminary chore before beginning what, to Manigault, must have been a much more interesting endeavor. Consequently, we find a greater number of careless spelling and punctuation errors in the Mexican War manuscript than in that of the Civil War to which Manigault no doubt devoted far greater thought and effort.

For instance, such a simple word as "village" — which Manigault certainly knew how to spell — turns up indiscriminately as "vilage" or "village." Punctuation also is casual, to say the least. Consequently, to preserve the flavor of Manigault's manuscript, the editors have retained, for the most part, the author's spelling and punctuation, changing them only where deemed necessary. These instances are few and the manuscript is essentially the way the general penned it shortly after his return home in 1865.

(Arthur M. Wilcox and Warren Ripley,
editors of the Mexican War narrative)

THE PREFACE

(The Narrative)

The Palmetto Regiment — which was mustered into service in the latter part of the year 1846 numbering Officers and men one thousand and forty (1,040) — after having taken a prominent part in the campaigns of Genl. Scott[1] in Mexico on the line from Vera Cruz to the capital, was mustered out in Mobile on their return to the U.S. in the latter part of June 1848.

Its losses had been very heavy, many having died of the diseases common to the climate of Mexico, made more fatal as is invariably the case when large numbers of men are brought together, large numbers were killed or wounded, and a few captured and never again heard of. The greater number of deaths, however, were from disease. As nearly as I can arrive at it, and I endeavoured on our return to the U.S. to make an estimate, I do not think that more than four hundred men out of the original number were alive when the Regiment was disbanded in Mobile.

To our first Colonel, P.M. Butler,[2] killed at Churubusco, the regiment was indebited for much of the reputation which it acquired during its term of service. He had the remarkable & valuable faculty of instilling into his men a pride in themselves and an esprit de corps which effectually detered them on more than one occasion from giving way when hard pressed by heavy odds & when others near them were doing so. On two occasions, in that portion of the field in which they were engaged together with a considerable portion of the army, they retrieved the fortunes of the day, saving their Generals from disgrace, and winning honor for themselves. By his management, tact and judicus discipline he succeeded in impressing each individual with the idea that he personally was responsible to a considerable extent in sustaining the reputation of his corps for courage, prompt and ready obedience to orders and other qualites essential to a good soldier. Altho not much of a drill officer he was an admirable disciplinarian and the good influence of his administration was invaluable to the Regt. and was felt to the end. For precision in drill and the ordinary duties of the soldier, we were indebted to Major (afterwards Colonel) A.H. Gladden[3] himself a good soldier and a bold leader.*

---

* The same Genl. Gladden of the Confederate States Army killed in April 1862 at the Battle of Shiloh. — A.M.M.

I think it has generally been conceded that the reputation of the Palmetto Regiment during the war with Mexico was second to no other amongst the voluntiers and only equaled by the 1st Mississipi commanded by Col. Jefferson Davis.[4] The material of which it was composed was from amongst the best citizens of the State of S.C. Most of them young men of good family and well to do in the world.

The regiment took part in the following named

Battles

1. Contreras	—	Valley of Mexico	—	Augst.	19,	1847
2. Churubusco	—	Do	—	,,	20	,,
3. Chapultapec	—	Do	—	Sptbr.	12/13	,,
4. Garita Balen						
(& City of Mexico)	—	Do	—	,,	13	,,
5. Seige of Vera Cruz	—	V.C.	—	March		,,

(It was also engaged in
(four or five skirmishes.

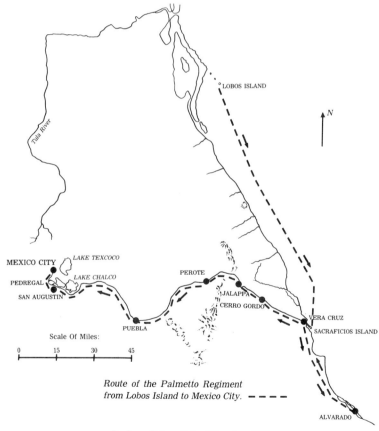

Route of the Palmetto Regiment
from Lobos Island to Mexico City. — — — —

Lobos Island to Mexico City

A Record Of My Military Services.

(The Narrative)

F inding that many of the events and actions in which I took part are becoming confused in my mind, as to dates &c., some of which I have forgotten, my note book having been lost, & the means of reference being very limited, I have here enumerated an outline of the campaigns, battles & skirmishes for future reference.

Was elected in June 1846 1st Lieutenant of the Charleston Voluntiers, Co. F. of the Palmetto Regiment, a regiment of volunteers (Infantry) raised for the war with Mexico, Pierce M. Butler being the Colonel. The regiment was not called into service until the month of November following when its organization was completed & in Decbr. it started by land for Mobile. At that point it was placed on board of transports & sailed for Lobos Island in the Gulf of Mexico to join the army of General Scott, rendezvousing at that place for an attack on Vera Cruz.

On this island we remained about three weeks & from thence we sailed to Point Anton Lizardo, reaching it in three days, here awaiting a favorable state of weather, wind &c. The entire army was collected in transports together with a considerable naval force & on the 10th of March 1847 the entire fleet set sail for Vera Cruz and on the same evening the greater part of the army landed on the coast about three miles south of V.C. & opposite the small Isld. of Sacraficios. On the 11th the Palmetto Regt. landed & were brigaded with the Georgia & Alabama Regts. commanded by Genl. Quitman.[5] The investment of the city was soon completed. The regiment was constantly engaged on the necessary works — construction of batteries & in doing picket and other military duties — from this period until the surrender of the city. Our batteries opened on the enemy on the 22nd of March, the bombardment continuing with but little intermission until the 29th when the surrender took place, the garrison of between 4 & 5,000 men under Genl. Landero[6] marching out & the United States forces marching in, Scotts effective force being at the time, if I remember rightly, about 13,000 men of all arms.

Early in May, a few days after the surrender, Genl. Quitman with his Brigade, a section of artillery (12 pdrs), (and) a squadron of cavalry, was ordered to march upon the small town of Alvarado situated near the mouth of the Alvarado river, distant South of Vera Cruz about (70) seventy miles. A United States vessel of war being ordered to meet him near that point to cooperate with the land forces.

Lieut. Hunter,[7] arriving before the infantry, finding that he could cross the bar & being informed that there was only a small & demoralized force in the batteris defending the town determined if possible to capture it before the arrival of the land forces, (and) made the effort. After a short cannonade the enemy evacuated the place & Lieut or Capt. Hunter took possession. On the following day Genl. Quitman arrived with his troops & was much mortified to find that the honor, if any could be gained from so small an affair, had been appropriated by the navy.

At Alvarado the command remained three days & were then hastily summonsed to return to Vera Cruz. Both on the march to & from Alvarado the time occupied was two days and a half over a bare sandy country exposed to a burning sun & almost destitute of drinking water. The men had been much reduced by their privations & exposure around V.C. The health of the command was bad, many being afflicted with fevers, chills & diarrhoea. Physically most of them were unfit for the severe and forced march to which they were subjected & the consequence of which was that many broke down, & from the miserable diet & worse water the seeds of those diseases were contracted, from which many poor fellows died in the course of the next six months & many more suffered from (them) for years. It must have cost the regiment two hundred and fifty men, lost to the service from the time of their return from this expedition. I have never suffered so much from fatigue & thirst as during these few days. During this march I saw for the first time in my life what is known as a mirage. The deception was complete, luring many in search of water from ponds and lakes, which were as plainly visible as tho they actually existed.

On our return to V.C. the greater part of the army had advanced in the direction of Jalappa on the high road to the City of Mexico. Our Brgd. remained in the vicinity of V.C. nearly a week & were then ordered forward to join the army an engagement being imminent. We were however too late to take part in the Battle of Cerro Gordo arriving there two days after it had been fought. Tho thirty miles distant from the action we could distinctly hear the discharge of artillery. The Battle of Cerro Gordo was fought on the (18) Apl. (1847) & was a complete victory on the part of the U.S. troops over the Mexicans. The loss on both sides was heavy, but far greater on the part of the enemy, including all their artillery.

At the beautiful town of Jalappa, about sixty miles from V.C. & situated at the point separating what is known as the Tierra Calliente country from the more elevated or healthy regions, we remained about one week. Here the other two regiments of our brigade from Georgia & Alabama, there term of service having expired (12 months), were sent back to the coast to be disbanded & their places supplied by a New York & Pensylvania Rgts, regiments far inferior to our old comrades in drill discipline and efficiency. There never was any good feeling between us & much of our subsequent loss was owing to a deficiency on their part, not very creditable to them, which we were on more than one occasion called upon to supply.

Genl. Worth[8] in the latter part of May was ordered by Genl. Scott to advance on Puebla, distant from Jalappa about 70 miles & the next city in size & importance to the Capital. Quitman's brigade was attached to his command. The Castle of Perote, a strongly fortified work built of heavy masonry and most admirably situated for defence, was evacuated by its garrisson on our approach & was quietly taken possession of. Here we remained one day & leaving the 1st Pensylvania Regt as a garrisson we again moved on in the direction of Puebla. Perote is very nearly equidistant between Vera Cruz & the City of Mexico & is situated in a level, open plain in a long valley, its width being from five to eight miles.

The country about (is) very poor & used but little for other purposes than for pasturage, immense herds of every discription of cattle here find subsistence.

On the 30th April whilst on the march a heavy demonstration was made on our column by a large body of cavalry, estimated to be about 2,500 strong & commanded by Santa Anna in person. They were easily driven off by our artillery, very few of the infantry being used for the purpose.

On the 1st of May (1847) the Civil authorites, with a flag of truce from Puebla, met the Genl. comdg. & surrendered the city, the military having retired, & on the same (day) we marched in & took possession. Our force being comparatively small, not exceeding 3,500 men, & not having much faith in Mexican assurances, there was much anxiety felt for several days on the part of all & many indications were apparent of an outbreak on the part of the citizens & Mexican soldiers who were known to be within the city disguised as civilians. The admirable precautions taken by our General, however, & strong guards & patrols constantly on duty effectually put a stop to any threatened rising which had it taken place, would have resulted in most unfortunately for the Mexicans, & with comparatively little harm to ourselves. Puebla contains about 80,000 inhabitants, is a large & beautiful city with regularly laid out streets, broad & well paved & kept very clean. There are many handsome buildings public and private & a large number of Churches & monastaries. The Cathedral, tho not as large as that of the City, (*Mexico City*) is I think a handsomer & more imposing looking building both as regards its exterior & interior appearance. Here we were quartered in the monastary of St. Augustin in which there was ample room for the accommodation of the entire regiment numbering some 700 men & about forty officers. During this month the remainder of the army gradually assembled here and for three months we had a very pleasant time of it. There was no dearth of amusement and the markets of all kinds were abundantly supplied & purchases could be made at very reasonable rates.

The army generally here suffered greatly from the diseases of the country to which the men were unacclimated, & became more liable from their imprudences & the too free indulgence in fruits which were abundant & to be obtained in large quantities for a mere trifle. The water also was abominable. This however is the case throughout Mexico but the injurious effects of its too free use began to be more apparent here. Many died, more became confirmed invalids & there services lost to the country from that time. The Mexicans themselves drink very little water and foreigners are always warned against doing so, the lower orders substituting "pulquie" a slightly fermented liquor obtained from the Maguay plant & the better classes, whilst pulquie is also freely used by them, as a general rule drink large quantities of claret & the lighter German wines. I do not remember ever to have seen a Mexican drinking water alone.

It was of course almost, indeed utterly impossible to prevent our soldiers & even officers from drinking water freely altho warned what the consequence would be. Indeed for very considerable periods it was water or nothing else, but they gradually became aware of the necessity for abstinence in this respect and after overcoming the repulsive taste of poulquie, which at first is neausuris in the extreme, by degrees became almost as fond of it as the natives themselves.

About the middle of May what is known as the rainy season sets in & usually lasts until the middle of August.

I was much surprised to find instead of a constant rain or rather a great quantity of it with damp drizzly murky weather where it would be scarcely possible to stir out with any degree of comfort, that it was one of the most delightful seasons of the year. At about from two to three O'clock there would be indications of a thunder storm which in the course of 30 or 40 minutes accompanied by thunder and lightning, would burst over the entire country & a steady & heavy rain lasting from two to three hours after which the clouds would disperse, the sun again appear & the remainder of the evening would be bright & clear with a cool bracing atmosphere. The streets & principal highways being well graded & paved, the system of surface draining almost perfect, you could within a few minutes after such a shower walk out with thin shoes without any fear of soiling them or getting your feet damp.

On the following day the sun would rise in a bright & cloudless sky, all nature appearing refreshed from the rain of the day before & until about the same hour in the afternoon there would be no indications of other than a hot dry spell of weather. For about three months the discription of one day will answer for all — of course there are some exceptions to this rule — & only on two or three occasions have I

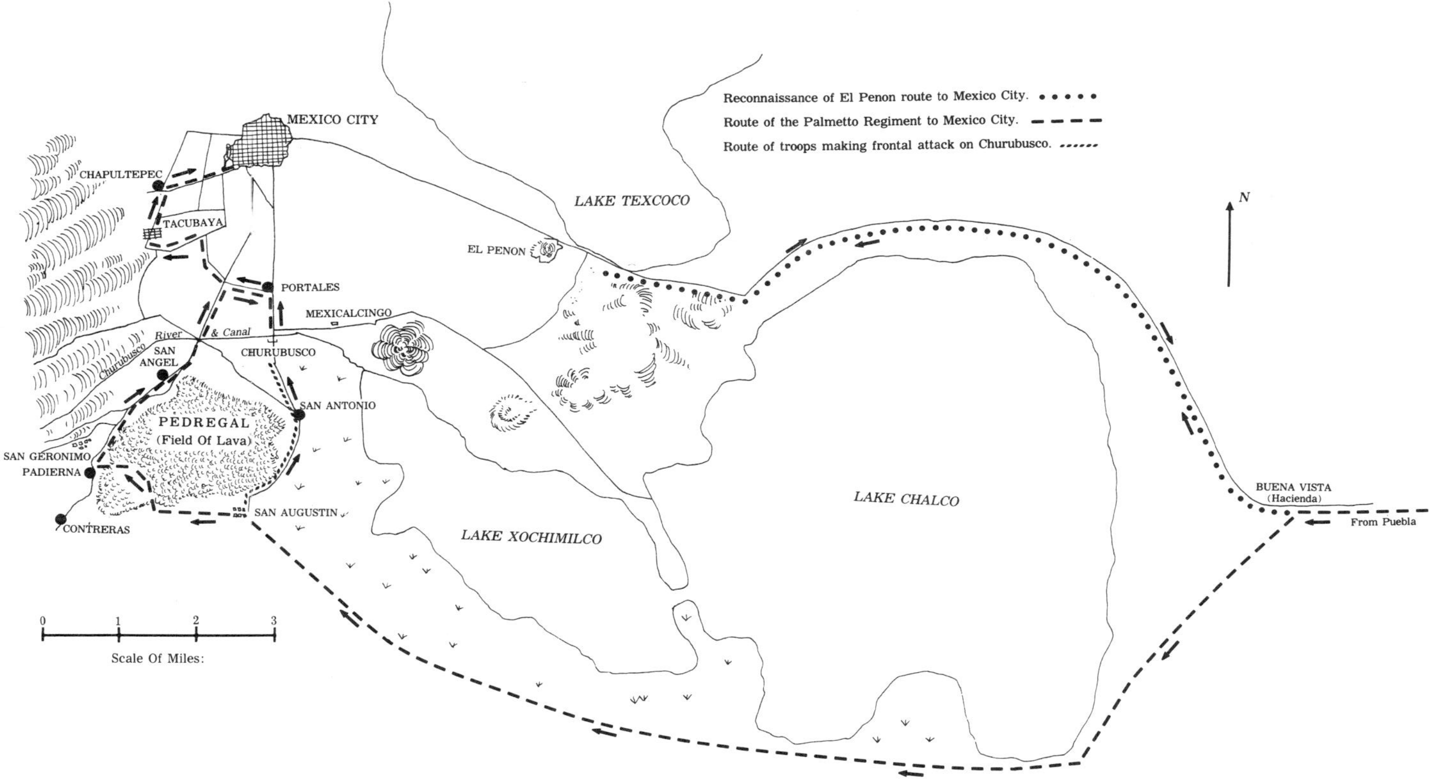

Reconnaissance of El Penon route to Mexico City. ••••••
Route of the Palmetto Regiment to Mexico City. — —
Route of troops making frontal attack on Churubusco. ‒‒‒‒‒‒

N

LAKE TEXCOCO

EL PENON

MEXICO CITY

CHAPULTEPEC

TACUBAYA

PORTALES

MEXICALCINGO

CHURUBUSCO

River & Canal

SAN ANGEL

SAN GÉRONIMO

PADIERNA

CONTRERAS

PEDREGAL
Field Of Lava

SAN ANTONIO

SAN AUGUSTIN

LAKE XOCHMILCO

LAKE CHALCO

BUENA VISTA
(Hacienda)

From Puebla

Scale Of Miles:

0   1   2   3

Lake Chalco to Mexico City

304

known it rain all night & as seldom have I known an entire day to be cloudy.

Puebla is on the first table land between V.C. & Mexico *(City)*. *(It)* is I believe about 7,000 feet above the level of the sea, the country around it very slightly undulating, the land fertile & highly cultivated, the sceenery very soft & pretty the climate delightful. The weather is very warm but not as much so as the low country of South Carolina, the nights cool — a blanket to cover with being necessary to comfort — & the evenings & mornings until 9 A.M. always pleasant.

During the month of July the health of the army gradually improved. It had lost heavily. Our regiment had been particularly unfortunate, the Alvarado trip told severely upon us & it was one of the causes of our severe losses.

On the 1st of August it became evident to all that our advance was about to be made and altho we had enjoyed ourselves much in this delightful city and our military duties had been by no means arduous we all hailed with delight the prospect of more active movements, the certainty of a conflict with the enemy, little dreaming of the hardships & heavy losses in life & limbs that we were about to meet with & the gratification our hopes & curiosity in a triumphal march into the City of Mexico.

On the 8th of August 1847 Genl. Twiggs[9] Division moved in advance on the high road to the city. Our Division followed on the 9th, Quitman now a major genl. comdg.. & Brigd. Genl. Shields[10] now our immediate comdr. having been given the 1st New York & our own regiment. On the two following days the two remaining Divisions also took up the same line of march.

At Buena Vista, a Hacienda near the foot of the mountain on the side of the Valey of Mexico, the army concentrated. Here they were distant about 12 or 15 miles from the city. Within three miles of it the high road passed by a causeway of some length. Across the lake *(Texcoco)* where the road again strikes the high land there is almost immediately opposite to it a remarkably high hill or mount composed of rock known as El Penion. Here the great bulk of the Mexican army lay prepared to defend any advance of the invaders upon their capital by this route. El Penion was fortified in the most approved manner with infantry & heavy artillery, battery rising above battery, with infantry breast works extending along its base & to the right and left extending to the lake on either side. The only approach to it being by a causeway less than forty feet wide with water on each side. The position was impregnable & it would have been folly to have attacked it. After pushing forward recognizances in several directions Genl Scott determined to endeavour to flank this position & to turn it by moving round the borders of the lake *(Chalco)* in the direction of St. Augustine & attacking the city from one of the other highways leading into it & where it was hoped that the defences would be found less formidable and elaborate, although the formidable Castle of Chapulta-pec would prove an obstacle not easily to be overcome. The objections to moving to our right & east of the city were said to be very great & the distance necessary in making the circuit, from the configuration of the country, very considerable.

The new movement was soon commenced & altho our movements were necessarily slow owing to the destruction of the roads, bridges &c. the former being narrow, badly constructed & being but little used (the lakes being the highway principally used by the inhabitants of this portion of the valley in their intercourse with the city) it was necessary in many instances to construct new ones over a rough & broken country. Our route lay near the foot of the inner range of Mts. (smaller ones) which encircale the Valley of Mexico, the edges of the lake *(Chalco)* being on our right or a swampy low country contiguous to the same. On the 1st August we were within a few miles of St. Augustine, quite a flurushing village about 9 miles from Mexico *(City)* our change of route made the distance from Puebla to the city fifty miles greater than by the direct road, passing the Penion Mt.

For a day or two previous some sharp skirmishing had been going on with the enemy who now began to develop themselves, having changed their front & anticipating our movements were fast getting into a state of preparedness to receive us. Their positions were at "Mexicalhingo" on the San Antonio road and at Contreras, a strong position on the road thro the village of "San Angel" to the city entering it at the gate of "Nino Perdido."

On the morning of the 19th, Quitman's command entered the village of St. Augustine. During the day heavy cannonading was heard in the directions of Contreras & on the San Antonio road. From the steeple of the Church (quite a high one) we could distinctly see the Mexican forces at Contreras distant about four miles busily engaged in throwing up works & strengthning their position, Pillow's[11] command at the time steadily feeling their way towards them. At about 3 OC in the afternoon the fire became very heavy & the battle in reality commenced. Shield's Brgd. (our Regt & 1st N.Y.) soon after received orders to move forward in this direction as well as a considerable portion of the army. At about 5 OC we came under fire of their artillery.

The position of the enemy was very strong. In their front lay the "Pedrigal," a volcanic formation composed of broken ruggid rocks varying in hight from 5 to 20 feet broken up into fizures of different widths & forming a heterogenious mass which from its sharp & jagged outlines made it an obstacle in our approach to the enemy almost insurmountable. Its width varied I should judge from ½ to 1¼ miles. Over this we toiled until dark making but little head way. The inequalities of the ground however gave much protection from the enemies fire, the greatest danger being from the fragments of rock splintered by the enemies cannon balls. As dark approached the firing gradually ceased, the night became dark & stormy & a steady rain set in. It having become evident to the commander in chief that an attack upon the enemies front could not well be undertaken with any prospect of success or only by a great sacrifice of life, Pillow's Division was ordered to remain in the enemies front with instructions to occupy the enemies attention during the night & in the morning at daylight to make a demonstration as if about to attack. The remainder of the troops, Riley's,[12] Persifer Smith's[13] & Shields' Brgds, were ordered if possible during the night to cross the "Pedrigal," move to our right & to the left of the enemies position at a point where the ground presented fewer obstacles & where only a force of cavalry had been posted to protect the flank of the Mexican army. Riley had succeeded just about dark in getting a position on the side of the Pedrigal nearest the enemy, the other two Brigades moved in the same direction in the dark. There was no road or even path way along which to march or prominent point visible in the dark by which to take the proper direction but under the leadership of Capt. Robt. E. Lee,[14] engineer officer, after a wearing march of five hours we halted almost broken down with fatigue & much bruised & sore from repeated & severe falls over this the roughest country that I ever saw, the distance we had come not being over three miles. The night was one of the darkest in my experience and altogether the most uncomfortable one that I ever passed. Day light showed that we were to the left & a little in rear of the enemy's position, hidden from their sight by an undulation of the ground & on the principal road by which the enemy could retreat from the position at Contreras to the City of Mexico. The other two brigades under the command of Genl. Persifer Smith were still further in their rear & preparing to assault which as soon as it commenced would be a signal for a general advance.

(Gabriel) Valencia, the Genl. comdg the Mexicans, seemed to be entirely unaware of the dangerous proximity of his enemies & was completely cut off an hemmed in by his enemies. His command numbered about 11,000 of the best troops in their army. Their cavalry numbering about 3,000 men, not included in the above estimate, behaved very badly. The light of morning showed them to us about a half mile beyond us on the road before mentioned, nearer to the city than we were & drawn up on a ridge to right & left of the road. In the direct attack upon the works our brigade took no part as we were held in reserve & furthermore it was necessary that some portion of troops in this part of the field should be in position to hold this formidable force of cavalry in check.

It was one of the most imposing sights that I had ever seen, this body of cavalry. They were quite near enough to be distinctly seen as they advanced towards us & as they formed on the sumit of a high hill gradually sloping down towards us the figures of men & horses. Their outlines distinctly visible against the grey sky, both horses and men looked as tho their proportions were immense (tho not really so) excitement and anxiety magnifying them no doubt to our vision. One could tell almost to a man the length of line occupied by each regiment, by the different colours of their horseman cloaks. Their long lances with their bright steel heads & red pennons made them look exceedingly venomous & a nearer acquaintance with them did not seem to be atall desirable. A stream much swolen by the rain of the preceeding night lay within 100 yards of our front which altho it might have been crossed, was really a serious impediment in their way & the result can hardly be considered doubtful had they attempted it. Some slight skirmishing took place between us. Their comdg officer seeing the difficulty in his way was evidently making dispositions to cross the stream higher up & beyond the fire of our guns & his columns had commenced the movement for this purpose when the action began by our attack on the enemies position. The departure of the greater part of the cavalry now allowed us to change our dispositions & to prepare for our part in the engagement. The firing had now become heavy & continuous the artillery & small arms keeping up a continuous war. We had just changed front & were prepared for action when several detached & considerable bodies of cavalry made their appearance rapidly retreating from the rear of the works. Our command now (was) facing the road leading to the position of the Mexicans. On our right was a stone wall enclosing a large orchard. The other angle of this wall extended along the road. On the oposite side & in our front the country was open but practicable for infantry only. Immediately after the cavalry came the head of a column of a large reserve of infantry who were rapidly retreating from the scene of action. They did not seem to be aware of our position until the leading companies began to clear the angle of the wall. Here our fire opened, checking for a short time their advance. Again they moved forward & endeavoured to deploy & partially succeeded but the withering fire poured into them by the S.C. Regt soon threw them into inextricable confusion. Regiment after Rgt endeavoured to execute the same movement, but with no better success. The fugitives from the works (which had by this time been carried by the combined attack of our forces) with artillery cavalry & wagons now pressed on the rear of the column with which we were engaged creating a great panic & the confusion became inextricable. The Mexican officers in many instances behaved with great galantry & did all they could to restore order & to save if possible their command. Our fire was replied to spiritedly but with little effect. The aim of the Mexicans was bad & the great bulk of their balls flew harmlessly over our heads. Finding that the combat was a hopeless one on their part & that if long continued would result in their total annihilation, officers & men threw down their arms & gave all the usual indications of a desire to surrender. Our firing ceased by order and steps were taken to secure our prisoners. Almost every man of the enemy who was not killed or wounded was captured & I think the number of prisoners could not have been less than 2,500. Our fire had been terribly effective, being almost entirely concentrated on the point of the road near where the enemy debouched from behind the wall of the orchard. Those in rear pressing forward those in front presented a living mass into which nearly every bullet told. I have never seen either before or since so many bodies of men killed or wounded collected over a space of a few acres as I did on this occasion. In many places they were lying one on top of another & hundreds of bodies in contact with each other. The killed & wounded must have amounted to from 1,800 to 2,000 men. Our own loss was comparatively trifling. The victory was a decisive & complete one. The attack & arrangements for it was masterly & about the only battle in this war & on this line where there was any military genius & skill displayed. The taking of this place now rendered it necessary that the enemy should abandon their other positions on the San Antonio Road and at Mexicalhingo as both these other points were turned. The loss of this Army to Mexico was a most serious blow. Altho Valencia with a considerable body of his men made their escape, they were too much demoralized by their defeat to be of any real service to their country for sometime to come. Santa Anna still had near 25,000 men with which to oppose the Americans & he immediately began to concentrate them at Churubusco about six miles from Contreras.

At the Vilage of Churubusco a formidable set of works had been thrown up & batteries armed with heavy artillery & field pieces had been constructed commanding the road leading into the city by the gate known as "Garita San Antonio Abad."

On the 20th August, 1847, the different detached columns of the U.S. army from different points moved by various roads & gradually converged on the new position of the enemy at Churubusco. At San Angel, that portion of the army which had been engaged at Contreras were collected about one O'Clock. The position of the enemy could be seen at various points where the view was unobstructed. The troops soon became aware from the movements of the generals & from portions of conversations overheard by them that an attack was in contemplation. Soon after some of them moved off. Several batteries of Artillery galloped by us & about two O.C. the first fireing began which rapidly increased giving evidence of the commencement of another battle. Shield's Brgd. was again apparently held in reserve. From our position we could catch an unsatisfactory view of the field of battle & like most young soldiers I believe that there were but few of our men (Palmetto Rgt.) who were not foolish enough to be exceedingly disappointed & mortified at our present state of inactivity, fearing that the battle would be fought & won without our being called upon & believing that the enemy could be as easily beaten again as at Contreras. Two hours later those who were left alive were certainly sadder & perhaps wiser men & I doubt if ever again they felt any desire to expose themselves voluntarily in battle merely as a pastime & for the excitement of the thing.

It soon became evident that our men in front had their hands full. The stragglers & wounded passing us on their way to the rear did not give very cheering accounts, the fire of our artillery also began to slacken and we soon learned that one battery (Taylors or Duncans, I do not remember which)[15] had been almost completely destroyed by the overwhelming fire of the enemys artillery. About this time Genl. Scott galloped by us with several of his staff having but just arrived upon the ground. My own impression has been & still continues to be, in spite of history & Genl. Scott's report, that the action was brought on without his order & most unexpectedly to him. The cause of his late arrival on the ground may be explained by the fact of really not knowing the condition of affairs at Contreras it taking him sometime to cross the Pedrigal to reach the battle field to this point. Communications from the Genls. advancing from other points — their roads being opened by the rapid retreat of the Mexicans caused by the defeat at Contreras — did not reach him until they themselves following up the retiring enemy found themselves again in the enemies front at Churubusco. A general order had, I also believe, been given to the different commanders to push forward their advances rapidly whenever the enemy should give way or retire. Each comdg officer of the three grand divisions of the Army, finding themselves in close proximity to the enemy & to each other, not believing that the enemy could offer a serious resistance to their advance, pushed forward to the attack, making only careless recognizance, each inflamed with a desire to out do the other, made them more careless than they would otherwise have been so that they hurried their men into an engagement without determining on any general plan of battle, even without having confered with one another. I myself heard the hasty report of an Officer of Engineers to the ranking Genl. of the body of troops to which we were attached to the effect "that there was only a one gun battery with a small supporting force in the way which could easily be captured." The receipt of the information was immediately followed by an order to advance. Most fortunately without any combination whatever & without knowing anything of the plans of the other, the attack commenced almost at the same time from three different points. On the arrival of Scott, it was too late to draw out & it was almost impossible to communicate his orders to each Genl. so simultaniously as to obtain concert of action. He could only make use of such troops as he could lay his hands upon or whom he found unimployed to the best advantage. From him an order soon came to us to move forward. Marching by a flank we made a short circuit of the enemies right, crossed the stream of Churubusco on a bridge, filed to the right thro a succession of corn fields in the last of which we found Genl. Pierce[16] (afterwards President) lying on the ground & complaining much of injuries received by a fall from his horse on the same morning or evening before, I have forgotten which.

He was just about 200 yards beyond the enemies fire. His own Brigade had preceeded ours. On emerging from this last field we found ourselves in a large open one unplanted a mile or so long and about 500 yards in width. Pierce's Brgd. which had been engaged had been beaten back loosing heavily. The N.Y. Regt. which had been in advance had not been under fire more than ten minutes & had had enough. Not more than 100 men or thereabouts who had gathered about their color were showing any front. The rear of a large row of buildings consisting of the stables and barns of the Hacienda of Portales was thronged with our soldiers who had taken refuge behind it. A low wall in front & the roof of the buildings were however occupied by the more daring spirits who were returning in a lively manner the enemies fire. Our Regt. had been much strung out by our rapid movement & consequently much time had been lost in forming our line & before the left was in position our right, which was necessarily for a longer time exposed, suffered severely.

Here we found ourselves in rear of the right wing of the Mexican line of battle & advancing on a large reserve force stationed on the road which passed thro their works & for the defence of which they were now battling. The line formed by this reserve was directly at right angles with that of the main line so that a figure very like that of the letter T showed the formation of the enemy. The force here opposed to us consisted of infantry, estimated at 7,000 men, strongly posted in the ditches on either side of the road. On our left flank & still higher up the same road were a large number of houses forming the Hacienda Portales. This place was held by a large body of cavalry, who altho they did not attempt to charge us annoyed us very much with a heavy flank fire. After advancing to within 250 to 300 yards of the enemy we opened fire on them but as the greater part of their persons were hidden in the ditch it could not be very effectual.

The enemies fire was very severe killing & wounding numbers of our men. As we were unsupported & the aim of the enemy was concentrated upon us it became evident that we must either fall back or be annihilated. We were too much reduced in numbers & the enemy too far exceeded us, to render it likely that a charge would be successful. An order soon came for us to retire which we did in good order, occasionally facing about & fireing. When near the buildings first mentioned, we were again halted. By some mistake a 2d order was given to advance which again (we) did for a short distance when it was countermanded. We now retired behind the farm buildings & our lines reformed & gaps closed. So far the battle had gone against us & in this portion of the field we were clearly beaten. Shields, who commanded here, exerted himself greatly to restore order & laboured to induce the other troops to reform & again engage the enemy. He was ably seconded by Col. Ransom[17] from Main comdg 9th U.S.I. & Col. Butler who immediately calling upon his regt. they promptly responding led them out again & established a nucleus on which to form a new line while the other regts were forming on us. Our men went down fast. The 9th Rgt. supported us handsomely. I have nothing to say in favor of any other. They were nothing more than handfuls of men who with the colors of their comds. formed in a confused manner upon our right & left.

Again we advanced to within a short distance of the enemy & poured a rapid fire into them. After a few minutes fireing they appeared much shaken. Inded the front line was now giving way & fugitives began to show themselves amongst the enemy reserve. The heavy firing in their rear caused by our movement had alarmed & demoralized the troops on the front line. Twiggs & Worth again throwing themselves against them at this critical moment succeeded in breaking their line at the same time that Shields now ordered us to charge. It did not take us two minutes to reach the enemy. Few waited to resist our charge & all in a moment was rout & confusion, and so far as the battle is concerned, it was ended. The enemy were pursued, such as were not killed wounded or captured, to within a few hundred yards of the lines encircling the city by our cavalry. It would have been better if the entire army had also advanced as had they done so there is little doubt but that it would have fallen into our hands before morning. Genl. Scott however thought differently & did not push forward with his army. It is true that the men were much overcome with the exertions of the two or three days preceeding, our losses heavy & physically we were almost unable to sustain much more fatigue to which there can be no doubt we would have been subjected to say nothing of the additional fighting which would have attended our advance & efforts to break thro their strongly fortified lines. The loss in our regiment was very nearly two hundred men out of about 440 carried into action. The gallant Colonel Butler was shot thro the head and instantly killed.* Shortly after our regiment had been reformed for the last charge he had previously been shot thro the leg. He retired for a few minutes to have his wound attended to & then again rejoined his regiment. Early in the action his horse had been shot under him. He was much beloved by his command, was a good soldier and disciplinarian and upon the whole the best man to command Volunteers that I ever met with. His loss was a severe one to us & no one ever filled his position with the same amount of satisfaction to us. Had he lived I have no doubt but that the regiment would have been even more distinguished than it became.

Lieut. Col. Dickinson[18] near the close of the battle was mortally wounded. He had seized the colors when the color bearer fell & was leading the Regt. when he was struck down. He was a brave officer.

Besides these, our two ranking officers, there were five others killed & many wounded & many of our best men here finished their career on earth. The army suffered severely in officers & men but our Regt. more than any other. It was a

---

*Pencilled in above and underlined is an apparent later correction by Manigault: "He had previously been shot thro the thigh." — Editors.

hard fought fight against great odds. Our force could not have exceeded 10,000 men in all whilst that of the enemy must have been at least 25,000. The position could have been turned & a careful recognizance, I feel satisfied, have brought about a result much more satisfactory to us and I think our loss would not have been near so heavy. Where we fought was the true point of attack but we were too few in number. The greater part of the army should have been put in at this point instead of attacking the enemy, just where they wanted us to do it & where all the advantage was on their side, but unfortunately before he was aware of it Scott found his army involved in a most serious battle from which it was scarcely possible extricate it & the best thing that he could do was to let it go on & to use to the greatest advantage such troops as he found unengaged or could *(get)* his hands upon. He certainly did so to advantage & in this way showed a good deal of skill & presence of mind. I think some other Genls. whilst hurrying pell mell into action had visions of the White House before their eyes. During the night a proposition for an armistice with a view to a treaty of peace was received from the enemy & during the following day it was definitely arranged.

The army encamped in various positions in the vicinity of San Angel, San Augustine, Tacubayia & other vilages & we were soon busily engaged in repairing losses, reorganizing & taking the proper steps to increase its efficiency. During this period our wounded were well cared for. A reasonable amount of drill was very properly required of us but still we had much time for amusement & I enjoyed myself much in riding from point to point where the different divisions & brigades of the army lay not more than a mile or two separated one from an other yet it was not safe to move between them unless with a party of three or four. I was much interested in these excursions, had some agreeable adventures & was delighted with the country.

Unfortunately this period of repose & enjoyment too soon came to an abrupt end. Santa Anna[19] and the Mexican authorities had overreached our Genl. & the U.S. commissioner.

Their purpose had only been to gain time & to make additional arrangements for the security of their capital. No definite or satisfactory terms for a peace could be agreed upon, yet our Genl. &c was encouraged to believe that in course of time an arragement agreeable to both governments would be effected. In the meantime in direct violation of one of the articles of agreement of the armistice the enemy was prosecuting his labors with great energy & their works and defences were being strengthened and additional troops brought into the city. This could not continue long without being discovered & the knowledge of the fact caused an abrupt termination of the truce on the 7th of Sept., I think.

On the 8th the Battle of "Molino Del Rey" was fought. Two Divisions under the command of Worth were engaged in it. Altho it resulted in a victory it was a dearly purchased one. Our loss exceeded 800 men & officers & the advantage derived was by no means commensurate *(to)* our loss. Both Genls Scott & Worth have been much blamed for this affair & each in turn throwing the blame on the other produced an ill will between the two & their partizans the ill effects of which was soon easily descernable & produced no little harm.

This whole affair has never been divested of the mystery which surrounded it and I ever have been & still am unable to form a satisfactory opinion in my own mind as to who was to blame & where the fault lay. I have heard the different accounts from the friends of each, both parties professing to be thoroughly posted & each swearing that his representation was correct, but am stil as mistifyed as ever.

On the morning of the day of the battle of Molino Del Rey at daylight our command (Quitman's) moved out from San Augustine & advanced towards Tacubayia near which place the engagement was fought. We could distinctly hear

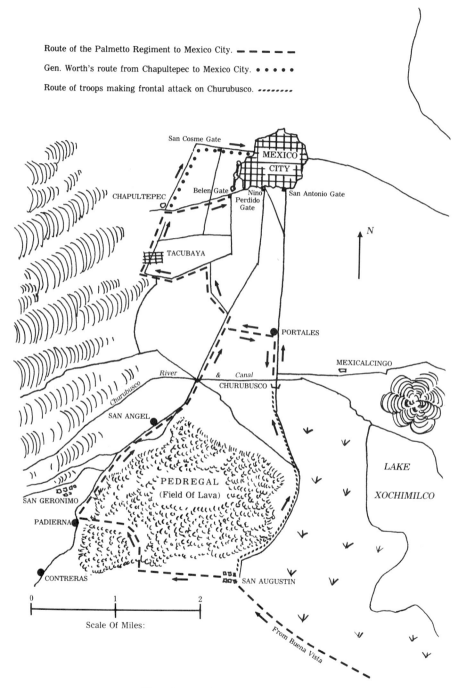

Route of the Palmetto Regiment to Mexico City. — — — — —

Gen. Worth's route from Chapultepec to Mexico City. • • • • •

Route of troops making frontal attack on Churubusco. ⸺⸺⸺

San Cosme Gate

MEXICO CITY

CHAPULTEPEC

Belen Gate

Nino Perdido Gate

San Antonio Gate

N

TACUBAYA

PORTALES

MEXICALCINGO

River   &   Canal

Churubusco

CHURUBUSCO

SAN ANGEL

LAKE

XOCHIMILCO

PEDREGAL

(Field Of Lava)

SAN GERONIMO

PADIERNA

CONTRERAS

SAN AUGUSTIN

0   1   2

Scale Of Miles:

From Buena Vista

San Augustin to Mexico City

312

The regimental colors of the Palmetto Regiment, raised over the City of Mexico after heavy fighting around the Castle of Chapultepec. The flag is in the Confederate Relic Room and Museum, Columbia, S.C. —Photo by William A. Jordan.

Medal for service in Mexico. One was struck for each officer and man of the Palmetto Regiment—gold for officers and silver for enlisted men —Photo by William A. Jordan.

A pair of silver cups given to Manigault by the Marion Artillery of Charleston. They were made by John Ewan of Charleston and inscribed: (left cup) "Vera Cruz, Contreras, Churubusco, Chapultepec, Garita De Belen." (Right cup) "presented by the MARION ARTILLERY to CAPT. ARTHUR M. MANIGAULT as a token of their admiration of his gallant conduct in MEXICO as First Lieut of the Charleston Volunteers" —Photo by William A. Jordan.

Gen. Manigault's field sword, given him by the citizens of New Orleans on his return from the Mexican War. During the fighting at Chickamauga, which Gen. Manigault described as the hottest he had ever experienced, it was struck by a rifle ball and the scabbard was broken —Photo by William A. Jordan.

Inscription: "Presented to Lieut. Arthur M. Manigault of the [Palmetto] Reg. by his fellow citizens in New Orleans [La.?] as a tribute to his valor displayed at Vera Cruz, Contreras, Churubusco, Chapultepec, and the taking of the City of Mexico."

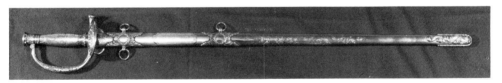

Silver mounted sword presented to Manigault by the City of Charleston on his return from the Mexican War —Photo by William A. Jordan.

Inscription: "Presented by the City Council of Charleston to Lt. ARTHUR M. MANIGAULT of the Charleston Co. Volunteers as a testimony of his GALLANT CONDUCT in the Mexican Campaign. July 28th 1848."

Joseph Manigault House, where Gen. A.M. Manigault was born in 1824. One of the handsomest of Charleston houses, it was built by Joseph's brother, Gabriel, a noted amateur architect. It is now owned by the Charleston Museum—Photo by William A. Jordan.

the cannonade & the rattle of musketry eight miles off. About 8 O.C. we were halted & went into quarters in the little village of *(name omitted)*. I remained here until the evening of the 11th Septbr. Orders were received to take up the line of march on that day & in the afternoon about 5 O.C. we took the direction of the city & moved towards the works defending the Garita of "Tenio Perdido" *(Nino Perdido?)* Some skirmishing occured but our regt. took no part in it. After dark, we moved to the left & after marching all night by a circuitous rout we formed ourselves a little before day entering the village of Tacubayia. This village is distant from the Castle of Chapultapec about 1,200 yards & the latter place situated on the summit of a steep isolated rock about 200 feet high completely commands it & the country sourrounding it on all sides.

Unmistakable evidences gave notice of the recommencement of active oppera- tions, the first scene of which would be an effort to gain possession of the formidable work just described. Large bodies of troops were in motion & the heavy artillery moving to the front to be placed in batteries, upon which our engineers were hard at work preparing them for the reception of the guns, which it was expected would open upon the doomed fortress as soon as it was light enough to see sufficiently to aim them. Large details were made from our command to aid in the rapid construction of the works also a sufficient force as a support & protection against any effort on the part of the enemy to get possession of them. The remainder of the troops remained out of view in the streets of the village.

During the night the enemy did not open upon us altho they must have heard & been aware of preparations making against them. It was intended to bombard and assail the works from the west & south sides. Genl. Quitman was entrusted with the attack on the South & on this front our Division was disposed. At about 6 A.M. of the 12th Sptbr 1847 the batteries on the west opened. Ours were not completed until eight O.C. or thereabouts when they began to reply to the enemies guns, the fire from which had been continuous & very severe ever since daylight. During the whole of the day a heavy & uninturrupted cannonade & shelling was kept up on both sides, our artillery was well served & its fire very effective the distance being about 600 yards.

At about 2 O.C. a recognizance in force was made by Genl. Quitman for the purpose of developing the entire strength of the Mexican position & to make him show his strength & the disposition of forces & guns in the lower works at the foot of the hill. The enemy regarding it as an assault, unmasked several batteries and the information desired *(was)* purchased at a severe loss to us. Towards evening the enemies fire sensibly declined, the lower wall was breached in several places & the main work itself, several guns having been dismounted, showed evident signs of the rough usage to which it had been subjected. The fireing from our batteries encreased as theirs deminished & continued during the whole night although after dark it was slower & principally confined to the mortars. At about midnight our company with others on the same duty had a sharp skirmish with a reconoitring party of Mexicans which we at first supposed to be a sally on their part & the entire command was under arms to repel it. After a short conflict they retired & we were not disturbed again that night. At break of day the bombard- ment commenced with renewed energy & spirit & for about two hours it was incessant. Dispositions were now made for an assault. Quitman's command, himself leading & Genl. Shields 2d in command, was formed in column of companies along the main street of Tacubayia out of view & was composed of the following regiments placed from right to left in the order named: 2d Pensylvania, Regiment of United S. Marines, 1st New York, Palmetto Regiment. We were again supported by *(a)* body of regulars and one or two light batteries of Artillery. A body of troops composed of Volunteers were already in position on the extreme right of the south attack, about 800 strong, who were directed to attack some strong earth or field works a little to the east of the castle. Directly parallel with the south front of the castle ran the road from Tacubayia in a direction almost east & west. After extending about 100 yards beyond the south east angle, it made nearly a right angle & led to the works before mentioned situated at the foot of the rock & which answered the double purpose of a protection to the main gate of Chapultapec & the causeway leading to the city by the "Garita Belen." Between the road and the lower wall & works of the castle lay an open field about 350 or 400 yards wide grown up in tall rank grass and intersected with numerous ditches from 5 to 8 feet wide, 3 to 4 feet deep & generally filled with water. On each side of this parallel road was a dry ditch. The orders being received by Genl. Q., the column advanced rapidly up the road & on the head of it reaching within a hundred or so yards of the angle mentioned they were halted to protect the men from the fire which was very severe every gun now being turned against the infantry & whilst awaiting for the concerted signal when the assault both on the west and south front would begin at the same moment. Genl. Quitman ordered the three leading regiments into the ditches on the road side. The Palmetto Regiment moving on found itself when halted on the left of the New Yorkers (safely ensconsced in the ditch & themselves in Column of Companies) in an open road exposed to a heavy fire of artillery & musketry by which they were losing men rapidly. We thought this hard as Genl. Q. had but a short time before assured our commander, Col. Gladden, that in consideration of our late heavy losses & admirable conduct, that the S.C. Rgt on this occasion would be exposed as little as possible & should only be placed in a prominent position in case of an emergency when of course no favoritism could be shown. & now here we were in a command of 2,000 men the only ones offered as a target for the enemy's practice. Fortunately for us we had not long to remain in this position. The signal for a general advance was given & our leading troops received their order to advance.

Some delay which I could not account for at the time took place at the right & I turned my attention to the attack on the west which had commenced & a great part of which I could distinctly see. So interesting & exciting was it, engaging my entire attention, that I almost forgot my danger & what was going on around me. It appears that when Genl. Q. gave the order for the 2d Pensylvania to advance they did not do so very promptly. Those that sprang out of the ditches immediately received a galling fire which produced much confusion. Every effort was made by Gens. Q. & Shields & their field officers to force the laggards out. Their conduct demoralized the more willing ones & it was found impossible as a regiment to use them to advantage. The U.S. Marines were then ordered to advance (as fine a looking & well disciplined a body of men as I ever saw). The evil influence of the bad conduct of the Pensylvanians had done its work. A repetition of the same thing occured. It was too hot outside. The ditch was the safest place. Genl. Quitman was in despair. Pillow's troops were rapidly advancing. Time was passing and disgrace threatened him. He believed that the South Carolinians would not fail him. What he thought about the New Yorkers I do not know but altho they being next in line, were nearest at hand, he skipped them and an Aid De Camp came galloping down the road to our Rgtl. commander. In a few hurried sentences he stated the difficulty to him. They were repeated by Col. Gladden in a loud tone of voice. At a double quick & with a cheer my gallant comrades in obedience to his order moved up the road to where Gnl. Quitman was, were wheeled into line & receiving the order to make the assault, dashed forward with a gallantry and steadiness that I have never seen surpassed. The entire line sprang over the heads of our comrades in the ditches & I have many a time since laughed heartily when I have remembered the cheers they sent after us as we rapidly left them in the rear. Our conduct on this occasion was never forgiven by our Northern friends and they regarded it as a reflection upon themselves which they lost no opportunity afterwards of resenting in the most cowardly & treacherous manner. I must say for the N.Y. Regt. however that they were not offered the opportunity of leading the attack, that when ordered to our support, they followed with alacrity & to a man, that after overcoming the obstacles at the lower wall they advanced with us on our left & a portion of their Regt. got into the main work before us. So also did the two Regts of which I have written follow us but they did not contribute in any way to the success of the day. Owing to the nature of the ground & the heavy loss in crossing this open field we were in much confusion when we gained the wall yet we carried everything before us. Getting rapidly thro the breaches, we were hastily reformed & driving the defenders of the lower works before us we went into the main work almost with the rearmost of them. Here we found that the attack from the west was also successful, Pillow's comd. having also affected an entrance. Such of the defenders as had not been killed or wounded in first fury of the forced entrance (for the blood of the men was up & it was almost impossible to restrain them from acts of cruelty to those of the enemy, who seeing that further resistance was useless, threw asside their arms) surrendered or took flight, passing out at other points, their familiarity with the works enabling them to do so & we being ignorant of those points of egress. Such as I have described it was the battle or properly speaking, the "storming of Chapultapec." I can only detail & vouch for the correctness of the description of the part taken by my own regiment & of such occurrences as came within my own view or knowledge & to all similar events this remark is also intended to apply.

During this action, and just as the So Ca Rgt. having received the order had started to make the attack a battery of field artillery* which had followed in the rear of the regiment, unlimbered & came into battery in the road & as soon as we had advanced about one hundred yards it commenced fireing using shell principally which it threw over our heads into the lower works. I was surprised to find that many of the officers & men, in discussing the fight afterwards, complained that the effect of this fire in their rear was injurious to them that they could not get rid of the idea that they might be shot in the back by their own artillery, a sensation so repulsive that they were almost more annoyed by this fire than the enemies. In my own instance the reverse was the case & it gave me more confidence, believing that the shell & shot of our artillery had much to do in distracting the aim of the enemies sharp shooters & causing a nervousness amongst them which contributed no little to our greater safety. The said guns were well served & I do not know an instance of a single man of ours being wounded by it & its effect upon the enemy I have no doubt resulted as I have described it.

An instance of uncontrolable panic & supernatural presentiment of evil occured about this same period of the engagement which I have since frequently seen exhibited but this was the first that I had noticed. During the charge a soldier who on several previous occasions had given evidence of great coolness & courage under fire, as the right wing of the Regt. was for a moment or two halted to allow the left who were a little in rear to regain their position on the line, completely lost control of himself from the effect of a discharge of grape shot which crashed through our company striking down killing and wounding several men. A large tree under which we were standing received several of the balls cutting two or three good sized boughs which fell amongst us. He turned to run and was rapidly passing me, who as a file closer was several paces in rear of the line. As he passed

*A section of Artillery comd by Lieut. Hunt — now Maj. Genl. Hunt, U.S.A. May 19th 1881 — well known in Charleston.[20] (The foregoing was pencilled by Manigault on the side of the MS.) — Editors.

rapidly near me, seeing his intention & that to all appearances he was not wounded, I seized him by the collar & shaking him violently whilst using threatening & upbraiding language thrust him back into his former position. I had scarcely removed my hand from him, when he fell, doubled up and mortally wounded, a large "escopet" ball having entered into his side.[21] About 12 O.C. that night after having returned to Tacubayia for rest & refreshment I received by a hospital attendant a message from G....[22] that he wished to speak to me. I immediately went to the hospital, near by, & there found stretched off on his blanket in the room set apart for those for whom there was no hope of life. He was calmly smoking his pipe which seemed to give him much comfort. After shaking his hand he remarked in a clear firm voice "Lieut, I cannot die without an explanation with you. My conduct this morning was such as to give you a very contemptable opinion of me & you now regard me in spite of my previous good character as a soldier, as a coward. I am not one. A presentiment of evil & a desire for self preservation over which I had no control, took possession of me. I did not know what I was about to do until you seized me, and your voice brought me back to my senses. You must not judge me harshly. The surgeons have told me that I cannot live & I feel that in a few hours I will be a dead man. Do I appear to fear death? I wish you to bear evidence of courage now & to set me right with my comrades when I am gone."

I offered to do anything in my power for him & to bear or communicate any message to his friends but he replied that he had not any & did not know whether his relatives were living or not. If they were they took no interest in him. He had been a soldier in the Brittish army & had been but a short time in America previous to voluntiering. He died an hour or two after as he had foretold.

Lieut Col. Dickinson died this morning just as his regiment was going into action. He had been mortally wounded at Churubusco three weeks previously. Our loss in this engagement ammounted to nearly a third of our force in the field & was particularly heavy in officers. It might have been greater had the enemy been able to explode their mines but the officers to whom this duty was entrusted were most fortunately for ourselves either killed or wounded & we were thereby saved much additional loss.

Chapultepec now being in our possession the two roads to the city were open to us, viz: by the causeways leading to the Garitas San Cosme & Balen but there were still strong works to overcome before we could reach the city. The causeways were cut in several places & batteries sweeping them were thrown up at intervals on each side. The country was either swampy or covered with water, the lake having formerly extended entirely around Mexico *(City)* but here they had gradually filled up & during and just after the rainy season the country on each side of these causeways is generally covered with water. Only here and there was there land visible & often it was of such a character as to render it impracticable for even infantry so that our only sure means of approach was by two causeways with an acqueduct in the centre leading from Chapultepec to the city & supplying the water used by the inhabitants from a large spring at the former place. This acquaduct was supported on heavy arches about twelve feet high, six feet wide & the space between them perhaps twelve feet. It was constructed of heavy masonry & brick & both on the San Cosme & Balen roads the one was a counterpart of the other. The advance upon the first was entrusted to Genl. Worth, on the latter to Genl. Quitman. The troops having been collected reformed & order restored were now pushed forward by their respective commanders. Our advance was composed of the Rifle Regiment which had reported to Genl. Q. and the Palmetto Rgt. The promises of Generals are not always to be relied upon for altho we had been assured of an easy time to day yet on that part of the field where we fought we certainly bore the brunt of the actions.

The credit for being a fighting regiment is not at all times a very desirable one, & on this occasion we would willingly have dispensed with it but Genl. Quitman I suppose was thinking more of his own reputation, than of our comfort & consequently could not spare us & if he did give us our fill of fighting he also certainly did not stint us in praise & compliments.

During the remainder of the day we fought side (by side) with the rifles & their metal was fully equal to our own & the mutual & prompt support given to each other on many trying occasions during this day produced a feeling of respect and friendship for each other which lasted until the close of the war and I have no doubt is still entertained at the present day by many of the survivors of either. After receiving our orders but little time was lost by us. Advancing rapidly along the causeway we soon again came under fire from a two gun battery accross the causeway but by watching for the discharges of the artillery & avoiding its ill effects by springing under cover of the arches at each discharge & again immediately springing out of them & moving at a double quick before they could reload their pieces, we were soon within a few yards of the enemy. Our Comdg. officer seeing his men well together & awaiting a favorable opportunity gave the final order which was succeeded by a rush & the work, guns & such Mexicans who stood to await the onset were ours.

Another battery still lay between us and the Garita. This was carried in like manner. Against the Garita, a much more formidable work at nearly the very entrance to the city, we had to advance more warily. We now also began to receive a heavy cross fire from the citadel on our left but still in advance of us & a battery to the right which we could not reach. A portion of Twiggs command, however, coming round far to our right, having made a circuit of several miles, fortunately & most opportunely for us made there appearance about this time & stormed this work on our right capturing and driving before them the infantry force protecting it. Relieved in a measure from this annoyance, the Rifles and ourselves simultaniously charged. A few bloody minutes followed & the Palmetto flag floated, the first American Color, over the walls of the city of Mexico, my friend Lieut Selleck[23] of Abbeville bearing them. A minute after he was carried to the rear severely wounded. A considerable number of prisoners, stores & ammunition with the artillery was captured here. The order was still onward, and again we advanced but our difficulties began to increase. Although virtually within what is known as the City of Mexico, we had still an open space between us & the margin of firm ground on which the city is built. This space must have been 300 yards. On our left lay the citadel separated by water from us some 200 yards. The road on which we were ran paralel with its South face. On our left another road, I forget the name, ran at right angles to & joined it at the Garita.* This latter one ran parralel with the west face of the citadel. There was no advancing but by these roads. On each side of them was deep water. On our left was the formidable work of "The Citadel," the last obstacle to the capture of the city, and 3 or 400 yards in our front was a heavy redoubt armed with artillery. The Mexican Infantry swarmed in an arround each of these positions & their fire was severe in the extreme. Had we to contend alone with the force & work in front the contest would have been soon decided, but the arches no longer afforded the protection that it had previously done as the fire from the citadel swept steadily through them & where you attempted to protect yourself on the opposite side the fire from the infantry & battery in front also bore every thing down before it. Again and again was the effort made to push up to the work in front but the Mexican gunners in the citadel

*City gates & Custom House — A.M.M.

317

had the range accurately & grape canister & musket balls swept like hail every foot of ground for 200 yards. Several heavy guns both of our own & captured artillery were brought up but unprotected as they were, they could produce no decided effect. The artillerists officers and men were stricken down again and again. Voluntier details from our Regt essayed to work them. They met with a like fate & no better success & eventually they were dismounted or rendered useless by the enemies artillery. Seeing our want of success the enemy made several efforts to take them & drive us back, but they paid dearly for their timerity.

Seeing that for the present that nothing more could be effected Genl. Q. ordered us back to the Garita at which point we were less exposed to the cross fire, where we remained until dark. Twilight was approaching when we fell back. During the night he intended constructing batteries to oppose the enemies, with the assistance of which he hoped on the following morning to effect his purpose.

Our Regiment much reduced in numbers (indeed it barely ammounted to two good companies, about 120 men, fatigued & worn out with an almost uninterrupted contest of twelve hours) was directed by Genl. Quitman after dark to return to the provision train at Tacubayia, there to make ourselves as comfortable as possible during the night & to return at daylight in the morning. He would not, he said, impose the drudgery of building batteries &c on men who had so conducted themselves during this severe day & that those who had been less exposed should do the manual labor & moreover he added that our physical exhaustion alone would preclude his using us for any such purposes.

Worn out with fatigue, we retraced our steps to Tacubayia over the ground which we had so hardly contested during the day, passing by & leaving behind us the bodies of our slain comrades. We reached our resting place after a march of three miles about 9 O.C. P.M. & after refreshing ourselves with such provisions as we could without too much trouble lay our hands upon we lay down to rest in the same quarters that we had been occupying the day before. Our wounded had all been brought in by the fatigue parties attached to the hospital corps. Amongst (them) was Major Gladden our only remaining field officer, suffering from a severe wound in the leg. In this second combat our loss exceeded that of Chapultepec. I myself was severely bruised & suffered not a little from injuries received by a pice of masonry splintered by a cannon ball from one of the arches which striking me on ribs near the back bone rolled me over & knocked the breath out of my body. It was some time before I could stand & for a minute I supposed myself mortally wounded, but gradually recovered & only suffered from the soreness occasioned by the blow.

I did not mention in the proper place, that at Churubusco I was twice struck by musket balls, once by a spent one full on the left fore arm, paralizing it for a day or two & exceedingly painful. A second time a bullet grazed the flesh on the inner part of my left thigh raising a conserable welt & passing between my legs.

This day also I had several very narrow escapes but the only injury received, I have already mentioned. I did not go upon the list of wounded.

On the following morning our bugles summonsed us to fall in at 4 OClock and our skeleton of a regiment again moved in the direction of the Garita. Our march was slow owing to many obstructions that we met with. On our way we gleaned much information on various matters connected with the operations of the other portions of the army on the previous day. Genl. Worth who directed the attack on the San Cosme road had also succeeded, a little before dark effecting a lodgment on the outskirts of the city. During the night he had shelled the city throwing many bombs in the direction of the "Grand Plaza." Quitman had also completed his batteries & had armed them. At both points all the arrangements had been matured for a final effort & there can be but little doubt as to what the result would have been.

During the night, however, Santa Anna, perceiving that further efforts to save the city would result only in a great sacrifice of life to little purpose, & that it must inevitably fall & anxious to spare it & its citizens the heavy misfortune & sufferings that would inevitably be the result of a contest in the streets, very wisely & humanely determined to withdraw his army & leave to the civil authorities the opportunity of making the best terms they could for themselves. Before day a flag of truce made its appearance in front of Quitman's advance. The offer of an unconditional surrender was accepted & at daylight he marched in and took possession. Shortly after Genl. Worth, a like deputation having waited on him, also moved his troops in.

Unfortunately for us when within a half mile of the Garita we were halted by Genl. Pierce who assumed the responsibility of retaining us for some purpose & we consequently did not enjoy the priviledge of being the first U.S. troops who led the way into this beautiful capital. We remained in the neighborhood of the garita two days performing various military duties & burying the dead and on the third day marched in & had assigned us as our quarters, as a compliment for our services, The Palace in the city. Here we were well provided for & had an abundance of everything. The principal suite of rooms in The Palace was reserved for Genl. Quitman, who was made military governor of the city, as also for the heads of several departments of the army. The remainder of the building was distributed amongst the different officers & companies, as quarters so that we had a plenty of room and apartments, such as no one of us had ever before occupied. Our duties were comparatively light & much time and liberty allowed us.

I will here mention that a few hours after Genl. Scott had taken possession of the city rather a serious rising took place. Many of the soldiers belonging to the Mexican Army deserted with their arms & remained behind. A large number of political offenders & criminals were released from the prisons by Genl. Santa Anna & arms given them. These with a considerable number of the lowest class of citizens having nothing to lose & much to gain in the way of plunder by inaugurating a system of anarchy & discord attacked & murdered several detached parties of guards & patrols & fired on bodies of troops & individuals from the tops of houses & various places of concealment. In this way a good deal of fighting took place in many parts of the city & a good deal of trouble & some loss of life was occasioned thereby & it was a day and a half before it was put a stop to & finally checked. The harshest measures were adopted to effect it & all who were found in arms or were with good reason suspected of fomenting these disturbances, were dealt with in a most summary manner. This system of treatment, the most effectual in my opinion that should be adopted in such occasions was a lesson which the Mexicans never forgot & during the remainder of the war the citizens of the capital were as orderly as could be desired & never again gave any serious trouble.

Our Regiment remained in the city until the latter part of December when our Brigade having changed commanders was ordered to San Angel. Genl. Quitman owing to failing health & Genl. Shields suffering from his wounds, the first received at Cerro Gordo, the 2d at Chapultepec, were furloughed early in Decbr. & returned to the U.S. Genl. Cushing[24] from Massachusetts assumed comd. of the Brigade composed of the N.York, 1st & 2d Pensylvania, 1st Massachusetts and our own regiment. Our military associations both with our Genl. & the Northern regiments from this time until we were finally mustered out of service was very disagreeable. Genl. Cushing did not like us & treated us discourteously on many occasions. With the other Regiments there was continual bickering quarelling & fighting & they never failed when in sufficient numbers, generally two to one, in assailing our men when they could meet with them in detached parties. Many serious riots took place & a general battle was on more than one occasion imminent. I must however except the Massachusetts Regt. Strange to say with them our intercourse was pleasant, both among the officers & men and on all occasions they sided with us.

At San Angel we remained until May. Occasionally detachments would be sent on military duty to various points within fifty miles of the city but all military opperations of any importance ceased from the day of the capture of the City of Mexico. The war was virtually over from that time. Towards *(the)* end of May 1848 a treaty of peace was made & shortly after the army evacuated the country. Our brigade was the first from the city to commence the movement. We arrived at Vera Cruz in June & sailed shortly after for Mobile where we were mustered out service. About the 25 July I reached Charleston having been absent about 20 months and my first experience of a military life having extended over a period of very nearly two years. In spite of the privations fatigue and dangers to which I was at times exposed they were perhaps the happiest & most romantic period of my life.

The City of Mexico, situated in the valley of Mexico is the largest by far of all the cities of that Republic & also the most wealthy & important & is the seat of government. The Mexicans are justly proud of it, a little too much so perhaps as they very generally regard it as second only to some of the great Capitals of Europe. It has many handsome public buildings built on a grand scale & ornamented without regard to cost & trouble. The Cathedral is perhaps the most conspicuous. It is a most imposing structure & the interior handsome in the extreme, altho had they been less profuse with colours, guilding & many tawdry ornaments, more taste would have been displayed. The property belonging to it is said to be enormous & they could well afford *(to)* expend a good portion of it on its construction & in a manner to produce an effect on the senses of the people who are perhaps the most biggoted & narrow minded even of Roman Catholics.

The Pallace tho a large, commodious & well planned building, can scarcely be called handsome. Its proportions are bad, style too severe (a very uncommon fault in Mexico) & is only remarkable for its great size. These two buildings form two of the sides of the Grand Plaza. On the other two are large & striking looking buildings, each one a solid block with a handsome colonade. The greater part of that one to the South is used by civil power governing the city & corresponding to our City Councils. The remainder of the same & the one on the west side, are divided into large & handsome stores.

Mexico is a city of Churches, Monastaries and other religious bodies. These buildings are generally spacious & handsome and add much to the appearance of the city.

The streets almost invariably run at right angles with each other. On many of them the buildings are large & ellegant & compare favorably with most of the larger cities on the Continent of Europe. The style differs so much from that of our cities in the U.S. that it is impossible to institute a comparrasson, but taking the city as a whole, it produces a much more picturesque & imposing effect than any other city that I have seen in America.

The sanitary condition of the place during the seven months of my stay either in or near it was exceedingly good. The streets were clean as also the houses and yards & every thing had a bright & lively appearance. It was some time after our entry before the more wealthy clases of citizens began to return perhaps a month & owing to the good order prevailing & protection of life and property afforded by our military authorities, all classes seemed to acquire a confidence & freedom from feeling insecurity by no means common to them heretofore. Business revived. Places of amusement were opened, handsome equipages were to be seen about the streets & the public walks & places of resort thronged with persons of each sex & of all classes in pursuit of pleasure.

Their theatre (Teatro Nacional) a splendid building complete in all its equipments & one of the finest that I have ever seen was a place of nightly resort for all our officers & was always filled it seemed to me. Many of their plays, Ballets & operas were very creditable. The first were excellent & I enjoyed them greatly.

The Spanish language seemed to me most admirably suited to the drama. Their actors were good, sceenery & costumes in the most perfect keeping & the latter strictly correct.

Their "Fondas" or resturants, were on a scale that I had never seen equaled before. Every comfort and luxury could be obtained at very reasonable rates & the crowds of well dressed and respectable looking people that one met there would lead you to suppose that it was a part of the business of every day life to spend several hours of the twenty four at these places. In each a room was set apart for gambling purposes & many tables at which the games of Monte, Roulette, Rouge et Noir and the American game of Faro, was played & the space around them almost always crowded by players & spectators. I have seen enormous sums of money lost and won in an hour or two. Gold was the stakes always played for. I never saw a bank bill while I was in Mexico. The Mexicans are a nation of gamblers from the little beggar boy in the street who pitched his "tlacos" to (the) man of wealth. All had imbibed the habit and seemed to be happy only whilst engaged in these games of chance.

The markets in Mexico during our stay was well supplied with beef, game, mutton, vegetables and fruit, and we were able to supply ourselves at very reasonable rates, far cheaper than than we could have done in this country. During a portion of our stay in the city I took my meals with a number of officers who formed a mess together at the house of an English lady who undertook to provide us dinner breakfast and supper for one dollar per day. Our fare was excellent, quite a variety always on table and the cooking quite satisfactory.

The climate of the Valley of Mexico I think was perfection. During the winter that we spent there I saw on three or four occasions, about sunrise in the morning, the thinest possible coating of ice on the surface of small pools of water so situated as to be protected from the action of the winds. At nights the atmosphere would be cool & bracing & during the day it would be balmy & pleasant during the sumer months altho much warmer than in winter. It was never oppressive during the day & the nights always pleasant & a blanket to cover with was always necessary. The change of temperature from 5 P.M. to 7 A.M. was sudden (and) very great from the other portion of the day. I never found summer clothing atall necessary but wore my wollens always. To this precaution I attribute the perfect health which I enjoyed, never during the whole period of my stay in Mexico or at any other time whilst in the army having suffered from indisposition of any kind & never once having been on the sick report of the Regt. One of the last charges that Mama[25] gave me was always to wear my wollen clothes & I believe that by following her advice my remarkable exemption from disease must be attributed.

Of the beauty of the scenery of the Valley of Mexico much has been said and the accounts given by travellers often appears exagerated. I can only say that no account that I have ever read coloured it too highly or gave a discription of it beyond what it deserved. I have seen in Europe (Switzerland & Savoy) sceenery more grand & striking but of a character entirely different.

Of its kind I believe it to unsurpassed. This valley, to make a circuit of which would be a journey of perhaps a hundred miles, is sourrounded by mountains many of great hight. Popocatapetl and Istahuawhatel (I do not know that I am quite accurate in the speling of the last named) are from 17 to 18,000 feet above the level of the sea. These two are snowclad always. Many others are often white from the same cause and all are of considerable altitude, and appear completely to enclose the valley. The table land within this circle is generally level and only begins to be slightly undulating as it approaches the mountains. Here and there interspersed throughout the valley are several, abrupt ellevations regular in shape & varying from one to three hundred feet in highth. These mountains if they may be so called together with water view afforded by several considerable lakes serve to relieve the eye and add much to the landscape.

Numerous villages are to be seen and Haciendas sourrounded by groves of noble trees. The quality of the soil is exceedingly rich and all in the highest state of cultivation. There is a softness of sceenery yet with a bold outline and a blending together of valley water and mountains which gives a character peculiar to this country which I have never seen equaled. It seemed to me that I could never get tired of beholding it and the more one saw of it, the more it pleased him. Were it not for the inhabitants & the miserable government with which this country is cursed I would if it were possible, of all other places in the world which it has been my fortune to see, select this valley in which to pass my life.

After leaving Vera Cruz about sixty miles the elevation as you approach the mountains is so great and the atmosphere so rarified that until the lungs become somewhat accustomed to it any over exertion causes much inconvenience and a great difficulty in breathing. This encreases as you approach the Capital & was the subject of much speculation amongst the soldiers until explained to them, but gradually we all became accustomed to it and it ceased to be an annoyance.

Another curious influence of the climate upon us was that all the pores of the skin become closed or to all appearances were for it did not matter how hot the weather was or how much exercise we took, I never knew anyone to be in a state of profuse perspiration. It would be so slight as to be scarcely perceptible.

The inhabitants of the country as far as I could judge seemed also to be in the same condition. I should suppose that this would be an unwholesome & unnatural condition of the human body yet the Mexicans tho small in stature are a very hardy and athletic race of men *(and)* appear to suffer little from disease and it is I believe a well established fact, that they are capable of enduring great fatigue and can subsist for a very considerable period on the smallest quantity of the commonest kind of food, and are at the same time able to accomplish tasks requiring great bodily exertion. I also never in my life enjoyed better health than I did in this climate.

Mexico is said to abound in game, but this I doubt. Excepting in the immediate vicinity of the mountains, the country is a very open one with but few forrests. It is true that I had no opportunity of personally satisfying myself on this point but from the character of the country thro which I passed, I do not think that they can be very numerous. I saw however several deer, many wolves, and in the lakes near the city, large numbers of wild duck.

The principal highways thro the country are exceedingly good being generally paved with square stones or McAdamized & carefully graded. Their bridges are solid heavy works of masonry built to last and never requiring repair. For these advantages the Mexicans are no doubt indebted to their former masters, the Spaniards.

Owing to some radical defect in the Mexican character unfitting them for self government the country has been cursed by one of republican form and they as a people are so dificient of stability and settled purpose that their rulers of yesterday are deposed today by a revolution headed by some unscrupulous politician or military chieftain who making great promises to the people undertakes to redress all grievances & bring about a state of affairs ensuring protection justice and security to all.

Just as soon as such a one is in power all promises are forgotten, and the real purpose of aggrandizement & power soon becomes apparent and a systematic course of plunder & robbery is instituted, for the benefit of the party in power and its personal adherents. After a short career another "pronunciamento" is published, the men in power are deposed an a repetition of the same events occour.

The consequence of all this is, that there being but little security for life or property but little internal improvement goes on. Capitalists bring but little money into the country. Those merchants and speculators who are successful in their efforts invest their gains and spare means elsewhere, in Europe or the U.S., and Mexico in spite of its delicious climate, firtile soil and imposing scenery remains at a stand still and its resources lie undeveloped.

One of the most striking features of the country are the Haciendas (plantations or farms) of the large land owners.

Many of them cover an immense area of country. The owners of these are as a general rule the true Aristocracy of the country and are often men of great wealth. Their Haciendas, which properly are the residences, together with the farm and other buildings attached to them, are of great size, are well furnished and are arranged pretty much on the following plan. For protection against robbery and violence all of the buildings are built as one, the form most frequently being a quadrangle or oblong square. On one front is the owners residence, a building of one or two stories and a little higher than the others which enclose the open space within sometimes consisting of several acres, say from two to six or eight. These consist of the residences of the servants, domestics & farm labourers and the barns, stables and such other accommodation necessary to a large agricultural establishment. At the four corners the buildings are so constructed as to form military towers and so arranged as to afford a flank fire on each other, the roof being flat with a wall of two or three feet high going entirely arround the buildings and their usually being but one large gateway passing thro the lower story of the larger building, strong and massive gates ready to be closed. They give you the idea of military works or fortresses as indeed they are and in visiting several of them I could not help associating them in my mind with the castles of the feudal ages and thought how, like those barrons, the possesor of one of these Haciendas might shut himself up in his stronghold with his garrisson of retainers his magazine well filled with bread, his herds safely secured within the four walls, and bid defiance to his foes, ready to repel an attack or fully prepared for a siege. The only feature wanting to make the.....* perfect was the absence of ditch and drawbridge.

I was assured that this state of things not unfrequently happened and was not altogether imaginary on my part.

Many of these Haciendas were indeed capable of a stout defence & could resist successfully an attack in considerable numbers where artillery was not brought into play against them for any considerable time. They were frequently fortified by the Mexicans during the war, whereever they could use them to advantage. All Haciendas, it must be understood, were not as described above, but only the larger and more important. Some of them had buildings only on one or two sides, the other sides being composed only of high walls.

As I have before remarked the lands in many portions of Mexico are very fertile, particularly so in the neighbourhood of Jalappa, Puebla & the valley, in the latter more so I have been told than in any other section of the Republic.

Comparatively very little labor is required to make a crop and the tools and utensils used are of the most primitive style, generally of wood. The system of irrigation in the valley was almost perfect and the water used for the crops during

*Word, perhaps "picture" or "scene," missing in MS. — Editors.

the season when no rain fell was carried over the country in small aquaducts a few feet above the surface of the ground and for the use of it each farmer paid a certain amount of tax to government according to the number of acres planted, and I believe that it is an important item in the internal revinue of the country.

Of the Mexican army I can say but little in its favor. On many occasions it fought creditably enough, but it should have accomplished much more than it did. As long as a considerable space separated the two lines, though within musket range, their soldiers fought & returned our fire with great spirit and caused us severe losses, but so soon as we went in for close fighting & threatened them with the bayonet and our men only showed determination in their advance, so certain was it that their lines would give way & nothing could induce them to await a charge and cross bayonets with their adversaries. Individually I do not regard them as deficient in courage but their armys were badly officered & the men had no confidence in their superiors. Any one atall familiar with the history of the corruptions of the government and the bad moral tone of the more conspicous civil & military leaders can easily understand the deficiencys and short comings of the army & how difficult under these circumstances it must have been to thorughally organize and make it anything like efficient.

The Mexican women are not handsome but are well made with good figures, small feet & an exceedingly graceful carriage, coquettish & ready always for a flirtation. Their costume is exceedingly pretty & becoming and altho coming into their country with an invading army, yet many of our officers found but little difficulty in mingling freely with them.

NOTES TO APPENDIX II

[1] Gen. Winfield Scott, one of the nation's most brilliant military leaders, was born near Petersburg, Va. in 1786. He entered the army as a captain of artillery in 1808 and by 1841 he had become general in chief. Ordered to take command of the army in Mexico, he drew many of the experienced troops from Gen. Zachary Taylor, who had been fighting near the Rio Grande, and assembled them at Lobos Island, about 75 miles southeast of Tampico. His army, including the Palmetto Regiment, landed at Vera Cruz in March 1847. Following capture of that city, Scott moved inland in a campaign that resulted in the eventual capture of Mexico City and the end of the war. At the start of the Civil War, Scott organized the defense of Washington and was one of the originators of the strategy of blockade and segmentation of the South which resulted in victory for the North five years later. He was too old to take active command, however, and resigned Nov. 1, 1861. He spent the remainder of his days at West Point where he died May 29, 1866. *Appletons' Cyclopaedia of American Biography,* (New York, 1894), Vol. V, 440-442. Hereafter cited as *Appletons'. The Encyclopedia Americana,* (New York, 1946), Vol. 24, 445-446. Hereafter cited as *Americana.* Allen Johnson (editor), *Dictionary of American Biography,* (New York, 1928), Vol. XVI, 505-511. Hereafter cited as *Dictionary.*

[2] Pierce Mason Butler was born in South Carolina April 11, 1798, and was appointed a lieutenant in the Army in 1818, rising to the rank of captain by 1825. He resigned in 1829 and settled at Columbia, S.C., where he became a successful banker. In 1836 he was elected governor of the state. At the outbreak of war with Mexico, he was named colonel of the Palmetto Regiment and led his unit in the siege of Vera Cruz and subsequent operations. During the early stages of the Battle of Churubusco, Aug. 20, 1847, he was wounded but continued to lead his regiment in the assault until killed by a musket ball. *Dictionary,* Vol. III, 365-366. *Palmetto Regiment, Documents 1846-1849,* (Department of Archives and History, Columbia, S.C.) 129, 153. Hereafter cited as *Documents. Letters Received by Gregg-Hayden & Co., 1852-1855, Regarding Medals for Members of the Palmetto Regiment,* (Department of Archives and History, Columbia, S.C.) 2A. Hereafter cited as *Letters.*

[3] Adley H. Gladden of Columbia, S.C., was appointed major of the Palmetto Regiment during the early stages of the Mexican War. At the Battle of Churubusco, Aug. 20, 1847, he succeeded to command of the regiment when both superior officers were killed. Promoted lieutenant colonel and then colonel, he led the regiment in subsequent battles being severely wounded during the assault at the Belen Gate. In 1861, he was appointed brigadier general and assigned to the Army of Tennessee. He was fatally wounded April 6, 1862, first day of the Battle of Shiloh. *Appletons',* Vol. II, 663. *Documents,* 129. David Duncan Wallace, *The History of South Carolina,* (New York, 1934), Vol. III, 112-114. Hereafter cited as *Wallace.*

[4] Later president of the Confederacy.

[5] John Anthony Quitman (1799-1858) moved to Mississippi from his native New York in 1821 and during the next few years engaged in law and politics. In 1836 he raised a body of troops to aid the Texans against Mexican incursions and on his return to Mississippi became a major general of militia. Appointed a brigadier general in the U.S. Army in 1846, he participated in the Battle of Monterey and the siege and capture of Vera Cruz. He led the army contingent in the combined army-navy expedition against Alvarado and was with the advance troops in the taking of Pueblo for which he was brevetted major general. Quitman's units stormed the works at Chapultepec and carried the Gates of Belen for which he was rewarded by being named governor of Mexico City. Following the war, he was elected governor of Mississippi and then served in the U S. Congress from 1855 until his death. *Appletons'* Vol. V, 156. *Documents,* 83, 208, 224. *Americana,* Vol. 23, 99. *Dictionary,* Vol. XV, 315-316.

[6] Gen. Juan Morales relinquished command of Vera Cruz to Brig. Gen, Jose Juan de Landero a short time before the surrender. *The Charleston (S.C.) Courier,* April 10 and 14, 1847. Hereafter cited as *Courier.* H. Judge Moore, *Scott's Campaign in Mexico,* (Charleston, S.C., 1849), 25-26. Hereafter cited as *Moore.*

[7] Lt. Charles G. Hunter of the steamer Scourge. In a letter to his brother, Henry Manigault, dated "Camp near Vera Cruz, April 9th, 1847," and published in 1914, Lt. Manigault described the action: "...As I mentioned before, we are at the present moment encamped on the plain to the South of Vera Cruz, within a quarter of a mile of the city, resting after a most severe march to & from Alvarado, which place to our great chagrin, on hearing of our approach yealded, without fireing a gun, to a midshipman & four men, who happened to enter the river in the boat of a small war steamer; he was much surprised as he approached the town to see a boat & white flag, making for him with the Alcaldi, who surrendered to him everything. Genl. Quitman was there within 15 miles of the town with 2,000 men, & when the news reached him, the very day he arrived there, he was not a little mortifyed. It was more than Comodore Perry *(M.C. Perry, commanding the fleet)* & himself could bear with, who had entered into an agreement with each other, that they both should make their appearance at the same time & have all the credit to themselves, but they were forestalled by one of inferior rank, & the unfortunate subaltern has been arrested to stand a court martial...." *The Southwestern Historical Quarterly,* Vol. XVIII, No. 2. October 1914, 215-218. Ernest McPherson Lander Jr., *Reluctant Imperialists, Calhoun, the South Carolinians, and the Mexican War,* (Baton Rouge, 1980), 86-87. *Moore,* 52.

[8] William Jenkins Worth (1794-1849), a New Yorker, had a distinguished military career in the War of 1812 and the Seminole Indian War. During the Mexican War, he served with Gen. Zachary Taylor, then joined Gen. Winfield Scott, for whom he had been an aide during the War of 1812. He fought in all the major battles from Veṛa Cruz to the taking of Mexico City. Following the war, Worth was placed in command of the Department of Texas where he died of cholera in 1849. *Appletons',* Vol. VI, 615-616. *Americana,* Vol. 29, 562. *Dictionary,* XX, 536-537.

[9] David Emanuel Twiggs (1790-1862) was a native of Georgia who served during the War of 1812 and remained in the army, attaining the rank of colonel by 1836. During th Mexican War, he first served under Gen. Zachary Taylor and later under Gen. Winfield Scott. He was promoted brigadier general in June 1846 and later was brevetted major general for gallantry at the Battle of Monterey. During operations against Mexico City, he commanded the 2nd Division. In February 1861,

Twiggs was commander of the Department of Texas. He surrendered his troops to the Confederates for which he was dishonorably dismissed from the U.S. Army. Appointed a major general in the Confederate Army May 22, 1861, he commanded the District of Louisiana but resigned his commission toward the end of the year. He retired to Augusta, Ga. where he died Sept. 15, 1862. *Appletons'*, Vol. VI, 191-192. *Dictionary*, Vol. XIX, 83.

[10] A native of Ireland, James Shields (1810-1879) was appointed brigadier general July 1, 1846, and served under Gen. Zachary Taylor on the Rio Grande, and Gen. John E. Wool in Chihuahua before joining Gen. Winfield Scott. He was brevetted major general at Cerro Gordo where he was shot through the lung. Following his recovery, he commanded the brigade containing the Palmetto Regiment and was wounded again at Chapultepec. Mustered out in July 1848, Shields was appointed governor of the Oregon Territory then served in the U.S. Senate 1849-55 and 1858-59. He was named a brigadier general of U.S. Volunteers Aug. 19, 1861 and was victorious in the Battle of Winchester, Va., March 23, 1862. A few months later, June 9, 1862, he was defeated by Gen. Thomas J. (Stonewall) Jackson at Port Republic. Shields resigned his commission March 28, 1863, and settled in California for a short time then moved to Carrollton, Mo., where he resumed a former law practice.*Documents*, 200, 201, 224. *Appletons'*, Vol. V, 509. *Americana*, Vol. 24, 709. *Dictionary*, Vol. XVII, 106-107.

[11] Gideon Johnson Pillow (1806-1878) was appointed brigadier general of Tennessee Volunteers in July 1846 and served with Gen. Zachary Taylor before joining Gen. Winfield Scott at Vera Cruz. He was wounded at Cerro Gordo and engaged in the Battles of Churubusco, Molino del Rey and Chapultepec, where he was again wounded. He was promoted to major general April 13, 1847. Following the war, Pillow returned to a law practice in Tennessee and in July 1861 was made a brigadier general in the Confederate Army. He was second in command at Fort Donelson in February 1862 and he and his superior were censured for escaping and leaving surrender of the post to a junior officer. He was relieved of command but subsequently led a cavalry detachment in the Southwest and also served as chief of conscription in the Western Department. *Appletons'*, Vol. V, 20. *Dictionary*, Vol. XIV, 603-604.

[12] Bennett Riley was born at Alexandria, Va., in 1787. A career soldier, he served in the War of 1812 and began the Mexican War as a regimental commander. He led a brigade in Gen. David E. Twiggs' division during the Mexican Valley campaign and was brevetted brigadier general April 18, 1847,for service at Cerro Gordo, and major general following the Aug. 20, 1847, engagement at Contreras. After the war, he commanded the Department of the Pacific and was appointed military governor of California. He became colonel of the 1st Infantry Regiment in 1850 and died at Buffalo, N.Y., in 1853. *Appletons'*, Vol. V, 254. *Dictionary*, Vol. XV, 608-609.

[13] Persifor Frazer Smith (1798-1858) fought in the Seminole Indian War and in May 1846 was appointed colonel of a rifle regiment. He commanded a brigade from September 1846 until the end of the Mexican war, being brevetted brigadier general for service at Monterey and major general following the Battles of Contreras and Churubusco, Aug. 20, 1847. He later became military governor of Vera Cruz and subsequently had charge of the departments of California and Texas. He was appointed to the full rank of brigadier general Dec. 30, 1856, and was serving at Fort Leavenworth, Kansas, at the time of his death. *Appletons'*, Vol. V, 583. *Dictionary*, Vol. XVII, 331-332.

[14] Robert Edward Lee (1807-1870), future commander of the Army of Northern Virginia, was one of the many young West Point graduates who, during the Mexican War, proved the value of the United States Military Academy and the wisdom of retaining a cadre of career officers in military sevice. *Americana*, Vol. 17, 185-186.

[15] The batteries of Col. James Duncan and Capt. Francis Taylor were both engaged in the Battle of Churubusco. However, Manigault refers here to Taylor's battery of 6-pounders. H. Judge Moore states that Capt. Taylor's battery suffered "...great & fearful loss of both men and horses, the battery was ordered to be withdrawn from the scene of action in an almost totally disabled condition which was done only about one half hour before the final surrender...." The loss was 22 men and 13 horses. *Moore*, 143. Bvt. Maj. Gen. George W. Cullum, *Biographical Register of the Officers and Graduates of the U.S. Military Academy at West Point, N.Y.* (New York, 1891), Vol. I, 344-345, 569-570. Hereafter cited as *Cullum*. Lester R. Dillon Jr., *American Artillery in the Mexican War, 1846-1847*, (Austin, Tex., 1975), 46.

[16] Franklin Pierce (1804-1869) was a New Hampshire lawyer and politician who had served in both the House and Senate of Congress prior to the Mexican War. In 1847, he went on active duty with the rank of colonel and served under Gen. Winfield Scott, winning promotion to brigadier general. Pierce resigned his commission immediately after the war and in 1852 was elected 14th president of the United States. *Appletons'*, Vol. V, 7-11. *Dictionary*, Vol. XIV, 576-580.

[17] Col. Truman Bishop Ransom (1802-1847) was a native of Vermont, not Maine. A teacher and later president of Norwich University, Ransom became a major general in the Vermont militia. He volunteered for active duty during the Mexican War and was appointed major of the 9th U.S. Infantry in February 1847. A month later, he became colonel of the regiment. He was killed leading his men during the Battle of Chapultepec. *Appletons'*, Vol. V, 181.

[18] Lt. Col. James Polk Dickinson was second in command of the Palmetto Regiment. He was wounded during the Battle of Churubusco Aug. 20, 1847, shortly after taking over command at the death of Col. P. Mason Butler, and died Sept. 11. *Letters*, 2A.

[19] Antonio Lopez de Santa Anna, soldier and several times president of Mexico, who had a colorful and tumultuous career both on the field and in politics. Defeated by Gen. Zachary Taylor at Buena Vista Feb. 22-23, 1847, he tried his hand against Gen. Winfield Scott with equally disastrous results, eventually losing his army and his capital. *Appletons'*, Vol. V, 393-394. *Americana*, Vol. 24, 276-277.

[20] Maj. Gen. Henry J. Hunt, one of the foremost United States artillerymen, was stationed in Charleston during 1875-77. *Cullum*, Vol. II, 9-13.

[21] Definitions of the escopet (also spelled escopeta, escopette, or esclopette) are many and varied. Most sources agree that it was a heavy caliber musket, but descriptions of its length vary from 18 to 48 inches. Probably all are basically correct and the name is a generic term for a weapon issued in two or more lengths — a short version for mounted troops and a longer type for infantry. Its reported accuracy and heavy ball — approximately an ounce — made it a weapon the United States troops viewed with considerable respect. *Moore*, 19. *Webster's Third New International Dictionary*, (Springfield, Mass., 1961), 775. *Oxford English*

Dictionary, (London, 1961), Vol. III, 286. Sidney B. Brinkerhoff and Pierce A. Chamberlain, *Spanish Military Weapons in Colonial America, 1700-1821,* 18-19, 21, 24-28, 47, 110, 111. John Quick, *Dictionary of Weapons and Military Terms,* (New York, 1973), 154.

[22] Based on casualty records of the Palmetto Regiment at the Department of Archives and History in Columbia, S.C., this was Pvt. Patrick S. Graham, a member of Co. F., Manigault's company. *Letters,* (Capt. William Blanding, commanding Co. F, to Gregg, Hayden & Co. 16 Dec. 1852, regarding a silver medal for "Priv. Patrick S. Graham"). *Documents,* 266.

[23] Frederick W. Selleck of Abbeville, S.C., 2nd. and later 1st. Lt. of Co. E, Palmetto Regiment. Selleck, a close friend of Manigault's, was severely wounded during the battle for the Gates of Belen. He was shot while raising the regimental flag over the conquered Mexican works at the gate. *Wallace,* Vol. III, 114. *Courier,* Nov. 14, 1847. J.F.H. Claiborne, *Life and Correspondence of John A. Quitman* (New York, 1860), Vol. I, 364. *Documents,* 64, 131, 212, 242.

[24] Caleb Cushing (1800-1879), a Massachusetts lawyer, raised a regiment at the start of the Mexican War and was elected colonel. He later was promoted brigadier general and led a brigade from Vera Cruz to Mexico City but arrived after the fighting had ended. Returning to civilian life, April 1860 found him in Charleston, S.C., as chairman of the Democratic Convention which adjourned when it was unable to agree on a candidate. The convention reopened later at Baltimore, Md., with Cushing again in the chair, and eventually nominated Stephen A. Douglas. Many of the electors walked out. Cushing joined them and chaired a convention of the seceders which nominated John C. Breckinridge. This split in the Democratic Party culminated in the election of Republican Abraham Lincoln. Cushing, who had preached in the North against the abolitionists and urged that the South be permitted to leave the Union, was sent by lame duck President James C. Buchanan to Charleston to try to stave off secession. Arriving Dec. 20, 1860, he learned that the ordinance had been passed earlier in the day. Returning north, he publicly announced his allegiance to the Union and served during the war in a legal capacity for President Lincoln. Following the war, he practiced law in Washington. *Appletons',* Vol. II, 38-39. *Dictionary,* Vol. IV, 623-630.

[25] His mother. Manigault's parents were Joseph Manigault and Charlotte Drayton Manigault.

INDEX
TO APPENDIX II

Manigault, Arthur Middleton — 297.

Manigault, Charlotte Drayton — 321, 329n.

Manigault, Henry — 326n.

Manigault, Joseph — 329n.

Meade, George G. — 297.

Mexicalcingo — 306, 308.

Mexico City — 300, 303, 305, 306, 311, 316, 317, 319, 320, 325n-327n, 329n. (Manigault's comments on, 318, 319, 320-326).

Mobile, Ala. — 299, 301, 320.

Molino Del Rey — 311, 327n.

Monterey (Battle) — 326n, 327n.

Morales, Juan — 326n.

Nino Perdido Gate — 306, 313.

Pedregal — 306, 308.

Perote — 302.

Perry, M.C. — 326n.

Pierce, Franklin — 297, 309, 319, 328n.

Pillow, Gideon Johnson — 306, 314, 315, 327n.

Point Anton Lizardo — 301.

Portales (Hacienda) — 309.

Puebla — 302, 303, 305, 323.

Quitman, John Anthony — 301, 302, 305, 306, 311, 313, 314, 316, 318, 319, 326n.

Ransom, Truman Bishop — 310, 328n.

Regiments:
1st. Massachusetts — 319.
1st. Mississippi — 300.
1st. New York — 302, 305, 306, 309, 313-315, 319.
1st. Pennsylvania — 302, 319.
2nd. Pennsylvania — 313, 314, 319.
9th. U.S. Infantry — 310, 328n.
Alabama — 301, 302.
Georgia — 301, 302.
Palmetto (South Carolina) — 297, 299-301, 306, 308, 310, 313-319, 325n, 327n-329n. (Flag, 316, 329n).
Rifle — 316, 317, 327n.
U.S. Marines — 313, 314.

Riley, Bennett — 306, 327n.

Sacraficios Island — 301.

San Angel — 306, 308, 311, 319, 320.

San Antonio Gate — 308.

San Antonio Road — 306, 308.

San Augustin — 305, 306, 311.

St. Augustin Monastary — 303.

San Cosme Gate — 316, 318.

Santa Anna, Antonio Lopez de — 302, 308, 311, 319, 328n.

Scott, Winfield — 299, 301, 302, 305, 308, 310, 311, 319, 325n-328n.

Selleck, Frederick W. — 317, 329n.

Shields, James — 305, 306, 308, 310, 313, 314, 319, 327n.

Shiloh — 299n, 325n.

Smith, Persifor Frazer — 306, 327n.

Tacubaya — 311, 313, 314, 318.

Taylor, Francis — 308, 328n.

INDEX

Officers listed held commissions in the Confederate Army, unless designated U.S.A., and are carried at the highest rank held.

Brown's Ferry, Tenn. — 119, 149.
Buck, Capt. Irving — 152.
Buck, Col. William A. — 56, 58, 64.
Buckner, Lt. Gen. Simon Bolivar — 83, 85-87, 90, 93, 99, 104, 105, 112, 113, 119, 147, 149, 150, 152.
Buell, Maj. Gen. Don Carlos (U.S.A.) — 31, 33, 38, 39, 42, 45-48, 86.
Bunker Hill, Tenn. — 36.
Burnside, Maj. Gen. Ambrose E. (U.S.A.) — 119, 148, 169.
Bush, Capt. Asahel K. (U.S.A.) — 64.
Butler, Maj. Gen. Benjamin F. (U.S.A.) — 148.
Butler, Lt. Col. William L. — 107, 131, 141, 265.
Butterfield, Maj. Gen. Daniel (U.S.A.) — 207.
Buzzard Roost, Ga. — 170.

Cain, Dr. Joseph P. — 60.
Calhoun, Ga. — 174, 183, 205, 206, 209.
Cameron & Co., Charleston, S.C. — 6.
Camp Dick Robinson, Ky. — 42.
Camp Marion, S.C. — 5, 11.
Cantey, Brig. Gen. James — 204, 205, 207, 264.
Cape Fear River, N.C. — 23.
Caperton's Ferry, Tenn. — 85.
Carter, Brig. Gen. John C. — 64.
Carter House, The — II.
Carthage, Tenn. — 32.
Cassville, Ga. — 174, 175, 184, 186, 187, 208, 209.
Cass Station, Ga. — 210.
Cat Island, S.C. — 6, 12.
Catlett's Gap, Ga. 111.
Cave City, Ky. — 38, 45.
Chalmers, Brig. Gen. James R. — 16, 28, 38, 45, 49, 63.
Chancellorsville, Va. — 69, 218.
Charleston, S.C. — II, V, VIII, IX, 5-7, 9, 13, 14, 19, 25, 116, 161, 170, 250, 259, 281
Charleston, (S.C.) *Courier* — 7, 29, 116.
Charleston Library Society — IX, XV.
Chattahoochee River, Ga. — 176, 194, 195, 198, 214, 215, 217, 220, 243, 252, 258, 266, 267, 280.

Chattanooga, Tenn. — VIII, XIV, 7, 26, 31, 32, 35, 36, 44, 46, 48, 52, 64, 71, 75-77, 79, 81-83, 85, 87-92, 94, 101, 103, 107, 109, 111, 112, 115, 117-119, 126, 127, 130, 145, 147, 149, 151, 153-155, 157, 158, 162, 169, 170, 173, 203, 243, 252, 256, 273, 279, 281.
Chattanooga Creek — 85.
Cheatham, Maj. Gen. Benjamin F. — I, 36, 45, 57, 62, 65, 70, 87, 89, 94, 96, 104, 112, 113, 146, 151, 153-155, 169-171, 176, 203, 207, 217, 218, 258-260, 262, 263, 274, 280, 289, 291.
Chesnut, Brig. Gen. James Jr. — 64.
Chesnut, Mary Boykin — 64.
Chickamauga, Battle of — I, VI, VIII, XI, XIV, 60, 64-66, 83, 86, 90, 95, 101, 103, 109-113, 115, 118, 119, 126, 127, 130, 145, 147, 149, 151, 153, 158, 170, 176, 216, 259, 274, 294.
Chickamauga Creek, Ga. — 35, 86, 87, 92, 93, 95, 96, 111, 112, 118, 142, 148, 152, 157.
Cincinnati, Ohio — 32, 33, 273.
Clayton, Maj. Gen. Henry L. — 231, 232, 237, 246, 262-265, 268, 269, 280, 291, 293.
Clear Creek, Miss. — 20.
Cleburne, Christopher — 169.
Cleburne, Maj. Gen. Patrick R. — 49, 65, 68, 86, 88, 89, 111, 120, 137, 146, 147, 149, 152, 155, 157, 169-171, 176, 203, 204, 210, 218, 225, 258, 259, 267, 269, 270, 280.
Cobb, Howell — 272.
Cockerill, Capt, Giles J. (U.S.A.) — 262.
Coles Island, S.C. — 14
Coltart, Col. John G. — 63, 226, 227, 260, 291.
Columbia, S.C. — 66, 161.
Columbia, Tenn. 67, 273.
Connasauga River, Ga. — 180, 183, 184, 206.
Cooper, Gen. Samuel — 28, 61, 147, 213.
Cooper's Gap, Ga. — 111.
Coosawhatchie, S.C. — 6.
Cordes, Capt. Theodore — 11.
Corinth, Miss. — VII, XIII, 7, 14-16, 18-22, 27, 29, 31, 44, 159.
Corse, Maj. Gen. John (U.S.A.) — 281.

McGavock House, Franklin, Tenn. — 274.

McLaws, Maj. Gen. Lafayette — 113.

McLemore's Cove, Ga. — 85-87, 89, 90, 93, 95, 104, 111, 112, 116, 124, 145.

McMinnville, Tenn. — 67, 150.

McNair, Brig. Gen. Evander — 85.

McNairy, Maj. Frank — 146.

McPherson, Maj. Gen. James B. (U.S.A.) — 173, 174, 176, 177, 179, 203, 204, 206, 212, 215, 217, 218, 230, 231, 258-260, 263, 289, 292.

Memphis & Charleston R.R. — 26, 30, 31.

Mercer, Brig. Gen. Hugh W. — 214.

Meridian, Miss. — 170.

Merrill Hill, Tenn. — II.

Mersy, Col. Augustus (U.S.A.) — 262, 294.

Mexican War — II, IX, X, 1, 4, 27, 28, 44, 64, 82, 110, 151, 270.

Mill Creek Gap, Ga. — 173, 203, 204.

Milledgeville, Ga. — 218.

Millen, Ga. — 281.

Missionary Ridge, Tenn.-Ga. — VIII, XI, XIII, 85, 88, 92, 103, 112, 115, 118-120, 124, 131, 134-136, 138, 152-154.

Missionary Ridge, Battle of — 137, 142, 151, 154, 155, 169, 203.

Mitchel, Maj. Gen. Ormsby M. (U.S.A.) — 26.

Mitchell, Col. Julius C.B. — 63, 79.

Mobile, Ala. — 14, 27, 35, 166.

Mobile & Ohio R.R. — 14, 20, 22.

Moccasin Point, Tenn. — 128.

Monterey, Tenn. — 18.

Montgomery, Ala. — 3, 9, 14, 23, 35, 220, 265, 272.

Moore, Brig. Gen. John C. — 151.

Moore, Stephen — 247.

Morgan, Maj. Gen. James D. (U.S.A.) — 281.

Morgan, Brig. Gen. John H. — 44, 48, 71, 215.

Morgan's, Ga. — 93, 111.

Morris Island, S.C. — 10.

Morris, Capt, Walter — 209.

Mount Pleasant, S.C. — 14.

Mount Vernon, Ky. — 42.

Munfordville, Ky. — VII, 16, 32, 38, 40, 47, 86.

Murfreesboro, Tenn. — 32, 48, 52, 54, 64, 65, 67-69, 72, 80.

Murfreesboro, Battle of — XI, XIII, 27, 28, 48, 58, 59, 61, 151, 294.

Murrell's Inlet, S.C. — 12.

Muscle Shoals, Ala. — 150.

Nashville, Tenn. — I, 24, 32, 33, 38, 45, 48, 53, 70, 119, 215, 220, 266, 270, 272-275.

Nashville, Battle of — 152, 154.

Nashville & Chattanooga R.R. — 48, 67, 74, 76, 127.

National Trust for Historic Preservation — V.

Negley, Maj. Gen. James S. (U.S.A.) — 85, 86, 116.

Nettles, Capt. J.R. — 58, 60.

New Hope Church, Ga. — 175, 178, 209.

Newman, Ga. — 265.

New Orleans, La. — 44, 82.

Neysmith, Sam — 229.

Nickagack Cave, Tenn. — 76.

Noonday Creek, Ga. — 191, 211.

North Carolina Military Institute — 110.

North Island, S.C. — 24.

North Santee River, S.C. — X, XII, 1, 6, 9, 12, 170.

Noyes Creek, Ga. — 175, 212.

Ohio River — I.

Oliver, Capt. Starke H. — 230, 263.

Oostanaula River, Ga. — 174, 180, 182, 183, 205.

Orchard Knob, Tenn. — 131, 132, 134, 138, 151, 153.

Orr, Col. James L. — 24, 25.

Otey, Bishop James H. — 70.

Pace's Ferry, Ga. — 215.

Palmer, Rev. B.M. — 109.

Palmer, Maj. Gen. John M. (U.S.A.) — 210.

Palmetto Regiment — IX, X.

Palmetto Station, Ga. — 254, 271, 272, 280.

Parham, Capt. R.T.B. — 60.

Parker, Lt. F.S. Jr. — 142, 153.

Pea Vine Church, Ga. — 112.

Pea Vine Ridge, Ga. — 94, 104.

Peachtree Creek, Ga. — 119, 200, 215, 217, 218, 223, 258, 262.